CAMBRIDGE TEXTS I

HISTORY OF POLITICAL

EDMUND BURKE

*Revolutionary Writings*

*Reflections on the Revolution in France*
and the first *Letter on a Regicide Peace*

# CAMBRIDGE TEXTS IN THE
# HISTORY OF POLITICAL THOUGHT

*Series editors*

RAYMOND GEUSS

*Professor in Philosophy, University of Cambridge*

QUENTIN SKINNER

*Barber Beaumont Professor of the Humanities, Department of History,*
*Queen Mary, University of London*

Cambridge Texts in the History of Political Thought is now firmly established as the major student textbook series in political theory. It aims to make available to students all the most important texts in the history of western political thought, from ancient Greece to the early twentieth century. All the familiar classic texts will be included, but the series seeks at the same time to enlarge the conventional canon by incorporating an extensive range of less well-known works, many of them never before available in a modern English edition. Wherever possible, texts are published in complete and unabridged form, and translations are specially commissioned for the series. Each volume contains a critical introduction together with chronologies, biographical sketches, a guide to further reading and any necessary glossaries and textual apparatus. When completed the series will aim to offer an outline of the entire evolution of western political thought.

*For a list of titles published in the series, please see end of book*

# EDMUND BURKE

# Revolutionary Writings

## Reflections on the Revolution in France and the first *Letter on a Regicide Peace*

EDITED BY

## IAIN HAMPSHER-MONK
*Professor of Political Theory, Department of Politics, University of Exeter*

CAMBRIDGE
UNIVERSITY PRESS

# CAMBRIDGE
## UNIVERSITY PRESS

University Printing House, Cambridge CB2 8BS, United Kingdom

Cambridge University Press is part of the University of Cambridge.

It furthers the University's mission by disseminating knowledge in the pursuit of education, learning and research at the highest international levels of excellence.

www.cambridge.org
Information on this title: www.cambridge.org/9780521605090

First published 2014

*A catalogue record for this publication is available from the British Library*

ISBN 978-0-521-84393-5 Hardback
ISBN 978-0-521-60509-0 Paperback

# CONTENTS

v

# Preface

Burke's *Reflections* has long been seen as an epitomic text, supposedly articulating an – indeed the first – theoretical defence of 'modern conservatism'. In keeping with the philosophy of the Series, this edition seeks to place it in the intellectual contexts in which its author conceived and wrote it, whilst also indicating those in which it came to be read. Alongside *Reflections* – Burke's early response to the Revolution – is included one of his last, the first *Letter on a Regicide Peace*, a work that reveals the development of his thought during the course of the Revolution and one that has helped to shape a particular view of international society.

The Introduction sketches a widening circle of contexts in which the works can be situated: beginning with the localised political circumstances faced by Burke at the time, and extending to the trans-historical and universal circumstances of human political agency to which Burke appeals in the course of his writing, and which have given his work a significance that has extended far beyond the specific conditions of the Revolution that gave rise to it – themselves of huge and still debated historical significance.

Neither Burke's prose style nor his references are easily accessible to modern readers. Accordingly both works have been generously annotated to assist in understanding the significance of his wide and nowadays often obscure allusions, whilst leaving readers as free as possible to interpret the text for themselves. Burke was prodigiously well-read in both classical and modern literatures. He possessed extraordinary recall and wove quotations into his speech and writing with great, and doubtless sometimes subconscious, facility. Identifying all of these would have completely changed the character of the edition, but it seemed important to give enough to provide some sense of how richly Burke's thinking is saturated in and conditioned by this literary and cultural heritage: a feature of the human mind which played such a central part in his political thinking.

Within the texts three kinds of aids have been provided for the reader. Burke's own notes are indicated by Roman numerals, whilst a second set of Arabic-numbered footnotes supplied by the present editor explain terminology, identify and translate quotations and other references. Significant events and brief biographies of persons mentioned more than once in the texts are explained in a separate set of Notes. The existence of such an entry is indicated by a superscript 'N' in the text. There is a separate Chronology of events relevant to Burke's life and engagement with the Revolution.

Finally there is a brief list of further reading. I have tried to identify writings which help the student to understanding and situate these works and to indicate some of the main schools of interpretation. The student should also consult the excellent companion volume to this, edited by Ian Harris: *Edmund Burke: Pre-Revolutionary Writings* (Cambridge, 1993).

# Acknowledgements

I am grateful to the British Academy and Leverhulme Trust for a Senior Research Fellowship, part of which was devoted to the preparation of this edition. Many thanks to the editors of the series Quentin Skinner and Raymond Geuss and to Richard Fisher of Cambridge University Press for their customary encouragement, help, advice (and patience) in developing this edition, and to Quentin Skinner and Richard Fisher for so much else as well. Special thanks to Malcolm Todd, my copy-editor, for help that went well beyond his editorial remit and for saving me a number of blushes. Thank you also to Samuel Hampsher-Monk for preparing the images on pp. 2 and 252.

Editors owe a huge debt to their scholarly predecessors. Three editions have been particularly helpful, even if I have not always followed their identifications or suggestions: E. J. Payne's nineteenth-century edition, now reprinted by the Liberty Fund with a new introduction by Frances Canavan (Indianapolis, 1999), the French translation introduced by Philippe Raynaud, with extensive notes by d'Alfred Fierro and Georges Liébert (Hachette, 1989) and the superb, and by far the best modern scholarly edition by J. C. D. Clark (Stanford, Calif., 2001). The first two also contain the *Letter on the Regicide Peace*. I have benefited over the years from conversations with many Burke scholars, recorded in other places. More recently I should particularly like to mention Ian Harris and Richard Bourke, who also read and commented on the Introduction.

Many thanks are due to colleagues in the Departments of Politics and History at Exeter who have indulged my obsession with Burke. Particular thanks are due to Jeremy Black for checking my footnotes, to Rebecca Langlands, who checked my translations from the Latin, and Chris Gill for identifying a particularly recalcitrant reference. Barbara Yates oversaw my French translation and helped research eighteenth-century French word usage. Huge thanks to Kate Berrisford for help in preparing and rationalising the text and notes. Needless to say, any errors that, despite all their efforts, remain, are my own.

# Editor's introduction

## I

Edmund Burke was born in Dublin in 1730 to a Catholic mother and a Protestant Father.[1] He was educated in Ireland at both Catholic and Quaker schools, and at Dublin's Anglican university, Trinity College, before studying law at the Middle Temple in London. His initial ambitions were literary and his first two works, the *Vindication of Natural Society* (1756) and – more particularly – the *Philosophical Enquiry into the Origin of our Ideas of the Sublime and the Beautiful* (1757), gained him public recognition, the company of London's literary elite and the editorship of the newly-founded *Annual Register*, a political and literary review. Need for a secure income led him into political service, briefly as secretary to William Hamilton MP, on the staff of Lord Halifax, the Lord Lieutenant of Ireland; but in 1765 he formed his major political connection, as secretary to Lord Rockingham, the leader of the Whig Party. Although twice briefly Paymaster General (1782 and 1783), his major role was as opposition pamphleteer, political fixer, and spokesman for the Rockingham Whigs. Burke produced polemical writings and speeches on a wide range of issues critical of the government, opposing its controversial taxation policy in the American Colonies, seeking reform of the tangled skein of national and royal domestic finances, of the East India Company's administration of British India, and, less publicly in

---

[1] The year of his birth is disputed. See the discussion of the case for 1729 and 1730 in by far the best and fullest modern biography by F. P. Lock: *Edmund Burke*, vol. 1: *1730–1784* (Oxford, 2006), pp. 16–17.

that stridently Protestant age, to relieve the restrictions imposed on Irish Catholics in his home country.[2]

As this brief list reveals, Burke's political life, down to 1789, was firmly identified with reform and, in party-political terms, opposed to the Tories. Of course the eighteenth-century Whig–Tory polarity does not map easily onto the modern radical–conservative distinction, which itself only emerged out of the revolutionary events that dominated the last eight years of Burke's life. Nevertheless his opposition to the French Revolution surprised many, seeming to reverse his life-long commitment to reform and to liberty.[3]

*Reflections* was quickly recognised by contemporaries – foes and friends alike – as a definitive statement of anti-revolutionary principles; and has since been widely characterised as the founding statement of modern conservatism. From the start therefore it has been an ideologically charged work. For nineteenth-century liberals it articulated a peculiarly British political path between the violence and danger of revolutionary republicanism and the political absolutism to which many Continental monarchies were still wedded. Burke was subsequently recruited by twentieth-century cold warriors – particularly in America – against communism. Yet paradoxically Burke has also had an appeal for radicals. Most of those who opposed him in the 1790s – James Mackintosh, Coleridge, Southey and Wordsworth – later, as Coleridge put it, snapped their 'squeaking baby trumpet of sedition'[4] and came to agree with him politically, helping to construct the culturally rich versions of the English past and society to which Burke's politics appealed and in which it could find root. Even the most un-Burkean writer of that decade – William Godwin, rationalist, individualist, atheist – later adopted positions on the role of habit and the emotions close to those which Burke had espoused.[5]

---

[2] Many of his writings connected with these issues have been collected, excerpted and introduced in the companion volume to this: *Edmund Burke: Pre-revolutionary Writings*, ed. Ian Harris (Cambridge, 1993).

[3] Tom Paine, who had met Burke in 1788, wrote describing the progress of the Revolution, clearly expecting Burke's approval of events (Paine to Burke 17 Jan. 1790, *Corr.* vi, p. 67). Similarly Baron 'Anacharsis' Cloots, to Burke (12 May 1790, *Corr.* vi, p. 109).

[4] S. T. Coleridge to George Coleridge *c.*10 March 1798, in *Collected Letters of Samuel Taylor Coleridge*, ed. Earl Leslie Griggs, 6 vols. (Oxford, 1956), vol. 1, p. 238.

[5] There were those too who moved the other way. Most famously William Cobbett, a Tory in the 1790s, returned from America in 1811 with the bones of Tom Paine, to inspire a new generation of radical pamphleteers.

The image of reflected light in the title is highly appropriate, since it both forms part of the internal strategy of the work and characterises its impact on the range of contexts in which it has been read and used. At one end of that range lies the local context of British, and even internal Whig Party, politics in which it was an intervention. At the other, there is a much wider context which sees in *Reflections* a conservative synthesis of a wide range of issues and a number of political-theoretical preoccupations and positions to be found in many early modern European states which were brought to a head in the French Revolution. Some of these – such as the doctrine of persisting natural rights – would, Burke believed, if allowed to prevail, be destructive of the political liberty enjoyed by modern, commercial, and constitutionally limited monarchies, a political form which he and many other leading thinkers then saw as the major achievement of the enlightened age. The triumph of the ideology of natural rights would, thought Burke, plunge Europe into a new age of barbarism – the emergence from which had only recently been charted by Scottish thinkers such as William Robertson and Edward Gibbon in his massive history of the long decline and fall of Rome. But in fact, during the past two centuries, it is increasingly the French Revolution that has been identified as the threshold event of political modernity, and the inspiration for similar revolutions. In denouncing that Revolution, *Reflections* challenges our conceptions of the transition to political modernity and makes a counterclaim to be the definitive text of that transition rather than the repudiation of it. Some have seen in it an even wider significance in which Burke is taken to be saying something about the very conditions of human social and political life, independent of the particular historical circumstances in which he wrote. Burke certainly thought himself to be making such claims; whether he succeeded is a much more contentious issue.

Indeed, given the surface features of Burke's writing – and his characteristically deprecatory remarks about theory – *any* claim that Burke writes at a level of theoretical abstraction can look distinctly odd. Readers coming to this text from the 'tradition' of early modern European political theory will be accustomed to the kind of systematic treatment we find in Hobbes, Locke, Rousseau, Hume or Kant, in which epistemological preliminaries lead up to (or are implicated in) an account of human nature and moral psychology, to which is joined some account of pre- or early social existence, and from which emerges, through contract or practice, political society. *Reflections* utterly confounds such expectations of orderly exposition. As his radical opponents complained, the work seems to ignore any organisational principles at all.[6] Instead, we have an apparently unsystematic[7] and rambling 'letter' of inordinate length. Burke's concerns seem at first entirely polemical and focussed on purely factual historical or sociological issues: What had *actually* happened in 1688? What *is* the social composition of the Constituent Assembly? How bad *were* French finances? Statements which look as if they might belong to political philosophy appear rather as isolated insights or maxims– we may agree or disagree with them, but it is difficult to locate such remarks within any systematic chain of argument. However we are to characterise Burke's achievements in these works, we must, it seems, approach him in a different way than we do those whose concern was evidently with a systematic presentation of their ideas.

Burke's contemporaries – whether they agreed with him or not – recognised that he had achieved something important.[8] No other attack on the Revolution in England was remotely so famous. His opponents, defending the Revolution's principles, recognised Burke and *Reflections* as *the* writer and *the* work to target: Burke thus clearly connected with his contemporary audiences; for them, at least – even his critics – his unsystematic exposition did not disqualify the importance of the work. They recognised that Burke wrote as a politician and a rhetorician, not as an academic or a philosopher. He wrote to persuade, not to satisfy canons of logic. Unlike philosophers, politicians and rhetoricians do not start from the most primordially imaginable propositions and derive conclusions from these; rather, they start from or appeal to propositions which may be unexamined but are thought by their audience to be true.[9] Burke's arguments start from, or often presuppose, assumptions Burke

---

[6] Thomas Paine excused his insertion of a 'miscelleneous' chapter in his reply to Burke, the *Rights of Man*, on the grounds that: 'Mr Burke's Book is *all* Miscelleny, His intention was to make an attack on the French Revolution but instead of proceeding with an orderly arrangement, he has stormed it with a mob of ideas tumbling over and destroying one another' (*Rights of Man* (Harmondsworth, 1969 [1791]), p. 116); Mary Wollstonecraft describes her 'indignation when I attempt methodically, to unravel your slavish paradoxes, in which I can find no fixed principle to refute' (*Vindication of the Rights of Men*, ed. Sylvana Tomaselli (Cambridge, 1995 [1790]), p. 7).

[7] In fact we know from at least one draft fragment that Burke worked out its structure very carefully (F. P. Lock, *Burke's Reflections* (London, 1985), pp. 59–60). For an excellent structural analysis of the work see the edition by J. C. D. Clark, pp. 5–9.

[8] There are good accounts of the reception in Lock, *Burke's Reflections*, ch. 5 and in his *Edmund Burke*, vol. 2 (Oxford, 2006), pp. 332–50.

[9] Aristotle, *Rhetoric* 1357a.

shared with his readers, and which he did not need to make explicit. And Burke could evoke the right kind of emotional links and associations the more easily since they shared with him, as we do not, a certain cultural repertoire. For them the genius of Burke was to have woven the political commonplaces and prejudices of the day into an argumentative fabric. Modern readers must recover these before we can assess Burke, let alone consider how his political thought might relate to our own age.

# II

Burke was not uninformed about France. He read and wrote the language competently, and had visited France at least once, for two months early in 1773. As early as 1769 he had commented that the French economy threatened an 'extraordinary convulsion' not only to France but to the whole of Europe.[10] Burke's initial response to the French Revolution, expressed in private letters, was one of astonishment. He thought: 'the progress of this whole affair is one of the most curious matters of Speculation that was ever exhibited'.[11] Through the autumn of 1789, however, his increasing concern at events – the growing boldness of the Paris mob, the abolition of feudal privileges (4 August), the rejection of an upper house in the new legislature (1 Sept.) and the attack on the royal bedroom in the Palace of Versailles (5–6 Oct.) – which would become one of the great rhetorical set-pieces of *Reflections* – all crystallised into a decidedly critical view of the Revolution.[12]

In November, Charles-Jean Francois Depont, the son of a French family who had stayed with the Burkes in 1785, wrote asking for assurance that the French were 'worthy to be free, could distinguish between liberty and licence, and legitimate government from despotic power'.[13] Burke wrote a substantial reply[14] expressing grave misgivings about the Revolution, but withheld it lest it compromise Depont, sending instead a now lost, brief and non-committal response. Depont wrote again reassuring Burke that he was in no danger and pressing him to send the original

---

[10] *W&S*, ii, p. 151.   [11] *Corr.* vi, p. 10.

[12] Burke followed reports of French events closely, reading 'the authorized, or rather the equally authentic documents on this subject, from the first instructions to the representatives of the several orders' (*Corr.* vi, p. 79).

[13] Depont to Burke, 4 November 1789, *Corr.* vi, p. 32.   [14] *Corr.* vi, pp. 39–50.

letter, which Burke then did.[15] The opening of *Reflections* refers not only to Depont's second letter and to the initially withheld, but finally sent letter, but also to a third letter ('a second and more full discussion on the subject', p. 4) which had grown into *Reflections*.

However, on the same day (4 November 1789) as Depont's letter, an event took place in London that would significantly change Burke's thought and writing on the subject.[16] On that day, the aged leading light of radical dissent, Richard Price,[N] had delivered to a meeting of the 'Revolution Society',[N] and subsequently published, an address on the 'Love of our Country'. The occasion was an annual celebration by Dissenters of the 'Glorious Revolution' of 1688[N] in which the Catholic James II had been ousted by parliamentary leaders in favour of the Protestants William and Mary. Price's sermon dismissed the 'blind and narrow principles' of conventional patriotism, urging his hearers instead to 'consider yourselves more as citizens of the world than as members of any particular community'.[17] But he proceeded provocatively to assert three principles on which (he claimed) that English Revolution was founded, and in which he called on the Society to instruct the public. These were the rights to 'choose our own governors . . . cashier them for misconduct . . . [and] frame a government for ourselves'.[18] He closed by stressing the insecurity of these principles, for 'though the Revolution was a great work, it was by no means a perfect work', and he exhorted his listeners and readers to redress the imperfect religious toleration it provided, and 'the inequality of our representation'.[19]

Burke had been aware of Price's pamphlet, but it was not until mid January that its content was drawn to his attention at a dinner party. 'Late as it was', he later recorded, he went home, read it, and immediately began composing a public response.[20] Thus, early in 1790 Burke seems to have had two works in mind, the 'more full discussion' of French developments in the projected letter to Depont, and the notes for a public response to Price. As early as 13 February *Reflections* was already being

---

[15] Depont to Burke, 29 Dec., *Corr.* vi, p. 59; Burke to Depont [Nov 1789], *Corr.* vi, p. 39 is the letter Burke eventually sent but not until early January 1790.

[16] In the introduction to *Reflections* that ascribes its origins to the correspondence with Depont, he refers to his sentiments (on the Revolution) having 'received another direction', which may well be the impact of Price's pamphlet discussed here.

[17] Price, *A Discourse on the Love of our Country* [1789], in *Political Writings*, ed. D. O. Thomas (Cambridge, 1991), pp. 179, 193.

[18] Ibid., pp. 193–4.    [19] Ibid., p. 193.

[20] To William Weddell, 31 Jan. 1792, *Corr.* vii, pp. 56–7.

advertised as 'in the press and speedily will be published', but its title at that point, *Reflections on certain proceedings of the Revolution Society of the 4ᵗʰ November, 1789, concerning the affairs of France*, reveals how much its original focus was England, and the work may at this time have simply comprised a response to Price.²¹ Still imminent in early March, it was to be transformed over the rest of the parliamentary session and the summer into a much larger work that integrated the two projects from which it had arisen.²²

We can date the completion of *Reflections* fairly closely. The latest event in France mentioned in the first edition is the correspondence between the 'Patriotic Society' at Nantes and the Revolution Society in London, reported in the *General Evening Post* for 4–7 September; whereas the French Finance minister, Necker, who resigned on 4 September, is described in *Reflections* as still in office.²³ So by early September Burke had completed the text, a fact corroborated by our knowledge that through most of the rest of September the Burkes were touring in the Malvern Hills and Wye Valley. They did not return to Beaconsfield, their country home, until about the 27th, by which date the work was printed and bound and advance copies sent to friends. It was published on 1 November.

## III

By 1790 Burke had become somewhat isolated within his own party, and *Reflections* has been seen as a bid to regain prominence within and influence over the Whigs.²⁴ There were a number of reasons for this isolation. Since 1786 Burke had been deeply committed, on behalf of the House of Commons, to managing the impeachment of Warren Hastings,

---

²¹ *St James's Chronicle*, 11–13 Feb., *Gazeteer*, 13 Feb., *The World*, 13 Feb.; cited in *Lock*, vol. 2, pp. 254–5. Burke's correspondents at this time, to whom he showed drafts for comment, described the work as a pamphlet about England, directed at Dissent, and defending the Anglican established Church. The advertisement's claim that the work was 'in the press' – i.e. being printed – seems inconsistent with the fact that Burke had only begun composing the work, and may well have been advertising hype. But it was his habit to send copy as he wrote to the printers to be set, and to revise from the printed proofs, so the early stages of composition may still have involved sheets being 'in the press'.

²² Parliament was dissolved on 11 June. Burke was still very busy with the Hastings impeachment.

²³ See p. 208, n. 303.

²⁴ This is the context for *Reflections* to which L. G. Mitchell gives almost exclusive prominence in the modern collected edition of *Writings and Speeches*, 9 vols. (Oxford), vol. 8 (1989), pp. 29ff.

Director of the East India Company and effective governor of British India.[25] Initially a huge celebrity trial, colleagues and the public had become bored with it. Cartoonists lampooned him dressed in a toga, pathetically imitating Cicero's prosecution of the provincial governor, Verres. Burke's dogged persistence threatened to bog down himself and his colleagues in an unpopular issue.[26]

Further tensions arose over King George III's temporary 'madness' of 1788/9. During this the out-of-office Whigs had incautiously become too identified with the heir and expected Regent, the Prince of Wales – from whom the King was deeply estranged. Burke was extremely uncomfortable with what he saw as this disloyalty, and relations between himself and Charles James Fox, the populist leader of the Whigs in the Commons, never recovered.[27] The King's return to health left the Whigs – already in opposition – dangerously exposed and Burke semi-detached from them. Finally, the French Revolution cut, in a raw and destructive way, across the Whigs' sense of their own identity as essentially paternalistic, aristocratic champions of the cause of popular liberty. These tensions would ultimately divide them, some joining Pitt's Tory government, others following the radical and populist Fox into the political wilderness. Initially, however, the Revolution separated Burke from the majority who hoped to maintain the unity of the Whig connection. Whigs saw themselves as the defenders of parliamentary liberty against the prerogatives of the Crown – principles embodied in the Glorious Revolution of 1688.[N] Many, particularly those around Fox, were eager to read into the earlier stages of the French Revolution a version of what had happened in Britain in 1688. But the Whigs of 1688 were heroes for many not only because they constitutionalised the monarchy, but because they avoided a repeat of 1649, when Parliamentary and military rebels had abolished it. Having tried and beheaded the King they had unleashed social forces and a range of political and religious ideas of a volatile and socially disruptive kind. It was with this second image of the Whigs, as safeguards against ideological discontinuity and social violence from below, that Burke now identified;

---

[25] The 'High Crimes and Misdemeanours' charged included breach of treaties with local rulers, extortion, illegal arrogation of powers, incitement to looting etc. ('Articles of Impeachment...', *W&S*, vi, pp. 125ff.).

[26] See cartoons 72, 93, 109 (rhetoric); 88 (Much Ado); 75 and 87 (Cicero); and 107 (coachman) in Nicholas K. Robinson, *Edmund Burke: A life in Caricature* (New Haven and London, 1996).

[27] F. O'Gorman, *The Whig Party and the French Revolution* (London, 1976), ch. 2 *passim*.

and it was he who warned that 1789 was to be 1649 again rather than 1688.

This is the party-political context in which Burke wrote and published *Reflections*. It explains his preoccupation with distinguishing the principles of 1688 from those of the French Revolution, and to call the Whigs back to their 'true principles' – an intention explicit and amplified in his *Appeal from the New to the Old Whigs* (1791). There was a personal twist to this party-political context. The dinner-party conversation at which Price's pamphlet had been brought to Burke's attention had not been about France, or even primarily about Price's views of the English constitution, but about the Dissenters' unwillingness to support the Whigs (despite much shared politics) because of their disapproval of Fox's dissolute private life.[28] Burke's personal morals were quite the opposite of Fox's, but it was their ingratitude to a friend and colleague who had so strenuously supported the Dissenters' case for toleration that had initially so irked him about Price's pamphlet.[29] Given Burke's support for Fox against Price's personal attack, for Fox to then side with Price over France must have increased Burke's dismay and added personal emotional fuel to his opposition to those seeking to identify French aspirations with British principles. The break between Burke and Fox on the identity of Whig principles and the attitude to France would become deep, personal and irrevocable.

This context highlights Burke as a defender of a specific interpretation of Whig politics. Although Burke's significance is much wider than this, it is not a view that would have been foreign to at least some of his contemporaries.[30] Moreover, locating Burke in this context enables a

---

[28] Fox, a hugely popular politician and clearly a charming and amusing companion, was a man of many and large appetites, a prodigious gambler at both horses and cards, a womaniser, drinker and gourmand. His gambling debts of £120,000 (approximately £11m in today's prices) were paid off by his father but they subsequently twice bankrupted him. Rational dissent, although in Burke's view doctrinally lax, was morally austere.

[29] 'the asperity with which I expressed myself against these Gentlemen arose from my resentment for their . . . treacherous animosity to Mr Fox' (Burke to Weddell, 31 Jan. 1792, *Corr.* vii, p. 57).

[30] Oliver Goldsmith's mock epitaph catches one view:

> Here lies our good Edmund, whose genius was such,
> We scarcely can praise it, or blame it too much;
> Who, born for the Universe, narrow'd his mind,
> And to party gave up what was meant for mankind.
>
> (*Retaliation*, ll. 29–33)

more acute appreciation of the rhetorical skill of some of Burke's best-known passages, such, for example, as the famous passage beginning 'Society is indeed a Contract . . . '.[31]

The idea of the social contract as a basis of political authority was a seriously ambiguous legacy of the Revolution of 1688[N], bequeathed by John Locke's defence of it to the Whigs in his much anthologised *Second Treatise*.[32] Whilst, as intended, this disposed of divine hereditary monarchical right, the idea of the constitution as a contract seemed to license dangerously radical readings of its ultimate status, in fact precisely those claimed by Price and attacked by Burke at the start of *Reflections*. The Whigs – as defenders of aristocratic and propertied government – had struggled for a century to tame the radical populist potential of this ideological inheritance. The Whig managers of the Sacheverall Trial[N] of 1714 had desperately played down the radical implications of 'the contract'.[33] David Hume – a philosophical Whig if a dispositional conservative – had denied the relevance of contract to government, claiming both derived their being and justification from considerations of utility, so 'we gain nothing by resolving the one into the other'.[34] Josiah Tucker, a major critic of Locke's influence in America, suggested 'The idea of a *Quasi – Contract* instead of an *actual* Contract'[35] as a way of outflanking radical, activist readings of Locke. But the Whigs were too deeply identified with 'contract' to be able to dismiss it, and Burke's rhetorical problem was to explain why it did not entail a radical, reformist, revisiting of that contract as Price claimed.

Burke seeks to solve this problem in two ways. Firstly, forensically, by trying to demonstrate that, as a matter of historical fact, if 1688 is construed as 'the contract' it was a very conservative one, and it failed to establish anything like the principles claimed by Price, let alone the

---

[31] Below, pp. 100–101.
[32] Locke's text distinguished between the social contract, or compact *establishing* civil society, and the *entrusting* of government to a magistrate. However, as so often, the precision to which the theorist aspires was sacrificed to ideological need and 'contract of government' was what the Whigs were saddled with.
[33] See Geoffrey S. Holmes, *The Trial of Dr Sacheverall* (London, 1973).
[34] David Hume, 'Of the Original Contract', p. 481 in *Essays, Moral, Political and Literary*, ed. E. Miller (Indianapolis, 1985) (originally in *Three Essays, Moral and Political* (London and Edinburgh, 1748).
[35] Josiah Tucker, *A Treatise Concerning Civil Government* (London, 1781 [repr. New York, 1967, same pagination]), p. 141.

French.[36] But in addition he rhetorically re-conceptualises the 'contract', so enlarging the time, space and agents within which and amongst whom the contract is construed that it both subverts the individualism and voluntarism implicit in the normal understanding of a contract and dignifies its terms and conditions beyond the possibility of utilitarian renegotiation. 'Society', he famously writes, 'is indeed a Contract', but whilst commercial contracts 'maybe dissolved at pleasure . . . The state . . . is to be looked on with other reverence; because it is not a partnership in things subservient only to the gross animal existence of a temporary and perishable nature. It is a partnership in all science; a partnership in all art; a partnership in every virtue, and in all perfection.' These noble aims are impossible to realise if the contract is construed as provisional, and revocable at will. Consequently 'it becomes a partnership not only between those who are living, but between those who are living, those who are dead, and those who are yet to be born'.[37] This is a justly famous passage, but we gain added appreciation of Burke's rhetorical skill in projecting the idea of contract onto a trans-historical dimension when we understand how the need to do so is framed by the dual imperatives of its unassailable place within Whig ideology and the need to deny its availability to radicals.

# IV

This invocation of the wider canvas against which politics is conducted is more than a clever piece of rhetorical invention. For although Burke did think that radicals, such as Price and the aristocrats who flirted with them, were wrong to read the principles of the French Revolution into the Whig political tradition, and although persuading his party to return to their true principles was part of his aim, Burke himself believed that far wider issues were at stake; and it would be quite wrong to identify his main intention in writing *Reflections*, let alone its significance as a work of political thought, as merely party political.[38] Burke wrote to a fellow Whig MP: 'I cannot say it was written solely within a view to the Service

---

[36] This is pursued at length in the first half of the *Appeal*, with direct quotations from the Sacheverall Trial[N], where establishing the moderate identity of 1688 was a major tactic of the prosecution.

[37] *Reflections*, pp. 100–101.

[38] Cf. Mitchell, *W&S*, viii, p. 29. This is a charge that Mary Wollstonecraft makes against him (*Vindication of the Rights of Men*, p. 45).

of that Party. I hope its views were more general. But . . . this was *one* of the Objects in my contemplation.'[39]

There is then already a second and much wider context implicit in Burke's claims that his version of Whig principles embodies English constitutionalism – that is a claim about the distinctive character of *English* thought about and conduct of their politics. Burke later wrote of *Reflections* that his 'intention had been to convey to a *foreign people* . . . the prevalent opinions and sentiments of a nation renowned for wisdom and celebrated in all ages for a well understood and well regulated love of freedom' (my italics).[40] But it is hard not to think that Burke is here being disingenuous. Addressing *Reflections* to a Frenchman provides a pretext for explaining, supposedly to the French, why they would be wrong to think the French Revolution was emulating the English one of 1688. But in fact *Reflections*, as we saw, originated both in a letter to a Frenchman and as a refutation of views expressed on England by an Anglophone writer, the Welshman Richard Price. Despite being written *to* a Frenchman, in publishing in English and in England Burke signalled that his primary concern was to persuade an English audience why they would be wrong to think the French Revolution to be a version of the English. This equivocation over the target audiences of *Reflections* enabled Burke to appear to speak on behalf of the English audience whom he is in fact addressing, a rhetorical device that invites their connivance with the author's aims and sentiments whilst enabling him to instruct them without seeming to. Once the direct attack on Price's sermon is over, the contrast between what the French do and the 'we' on behalf of whom Burke speaks inveigles an English reader into accepting that the political thought of *Reflections* is not just Burke's nor just Whig, but their own, English.

The English, who were increasingly becoming the British, thought of themselves and were seen by others, with some justification, as having generated quite distinctive political institutions and culture. The over-throw of James II in the Glorious Revolution[N] established a balance between the powers of the King and the representative institutions very different from that of most other European monarchies. This balance was further tipped in Parliament's favour by a succession of monarchs increasingly dependent on parliament. So curbed were the powers of the British King that Montesquieu had famously described England as:

---

[39] Burke to Weddell, 31 Jan. 1792, *Corr.* vii, pp. 54, 52.
[40] Burke, *Appeal from the New to the Old Whigs* (1791), p. 3 (and in *Further Reflections on the Revolution in France*, ed. D. E. Ritchie (Indiana, 1992), p. 56).

'a nation where the republic hides itself under the form of a monarchy'.[41] Whilst this constitutional balance was delicate – and the precise allocation of powers within it a matter of frequent debate – its existence was held to guarantee the liberty of the subject by preventing 'the Crown' – the Monarch or an executive acting in his name – from encroaching on the freedoms of individuals or of corporate bodies – the Church, parliament, the law courts etc.

The idea of the mixed or balanced constitution – combining elements of monarchy, aristocracy and democracy in the various offices of the constitution – was one which went back to antiquity, to the texts of Aristotle, Polybius and Cicero, some at least of which the educated would have read, and – as Burke does – quoted freely and from memory in the original. The 'balance' of the English constitution was celebrated in the work of William Blackstone, the foremost constitutional and legal scholar of the time. 'Balance' becomes, in eighteenth-century England, a pervasive political virtue. In contrast to the French concern to pursue a single principle in the establishment of their institutions, in England, wrote Burke, 'We compensate, we reconcile, we balance.'[42] A vital issue in retaining this balance and thereby restraining the Crown was to maintain the independence of the Commons, an aim which was believed to require the independence of the electorate themselves, both as a body and as individuals. To enfranchise those who were dependent, either because of poverty or moral weakness, laid the way open to the capture of the Commons by those able to sway the electorate through bribery, rhetoric or fear. If political liberty required balance, then to be opposed – as Burke famously was – to the concentration of power in the Crown, did not at all imply enthusiasm for the extension of it to the economically dependent populace. To enfranchise the poor would not extend freedom, but endanger it. Independence is not, today, a fashionable political virtue, if indeed it is one at all, but for Burke and his contemporaries it was central: worries about independence and balance pervade his analysis of the new French Constitution.

In England, a major constraint on the executive was parliament's control over taxation and the purposes to which it could be put. Such considerations of political economy preoccupy Burke throughout large tracts of *Reflections*. Financially troubled absolutist regimes such as France

---

[41] 'une nation où la république se cache sous la forme de la monarchie', *Esprit des Lois* (Paris, 1951), v.19, p. 304.
[42] *Reflections*, p. 172.

might at any time declare bankruptcy –a policy option under frequent consideration there in the 1780s. A bankruptcy would convert the state's debts into losses for the regime's creditors. This risk increased the cost of borrowing for absolutist regimes: creditors simply charged higher interest rates to offset the increased risk of losing the capital value of their loan. It was the French monarchy's failure to retain a sufficient tax-base to pay the interest on its loans that had forced the calling of the Estates General[N] in the first place and so set the Revolution in train. However, in a parliamentary regime such as Britain's, many members of the legislature were themselves creditors: they had an interest in ensuring the stability and viability of both the political regime and its finances. Because its political leaders were incentivised to secure the property rights of creditors, a parliamentary regime could borrow money more cheaply. Economic stability and political liberty – in the sense of protection from arbitrary sovereigns – were brought into harmony and secured by harnessing both to a class interest – that of the property-owners.

The stability of property rights was also the foundation of what Burke saw as another basis of a free society – the existence of independent corporations or establishments, such as the Church, universities, charitable trusts and other elements of what we would now call civil society. Their ability to act with political and social independence rested ultimately on their economic autonomy, which, in turn, their property rights guaranteed. One of Burke's major criticisms of the revolutionaries was their expropriation of Church property and the change in the status of priests and other clerics from members of an independently funded corporation into state employees with, he foretold, a resulting loss of autonomy. This had further ideological implications. Burke, although personally devout, was disarmingly frank about religion's part in creating and disciplining social order. The fear of eternal punishment played a vital role in sustaining morality and inhibiting the poor from instigating, or allowing themselves to be recruited into, destructive social experiments. The disestablishment of the French Church in order to resolve the state's financial crisis seemed to him to break a virtuous circle in which the stability of property sustained an independent church which provided moral instruction that inhibited attacks on the social order, including property rights. Indeed, disestablishment could be seen – and he so presented it – as a calculated attempt to break the mutually supportive political, financial and moral elements of the eighteenth-century polity. On this view the revolutionaries' strategy positively *required* the destruction of Christian morality in order to overcome the inhibitions it placed on radical social change. The appropriation of Church property thus – from a revolutionary point of view – turned two problems into a single solution. At a stroke it provided much needed capital for a regime which had inherited a bankrupt economy and guaranteed the security of the national debt (the holders of which were themselves, thought Burke, the real force behind the Revolution), and it simultaneously undermined the very institution – the Church – that had provided ideological protection against such action. The revolutionaries went on to claim this as a breakthrough to a new kind of social order, one that would achieve stability through social equality, not ordered ranks, with secular, not religious values and ideals, and with paper money (backed by land), rather than gold or silver.[43]

Burke denied that this could provide the basis for a stable social order. The reason was not only the rejection of Christianity or the moral repugnance of robbing the Church of its land: there was also an economic argument – which is still with us today – about the relative autonomy of the economy in the face of political intervention.

The revolutionary financial strategy was to restore the creditworthiness of the government and its new paper currency by nationalising the Church lands as security. These would be sold piecemeal over time, the proceeds amortising the national debt and creating confidence in the paper money – the *assignat*. The *assignat* was effectively a share in the national debt, a debt secured by the Church lands – indeed the original plan had been to offer *assignats* as certificates of investment in landed stock. It was the failure of the market to buy them that led the revolutionaries to impose them as currency. But this meant that parcels of expropriated land coming onto the market could be bid for in *assignats*, the value of which was itself pegged to the value to be realised by the sale of land determined by such bids. The plan reduced the unit of currency itself to a holding in a volatile stock market, the value of which would be set through speculation. Burke points out that this is not a market one can choose to enter, since merely to hold or use the currency is to be drawn into and subjected to it.

---

[43] The classic analysis of this aspect of *Reflections* remains J. G. A. Pocock's 'Political Economy of Burke's Analysis of the French Revolution', pp. 193–212 in *Virtue, Commerce and History* (Cambridge, 1985).

Burke is often held by libertarians, on the basis of his tract on grain prices,[44] to be an enthusiastic supporter of free markets. However, like most eighteenth-century social thinkers (and unlike most modern market apologists) Burke was quite discriminating about the diverse character-istics of markets in different commodities. Indeed it is not clear that he possessed – and he certainly did not endorse – a conception of 'the market' as an abstractly modelled set of relationships in the modern sense. Like many eighteenth-century social theorists he was particularly concerned about the volatility of speculative *financial* markets, likening them to gam-bling dens, and suspicious of the kinds of morals, mentality and resulting behaviour needed to succeed in such an environment. He charged the revolutionaries with being the first and only people to have 'founded a commonwealth upon gaming, and infused this spirit into it as its vital breath. The[ir] great object in these politics is to metamorphose France from a great kingdom into one great play-table; to turn its inhabitants into a nation of gamesters; to make speculations as extensive as life; to mix it with all its concerns.'[45]

The volatility of the currency as itself an object of speculation would, he thought, discourage industry, learning and investment, for 'who will labour without knowing the amount of his pay? Who will study to encrease what none can estimate? who will accumulate, when he does not know the value of what he saves?'[46] Even should the Revolution achieve some stability, the only ones to gain – and here as elsewhere Burke insinuates a conspiracy theory of the Revolution – will not be the poor, or even the idealistically motivated but foolish and gullible ideologues, but the urban financiers who understand the way these markets work:

> France will be wholly governed by the . . . directors of assignats, and trustees for the sale of church lands, attornies, agents, money-jobbers, speculators, and adventurers, composing an ignoble oli-garchy founded on the destruction of the crown, the church, the nobility, and the people. Here end all the deceitful dreams and visions of the equality and rights of men.[47]

In his diatribe against the gambling-economy of revolutionary France Burke makes great play on the ambiguity of 'speculation',[48] which denotes

---

[44] 'Thoughts and details on scarcity', a paper on managing the grain shortage of the winter of 1795, was discovered in his papers after his death, and published in 1800.
[45] *Reflections*, p. 196.  [46] *Reflections*, p. 197.  [47] *Reflections*, p. 199.
[48] The word or its cognates appears no less than thirty-four times in the text.

risk and irresponsibility in both philosophy and economics, and desta-bilises both meaning and social life. Increasing the speculative character of social life would disrupt continuity and expectations, leaving genera-tions unanchored in any of the shared values or practices constitutive of society. It misreads Burke to present him as an unqualified enthusiast for an abstractly conceived 'market', the workings of which, he once pointed out, were, in the absence of its embodiment in particular situations and practices, at best established 'a priori'.[49]

For Burke, cognitive instability is not just a concomitant of a specula-tive economy, it is a consequence of the way the French have chosen to reflect on and think about their society. The English based their politics, and political principles, like their law, on existent practices – on custom and precedent. The French revolutionaries by contrast, Burke points out, deduce their politics from abstract principles – the rights of men. This was more than a difference between the intellectual and moral resources available within two contrasting national political cultures, it was a con-scious (if perverse) decision: an 'unforced choice, [a] ... fond election of evil'.[50] Burke clearly thought the French might (like the English) have sought to reform on the basis of their (different) inherited institutions.[51] The French turn to abstraction was a fundamental difference in political principle.

This is a third, much larger and more abstract context in which to read Burke. He not only sought to represent the Whig tradition as opposed to the populist politics of Fox, and English politics and political economy as opposed to that of revolutionary France; he also describes two different conceptions of politics.

# V

One way of characterising that difference is between rationalist, reformist politics and a procedurally conservative politics. The rationalist starts

---

[49] In cases of conflict between political management and the dictates of untried market mechanisms Burke invariably sought to judge the issue on its merits and expressed his 'insuperable reluctance in giving [his] hand to destroy any established institution of government, upon a theory, however plausible it may be' ('Speech on Foxes India Bill', *W&S*, v, p. 387).

[50] *Reflections*, p. 41.

[51] Many, even moderate Frenchmen disagreed. They thought there were insufficient resources within the *ancien régime* to regenerate liberty from them. Amongst English replies to Burke James Mackintosh's *Vindiciae Gallicae* pursued a similar line.

from a set of principles – in this case those of natural right, or the rights of man – and seeks to deduce the features of a morally defensible political order from those principles. The presumption is that, if the principles are right, then all that is (legitimately) deduced from them will be so too. The task of politics is then conceived to be the reconstruction of the social world according to the principles. The procedural conservative,[52] by contrast, begins with 'really existing' institutions and ideas which they take to be constitutive of a given political reality and then proceeds to sustain that reality, reforming as and where necessary in a piecemeal way so as always to maintain the functional integrity of the whole. This is to put the matter very abstractly, but not at a level unavailable to reflective eighteenth-century protagonists. Burke clearly had particular views about specific aspects of the English constitution which he thought enabled it to function so well. But he did not regard constitutional monarchy as the uniquely eligible form of government. Republics, where they existed, he thought perfectly legitimate, and even regarded what he called a 'spirit of republicanism' as a possible – indeed sometimes the only – source of reform within monarchies.[53] But he thought the attempt to transform a whole political culture according to some principle extrinsic to its own history and practices was hugely dangerous, and he thought the attempt to reform on the principle of unqualified democracy (even though, as he pointed out, the institutional arrangements did not conform to it) was disastrous, as indeed it turned out to be.

Burke thought that normative natural-rights claims – if successful – effectively overturn this inherited experience and restart institutional history with a clean slate. French protagonists and Thomas Paine make this quite explicit: it was because 'the world is as new [to every child] as it was to the first man that existed, and his natural right in it is of the same kind' that inherited institutional arrangements have only as much authority as successive generations choose to give them: 'Every age and generation must be as free to act for itself, *in all cases*, as the ages and generations which preceded it.'[54]

---

[52] The adjective 'procedural' is used to signal a distinction between it and another kind of conservative, the substantive conservative, who defends one particular unchanging order – often religiously sanctioned – and who becomes indistinguishable from a reactionary, as that order recedes into the past.

[53] Letter to William Elliot, 26 May 1795, in *Two letters on the Conduct of our Domestic Parties, with regard to French Politics* (1797), *W&S*, ix, p. 42.

[54] Thomas Paine, *Rights of Man* (Harmondsworth, 1969 [1791]), pp. 66, 41. And see the speech, recorded by Burke, of the Deputy Rabaud de St. Etienne, for whom

Burke thought such claims foolishly overestimate the capacity of individual human reasoning and ignored the accumulation of experience which is embodied in institutions and social practices – 'Old establishments are tried by their effects... we conclude that to be good from whence good is derived'.[55] The radical also presupposed an *individual* competence to judge and act on these matters, when in fact political wisdom is, Burke thought, necessarily social, collectively gained and held in institutions. We should be 'afraid to put men to live and trade each on his own private stock of reason; because we suspect that this stock in each man is small, and... [they] would do better to avail themselves of the general bank and capital of... ages.'[56] The rejection of inherited practices constituted an act of epistemological and volitional original sin – pride. Since our contemporary societies take for granted not only a right to change but a virtual presumption in favour of the new over the old, it is worth underscoring the sense in which this – as Paine rightly sees – was the core issue. It is also worth bearing in mind that the concept of 'democracy' that Burke attacks is not what we call 'liberal democracies' today – which he might well have thought of as 'tempered oligarchies'.

Claims about the capacity or competence of reason invoke philosophical questions at the highest level. These formed fundamental issues for philosophers from Descartes to Kant and thus had wider echoes in European and Enlightenment thinking. *Reflections* is a piece of persuasive, rhetorical writing, and though it presupposes them does not explicitly ground political philosophy in them. But Burke's scepticism about the powers of individual reason was not mere prejudice. It had its basis in a philosophical epistemology quite as reflective as that of any of his Enlightenment predecessors. Two of Burke's earliest works are preoccupied with the nature and limits of human knowledge and the implications of these for politics. The *Philosophical Enquiry into the Origins of our Ideas of the Sublime and the Beautiful* (1757) deals with aesthetics, but for Burke and his immediate contemporaries, aesthetics derived from epistemology and both were implicated in issues of morals and religion. Burke thus connected his work with the wider field of the philosophy of knowledge and

---

Frenchmen 'must be refashioned, have their ideas changed, their laws changed, their customs changed;... men changed; things changed; words changed;... everything destroyed; yes, destroy everything; since everything is to be made anew' (*Reflections*, p. 171 fn. 322).

[55] *Reflections*, p. 175.    [56] *Reflections*, p. 90.

the psychology of belief and insisted on its importance for 'any whose business it is to affect the passions'.[57]

Burke's arguments were rooted in the debate provoked by John Locke's *Essay Concerning Human Understanding* (1690). Locke made a number of central claims. The first was that the constituents of our mental world – ideas – derived exclusively from impressions of the senses. There were therefore no innate, pre-experiential ideas. Human understanding was built up piecemeal through individual experience and the 'operations of the mind' on it. Reason, one of the 'operations of the mind', was the 'comparison of clear and distinct ideas' from which conclusions could be drawn about the different (or similar) properties of those ideas.

Locke's concern was to identify the *limits* of reason and understanding in relation to religious faith, but his legacy was ambiguous. Identifying the limits of reason could be used – as was Locke's intention – to prevent theologians invoking reason to make extravagant and dogmatic claims in the field of religion, thereby grounding religious toleration in a congenitally necessary human agnosticism. But Locke's criterion – of reason as the comparison of clear and distinct ideas – could also be used as a critical principle: to dismiss as *ir*rational such ideas as the Trinity, or the virgin birth, which were not 'clear and distinct' enough to be reasoned about. The devout responded by stressing that this merely showed the limits of reason, not the implausibility of faith. Whilst we now tend to think of scepticism as an anti-religious position, in the eighteenth century scepticism about the claims of reason was an essential weapon of the devout against the rationalist's critiques of religious claims. Those making such attacks (or thought to be doing so) were known as deists, and those who thought of themselves as orthodox ('true') Christians devoted enormous intellectual energy to identifying and denouncing them.

Burke was much exercised by these issues. He had not thought deists posed a threat to the religious basis of English political culture, although he feared their becoming numerous or influential as they had in revolutionary France; it was an influence he sought to oppose in *Reflections*. Nevertheless the philosophical arguments about the strength and weakness of reason earlier in the century had left a deep impression on him. His first published work had satirised the notorious deist Lord Bolingbroke. In the 'Preface' added to the second edition Burke explained that he had wanted 'to shew that, without the Exertion of any

---

[57] *Enquiry*, *W&S*, i, p. 282.

considerable Forces, the same Engines [i.e. arguments] which were employed for the Destruction of Religion, might be employed with equal Success for the Subversion of Government.' Over-confidence in our powers of reason could result in 'attack[ing] everything the most excellent and venerable'.[58] What would become of the world, he asked, 'if the Practice of all moral Duties, and the Foundations of Society, rested upon having their Reasons made clear and demonstrable to every Individual?'[59] In 1756 Burke's question was entirely rhetorical, inviting the reader to agree how ridiculous and destructive such a demand was. But, now, thirty-five years later, the claim that inherited institutions should be made justifiable to the ordinary man – and even woman – was indeed being proclaimed by the French Revolution and its imitators in Britain and Ireland, who argued in real earnest what Burke had sketched as a satirical absurdity.

In his *Philosophical Enquiry*, published in 1757, Burke engaged in a more detached way with these issues. The points of relevance to his later political theory are that clear ideas – which are for that reason capable of being subjected to the rationalising operations of the mind – affect us less strongly than what he calls sublime ideas. Sublime ideas escape the operations of reason, because of their obscurity, enormity, antiquity, or some other dimension of unboundedness which makes it impossible for them to be clear and distinct, compared, and so rationalised. A clear idea, he concludes, is 'another name for a little idea'.[60] However attractive the rational clarity and simplicity of 'natural right', these very qualities, Burke thinks, will disqualify them from providing an enduring and stable basis for political allegiance. Clear arguments affect us far less than imposing, if unclear ones, and politics is about affect, not reason. For human beings to be subject to political order, Burke thinks, their imagination needs to be affected by the sublime: in England it is the antiquity and continuity of the constitution that provides this. The political use of the sublime cannot be made explicit since, as Burke concedes, once we know how the sublime affects us, the contrivance of the argument – its clarity – weakens its effect.[61] Burke, although frequently deploying the sublime in *Reflections*, is there inexplicit about its mode of operation.

---

[58] *A Vindication of Natural Society*, 'Preface' to the Second Edition (1757), in *Burke: Pre-revolutionary Writings*, ed. Harris, p. 10.

[59] Ibid., p. 11.    [60] *Enquiry*, *W&S*, i, p. 235.

[61] 'great clearness helps but little toward affecting the passions, as it is in some sort an enemy to all enthusiasms whatsoever' (*Enquiry*, *W&S*, i, p. 232).

In insisting on the distinction between the logical properties of ideas and their persuasive power, Burke moves from the terrain of Enlightenment philosophy to that of ideology. This is not an intention we can impute to him in those terms – the word 'ideology' would not be invented until shortly after his death – but it is a way of thinking about political argument to which Burke increasingly appeals, stressing that it is not the deductive consequences of natural rights, for example, to which we should pay attention, but the likely consequences of their being believed. It is a way of thinking about political ideas which was to become increasingly prevalent in modernity and post-modernity. Belief in such an ultimately relativist world cannot be attributed to Burke, a sincere religious believer in an ultimately objective morality and epistemology. Nevertheless, he did not believe that our access to these objectivities was unproblematic: we are, rather, forced to interpret them from within our own historicised experience. This can make him appear very close to modern sceptical conservatives such as Michael Oakeshott, and even to share ground with certain post-modern positions.[62]

# VI

We have already hinted at one wider political context – that of a Christian Europe – in which Burke's arguments can be located and it is there that he increasingly situated his opposition to the Revolution, seeking polemically, politically and diplomatically to invest that opposition with the character of a continental crusade against what he saw as an atheistical, philistine attack on the property, institutions and culture of the whole Christian order of Europe that *ancien régime* France represented to him. Burke insists less on the military and more and more on the ideological and universal threat posed by the Revolution. How, he wonders, could an abstract doctrine such as the (universal) 'rights of man' be proclaimed true *only in France*? Those asserting it cannot be thought to limit its (or their) claims to France itself. Their theory of (popular) sovereignty denied the very legitimacy of the courts and rulers with whom they conducted their diplomatic relations. It was clear to him that such a theory of sovereignty was intended to undermine all those states that failed to subscribe to it,

---

[62] M. Oakeshott, 'Political Education', in *Rationalism in Politics and Other Essays*, 2nd edn (Indianapolis, 1991); on filiations between Burke and post-modern positions see Stephen K. White, *Edmund Burke: Modernity, Politics, and Aesthetics* (London and Thousand Oaks, 1994), pp. 83–4.

and the truth of this was manifested in the French attempts to export their revolution to neighbouring countries, something Burke had predicted and insisted to a neutralist British government they would do, not only by propaganda, but, as they did from 1792 onwards, by force of arms.[63]

The Revolution therefore differed from the usual political changes of 'persons and forms' that states undergo, and international relations with its regime could not be conducted according to the normal criteria of power politics. By contrast, Burke insisted, it was '*a Revolution of doctrine and theoretick dogma.* It has a much greater resemblance to those changes which have been made upon religious grounds, in which a spirit of proselytism makes an essential part.'[64] Burke thought it vital to the survival of Christian Europe not merely to prevent the Revolution from being exported, but that international intervention should ensure its overthrow. On reading *Reflections* a close friend of Burke's wrote to him that 'your appeal is to all Europe',[65] and as the 1790s wore on, the grounds on which he argues his case became increasingly European rather than specifically English.

Since 1791 Burke had pursued a kind of personal diplomacy aimed at persuading his own party, the government and foreign powers to declare war. Once the French had themselves done so, he sought to make that war one of regime change rather than a merely conventional power-conflict. In the pamphlets written between *Reflections* and his death in 1797,[66]

---

[63] Burke had arranged for a translation of, and had written an introduction to, Brissot's *Address to his constituents* of 1792 in which the exportation of revolution figures importantly. The translation was published in 1794 (*W&S*, viii, p. 500).

[64] *Thoughts on French Affairs, W&S*, viii, p. 341 (Burke's italics).

[65] Sir Gilbert Elliot, even more impressed, wrote: 'I knew that you was going to give a great lesson to your own country and to the world...But...your book contains the fundamental Elements of *all* Political knowledge, and clearly lays open to us the just foundations of *all* Social wisdom...(it is) the new and better Aristotle, in which we are to end our Study and prove our qualification to act and teach in our turn.' (Elliot to Burke, 13 Nov. 1790, *Corr.* vi, pp. 155–6).

[66] The unpublished pamphlets, all published posthumously, were *Hints for a memorial to be delivered to Monsieur de M.M.* (1791), *Thoughts on French Affairs* (1791), *Heads for Consideration* (1792) and *Remarks on the Policy of the Allies* (1793), collectively published posthumously as *Three Memorials on French Affairs* (1797). *Observations on the Conduct of the Minority* (1793), originally a private letter to the Whig leaders the Duke of Portland and the Earl Fitzwilliam, and the *Letter to William Elliot* (1795), a response to an attack on Burke's construal of Whig principles by the Duke of Norfolk, and, unlike the others, actually intended for publication, were also published in 1797 as *Two Letters on the Conduct of our Domestic Politicks*. To these could be added the 'Letter to Lord Fitzwilliam' which was begun in 1795 but set aside whilst he wrote the *Two Letters on a Regicide Peace*, before he resumed work on it, intending it as a further letter in the regicide peace series. Thus

Burke wrote, 'I had but one single principle . . . – that the extinction of Jacobinism in France, was the sole worthy object of the Arms and politicks of this time.'[67] Pitt did not share Burke's alarmism about the apocalyptic implications of French ideology and never accepted regime change as a war aim.[68]

When in 1795 Lord Auckland sent Burke[69] a copy of a pamphlet – *Remarks on the apparent Circumstances of the War* (1795) written at Pitt's instigation, suggesting peace overtures – Burke was 'filled with a degree of grief and dismay' which he confessed 'I cannot find words to express'.[70] But he nevertheless began writing what was later to be presented by his executors as a series of four letters 'on a regicide peace'. Within Burke's lifetime the first *Two Letters on a Regicide Peace* were published, the first of which is reprinted here.[71]

Some have claimed these works show Burke losing his sense of judgement and proportion over the war. But the germ of his claim (though not the particular arguments) is present in Burke's thinking from very early on, and it has increasingly been recognised as important because it provides a conception of international relations grounded in international society which contrasts with that based either on natural right (which his revolutionary opponents supported) or what has come to be labelled as a more Hobbesian, 'realist' conception. In *Reflections* Burke rejected the idea of the state as comprised of individuals, understood as isolated rights-holders, and prior to any shared political culture or structures. Instead the ongoing political cultures and institutions into which we are each born are the only practical sources of protection for individuals – or, he now argued, moral or legal resource for states. This view is irredeemably

the only works Burke himself published on France (as opposed to letters pirated by others and the *Appeal*, which has a domestic, and the *Letter to a Noble Lord*, which has a personal context) between *Reflections* and the first *Letter on a Regicide Peace* were the *Letter to a Member of the National Assembly* (1791) and the preface to his cousin's translation of *Brissot's Address to his constituents* (1794). For a detailed account of the arguments advanced in these works, and reasons for Burke's decisions about circulating them, see I. Hampsher-Monk, 'Edmund Burke's Changing Justification for Intervention', *Historical Journal* 48(1) (2005), pp. 65–100.

[67] To Lord Loughborough, 12 Jan. 1794, *Corr.* vii, pp. 517–18.

[68] Reportedly condescending to him at a dinner party where Burke had sought to express his worries for the future of European civilisation: 'Never fear, Mr Burke: Depend on it, we shall go on as we are until the Day of Judgement.' Cited in Jennifer Mori, *William Pitt and the French Revolution* (Keele, 1997) p. 101.

[69] On 28 October 1795, *Corr.* viii, p. 333.

[70] Burke to Auckland, 30 October 1795, *Corr.* viii, p. 335.

[71] On the complex history of these texts see the Note on the texts, p. lix.

historical, and places huge emphasis on the need for individuals to be socialised into accepting their place and the institutions that govern them if the social order which keeps the state of nature at bay is to work. He accepted that political institutions are the apparently contingent products of historical circumstance (the 'gifts of nature or of chance'[72] ), and to that extent arbitrary. But the contingent origin of our political institutions is not (as so often claimed by the radical) a reason for abandoning, or at least a presumption against them; on the contrary, it is all the more reason for holding on to them. For Burke the contrast is not (as it is for the radical) between an arbitrary set of institutions and a better, more rational set, but between having the good fortune to possess stable institutions *at all* and the anarchy that we risk from rejecting what 'time and chance' have given us. Far from its being the case that stable institutions can be deduced from abstract principles, Burke thought that, in the absence of shared conventions – which only a specific historical culture provides – reason was incapable of deducing any specific arrangements. Moreover there are no 'default' institutions or natural practices to which we can be thought to revert once reason persuades us to abandon our inherited political forms. Even the device of majority decision-making, he thought, far from being a basis on which to establish political institutions was 'one of the most violent fictions of positive law . . . nature knows nothing of it; . . . [rather it] must be the result of a very particular and special convention, confirmed . . . by long habits of obedience'.[73]

In his early arguments for intervention Burke appealed to the eminent Swiss international jurist Emmerich de Vattel.[74] Vattel depicted states (like individuals in early modern contractualist theories) in a state of nature, with natural autonomy: states had no right to interfere in the internal affairs of each other. Burke ransacked Vattel for exceptions to this underlying principle, but had not found any to permit the case he wished to make for intervention in France. In the *Letter*, instead of appealing to international application of natural law, he turns to Roman domestic law. He first points out the importance of manners (by which he means customs, conventions and informal practices) and law in defining a political community. He then argues that Europe, in view of its similarity of manners and shared Roman legal heritage, could be considered a single

---

[72] *Reflections*, p. 161. Although in the wider sense he sees history as providential and guided by God, it is not clear to human minds what the significance of events is.

[73] Burke, *Appeal* (1791), p. 126 (*Further Reflections*, ed. Ritchie, p. 105).

[74] Emmerich de Vattel, *Le droit des gens*, 2 vols. (Washington, 1916 [1758]).

juridical community (and in this many contemporary writers such as Gibbon agreed). Granted this, the appropriate legal model for thinking about conflict would not be international law but Roman domestic law, which, he points out, provided for pre-emptive intervention to prevent a neighbour damaging one's property through neglect or misuse of their own.

The details of this claim in Roman law were, and have certainly become, less important than the framework of the argument. Burke's claim that there existed an international community with shared conventions of diplomacy, expectations of treaty-obligation and deference to common customs, and a right of intervention to preserve such a community, presented a view of international relations in complete contrast to either the abstract universalist ideology of the French or the stark realism identified as Hobbesian. The view of states as legitimated by a combination of their own historical and institutional history and the mutual recognition of those with whom they form a community of diplomatic practice and political and legal culture is a view which has, and continues to have, an important, if controversial, place in our modern thinking about international relations.[75]

[75] See for example Tim Dunne, *Inventing International Society: A History of the English School* (Basingstoke and New York, 1998).

# Further reading

The secondary literature on Burke is now vast and diverse. The titles below are only representative of some of the main lines of interpretation and topics where they relate primarily to *Reflections* or its major themes. I have not listed works focussing on other aspects of Burke's career, or the wider context of the Revolution itself, either in France or in England.

## Other Editions of the Texts

*Reflections on the Revolution in France*, ed. J. C. D. Clark (Stanford, Calif., 2001) is the best modern edition of the text of *Reflections*, with generous footnoting and supporting apparatus. Unusually it uses the text of the first edition, footnoting subsequent changes and with additions in appendices.

*Writings and Speeches of Edmund Burke*, vol. 8: *The French Revolution 1790–1794*, ed. L. G. Mitchell (Oxford, 1989) is the volume of the current scholarly edition of Burke's collected works containing *Reflections*. Like most modern editions it uses the ninth edition (1791), the last corrected by Burke, but also includes the footnotes added by Burke in preparation for the text of his posthumously published *Works* (London, 1802). The introduction contextualises the work well but, for the political theorist, in very localised historical detail, and from the modern student's perspective, it is sparsely referenced. This volume includes all the works by Burke relating to the Revolution down to 1794. Surprisingly, however, it does not include Burke's defence of the political principles underpinning *Reflections* in his *Appeal from the New to the Old Whigs* (1791).

*Writings and Speeches of Edmund Burke*, vol. 9: *I The Revolutionary War 1794–1797, II Ireland* (Oxford, 1991) contains the *Letters on a Regicide Peace*.

*Reflections on the Revolution in France*, ed. Conor Cruise O'Brien (Harmondsworth, 1968): the Penguin edition, widely available, with an introduction stressing Burke's Irish identity and suggesting his 'closet' radicalism.

*Reflections on the Revolution in France*, ed. L. G. Mitchell (Oxford, 1993), another widely available edition. It usefully includes Burke's *Letter to a member of the National Assembly* (1791): Burke's first defence of *Reflections*' view of the Revolution.

*Reflections on the Revolution in France*, ed. J. G. A. Pocock (Indianapolis, 1987). The Introduction locates Burke in the wider context of eighteenth-century political thought that Pocock has done so much to recover.

*Select Works of Edmund Burke*, vol. 2 (Indianapolis, 1999). A new imprint of the Payne edition, which claims to use the 'eleventh edition' (1791) but with some alterations in punctuation and includes the footnotes from the first collected *Works* (1803 edn). Payne's introduction and extensive and informative notes are included. Foreword and Biographical Note by the modern editor, Francis Canavan. Vol. 3 contains the *Four Letters on a Regicide Peace*, which is the title given by the editors of his collected *Works*, who added two works to the *Two Letters* originally published by Burke himself. These are also available online at http://oll.libertyfund.org/index.

# Biography

F. P. Lock, *Edmund Burke*, vol. 1: *1730–1784*, vol. 2: *1784–1797* (Oxford, 2006) is the modern standard for scholarly biography. Stanley Ayling's *Edmund Burke* (London, 1968) is lighter. T. H. D. Mahoney, *Edmund Burke and Ireland* (Cambridge, Mass., 1960) and Conor Cruise O'Brien, *The Great Melody: A Thematic Biography of Edmund Burke* (London, 1992), as the title of the former suggests, stress issues of Burke's Irishness. The latter, like his edition of *Reflections* (Harmondsworth, 1968), emphasises a suppressed radicalism in his writings. Psychological tensions in Burke's politics are also explored in Isaac Kramnick's *The Rage of Edmund Burke* (New York, 1979). Nicholas K. Robinson's *Edmund Burke: A Life in Caricature* (New Haven, 1996) is a superbly presented collection of contemporary cartoons in which Burke makes an appearance, a large number of which focus on his response to the French Revolution.

## The Text of *Reflections* and its respondents

The printing chronology of the editions is covered in William P. Todd's *A Bibliography of Edmund Burke* (London, 1964). F. P. Lock, *Burke's Reflections on the Revolution in France* (London, 1985) is still an excellent account of the creation of the text, a contextual reading of it, and its reception and critical history. The responses to Burke are arrayed in G. S. Pendleton's 'Towards a Bibliography of the *Reflections* and *Rights of Man* Controversy', *Bulletin of Research in the Humanities*, 85 (1982), and some of them are excerpted in Marilyn Butler (ed.), *Burke, Paine, Godwin and the Revolution Controversy* (Cambridge, 1984) and in I. W. Hampsher-Monk (ed.), *The Impact of the French Revolution* (Cambridge, 2005) with many full texts available in Gregory Claeys (ed.), *Political Writings of the 1790s*, 8 vols. (London, 1995).

## Interpretative traditions

Reading Burke as a Thomist **natural law theorist** is an approach adopted primarily in American (US) scholarship and popular amongst neo-conservative ideologues of the cold-war era. Perhaps the most balanced such reading is B. T. Wilkins, *The Problem of Burke's Political Philosophy* (Oxford, 1967). See also Francis Canavan, SJ, *The Political Reason of Edmund Burke* (Durham, N.C., 1960) and P. J. Stanlis, *Edmund Burke and the Natural Law* (Ann Arbor, Mich., 1958). An older, nineteenth-century tradition, exemplified by several works by John Morely, offered a soft **utilitarian liberal** reading of Burke. This is juxtaposed with and compared to the natural law reading by J. R. Dinwiddy, 'Utility and Natural Law in Burke's Thought: A Reconsideration', *Studies in Burke and his Time* 16 (1974) (and in Iain Hampsher-Monk (ed.), *Edmund Burke* (Farnham, 2009)). F. Dreyer, *Burke's Politics: A Study in Whig Orthodoxy* (Ontario, 1979), as the title suggests, reads Burke as an **'orthodox'** (*sc.* **Lockean**) **Whig**. C. B. Macpherson, *Burke* (Oxford, 1980) gives a **Marxist reading** of Burke as an ideological apologist for a market-based social order, the inhumanity of which required to be masked by a traditional aesthetic. Readings from a modern **literary-critical perspective** include Tom Furniss, *Edmund Burke's Aesthetic Ideology* (Cambridge,

1993) and Steven Blakemore, *Burke and the Fall of Language: The French Revolution as Linguistic Event* (Providence, R.I., 1988), whilst J. T. Boulton's *The Language of Politics in the Age of Wilkes and Burke* (London, 1963) provides a more conventional focus on the stylistic resources of debate. Reading a philosophical **link between Burke's politics and his aesthetics**, an issue originally raised by Neal Wood, 'The Aesthetic Dimension in Burke's Political Thought', *Journal of British Studies* 4 (1964), is pursued by Iain Hampsher-Monk, 'Rhetoric and Opinion in the Politics of Edmund Burke', *History of Political Thought* 9(3) (1988); Paul Hindson and Tim Gray, *Burke's Dramatic Theory of Politics* (Aldershot, 1988); and Stephen K. White, *Edmund Burke: Modernity, Politics and Aesthetics* (London, 1994). On Burke's relationship to the **Enlightenment**, a classic is still Alfred Cobban's *Edmund Burke and the Revolt against the Eighteenth Century* (London, 1929). More recently see the essays in Seamus Deane's *Foreign Affections: Essays on Edmund Burke* (Cork, 2005) and Richard Bourke's 'Burke, Enlightenment and Romanticism', in David Dwan and Christopher Insole (eds.), *The Cambridge Companion to Burke* (Cambridge, 2012).

## More specific interpretative issues

Stressing, in different ways, Burke's **debt to legal argument** are J. G. A. Pocock's 'Burke and the Ancient Constitution: A Problem in the History of Ideas', *Historical Journal* 3 (1960) (also in J. G. A. Pocock (ed.), *Virtue, Commerce and History* (Cambridge, 1985) and I. Hampsher-Monk (ed.), *Edmund Burke* (Farnham, 2009)), and Paul Lucas, 'On Edmund Burke's Doctrine of Prescription: or an appeal from the New to the Old Lawyers', *Historical Journal* 11 (1968). Burke's analysis of **the sociology and political economy of the revolution** is pursued in Michael Freeman, *Edmund Burke and the Critique of Political Radicalism* (Oxford, 1980), and by J. G. A. Pocock, 'The Political Economy of Burke's Analysis of the French Revolution', *Historical Journal* 25 (1982), reprinted in his *Virtue, Commerce and History* (Cambridge, 1985) and in Hampsher-Monk, *Edmund Burke* (2009). Studies focussing specifically on the *Regicide Peace* are few, but see R. J. Vincent, 'Edmund Burke and the Theory of International Relations', *Review of International Studies* 10 (1984); Jennifer Welsh, 'Edmund Burke and the Commonwealth of Europe: The Cultural Bases of International Order', in *Classical Theories of International Relations*, ed. I. Clark and I. B. Neumann (Basingstoke, 1966) and Iain Hampsher-Monk, 'Edmund Burke's Changing Justification for Intervention', *Historical Journal* 48(1) (2005).

**Comparison between Burke and his near contemporaries,** although not a currently fashionable genre, can be instructive: R. R. Fennessy, *Burke, Paine and the Rights of Man: A Difference of Political Opinion* (The Hague, 1963); C. P. Courtney, *Montesquieu and Burke* (Oxford, 1963); David R. Cameron, *The Social Thought of Rousseau and Burke: A Comparative Study* (London, 1973); A. M. Osborn, *Rousseau and Burke: A Study in the Idea of Liberty in Eighteenth-Century Political Thought* (Oxford, 1940).

## Influence and Legacy

For the immediate British reception see F. P. Lock, *Burke's Reflections on the Revolution in France* (1985) above; for Burke's immediate European influence see still Rod Preece, 'Edmund Burke and his European Reception', *The Eighteenth Century* 21 (1980). For modern appreciations of Burke by contemporary conservatives see several of the essays in Ian Crowe (ed.), *Edmund Burke: His Life and Legacy* (Dublin, 1997) and Roger Scruton, 'Man's Second Disobedience: A Vindication of Burke', in Ceri Crossley and Ian Small (eds.), *The French Revolution and British Political Culture* (Oxford, 1989).

# Chronology

Important events in Burke's life and those relevant to, or mentioned in, *Reflections*

1729/30  Born in Dublin to a Catholic mother and Protestant father.
1741  Enters a school run by the Quaker Abraham Shackleton at Ballitore.
1743–8  Attends Trinity College, Dublin.
1750  Arrives in London to study law at Middle Temple.
1750–6  The so-called 'lost years': no firm evidence of Burke's activity.
1756  *A Vindication of Natural Society* published.
1757  Burke marries Jane Nugent. *Philosophical Enquiry into the Origin of our Ideas of the Sublime and the Beautiful* published.
1758  Appointed editor of the *Annual Register*.
1765  Elected MP for Wendover. Increasingly politically prominent as private secretary to Lord Rockingham and political pamphleteer for the Whigs.
1773  Visits Paris and Auxerre in Burgundy. Shocked at the *philosophes*' irreligion.
1774  Elected MP for Bristol. Delivers noted speeches on role of MP and *On American Taxation*.
1775  Speech in Parliament *On Conciliation with America*. Fighting begins in America.
1780  Withdraws from Bristol election, anticipating defeat. Elected for Malton, Yorkshire.

1782    Second Rockingham Whig administration, Burke briefly becomes paymaster-general. Rockingham dies (July), succeeded by Shelburne. Burke resigns.

        Fox–North coalition, Burke again paymaster-general. American War of independence ends.

        December: Whig Coalition falls; Pitt becomes first minister; Burke goes into opposition.

1787    Budgetary crisis in France; Louis agrees to summon the Estates General.

1789    Abbé Sieyes publishes *What is the Third Estate?*

        5 May: French Estates General opens in Versailles near Paris.

        17 June: Third estate withdraws from the other two and declares itself the 'National' Assembly, swearing the 'Tennis Court Oath' (20th) not to dissolve 'until the [new] Constitution of the Kingdom is established'.

        14 July: Storming of the Bastille by Parisians.

        4–11 August: National Assembly declares intention to abolish the feudal regime, and the rights and duties imposed by it: hunting made free, tithes and alienated taxes abolished, tax and other legal privileges abolished, all professions declared open, etc. A National Guard (citizen militia) established.

        27 August: Assembly publishes the Declaration of the Rights of Man and Citizen.

        6 October: Paris mobs force the King and Queen to return to Paris from Versailles.

        2 November: National Assembly expropriates property of the French Church.

        4 November: Charles Depont writes to Burke asking his opinion of the Revolution; Richard Price addresses the London Revolution Society 'On the Love of our Country', praising the French and claiming that 1688 anticipated its principles.

        19 December: French Assembly issues the paper money *assignat*.

1790    January: Reads Price's sermon and begins *Reflections*.

        9 February: First denunciation of the Revolution in his Speech on the Army Estimates.

1 November: *Reflections* published in London.

29 November: Mary Wollstonecraft's *Vindication of the Rights of Men* is published. *Reflections* published in Paris.

1791    January: Begins to urge intervention in France, publishes *A Letter to a Member of the National Assembly* to correct 'some faults [in *Reflections*]'.

13 March: Paine's *Rights of Man* [Part I], responding to *Reflections*, published.

May: Mackintosh's *Vindiciae Gallicae*, responding to *Reflections*, published

6 May: Burke announces his public separation from Fox, splitting the Whig party.

20–1 June: The 'Flight to Varennes': French royal family arrested whilst attempting to escape to the east, and returned under guard to the Tuileries Palace in Paris. First suggestions of establishing a French Republic.

August: Publishes *Appeal from the New to the Old Whigs* to try to force the party to choose between himself and Fox and denounce the principles of the French Revolution.

3 September: French Constitution of 1791 declares a constitutional monarchy.

1792    10 August: Fall of the French Monarchy.

21 September: New French Convention declares a republic.

1793    21 January: Louis executed.

August–September: Privately circulates *Observations on the conduct of the Minority*, not published until 1797.

5 September: The Terror begins: execution of suspected enemies of the Revolution.

October: Introduction of Revolutionary (secular) Calendar. Execution of Marie Antoinette (16th), Girondins and other political opponents.

1794    21 June: Burke retires from Parliament.

28 July: Robespierre executed, end of the Terror.

25 October: Prussia starts to negotiate with France.

1795    2 March: Prussia makes a separate peace with France.

16 May: Holland makes peace.

22 July: Spain makes peace.

October: British Government considers peace negotiations. Lord Auckland's pamphlet *Some Remarks on the Apparent Circumstances of the War*, urging negotiation, published, having been sent to Burke for comment.

December: Burke starts to compose the *Letters on a Regicide Peace*, in response to Auckland's pamphlet.

1796    Summer: Government initiates peace overtures

19 October: *Two Letters on a Regicide Peace* published.

1797    9 July: Burke dies at Beaconsfield.

September: *Three Memorials on French Affairs* published posthumously.

# Notes

Individuals, institutions and events referred to more than once in the texts

**D'Alembert, Jean le Rond** (1717–83) French scientist, philosopher and musicologist. A notorious atheist, with Denis Diderot he was editor of, and prolific contributor to the *Encyclopedie*, the huge multi-volume compendium of human knowledge representative of the French Enlightenment.

**Assignat** Revolutionary paper currency. Originally issued as interest-bearing bonds by the Caisse d'Extraordinaire set up for the purpose in December 1789, and backed by the value of the expropriated Church (and later émigré royalists') lands, their purpose was to amortise the national debt inherited from the *ancien régime*. However – at least in part due to the market's sluggish interest in them – in April 1790 a decree declared them also to be negotiable currency and their rate of exchange with existing notes from the Caisse d'Escompte was imposed by the Treasury (*DocS*, §26). Because of this attempt to impose their value politically, and because of the excessive amount printed, they created – as Burke predicted – huge inflation. They were withdrawn as legal tender in 1797.

**Bailly, Jean Sylvain** (1736–93) French astronomer, member of the Academy of Sciences and politician. Elected for Paris in the Estates General, President of the Third Estate (1789) and subsequently Mayor of the new commune of Paris, he fell from favour after dispersing the crowd on the Champs de Mars (1791) and was guillotined two years later. His *Mémoires d'un Témoin* are an important source for the period.

**Bill of Rights** See Declaration of Right.

**Blackstone, Sir William** (1723-80) Foremost constitutional authority during Burke's lifetime, his *Commentaries on the Laws of England* (1765-9) being the authoritative account of English law, including constitutional law.

**Bolingbroke, Henry St John, Viscount** (1678-1751) Tory statesman and writer. Secretary of State under Harley (1710-14), dismissed at the accession of George I, when he fled to France, joined the court of the Pretender Charles Stuart and was stripped of his title and lands. Following the failure of the Stuart uprising in 1715 he sought a pardon, eventually granted in 1725. In later life he returned to English politics to join the attack on Walpole's Whigs in *The Craftsman* and in famous pamphlets such as *The Dissertation on Parties* – drawn from *Craftsman* articles (1733-4) – episodes also referred to by Burke in the two texts reproduced here. Bolingbroke was also notorious for his deist philosophy, written in exile and published posthumously. These works were satirically attacked by Burke in his first adult publication, the *Vindication of Natural Society* (1756).

**Brunswick, House of** Original family title of the Dukes of Hanover, from which descended the British monarchs from George I onwards. Hence the name of that dynasty.

**Caisse d'Escompte** Financial institution set up in 1776 under French Finance minister Turgot in an attempt to lower rates of interest by creating a more flexible market in credit, offering to discount commercial bills and dispersing French debt more widely in Europe. It did not, however, have the power to issue specie. It was abolished in 1793.

**Calonne, Charles Alexandre de** (1732?4–1802) French statesman. As controller of finances for Louis XVI (1783-7) he had persuaded Louis to call the Assembly of Notables (1787) to institute a property tax to overcome the national debt. Dismissed, he went into exile in England, where he wrote *De l'état de la France* ['On the present and future state of France'] (1790), an assessment of the French nation's political and economic condition. Burke corresponded with him and drew on *De l'état* in his revisions in the 3rd edition of *Reflections* (16 Nov. 1790).

**Carnot, Lazare-Nicholas-Marguerite** (1753–1823) Member of the National Convention, he voted conspicuously for the King's execution. Later (1793) member of the notorious Committee of Public Safety, creator of, and General in, the Revolutionary Army, founder Director in the regime called the 'Directory' (1795–7).

**Coke, Sir Edward** (1549–1634) Famous seventeenth-century Lord Chief Justice and MP. Defended the rights of Parliament against Charles I. His *Institutes of the Laws of England* (4 vols., 1628–44) became a standard resource until Blackstone's work (q.v.) and he compiled other important legal texts: *Commentaries upon Littleton* and *Law Reports*. See *The Selected Writings of Sir Edward Coke*, ed. Stephen Sheppard, 3 vols. (Indianapolis, 2004).

**Colignis [Coligny]** French military family. The three sons of Gaspar I, Marshal of France – Gaspar II, Odet and François – were all prominent Huguenots during the French wars of religion, killed or exiled in the massacres of 1572.

**Condé** Noble French family. Louis of Bourbon (1621–86), first Prince of Condé, was a prominent Protestant leader during the French wars of religion. A later Duc de Condé – Louis-Joseph (1736–1804) – commanded the émigré royalist army opposed to the revolutionary governments.

**Constitutional Society** The Society for Constitutional Information was formed in 1780 by a group of reform-minded urban Whigs and dissenters including Major Cartwright (see J. Osborne, *Major Cartwright* (Cambridge, 1972)), Granville Sharp, Duke of Richmond, Richard Price and others. Its founding document, probably written by John Cartwright, declared its aim to be 'to supply, as far as may be, the want of those destroyed records (of our ancient constitution) and to revive in the minds of their fellow-citizens, THE COMMONALTY AT LARGE, a knowledge of their lost rights'. The attached 'DECLARATION of the rights of the Commonalty of Great Britain without which they cannot be FREE' stated that '*everyman* of the community . . . is, of common right, and by means of the laws of God, a *Freeman*, and entitled to the full enjoyment of *Liberty*' and 'That liberty . . . consists in having an actual share in the appointing of those who frame the laws' and 'That they who have no voice or vote . . . are absolutely enslaved to those who have votes' (*Address to the Public from the Society for Constitutional Information* (London, 1780)). The leading members of the society were tried for treason in 1794 but acquitted. Such societies were suppressed by the Government from 1794 onwards.

**Cromwell, Oliver** (1599–1658) Rose from the lower gentry to become a parliamentary leader and General of the New Model Army in the English Civil War. In 1653, following the execution of Charles I, and the failure of the Rump and Barebones Parliaments, he was created Lord Protector (the highest office) during the Commonwealth. Burke associates him with military rule.

**Declaration of Right** *An Act for Declaring the rights and liberties of the subject and settling the succession of the Crown* (1689), by which Parliament declared that James II had 'endeavoured to extirpate the protestant religion, and the laws and liberties of his kingdom', had abdicated, and was replaced by William and Mary, and then enunciated the various 'ancient rights and liberties' which were to be preserved by them. To avoid the future danger of a Catholic succeeding to the throne, the Act specified the line of succession through the nearest living Protestant descendants in the event of the incumbent monarchs failing to produce heirs (as in fact happened), firstly to William and Mary (daughter of James II), then to Princess Anne of Denmark. (W & M sess. 2, c. 2) Later supplemented by the Act of Settlement (q.v.).

**Diderot, Denis** (1713–84) Prominent French *philosophe*, vitalist, materialist and atheist. With d'Alembert (q.v.), co-editor of, and contributor of several important articles to, the *Encyclopedie*.

**Dissenters** Protestant Christians who were Nonconformists, i.e. not members of the Church of England, and who were thereby disqualified from certain public offices and professions.

**Empedocles** (*c*.490–430 BC) Sicilian philosopher who established the belief – which persisted into early modernity – that the world comprised four elements: earth, air, fire and water. Hence for Burke, a byword for any systematic materialist.

**Estates General** The French equivalent of Parliament, convened in 1789 to deal with the national debt crisis, had not met since 1614. It comprised representatives of the three 'estates' or 'orders': the Nobles, the Clergy and the *Tiers Etat* or 'Third Estate' (q.v.) of Commoners, which (joined by some other members) withdrew and declared itself a National Assembly (q.v.) with constitutive powers.

**Glorious Revolution of 1688** Events surrounding the ousting of the Catholic James II and his replacement by Protestant William of Orange and Mary, his wife, claimant to the throne through her father James II.

**Guise** Family name of the Dukes of Lorraine, an important political family throughout the early modern period in France: **Henry**, Duc de Guise (1550–88), with his brother **Charles, Cardinal of Lorraine** (q.v.), planned the notorious **St Bartholomew's Day massacre** (q.v.) and subsequently plotted to obtain the throne himself. Both were murdered in the Château de Blois by Henry III.

**Helvetius, Claude Adrien** (1715–71) French Enlightenment *philosophe*, author of a leading sceptical and materialist treatise *De l'Esprit* (1758), denying an immaterial soul or the existence of a transcendent source of morality; widely denounced (and read) at the time.

**Henry IV of France and Henry III of Navarre** (1553–1610) Ended the French wars of religion by converting to Catholicism and establishing toleration for Protestants in the *Edict of Nantes*. A proverbially 'good king', he was credited with a desire to ensure that 'every Frenchman could afford a chicken for his Sunday pot'. Assassinated by a Catholic zealot. Burke's insistence on not idealising his mildness is corroborated by his own claim that he ruled 'with a weapon in his hand and his arse on the saddle'.

**Jacobins** An extra-parliamentary political club which emerged during the French Revolution, so called because its Paris base was in an old Dominican ('Jacobin') monastery. Following the execution of the King they became one of the most radical groups in the National Convention, which they increasingly dominated. Under their leader, Robespierre, and with the help of the Parisian mob, they initiated the 'reign of terror' in 1794, under which opponents, and eventually Robespierre himself, were guillotined as enemies of the Republic.

**Lally-Tollendal, Gérard, Marquis de** (1751–1830) Grandson of an Irishman ennobled by the old Pretender – the would-be James III – whose family settled in France. Early in the Revolution Tollendal led the French moderates, the 'monarchiens', who had urged reform within the existing monarchical constitution. Burke had called on this case to support his own view of the Revolution but Tollendal disputed Burke's account. He joined the *émigrés* in England but later returned to France and became a peer under the Bourbon restoration in 1815.

**Lorraine, Cardinal of** Charles, Duke of Chevreuse, of the House of Guise (q.v.) (1524–74), devious and highly political churchman with a reputation for scheming and religious scepticism. Although, as Burke concedes, he was in Rome at the time of the St Bartholomew's Day massacre (q.v.), he was suspected of complicity in the plot.

**Louis XIV** (1637–1715) The 'Sun King', longest-reigning European monarch, who centralised French power, briefly gained French military pre-eminence in Europe and established at Versailles the most extravagant court in Europe, through which he tamed the French nobility and presided over a great flowering of the arts.

**Lucan[us], Marcus Annaeus** (AD 39–65) Latin Roman poet. Grandson of Seneca and protégé of Nero, against whom he subsequently conspired and who forced his suicide. His *Pharsalia* was a history of the civil war between Julius Caesar and Pompey. A favourite writer of Burke's.

**Machiavelli, Niccolò** (1469–1527) Florentine politician and writer. His most famous work, *The Prince*, was a scandalous and amoral guide to political efficacy, banned by the Catholic Church; hence 'Machiavellian': unscrupulous and devious in achieving one's ends.

**Magna C[h]arta** The 'Great Charter' extracted from King John by his barons at Runnymede in 1215, becoming a foundational statement of English liberty. It guaranteed the rights of 'freemen' to inheritance, security of property, due process of law and trial by peers etc.

**Mounier, Jean-Joseph** (1758–1806) A reforming judge from Grenoble, he was elected to the Estates General. He proposed the Tennis-Court Oath by which the Third Estate bound itself to stay in session until the constitution was established. Delivered the first report on the constitution to the Assembly, of which he was subsequently president. Leader of the *monarchiens*, the constitutional-monarchists. Disagreed violently with the treatment of the royal family during the attack on Versailles and returned to Grenoble the following week. In May 1790 he fled to Switzerland, where he remained until being recalled by Napoleon.

**National Assembly** The 'National Assembly' was the title claimed by the seceding members of the Estates General in August 1789, who formed a constituent assembly and drew up the initial draft constitution before giving way to the Legislative Assembly on 1 October 1791 (*DocS*, 8, 9).

**Necker, Jacques** (1732–1804) Genevan citizen, director of French finances 1776–81. Achieved great popularity by substituting borrowing for taxation and massaging accounts to create an appearance of financial solidity. Reinstated briefly in 1788, he urged calling the Estates General, and had drawn up a procedure for doing so. His dismissal in 1789 triggered the attack on the Bastille, and the Constituent Assembly reappointed him, but he resigned soon after. Burke evidently accepted Necker's doubtful claim that the debt could have been managed.

**Newgate** The largest and most notorious prison and place of execution in London. The Newgate 'ordinary' was the prison chaplain.

**Old Jewry** District in the City of London, originally the Jewish Ghetto until their expulsion in 1290. The location of a famous Nonconformist meeting house where Richard Price preached.

**Parlements** The thirteen French *parlements* were regional courts of legal appeal, but as local registers of new laws and decrees they also (and increasingly) claimed rights of assent (and by implication dissent) to those laws. They resisted the imposition of tax reform, and, being comprised of representatives of the nobility and bourgeoisie, were perceived as bastions of local privilege. They were finally abolished in 1790 – an example of the continuity of centralisation of power through the monarchy and the Revolution to which de Tocqueville later drew attention (Alexis De Tocqueville, *L'Ancien Régime et la Révolution* (1856), trs. Bevan as *The Ancien Régime and the French Revolution* (Harmondsworth, 2008)).

**Peter[s], Rev. Hugh** (1598–1660) Nonconformist Parliamentary Army chaplain and preacher during the Civil War and Commonwealth, notorious for his incendiary sermons asserting the religious significance of the Parliamentary cause. He supported the execution of Charles I, was excluded from the Act of Indemnity and executed for high treason with other regicides at the restoration in 1660.

**Petition of Right** (1628) A petition to the King (Charles I) from Lords and Commons, presented as a parliamentary Bill, assented to by Charles I, asserting, on the basis of Magna Carta and many subsequent laws, the right of subjects not to be taxed without Parliament's consent, not to be imprisoned without trial before peers, nor required to pay tax or other contribution without parliamentary consent.

**Pitt, William, 'the younger'** (1759–1806) Prime Minister (1783–1801; 1804–6) throughout the period of the French Revolution, having replaced the short-lived Fox–North coalition.

**Price, Dr Richard** (1723–91) Leading dissenting minister and philosopher. Author of *A Review of the Principal Difficulties in Morals* (1758) and *Observations on Civil Liberty* (1776, and numerous editions) defending American liberty during the conflict with Britain. His sermon *A Discourse on the Love of our Country* (1789) provoked and is targeted by Burke in *Reflections*. See *Price: Political Writings*, ed. D. O. Thomas (Cambridge, 1991).

**Priestley, Dr Joseph** (1733–1804) Nonconformist (Unitarian) minister, scientist and philosopher. Famous for attacks on the establishment of Anglicanism as a state church, and on the doctrine of the Trinity. He experimented on air at Lord Shelburne's Bowood House, and subsequently at the scientific 'Lunar Society' in Birmingham, where his congregation was. His support for the French Revolution led to his house being attacked in 1791 by a 'Church and King' mob, wrecking his laboratory. He escaped to London and eventually to the United States.

**Punic(k)** Of or relating to Carthage, the north African city against which the Romans fought three wars in the third and second centuries BC (the 'Punic Wars'). According to Roman historians the Carthaginians became notorious for their failure to keep treaties, hence 'punick perfidy'.

**Revolution of 1688** See **Glorious Revolution**.

**Revolution Society[-ies]** Associations formed throughout the country to commemorate the anniversary of the 1688 Revolution, meeting on William III's birthday, 4 November. By the 1780s many had become defunct, but the London Revolution Society, dominated by Nonconformists, but including a number of titled gentlemen, had been revivified for the centenary when a huge dinner was held with radical politicians invited and the following principles endorsed: 'That all civil power is derived from the people; That abuse of power justifies resistance; That the right of private judgement, liberty of conscience, trial by jury, freedom of the press and freedom of election ought ever to be held sacred and inviolable' (Albert Goodwin, *The Friends of Liberty*, (London, 1979)). It was at the Revolution Society dinner the following year (1789) that Richard Price (q.v.) delivered the famous *Discourse* that Burke attacked in *Reflections*.

**Richelieu** (i) Cardinal (1585–1642), principal minister of Louis XIII, famous political intriguer and anti-Protestant; (ii) his descendant, Duc de Richelieu, a turbulent soldier and conspirator (1696–1788).

**Rochefoucault / de la Rochefoucauld** A prominent French titled family, including the moral philosopher François VI, Duc de La Rochefoucauld (1613–80). Members contemporary with Burke include the Duc Louis Alexandre de Rochefoucauld (1743–92), deputy of the Nobility for the Estates General of 1789, a moderate reforming royalist who was assassinated in the September massacres of 1792, and Cardinal de Rochefoucauld, Archbishop of Rouen (1713–1800), who emigrated following the abolition of the monarchy.

**Rousseau, Jean-Jacques** (1712–78) French political and social thinker and polymath. Famous for his attacks on the moral evils of modern society in the discourses *On... the Arts and Sciences* and *On the Origins of Inequality*, and for his educational writings, *Emile* and *La Nouvelle Héloïse*. His *Social Contract* was posthumously credited with providing an ideological underpinning for the French Revolution.

**Ryswick, Peace of** (1697) Ended the 'war of the League of Augsburg' and the Grand Alliance against France, one important consequence of which for Britain was the recognition of the legitimacy of William and Mary.

**Sacheverall, Dr, Trial of** (1714) The trial of the high Tory priest Henry Sacheverall for a supposedly (and paradoxically) treasonable sermon praising the doctrine of political non-resistance and therefore implicitly critical of a radical reading of 1688 (and hence of the legitimacy of the existing regime). This became a *locus classicus* for those seeking to identify the evasive principles of the Revolution settlement of 1688. Whilst the trial provided Whig prosecutors with an opportunity to articulate their view of the principles of 1688, the difficulty of claiming loyalty to the monarch (Anne) on the grounds of a right of resistance to monarchy in general led to a circumspect case being presented. This bequeathed a distinctly ambivalent legacy of 'revolution principles' to the succeeding century. The case was used by Burke in his *Appeal from the New to the Old Whigs*, to show that his conservative politics were not a disavowal of original Whig principles, and that it was Fox and the Whigs flirting with the new urban radicals who had departed from them.

**St Bartholomew's Day massacre** Name given to a notorious massacre of French Calvinists (Protestants) held on that saint's day (24 August) in 1572. Initiated by royal guards on the instructions of the King in apprehension of the succession of the Protestant Henri of Navarre, it was enthusiastically taken up by Catholic mobs in Paris and throughout the country.

**Settlement, Act of** (1701) Further specified the line of Protestant succession due to the failure of those named in the Bill of Rights (q.v.) and Act of Succession (William and Mary, together or separately, or Anne, Mary's sister and named successor) to produce surviving offspring. It designated the succession to Electress Sophia of Hannover and her off-spring provided they did not marry Catholics. The latter proviso remains at the time of writing.

**Seyes/Sieyes, Abbé** (1748–1836) [sometimes Sieys, Sieyès and Siéyes, normally now, Sieyes] French priest and political writer. His famous pamphlet *Qu'est que c'est le tiers état?* ('What is the third estate?'), published on the eve of the meeting of the Estates General, answered 'the nation', claiming – in direct conflict with Burke's view that the nation is an ordered and differentiated corporate entity – that the French nation was the undifferentiated, third estate: the people.

**Society for Constitutional Information** See **Constitutional Society**.

**Somers, John, first Baron** (1651–1716) Whig parliamentary leader who supported the invitation to William and Mary to replace James II. Somers drew up the *Declaration of Right* (q.v.), widely regarded as the foundational document of the 'revolution settlement'. Subsequently Lord Chancellor (1697–1700) to William and Mary.

**Stanhope, Charles, Earl** (1753–1816) MP for High Wycombe until 1783, when he succeeded to the title. Reforming politician, founding member of the Society for Constitutional Information, early supporter of the French Revolution, and correspondent with the National Assembly.

**States General** See **Estates General**.

**Sully, Duc de** (1560–1641) French Protestant soldier and statesman, sought to overcome religious animosity between Catholics and Protestants in France, following the wars of religion and St Bartholomew's Day massacre (q.v.). Renowned for his integrity and application.

**Tallien, Jean-Lambert** Member of the Committee of Public Safety, 1794.

**Third Estate** (and) **Tiers Etat** The lower house of the Estates General, comprising the representatives of the French commoners, to whom, as a status group, the term could also be applied.

**Tour du Pin, Jean-Frédéric, M. [Comte] de la** (1727–94) French nobleman and career soldier, Minister of War August 1789–November 1790. Burke refers to his report to the National Assembly in June 1790, when he was thanked for re-establishing discipline in the Army. Although he voted for the abolition of feudal privileges it is not clear that he was such an enthusiastic revolutionary as Burke suggests here. Recalled by the King as late as 1792 and tainted for speaking in favour of Marie Antoinette at her trial, he was guillotined in 1794.

**Utrecht, Treaty of** (1714) Ended the thirteen-year War of the Spanish Succession, fought by many European Powers to prevent the consolidation of the Spanish and French thrones under a single monarch, thus disrupting the power balance in Europe. The treaty is claimed to inaugurate the modern European state system, involving mutual recognition of the sovereignty and territorial integrity of states.

**Voltaire, Francois Marie Arouet de** (1694–1778) French writer, dramatist and satirist. Waspishly critical of the *ancien régime* and of religious credulity, he was retrospectively credited with influencing the emergence of revolutionary and anti-clerical dispositions, and his remains were moved to the Pantheon, the desacralised church of St Genevieve, where heroes of the revolution were buried.

**Walpole, Robert** (1676–1745) Whig politician, First Lord of the Treasury (1721–41), and as manager of the House of Commons, the first 'prime minister'.

**William III (of Orange)** Dutch husband of Mary, daughter of the deposed King James II. The two were joint sovereigns of England following the Glorious Revolution of 1688 (q.v.).

# A note on the texts of *Reflections* and the *Letter on a Regicide Peace*

## The text of *Reflections*

The print history of *Reflections* is not overly complex. The various print-ings in Burke's lifetime are listed by William B. Todd in his *A Bibliography of Edmund Burke*. The way these describe themselves on their title pages does not always map onto Todd's modern bibliographic categories. Todd reserves the term 'edition' for printings where at least one frame of print has been broken and reset, whereas Burke's publisher often listed as a new 'edition' an impression or printing where only minor changes have taken place, and sometimes (as between the 'Eighth' and 'Eleventh' edi-tions) none.[1] Consequently Todd lists only four editions, with various 'impressions', but the last of these describes itself on its title page as 'the twelfth edition'.

The *First Edition* of 4,000 copies was published on 1 November 1790, with a further five printings of the same edition following by the 16th of the month, comprising 13,000 copies in all. Substantial changes to the text were made by Burke in the *Third Edition* (16 November), which included important references to a French work on the Revolution by an ex-Controller-General of the French Finances, Charles Alexandre de Calonne's *De L'État de la France*. The last printing sanctioned by Burke is the fifth impression of Todd's Third Edition, calling itself the 'Seventh

---

[1] William B. Todd, *A Bibliography of Edmund Burke* (London, 1964), p. 12.

edition' and published in December 1790.[2] Before his death in 1797 Burke subsequently added five footnotes to the text prepared for his collected works (1802). By that time some 30,000 copies had been printed.[3]

In addition to the London printings, *Reflections* was printed in Dublin (1790), Calcutta (1790), New York (1791) and Philadelphia (1792). Early translations, in some cases of excerpts, were published in French in Paris (1790), Lyons (1791) and Strasbourg (1791); in German in Vienna (1791) and Berlin (1793) (by Genz), in Italian at Rome and Colonia (1791) and Venice (1798), and in Spanish in Mexico (1826).[4]

This edition follows most modern editions in using the last corrected text of the single edition described as 'the ninth edition' with the few footnotes subsequently sanctioned by Burke in preparing his 'collected works' as identified by Todd (*Todd*, 53j). The case in favour of this edition is that it represents the author's 'last thoughts' on the text, and so the one he intended to pass on to posterity. However, in the case of a polemical work which reacted to an initial and very specific historical situation, and triggered immediate responses by others, there is an argument – urged by J. C. D. Clark in his edition[5] – for reproducing the text of the First Edition, on the grounds that this was the edition used by Mary Wollstonecraft and in all probability, Tom Paine, in their responses to Burke.[6]

Clark's argument seems to me, even for a student edition, to carry some – although not, in the end, decisive – weight. Accordingly I have indicated the substantive changes Burke made from the first edition by placing them in square brackets [] with a footnote detailing the variation. I have not tried to identify changes judged to be obvious grammatical, spelling or typographical corrections.

## The text of the *First Letter on a Regicide Peace*

The history of what became, only after Burke's death, the *Four Letters on a Regicide Peace* is considerably more complex than that of *Reflections*.

---

[2] *Todd*, item 53j. A further five impressions are listed by Todd as unrevised reprints of this item.

[3] *Todd*, p. 150.

[4] All listed by *Todd*, pp. 153-66, and see Wyger Velema, Appendix I, in *Reflections on the Revolution in France*, ed. Pocock (Indianapolis, 1987).

[5] Edmund Burke, *Reflections on the Revolution in France*, ed. J. C. D. Clark (Stanford, Ca., 2001).

[6] Wollstonecraft's *Vindication of the Rights of Men* appeared in print on 29 November 1790, and the first edition of Paine's *Rights of Man* in January 1791.

The *First Letter* reproduced here, was originally published in *Two Letters Addressed to a Member of the Present Parliament, on the Proposals for Peace with the Regicide Directory of France* in October 1796. Burke's original printer, John Owen – in dispute with him over the printing of both this and Burke's *Letter to a Noble Lord* – had produced a pirated edition from the proof pages through which Burke habitually worked up to the final versions of his texts.[7] The pirated edition is itself of interest, since it represents not – as is usually the case – the corruption of an authenticated text, but an earlier stage in the author's development of the finally published, acknowledged text. In this case the pirated version preserves for us an interesting passage (reproduced here as an Appendix) on the 'war against opinions' in which Burke considers – and rejects – the view, later famously championed by J. S. Mill, that opinions ought to be beyond the competence of law and government, a passage that Burke eventually suppressed in his authenticated text. The result of the piracy, however, was that Burke's own edition,[8] published by Rivington, was produced in a rush, and from *earlier* page proofs – the later ones having been sequestered by Owen. Consequently there were many errors, and the printer's attempts to incorporate unclear corrections compounded the problems.[9] The text of the editions describing themselves as the tenth, eleventh and twelfth,[10] which vary only slightly, and represent the last texts authenticated by Burke,[11] is the one reproduced here.

As the Owen affair had shown, writings by Burke commanded both public interest and commercial value, and after Burke's death his literary executors published a *Third Letter on the Proposals for a Regicide Peace*, constructed by them from printer's proof sheets recovered from Owen and unincorporated in the *Two Letters*, together with other 'sentiments' of Burke, culled, as they acknowledged, 'from repeated conversation . . . his own private letters, and from some letters to him, which he was pleased to commend and to preserve'. In the second edition they even identified the various sources from which they had constructed 'Burke's' *Third Letter!*[12] The first edition of Burke's collected *Works* also included a major private letter of Burke's, which he had begun in late 1795 and laid aside in order

---

[7] *Todd*, item 66a, p. 193.    [8] *Todd*, item 66b.

[9] *Todd*, pp. 196-8, 203.    [10] *Todd*, items 66k, 66l, 66m.

[11] There is some doubt as to whether the changes to the last in this series (item 66m), appearing as it did five months after Burke's death on 9 July 1797, were made by Burke himself. But although more than grammatical, they are few and do not substantially affect the meaning. See *Todd*, p. 205.

[12] See the 'Advertisement' to the fourth 'issue' (*Todd*, 71d), excerpted at *Todd*, p. 222.

to write the *Two Letters*. This was a letter to the leader of the non-Foxite Whigs, Earl Fitzwilliam, warning him against the peace policy. This private letter was now labelled the *Fourth Letter on a Regicide Peace* and published as if part of a Burke-sanctioned series of four, a presentational practice continued by many other editors of Burke's works.[13] What has come down to us as the *Four Letters on a Regicide Peace*, of which this is the first, is therefore very much a posthumous fabrication. Only two of the *Letters* were published by Burke as a unit, while one was not written for publication and the third was not written by Burke at all! Moreover the order in which they were composed is different to the numbers they have been given. *The Fourth Letter* was in fact the first to be written, followed by one and two, whilst *The Third Letter* contains material omitted from the *First* as well as earlier Burke texts and material from other sources altogether.

*Two Letters on a Regicide Peace* was printed in Dublin (1796) and Philadelphia (1797) and translated into French (Paris, 1796; London, 1797; Lille, 1797) and German (Frankfurt and Leipzig, 1797 and 1798).[14]

[13] The original edition of his works in which the *Four Letters on a Regicide Peace* were so presented was *The Works of The Right Honourable Edmund Burke*, 4 vols. (London, 1802), and the extension of that edition in *The Works of the Right Honourable Edmund Burke*, 12 vols. (London 1812–27). Later editions followed the practice: *Select Works of Edmund Burke*, ed. E. J. Payne (republished, Indianapolis, 1999), *Writings and Speeches of the Right Honourable Edmund Burke*, 12 vols. (Boston, 1901), and the Bohn's Standard Edition of *The Works of the Right Honourable Edmund Burke*, 6 vols. (London, 1886).

[14] *Todd*, pp. 205–7.

# Abbreviations

*C18C*   The Eighteenth Century Constitution: Documents and
         Commentary, ed. E. N. Williams (Cambridge, 1970)
*Clark*  Reflections on the Revolution in France, ed. J. C. D. Clark
         (Stanford, Calif., 2001)
*Corr.*  The Correspondence of Edmund Burke, ed. Thomas Copeland
         et al., 10 vols. (Cambridge, 1958–78)
*DocS*   John Hall Stewart, A Documentary Survey of the French
         Revolution (New York–London, 1951)
*Lock*   F. P. Lock, Edmund Burke, 2 vols. (Oxford, 2006)
*SW*     Selected Works of Edmund Burke [ed. E. J. Payne, Oxford,
         1874-8], ed. F. Canavan (Indianapolis, 1999). Online at
         http://oll.libertyfund.org/index.
*Todd*   William B. Todd, A Bibliography of Edmund Burke (London,
         1964)
*W&S*    The Writings and Speeches of Edmund Burke, ed. Paul Langford
         et al., 9 vols. (Oxford, 1981–)

# *Reflections on the Revolution in France*

# Reflections on the revolution in France, and on the proceedings in certain societies in London relative to that event. In a letter intended to have been sent to a gentleman in Paris. By the Right Honourable Edmund Burke

*It may not be unnecessary to inform the Reader, that the following Reflections had their origin in a correspondence between the Author and a very young gentleman at Paris, who did him the honour of desiring his opinion upon the important transactions, which then, and ever since, have so much occupied the attention of all men. An answer was written some time in the month of October, 1789; but it was kept back upon prudential considerations.[1] That letter is alluded to in the beginning of the following sheets. It has been since forwarded to the person to whom it was addressed. The reasons for the delay in sending it were assigned in a short letter to the same gentleman. This produced on his part a new and pressing application for the Author's sentiments.[2]*

---

[1] Charles-Jean-François Depont to Burke, 4 Nov. 1789, *Corr.* vi, pp. 31–2; Burke to C.-J.-F. Depont [Nov. 1789?], pp. 39–40.

[2] Depont's second letter to Burke pressing him for a fuller analysis of the prospects of the Revolution in gaining liberty, evidently written before he received the [Nov. 1789] letter referred to above, is Depont to Burke 29 Dec. 1789, *Corr.* vi, pp. 59–61. It is this request to which Burke refers at the start of *Reflections*. Depont, by this time a member of the Jacobins, was so appalled at the views expressed in *Reflections* that he published a reply to Burke telling him 'that if your opinions had been then known to me, far from engaging you to disclose them, I should have intreated you to withhold them from the public' (*Answer to the Reflections of the Right. Hon. Edmund Burke.* (London, 1791), p. 3).

3

The Author began a second and more full discussion on the subject. This he had some thoughts of publishing early in the last spring; but the matter gaining upon him, he found that what he had undertaken not only far exceeded the measure of a letter, but that its importance required rather a more detailed consideration than at that time he had any leisure to bestow upon it. However, having thrown down his first thoughts in the form of a letter, and indeed when he sat down to write, having intended it for a private letter, he found it difficult to change the form of address, when his sentiments had grown into a greater extent, and had received another direction. A different plan, he is sensible, might be more favourable to a commodious division and distribution of his matter.

DEAR SIR,

You are pleased to call again, and with some earnestness, for my thoughts on the late proceedings in France. I will not give you reason to imagine that I think my sentiments of such value as to wish myself to be solicited about them. They are of too little consequence to be very anxiously either communicated or withheld. It was from attention to you, and to you only, that I hesitated at the time, when you first desired to receive them. In the first letter I had the honour to write to you, and which at length I send, I wrote neither for nor from any description of men; nor shall I in this. My errors, if any, are my own. My reputation alone is to answer for them.

You see, Sir, by the long letter I have transmitted to you, that, though I do most heartily wish that France may be animated by a spirit of rational liberty, and that I think you bound, in all honest policy, to provide a permanent body, in which that spirit may reside, and an effectual organ, by which it may act, it is my misfortune to entertain great doubts concerning several material points in your late transactions.

You imagined, when you wrote last, that I might possibly be reckoned among the approvers of certain proceedings in France, from the solemn public seal of sanction they have received from two clubs of gentlemen in London, called the Constitutional Society, and the Revolution Society.

I certainly have the honour to belong to more clubs than one, in which the constitution of this kingdom and the principles of the glorious Revolution, are held in high reverence: and I reckon myself among the most forward in my zeal for maintaining that constitution and those principles in their utmost purity and vigour. It is because I do so, that I think it necessary for me, that there should be no mistake. Those who cultivate the memory of our revolution, and those who are attached to the constitution of this kingdom, will take good care how they are involved with persons who, under the pretext of zeal towards the Revolution[3] and Constitution, too frequently wander from their true principles; and are ready on every occasion to depart from the firm but cautious and deliberate spirit which produced the one, and which presides in the other. Before I proceed to answer the more material particulars in your letter, I shall beg leave to give you such information as I have been able to obtain of the two clubs which have thought proper, as bodies, to interfere in the concerns of France; first assuring you, that I am not, and that I have never been, a member of either of those societies.

The first, calling itself the Constitutional Society, or Society for Constitutional Information,[N] or by some such title, is, I believe, of seven or eight years standing. The institution of this society appears to be of a charitable, and so far of a laudable, nature: it was intended for the circulation, at the expence of the members, of many books, which few others would be at the expence of buying; and which might lie on the hands of the booksellers, to the great loss of an useful body of men. Whether the books so charitably circulated, were ever as charitably read, is more than I know. Possibly several of them have been exported to France; and, like goods not in request here, may with you have found a market. I have heard much talk of the lights to be drawn from books that are sent from hence. What improvements they have had in their passage (as it is said some liquors are meliorated by crossing the sea[4]) I cannot tell: But I never heard a man of common judgment, or the least degree of information, speak a word in praise of the greater part of the publications circulated by that society; nor have their proceedings been accounted, except by some of themselves, as of any serious consequence.

Your National Assembly[N] seems to entertain much the same opinion that I do of this poor charitable club. As a nation, you reserved the whole stock of your eloquent acknowledgments for the Revolution Society;[N] when their fellows in the Constitutional were, in equity, entitled to some

---

[3] I.e. the English, 'Glorious' Revolution of 1688,[N] not the French.

[4] Long sea passages often spoiled wines transported in the barrel. Port, most famously, but also other 'fortified' wines were mixed with spirit or imported in re-used brandy barrels, to prevent the wine from spoiling on the voyage. Adding spirit killed the yeast before the natural fermentation process was complete, resulting in a sweeter wine which was also more alcoholic than normal fermentation allows, since yeast is killed in concentrations above about 15%.

share. Since you have selected the Revolution Society as the great object of
your national thanks and praises, you will think me excuseable in making
its late conduct the subject of my observations. The National Assembly[N]
of France has given importance to these gentlemen by adopting them;
and they return the favour, by acting as a committee in England for
extending the principles of the National Assembly.[5] Henceforward we
must consider them as a kind of privileged persons; as no inconsiderable
members in the diplomatic body. This is one among the revolutions which
have given splendour to obscurity, and distinction to undiscerned merit.
Until very lately I do not recollect to have heard of this club. I am quite
sure that it never occupied a moment of my thoughts; nor, I believe,
those of any person out of their own set. I find, upon enquiry, that on
the anniversary of the Revolution in 1688,[N] a club of dissenters,[N] but
of what denomination I know not, have long had the custom of hearing
a sermon in one of their churches; and that afterwards they spent the
day cheerfully, as other clubs do, at the tavern. But I never heard that
any public measure, or political system, much less that the merits of
the constitution of any foreign nation, had been the subject of a formal
proceeding at their festivals; until, to my inexpressible surprise, I found
them in a sort of public capacity, by a congratulatory address, giving an
authoritative sanction to the proceedings of the National Assembly in
France.[6]

In the antient principles and conduct of the club, so far at least as they
were declared, I see nothing to which I could take exception. I think it very
probable, that for some purpose, new members may have entered among
them; and that some truly christian politicians, who love to dispense
benefits, but are careful to conceal the hand which distributes the dole,
may have made them the instruments of their pious designs.[7] Whatever I

---

[5] The Assembly made much of the contact with British reformers. *Le Moniteur* (10 Nov.
1789) published resolutions and a letter from the Revolution Society, and reported the
'great sensation' the reading of them had produced in the Assembly, and the fact that the
Assembly had unanimously instructed the president to write to Lord Stanhope[N] 'pour lui
témoigner la vive et profond sensibilité de l'Assemblée à la démarche que fait près d'elle
la Société de la Révolution' ['to testify to him the lively and profound appreciation of the
Assembly of the overtures made to them by the Revolution Society'].

[6] The Society, like other reform and radical societies, had begun to send congratulatory
letters to the leaders of the Revolution.

[7] Burke insinuates that an innocuous society may have been infiltrated for political purposes.
It is certainly clear that the Society, which had earlier provided benefits for poor ministers,
had been revivified following the 1788 centenary dinner, publishing a history in which it
claimed a continuous (and political) existence: although conceding that 'no records have

may have reason to suspect concerning private management, I shall speak of nothing as of a certainty, but what is public.

For one, I should be sorry to be thought, directly or indirectly, concerned in their proceedings. I certainly take my full share, along with the rest of the world, in my individual and private capacity, in speculating on what has been done, or is doing, on the public stage; in any place antient or modern; in the republic of Rome, or the republic of Paris: but having no general apostolical mission, being a citizen of a particular state, and being bound up in a considerable degree, by its public will, I should think it, at least improper and irregular, for me to open a formal public correspondence with the actual government of a foreign nation, without the express authority of the government under which I live.

I should be still more unwilling to enter into that correspondence, under anything like an equivocal description, which to many, unacquainted with our usages, might make the address, in which I joined, appear as the act of persons in some sort of corporate capacity, acknowledged by the laws of this kingdom, and authorized to speak the sense of some part of it. On account of the ambiguity and uncertainty of unauthorized general descriptions, and of the deceit which may be practised under them, and not from mere formality, the house of Commons would reject the most sneaking petition for the most trifling object, under that mode of signature to which you have thrown open the folding-doors of your presence chamber, and have ushered into your National Assembly,$^N$ with as much ceremony and parade, and with as great a bustle of applause, as if you had been visited by the whole representative majesty of the whole English nation. If what this society has thought proper to send forth had been a piece of argument, it would have signified little whose argument it was. It would be neither the more nor the less convincing on account of the party it came from. But this is only a vote and resolution. It stands solely on authority; and in this case it is the mere authority of individuals, few of whom appear. Their signatures ought, in my opinion, to have been annexed to their instrument. The world would then have the means of knowing how many they are; who they are; and of what value their opinions may be, from their personal abilities, from their knowledge, their experience, or their lead and authority in this state. To me, who am but a

regularly been preserved', they claimed 'there is no doubt . . . that it has annually met without interruption from [the Revolution of 1688] to the present' (*An abstract of the history and proceedings of the Revolution Society, in London. To which is annexed a copy of the bill of rights* (London, 1789), p. 6).

plain man, the proceeding looks a little too refined, and too ingenious; it has too much the air of a political stratagem, adopted for the sake of giving, under an high-sounding name, an importance to the public declarations of this club, which, when the matter came to be closely inspected, they did not altogether so well deserve. It is a policy that has very much the complexion of a fraud.

I flatter myself that I love a manly, moral, regulated liberty as well as any gentleman of that society, be he who he will; and perhaps I have given as good proofs of my attachment to that cause, in the whole course of my public conduct. I think I envy liberty as little as they do, to any other nation. But I cannot stand forward, and give praise or blame to any thing which relates to human actions, and human concerns, on a simple view of the object, as it stands stripped of every relation, in all the nakedness and solitude of metaphysical abstraction. Circumstances (which with some gentlemen pass for nothing) give in reality to every political principle its distinguishing colour, and discriminating effect. The circumstances are what render every civil and political scheme beneficial or noxious to mankind. Abstractedly speaking, government, as well as liberty, is good; yet could I, in common sense, ten years ago, have felicitated France on her enjoyment of a government (for she then had a government) without enquiry what the nature of that government was, or how it was administered? Can I now congratulate the same nation upon its freedom? Is it because liberty in the abstract may be classed amongst the blessings of mankind, that I am seriously to felicitate a madman, who has escaped from the protecting restraint and wholesome darkness of his cell, on his restoration to the enjoyment of light and liberty? Am I to congratulate an highwayman and murderer, who has broke prison, upon the recovery of his natural rights? This would be to act over again the scene of the criminals condemned to the gallies, and their heroic deliverer, the metaphysic Knight of the Sorrowful Countenance.[8]

---

[8] *Knight of the Sorrowful Countenance*: a reference to Don Quixote. In Cervantes' story, Quixote misguidedly frees a group of criminals bound to be galley-slaves under the misapprehension that they have been illegally impressed for military service. Once free they set on him. The image of Quixote, the untimely chivalric knight-errant, came back to haunt Burke, who was himself lampooned as the old-fashioned knight in print and cartoon. See Frederick Byron, 'The knight of the wo[e]ful countenance going to extirpate the national assembly' (1790), reproduced in Nicholas K. Robinson, *Edmund Burke: A Life in Caricature* (New Haven and London, 1996), p. 142; and in Iain Hampsher-Monk, *The Impact of the French Revolution* (Cambridge, 2005), p. 103.

When I see the spirit of liberty in action, I see a strong principle at work; and this, for a while, is all I can possibly know of it. The wild *gas*, the fixed air[9] is plainly broke loose: but we ought to suspend our judgment until the first effervescence is a little subsided, till the liquor is cleared, and until we see something deeper than the agitation of a troubled and frothy surface. I must be tolerably sure, before I venture publicly to congratulate men upon a blessing, that they have really received one. Flattery corrupts both the receiver and the giver; and adulation is not of more service to the people than to kings. I should therefore suspend my congratulations on the new liberty of France, until I was informed how it had been combined with government; with public force; with the discipline and obedience of armies; with the collection of an effective and well-distributed revenue; with morality and religion; with the solidity of property; with peace and order; with civil and social manners. All these (in their way) are good things too; and, without them, liberty is not a benefit whilst it lasts, and is not likely to continue long. The effect of liberty to individuals is, that they may do what they please: we ought to see what it will please them to do, before we risque congratulations, which may be soon turned into complaints.[10] Prudence would dictate this in the case of separate insulated private men; but liberty, when men act in bodies, is *power*. Considerate people, before they declare themselves, will observe the use which is made of *power*; and particularly of so trying a thing as *new* power in *new* persons, of whose principles, tempers, and dispositions, they have little or no experience, and in situations where those who appear the most stirring in the scene may possibly not be the real movers.

All these considerations however were below the transcendental dignity of the Revolution Society.[N] Whilst I continued in the country, from whence I had the honour of writing to you, I had but an imperfect idea of

---

[9] *Wild gas, the fixed air*: $CO_2$. According to contemporary scientific theory, carbon dioxide was a kind of air (gas) that was fixed in material but given up on combustion – so initially fixed but then free – wild. The most famous contemporary experimental chemist to subscribe to this view was Joseph Priestley,[N] whom Burke met and knew – and later castigates for his political and religious dissidence. However the term 'wild' air or spirit (*spiritus silvestre*) predates Priestley, being associated with the founder of gas chemistry, the Fleming, Jan Baptist van Helmont (1580–1644).

[10] Cf. Montesquieu: 'dans les démocraties le people paroit faire ce qu'il veut; mais la liberté politique ne consiste point à faire ce qu'il veut' ['in democracies the people may do what they wish; but political liberty does not at all consist in doing what they wish'] (*De l'Esprit des Lois*, Bk XI, ch. 3).

their transactions. On my coming to town, I sent for an account of their proceedings, which had been published by their authority, containing a sermon of Dr. Price,[N] with the Duke de Rochefoucault's[N] and the Archbishop of Aix's letter,[11] and several other documents annexed.[12] The whole of that publication, with the manifest design of connecting the affairs of France with those of England, by drawing us into an imitation of the conduct of the National Assembly, gave me a considerable degree of uneasiness. The effect of that conduct upon the power, credit, prosperity, and tranquillity of France, became every day more evident. The form of constitution to be settled, for its future polity, became more clear. We are now in a condition to discern, with tolerable exactness, the true nature of the object held up to our imitation. If the prudence of reserve and decorum dictates silence in some circumstances, in others prudence of an higher order may justify us in speaking our thoughts. The beginnings of confusion with us in England are at present feeble enough; but with you, we have seen an infancy still more feeble, growing by moments into a strength to heap mountains upon mountains, and to wage war with Heaven itself. Whenever our neighbour's house is on fire, it cannot be amiss for the engines to play a little on our own. Better to be despised for too anxious apprehensions, than ruined by too confident a security.

Solicitous chiefly for the peace of my own country, but by no means unconcerned for your's, I wish to communicate more largely, what was at first intended only for your private satisfaction. I shall still keep your affairs in my eye, and continue to address myself to you. Indulging myself in the freedom of epistolary intercourse, I beg leave to throw out my thoughts, and express my feelings, just as they arise in my mind, with very little attention to formal method. I set out with the proceedings of the Revolution Society; but I shall not confine myself to them. Is it possible I should? It looks to me as if I were in a great crisis, not

---

[11] *Archbishop of Aix*: Jean de Dieu Raymond de Boisgelin de Cucé (1732–1804), a prominent moderate churchman, representative of the Clergy to the Estates General[N] who left with the Third Estate[N] and was for five days President of the National Assembly 25–30 November. A constitutional royalist, he supported the abolition of feudal rights but opposed the nationalisation of Church property and the Civil Constitution of the Clergy (*Exposition des principes . . . par les évêques deputes à l'Assemblée nationale de France* (1791)). He emigrated to England in 1792, but returned under Napoleon's *Concordat* in 1801 and as Cardinal Archbishop of Tours.

[12] The third edition of Price's *Discourse on the Love of our Country* contained an appendix printing these enthusiastic reactions that the first edition had elicited in the National Assembly.

of the affairs of France alone, but of all Europe, perhaps of more than Europe. All circumstances taken together, the French revolution is the most astonishing that has hitherto happened in the world. The most wonderful things are brought about in many instances by means the most absurd and ridiculous; in the most ridiculous modes; and apparently, by the most contemptible instruments. Every thing seems out of nature in this strange chaos of levity and ferocity, and of all sorts of crimes jumbled together with all sorts of follies. In viewing this monstrous tragi-comic scene,[13] the most opposite passions necessarily succeed, and sometimes mix with each other in the mind; alternate laughter and tears; alternate scorn and horror.

It cannot however be denied, that to some this strange scene appeared in quite another point of view. Into them it inspired no other sentiments than those of exultation and rapture. They saw nothing in what has been done in France, but a firm and temperate exertion of freedom; so consistent, on the whole, with morals and with piety, as to make it deserving not only of the secular applause of dashing Machiavelian politicians, but to render it a fit theme for all the devout effusions of sacred eloquence.

On the forenoon of the 4th of November last, Doctor Richard Price,[N] a non-conforming minister of eminence, preached at the dissenting meeting-house of the Old Jewry,[N] to his club or society, a very extraor-dinary miscellaneous sermon, in which there are some good moral and religious sentiments, and not ill expressed, mixed up in a sort of por-ridge of various political opinions and reflections: but the revolution in France is the grand ingredient in the cauldron.[14] I consider the address transmitted by the Revolution Society to the National Assembly, through Earl Stanhope,[N] as originating in the principles of the sermon, and as a corollary from them. It was moved by the preacher of that discourse. It was passed by those who came reeking from the effect of the sermon,

---

[13] *Tragi-comic*: Tragedy and Comedy – two distinct dramatic genres. Hence 'tragi-comic' exemplifies the 'monstrous' mixed responses Burke is describing. But further – in Classical drama tragic characters were noble and high-born, comedic ones common and low-life. Given his later reference to the 'swinish multitude' intruding into high politics, Burke may also have had this mixture in mind.

[14] Possible reference to *Macbeth*, 4.i, where the three witches recite the list of ingredients as they

> Round about the cauldron go;
> In the poison'd entrails throw . . .

But certainly part of Burke's attempt to associate the revolutionaries with the world of the occult.

without any censure or qualification, expressed or implied. If, however, any of the gentlemen concerned shall wish to separate the sermon from the resolution, they know how to acknowledge the one, and to disavow the other. They may do it: I cannot.

For my part, I looked on that sermon as the public declaration of a man much connected with literary caballers, and intriguing philosophers; with political theologians, and theological politicians, both at home and abroad. I know they set him up as a sort of oracle; because, with the best intentions in the world, he naturally *philippizes*,[15] and chaunts his prophetic song in exact unison with their designs.

That sermon is in a strain which I believe has not been heard in this kingdom, in any of the pulpits which are tolerated or encouraged in it, since the year 1648, when a predecessor of Dr. Price,[N] the Reverend Hugh Peters,[N] made the vault of the king's own chapel at St. James's ring with the honour and privilege of the Saints, who, with the 'high praises of God in their mouths, and a *two*-edged sword in their hands, were to execute judgment on the heathen, and punishments upon the *people*; to bind their *kings* with chains, and their *nobles* with fetters of iron[i].'[16] Few harangues from the pulpit, except in the days of your league in France,[17] or in the days of our solemn league and covenant in England,[18] have ever breathed less of the spirit of moderation than this lecture in the Old Jewry. Supposing, however, that something like moderation were visible in this political sermon; yet politics and the pulpit are terms that have little agreement. No sound ought to be heard in the church but the healing voice of Christian charity. The cause of civil liberty and civil government

---

[i] Psalm cxlix.

[15] To *phillipize*: 'to speak or write as one who has been wrongly or corruptly inspired or influenced' (*OED*). Demosthenes had claimed that the Delphic Oracle gave prophecies in the interests of Philip of Macedon, hence 'Phillipized'. Burke insinuates Price's misuse of prophetic and inspirational language.

[16] Burke quotes approximately. Psalm 149:6–8.

[17] *Your league*: under the Ducs de Guise[N] the Catholic League's preachers helped to stir up fervent political opposition to Henry III, claiming theirs was a 'union of Catholics with God and between themselves' (R. Bonney, *European Dynastic States 1494–1660* (Oxford, 1991), p. 411).

[18] The *Solemn League and Covenant* of 1643 was an agreement between Parliament and the Scots against Charles I for mutual aid, and 'the preservation of the reformed religion in the Church of Scotland, in doctrine, worship, discipline, and government, against our common enemies; the reformation of religion in the kingdoms of England and Ireland, in doctrine, worship, discipline, and government, according to the Word of GOD, and the example of the best reformed Churches' (Art. 1).

gains as little as that of religion by this confusion of duties. Those who quit their proper character, to assume what does not belong to them, are, for the greater part, ignorant both of the character they leave, and of the character they assume. Wholly unacquainted with the world in which they are so fond of meddling, and inexperienced in all its affairs, on which they pronounce with so much confidence, they have nothing of politics but the passions they excite. Surely the church is a place where one day's truce ought to be allowed to the dissensions and animosities of mankind.

This pulpit style, revived after so long a discontinuance, had to me the air of novelty, and of a novelty not wholly without danger. I do not charge this danger equally to every part of the discourse. The hint given to a noble and reverend lay-divine, who is supposed high in office in one of our universities,[ii] and to other lay-divines 'of *rank* and literature,' may be proper and seasonable, though somewhat new.[19] If the noble *Seekers*[20] should find nothing to satisfy their pious fancies in the old staple of the national church, or in all the rich variety to be found in the well-assorted warehouses of the dissenting congregations, Dr. Price[N] advises them to improve upon non conformity; and to set up, each of them, a separate meeting-house upon his own particular principles[iii].[21] It is somewhat remarkable that this reverend divine should be so earnest for setting up new churches, and so perfectly indifferent concerning the doctrine which may be taught in them. His zeal is of a curious character. It is not for the propagation of his own opinions, but of any opinions. It is not for

---

[ii]   Discourse on the Love of our Country, Nov. 4, 1789, by Dr. Richard Price, 3d edition, p. 17 and 18.

[iii]   'Those who dislike that mode of worship which is prescribed by public authority ought, if they can find *no* worship *out* of the church which they approve, *to set up a separate worship for themselves*; and by doing this, and giving an example of a rational and manly worship, men of *weight* from their *rank* and literature may do the greatest service to society and the world.' P. 18. Dr. Price's Sermon.

---

[19]   In claiming that love of country must include a zeal for religious reformation, Price claimed he was doing no more than some of 'the wisest and best' urging reform from within the Anglican Church. In a footnote (omitted from the Cambridge edn) Price had cited a pamphlet *Hints, &c submitted to the serious attention of the Clergy, Nobility and Gentry* by A Layman [the Duke of Grafton]. Grafton had been briefly (1768–70) prime minister. Despite becoming a dissenter and a member of the Revolution Society, he was Chancellor of the University of Cambridge.

[20]   *Seekers*: name given to radical religious antinomians during the English Civil War, who rejected all prescribed 'outward forms' of worship, and, some claimed, any moral rules at all, relying on inspiration by the spirit.

[21]   Price, *Discourse on the Love of our Country* [1789], in *Political Writings*, ed. D. O. Thomas (Cambridge, 1991), p. 183.

the diffusion of truth, but for the spreading of contradiction. Let the noble teachers but dissent, it is no matter from whom or from what. This great point once secured, it is taken for granted their religion will be rational and manly. I doubt whether religion would reap all the benefits which the calculating divine computes from this 'great company of great preachers.'[22] It would certainly be a valuable addition of nondescripts to the ample collection of known classes, genera and species, which at present beautify the *hortus siccus*[23] of dissent. A sermon from a noble duke, or a noble marquis, or a noble earl, or baron bold, would certainly increase and diversify the amusements of this town, which begins to grow satiated with the uniform round of its vapid dissipations. I should only stipulate that these new *Mess-Johns*[24] in robes and coronets should keep some sort of bounds in the democratic and levelling principles which are expected from their titled pulpits. The new evangelists will, I dare say, disappoint the hopes that are conceived of them. They will not become, literally as well as figuratively, polemic divines,[25] nor be disposed so to drill their congregations that they may, as in former blessed times, preach their doctrines to regiments of dragoons,[26] and corps of infantry and artillery.[27] Such arrangements, however favourable to the cause of compulsory freedom, civil and religious, may not be equally conducive to the national tranquillity. These few restrictions I hope are no great stretches of intolerance, no very violent exertions of despotism.

But I may say of our preacher, '*utinam nugis tota illa dedisset tempora saevitiae.*'[28] – All things in this his fulminating bull[29] are not of so innoxious a tendency. His doctrines affect our constitution in its vital

---

[22] *Calculating divine*: double-edged reference to Price's reputation as a statistician. (See further fn. 179.)

[23] *Hortus siccus*: literally 'dry garden' – a collection of dried plant specimens.

[24] *Mess-John*: Lowland Scots slang for a minister of religion – possibly a corruption of 'mass john'.

[25] *Divine*: a minister of religion.

[26] *Dragoons*: cavalry armed with muskets – notoriously fearsome.

[27] The whole is a reference to the puritan priests who preached to the Parliamentary soldiers during the English Civil War (1642–9).

[28] Juvenal, *Satires* IV, ll. 150–1:

> ... utinam his potius nugis tota illa dedisset
> tempora saeuitiae

'if only he [the Emperor Domitian] had devoted to such empty pursuits, the time given to cruelty'

[29] *Bull*: a formal document or pronouncement issued by the Pope, often condemnatory.

parts. He tells the Revolution Society, in this political sermon, that his majesty 'is almost the *only* lawful king in the world, because the *only* one who owes his crown to the *choice of his people.*' As to the kings of *the world*, all of whom (except one) this archpontiff of the *rights of men*, with all the plenitude, and with more than the boldness of the papal deposing power in its meridian fervour of the twelfth century,[30] puts into one sweeping clause of ban and anathema, and proclaims usurpers by circles of longitude and latitude, over the whole globe, it behoves them to consider how they admit into their territories these apostolic missionaries, who are to tell their subjects they are not lawful kings. That is their concern. It is ours, as a domestic interest of some moment, seriously to consider the solidity of the *only* principle upon which these gentlemen acknowledge a king of Great Britain to be entitled to their allegiance.

This doctrine, as applied to the prince now on the British throne, either is nonsense, and therefore neither true nor false, or it affirms a most unfounded, dangerous, illegal, and unconstitutional position. According to this spiritual doctor of politics, if his majesty does not owe his crown to the choice of his people, he is no *lawful* king. Now nothing can be more untrue than that the crown of this kingdom is so held by his majesty. Therefore if you follow their rule, the king of Great Britain, who most certainly does not owe his high office to any form of popular election, is in no respect better than the rest of the gang of usurpers, who reign, or rather rob, all over the face of this our miserable world, without any sort of right or title to the allegiance of their people. The policy of this general doctrine, so qualified, is evident enough. The propagators of this political gospel are in hopes their abstract principle (their principle that a popular choice is necessary to the legal existence of the sovereign magistracy) would be overlooked whilst the king of Great Britain was not affected by it. In the mean time the ears of their congregations would be gradually habituated to it, as if it were a first principle admitted without dispute. For the present it would only operate as a theory, pickled in the preserving juices of pulpit eloquence, and laid by for future use. *Condo et compono quae mox depromere possim.*[31] By this policy, whilst our government is soothed with a reservation in its favour, to which it has no claim, the

---

[30] *Papal deposing power*: Medieval popes claimed the right to depose secular rulers. Pope Innocent III (1198–1216) had not only excommunicated King John, but released his subjects from their vows of obedience and invited the French King (Philip II) to invade England. Burke had told the story in his *Abridgement of English History*, *W&S*, i, p. 535–6.

[31] Horace, *Epistles*, 1.1.12: 'I store and order what I may presently use.'

security, which it has in common with all governments, so far as opinion is security, is taken away.

Thus these politicians proceed, whilst little notice is taken of their doctrines; but when they come to be examined upon the plain meaning of their words and the direct tendency of their doctrines, then equivocations and slippery constructions come into play. When they say the king owes his crown to the choice of his people, and is therefore the only lawful sovereign in the world, they will perhaps tell us they mean to say no more than that some of the king's predecessors have been called to the throne by some sort of choice; and therefore he owes his crown to the choice of his people. Thus, by a miserable subterfuge, they hope to render their proposition safe, by rendering it nugatory. They are welcome to the asylum they seek for their offence, since they take refuge in their folly. For, if you admit this interpretation, how does their idea of election differ from our idea of inheritance? And how does the settlement of the crown in the Brunswick line[32] derived from James the first, come to legalize our monarchy, rather than that of any of the neighbouring countries? At some time or other, to be sure, all the beginners of dynasties were chosen by those who called them to govern. There is ground enough for the opinion that all the kingdoms of Europe were, at a remote period, elective, with more or fewer limitations in the objects of choice;[33] but whatever kings might have been here or elsewhere, a thousand years ago, or in whatever manner the ruling dynasties of England or France may have begun, the King of Great Britain is at this day king by a fixed rule of succession, according to the laws of his country; and whilst the legal conditions of the compact of sovereignty are performed by him (as they are performed) he holds his crown in contempt of the choice of the Revolution Society,[N] who have not a single vote for a king amongst them, either individually or collectively; though I make no doubt they would soon erect themselves into an electoral college, if things were ripe to give effect to their claim. His majesty's heirs and successors, each in his time and order, will come to the crown with the same contempt of their choice with which his majesty has succeeded to that he wears.

---

[32] *Brunswick line*: descended from Sophia of Hanover, granddaughter of James I – the line established by the Act of Settlement[N] as defining the rightful succession to the English throne.

[33] Tacitus described the ancient German kings as 'chosen from the nobles' (*Germania*, 7). Burke's own account of the means of succession of Saxon kingship included 'popular election' (*Abridgement of English History*, p. 406).

Whatever may be the success of evasion in explaining away the gross error of *fact*, which supposes that his majesty (though he holds it in concurrence with the wishes) owes his crown to the choice of his people, yet nothing can evade their full explicit declaration, concerning the principle of a right in the people to choose, which right is directly maintained, and tenaciously adhered to. All the oblique insinuations concerning election bottom in this proposition, and are referable to it. Lest the foundation of the king's exclusive legal title should pass for a mere rant of adulatory freedom, the political Divine proceeds dogmatically to assert[iv], that by the principles of the Revolution[34] the people of England have acquired three fundamental rights, all which, with him, compose one system, and lie together in one short sentence; namely, that we have acquired a right

1. 'To choose our own governors.'
2. 'To cashier them for misconduct.'
3. 'To frame a government for ourselves.'[35]

This new, and hitherto unheard-of bill of rights, though made in the name of the whole people, belongs to those gentlemen and their faction only. The body of the people of England have no share in it. They utterly disclaim it. They will resist the practical assertion of it with their lives and fortunes. They are bound to do so by the laws of their country, made at the time of that very Revolution, which is appealed to in favour of the fictitious rights claimed by the society which abuses its name.

These gentlemen of the Old Jewry,[N] in all their reasonings on the Revolution of 1688,[N] have a revolution which happened in England about forty years before,[36] and the late French revolution, so much before their eyes, and in their hearts, that they are constantly confounding all the three together. It is necessary that we should separate what they confound. We must recall their erring fancies to the *acts* of the Revolution which we revere, for the discovery of its true *principles*. If the *principles* of the Revolution of 1688 are any where to be found, it is in the statute called the *Declaration of Right*.[N] In that most wise, sober, and considerate declaration, drawn up by great lawyers and great statesmen, and not by warm and inexperienced enthusiasts, not one word is said, nor one

---

iv  P. 34, Discourse on the Love of our Country, by Dr. Price.

34  *Revolution*: not the French but the English 'Glorious Revolution' of 1688.
35  Price, *Discourse*, ed. Thomas, pp. 189–90.
36  I.e. the Great Rebellion and Commonwealth 1642–60.

suggestion made, of a general right 'to choose our own *governors*; to cashier them for misconduct; and to *form* a government for *ourselves*.'

This Declaration of Right[N] (the act of the 1st of William and Mary, sess. 2. ch. 2.) is the corner-stone of our constitution, as reinforced, explained, improved, and in its fundamental principles for ever settled. It is called 'An act for declaring the rights and liberties of the subject, and for *settling* the *succession* of the crown.' You will observe, that these rights and this succession are declared in one body, and bound indissolubly together.

A few years after this period, a second opportunity offered for asserting a right of election to the crown. On the prospect of a total failure of issue from King William,[N] and from the Princess, afterwards Queen Anne, the consideration of the settlement of the crown, and of a further security for the liberties of the people, again came before the legislature. Did they this second time make any provision for legalizing the crown on the spurious Revolution principles of the Old Jewry? No. They followed the principles which prevailed in the Declaration of Right; indicating with more precision the persons who were to inherit in the Protestant line. This act also incorporated, by the same policy, our liberties, and an hereditary succession in the same act.[37] Instead of a right to choose our own governors, they declared that the *succession* in that line (the protestant line drawn from James the First) was absolutely necessary 'for the peace, quiet, and security of the realm,' and that it was equally urgent on them 'to maintain a *certainty in the succession* thereof, to which the subjects may safely have recourse for their protection.' Both these acts, in which are heard the unerring, unambiguous oracles of Revolution policy, instead of countenancing the delusive, gypsey predictions of a 'right to choose our governors,' prove to a demonstration how totally adverse the wisdom of the nation was from turning a case of necessity into a rule of law.

Unquestionably there was at the Revolution, in the person of King William, a small and a temporary deviation from the strict order of regular hereditary succession; but it is against all genuine principles of jurisprudence to draw a principle from a law made in a special case, and regarding an individual person. *Privilegium non transit in exemplum.*[38] If

---

[37] *This act*: the 'Act of Settlement'[N] 1701, 'An act for the further limitation of the crown, and better securing of the rights and liberties of the subject'. 12 & 13 William III, c. 2. *C18C*, pp. 56–60.

[38] A Roman Law maxim: 'A privilege should not become a precedent.' 'Privilege' in the legal sense of an exception to a rule granted to a particular individual.

ever there was a time favourable for establishing the principle, that a king of popular choice was the only legal king, without all doubt it was at the Revolution. Its not being done at that time is a proof that the nation was of opinion it ought not to be done at any time. There is no person so completely ignorant of our history, as not to know, that the majority in parliament of both parties were so little disposed to any thing resembling that principle, that at first they were determined to place the vacant crown, not on the head of the prince of Orange,[39] but on that of his wife Mary, daughter of King James, the eldest born of the issue of that king, which they acknowledged as undoubtedly his. It would be to repeat a very trite story, to recall to your memory all those circumstances which demonstrated that their accepting king William was not properly a *choice*; but, to all those who did not wish, in effect to recall King James, or to deluge their country in blood, and again to bring their religion, laws, and liberties into the peril they had just escaped,[40] it was an act of *necessity*, in the strictest moral sense in which necessity can be taken.

In the very act, in which for a time, and in a single case, parliament departed from the strict order of inheritance, in favour of a prince, who, though not next, was however very near in the line of succession, it is curious to observe how Lord Somers,[N] who drew the bill called the Declaration of Right, has comported himself on that delicate occasion. It is curious to observe with what address this temporary solution of continuity is kept from the eye; whilst all that could be found in this act of necessity to countenance the idea of an hereditary succession is brought forward, and fostered, and made the most of, by this great man, and by the legislature who followed him. Quitting the dry, imperative style of an act of parliament, he makes the lords and commons fall to a pious, legislative ejaculation, and declare, that they consider it 'as a marvellous providence, and merciful goodness of God to this nation, to preserve their said majesties *royal* persons most happily to reign over us *on the throne of their ancestors,* for which, from the bottom of their hearts, they return their humblest thanks and praises.' – The legislature plainly had in view the act of recognition of the first of Queen Elizabeth, Chap. 3d, and of that of James the First, Chap. 1st, both acts strongly declaratory of the inheritable nature of the crown; and in many parts they follow, with

[39] One of William III's titles was William of Orange, from the principality of Orange in southern France originally held by the Lords of the Burgundian Netherlands.
[40] I.e. in the English Civil Wars.

a nearly literal precision, the words and even the form of thanksgiving, which is found in these old declaratory statutes.[41]

The two houses, in the act of king William,[N] did not thank God that they had found a fair opportunity to assert a right to choose their own governors, much less to make an election the *only lawful* title to the crown. Their having been in a condition to avoid the very appearance of it, as much as possible, was by them considered as a providential escape. They threw a politic, well-wrought veil over every circumstance tending to weaken the rights, which in the meliorated order of succession they meant to perpetuate; or which might furnish a precedent for any future departure from what they had then settled for ever. Accordingly, that they might not relax the nerves of their monarchy, and that they might preserve a close conformity to the practice of their ancestors, as it appeared in the declaratory statutes of Queen Mary[v,42] and queen Elizabeth, in the next clause they vest, by recognition, in their majesties, *all* the legal prerogatives of the crown, declaring, 'that in them they are most *fully*, rightfully, and *intirely* invested, incorporated, united, and annexed.' In the clause which follows, for preventing questions, by reason of any pretended titles to the crown, they declare (observing also in this the traditionary language, along with the traditionary policy of the nation, and repeating as from a rubric the language of the preceding acts of Elizabeth and James) that on the preserving 'a *certainty* in the SUCCESSION thereof, the unity, peace, and tranquillity of this nation doth, under God, wholly depend.'

They knew that a doubtful title of succession would but too much resemble an election; and that an election would be utterly destructive of the 'unity, peace, and tranquillity of this nation,' which they thought to be considerations of some moment. To provide for these objects, and therefore to exclude for ever the Old Jewry[N] doctrine of 'a right to choose our own governors,' they follow with a clause, containing a most solemn

---

[v] Ist Mary, Sess. 3. ch. I.

[41] Acts of recognition endorsing the new monarch were passed by parliament on the accession of Elizabeth I, c. 3 (1558) 'An act for recognition of the Queen's highness to the imperial crown of this realm', and James I: I Jac. I, c. I (1604), 'A most joyful and just recognition of the immediate, Lawful and undoubted succession, descent and right of the crown.' They both stressed the right to inherit the crown by descent.

[42] I Mary, sess. 3. Ch. 1, declared 'the imperial crown of this realm ... is most lawfully, justly and rightfully descended and come unto the queen's highness that now is, being the very, true and undoubted heir and inheretrix thereof.'

pledge, taken from the preceding act of Queen Elizabeth, as solemn a pledge as ever was or can be given in favour of an hereditary succession, and as solemn a renunciation as could be made of the principles by this society imputed to them. 'The lords spiritual and temporal, and commons, do, in the name of all the people aforesaid, most humbly and faithfully submit *themselves, their heirs and posterities for ever*; and do faithfully promise, that they will stand to, maintain, and defend their said majesties, and also the *limitation of the crown*, herein specified and contained, to the utmost of their powers,' &c. &c.

So far is it from being true, that we acquired a right by the Revolution to elect our kings, that if we had possessed it before, the English nation did at that time most solemnly renounce and abdicate it, for themselves and for all their posterity for ever.[43] These gentlemen may value themselves as much as they please on their whig principles; but I never desire to be thought a better whig than Lord Somers;[N,44] or to understand the principles of the Revolution better than those by whom it was brought about; or to read in the declaration of right any mysteries unknown to those whose penetrating style has engraved in our ordinances, and in our hearts, the words and spirit of that immortal law.

It is true that, aided with the powers derived from force and opportunity, the nation was at that time, in some sense, free to take what course it pleased for filling the throne; but only free to do so upon the same grounds on which they might have wholly abolished their monarchy, and every other part of their constitution. However they did not think such bold changes within their commission. It is indeed difficult, perhaps impossible, to give limits to the mere *abstract* competence of the supreme power, such as was exercised by parliament at that time; but the limits of a *moral* competence, subjecting, even in powers more indisputably sovereign, occasional will to permanent reason, and to the

---

[43] It was precisely this incapacity of subsequent generations to swear away established rights and institutions ('the vanity and presumption of governing beyond the grave') that Paine was to deny: 'I am contending for the rights of the *living*, and against their being willed away, and controlled and contracted for, by the manuscript assumed authority of the dead . . . on what right could the parliament of 1688, or any other parliament, bind posterity forever?' Paine, *Rights of Man* (Harmondsworth, 1969), pp. 41–2.

[44] Burke's reading of 1688 was tendentious to say the least; but his invocation of Somers in support of the inalienability of hereditary succession is perhaps his most distorting claim. Somers' famous tract *Judgment of Whole Kingdoms and Nations* (1710) prominently affirmed on its title page 'that all Magistrates and Governours proceed from the People' and declared 'the Rights of the People and Parliament of *Britain* to Resist and Deprive their Kings for Evil Government'.

steady maxims of faith, justice, and fixed fundamental policy, are perfectly intelligible, and perfectly binding upon those who exercise any authority, under any name, or under any title, in the state. The house of lords, for instance, is not morally competent to dissolve the house of commons; no, nor even to dissolve itself, nor to abdicate, if it would, its portion in the legislature of the kingdom. Though a king may abdicate for his own person, he cannot abdicate for the monarchy. By as strong, or by a stronger reason, the house of commons cannot renounce its share of authority. The engagement and pact of society, which generally goes by the name of the constitution, forbids such invasion and such surrender. The constituent parts of a state are obliged to hold their public faith with each other, and with all those who derive any serious interest under their engagements, as much as the whole state is bound to keep its faith with separate communities. Otherwise competence and power would soon be confounded, and no law be left but the will of a prevailing force. On this principle the succession of the crown has always been what it now is, an hereditary succession by law: in the old line it was a succession by the common law; in the new, by the statute law, operating on the principles of the common law, not changing the substance, but regulating the mode, and describing the persons. Both these descriptions of law are of the same force, and are derived from an equal authority, emanating from the common agreement and original compact of the state, *communi sponsione reipublicae*,[45] and as such are equally binding on king, and people too, as long as the terms are observed, and they continue the same body politic.

It is far from impossible to reconcile, if we do not suffer ourselves to be entangled in the mazes of metaphysic sophistry, the use both of a fixed rule and an occasional deviation; the sacredness of an hereditary principle of succession in our government, with a power of change in its application in cases of extreme emergency. Even in that extremity (if we take the measure of our rights by our exercise of them at the Revolution) the change is to be confined to the peccant[46] part only; to the part which produced the necessary deviation; and even then it is to be effected without a decomposition of the whole civil and political mass,

---

[45] *Communi sponsione reipublicae*: 'by the collective contract of the commonwealth'. Not hitherto traced. Payne suggested Burke invented the phrase to give his sentiment more authority (*SW*, note, p. 108). However 'communis Reipublicae sponsio' occurs, describing the source of law, in Justinian, *Digest*, BK I. 3. 1 & 2.

[46] *Peccant*: corrupt or in error.

for the purpose of originating a new civil order out of the first elements of society.

A state without the means of some change is without the means of its conservation. Without such means it might even risque the loss of that part of the constitution which it wished the most religiously to preserve. The two principles of conservation and correction operated strongly at the two critical periods of the Restoration and Revolution, when England found itself without a king. At both those periods the nation had lost the bond of union in their antient edifice; they did not, however, dissolve the whole fabric. On the contrary, in both cases they regenerated the deficient part of the old constitution through the parts which were not impaired. They kept these old parts exactly as they were, that the part recovered might be suited to them. They acted by the ancient organized states in the shape of their old organization, and not by the organic *moleculæ* of a disbanded people.[47] At no time, perhaps, did the sovereign legislature manifest a more tender regard to their fundamental principle of British constitutional policy, than at the time of the Revolution, when it deviated from the direct line of hereditary succession. The crown was carried somewhat out of the line in which it had before moved; but the new line was derived from the same stock. It was still a line of hereditary descent; still an hereditary descent in the same blood, though an hereditary descent qualified with protestantism. When the legislature altered the direction, but kept the principle, they shewed that they held it inviolable.

On this principle, the law of inheritance had admitted some amendment in the old time, and long before the æra of the Revolution. Some time after the conquest[48] great questions arose upon the legal principles of hereditary descent. It became a matter of doubt, whether the heir *per capita* or the heir *per stirpes* was to succeed;[49] but whether the heir *per capita* gave way

---

[47] *Moleculæ*: molecules, in Burke's time equivalent to atoms: the smallest sustainable particle, i.e. the individual. Burke's insistence on the corporate identity of France becomes a major theme in the *Letters on a Regicide Peace*.

[48] *The conquest*: the Norman Conquest of England of 1066.

[49] *per stirpes . . . per capita*: two different rules governing inheritance. Under the first (*per stirpes*), each *branch* of the family descended from the children of the testator has an equal claim to the inheritance, which is divided equally amongst the survivors within that branch. Thus the strength of the claim of individuals will vary depending on the number of children within the branch. Under the second (*per capita*) the inheritance is shared equally amongst *all* the surviving *individuals*, irrespective of their parentage. The relevance of this is to the relative strength of the claims of James II (son of Charles I) and William of Orange and Mary – both grandchildren of Charles I. The combined weight of William and Mary's claim, under the *per stirpes* rule, may be thought to equal that

when the heirdom *per stirpes* took place, or the Catholic heir, when the Protestant was preferred, the inheritable principle survived with a sort of immortality through all transmigrations – *multosque per annos stat fortuna domus et avi numerantur avorum.*[50] This is the spirit of our constitution, not only in its settled course, but in all its revolutions. Whoever came in, or however he came in, whether he obtained the crown by law, or by force, the hereditary succession was either continued or adopted.

The gentlemen of the Society for Revolutions[51] see nothing in that of 1688 but the deviation from the constitution; and they take the deviation from the principle for the principle. They have little regard to the obvious consequences of their doctrine, though they must see, that it leaves positive authority in very few of the positive institutions of this country. When such an unwarrantable maxim is once established, that no throne is lawful but the elective, no one act of the princes who preceded the aera of fictitious election can be valid. Do these theorists mean to imitate some of their predecessors, who dragged the bodies of our antient sovereigns out of the quiet of their tombs? Do they mean to attaint and disable backwards all the kings that have reigned before the Revolution, and consequently to stain the throne of England with the blot of a continual usurpation? Do they mean to invalidate, annul, or to call into question, together with the titles of the whole line of our kings, that great body of our statute law which passed under those whom they treat as usurpers? to annul laws of inestimable value to our liberties – of as great value at least as any which have passed at or since the period of the Revolution? If kings, who did not owe their crown to the choice of their people, had no title to make laws, what will become of the statute *de tallagio non concedendo?* – of the *petition of right?* – of the act of *habeas corpus?*[52] Do these new doctors of the rights of men presume to assert, that King James the Second, who came to the crown as next of blood, according to the rules of a then

---

of James II. In any event Burke's claim is that the 'principle of inheritance' admits of a variety of definitions, so that whether the immediate heir, or another relative, later in line of descent, succeeds, the *principle* of inheritance is maintained.

[50] Virgil *Georgics*, 4.208–9: 'so through many years the fortune of the house stands firm and the ancestors of the ancestors may be counted'.

[51] *The Society for Revolutions*: note Burke's tendentious satirical alteration of the title of the Revolution Society.

[52] All famous guarantees of English liberty: the Charter (1297) *Tallagio non concedendo* bound the monarch not to impose taxes without the consent of parliament. The common law writ of *habeas corpus* required anyone held in custody to be brought before a court, thus guaranteeing their access to legal process. The *Petition of Right*[N] (1628) asserted both.

unqualified succession, was not to all intents and purposes a lawful king of England, before he had done any of those acts which were justly construed into an abdication of his crown? If he was not, much trouble in parliament might have been saved at the period these gentlemen commemorate. But King James was a bad king with a good title, and not an usurper. The princes who succeeded according to the act of parliament which settled the crown on the electress Sophia and on her descendants, being Protestants, came in as much by a title of inheritance as King James did. He came in according to the law, as it stood at his accession to the crown; and the princes of the House of Brunswick[N] came to the inheritance of the crown, not by election, but by the law, as it stood at their several accessions of Protestant descent and inheritance, as I hope I have shewn sufficiently.

The law by which this royal family is specifically destined to the succession, is the act of the 12th and 13th of King William.[N] The terms of this act bind 'us and our *heirs*, and our *posterity*, to them, their *heirs*, and their *posterity*,' being Protestants, to the end of time, in the same words as the declaration of right had bound us to the heirs of King William and Queen Mary. It therefore secures both an hereditary crown and an hereditary allegiance. On what ground, except the constitutional policy of forming an establishment to secure that kind of succession which is to preclude a choice of the people for ever, could the legislature have fastidiously rejected the fair and abundant choice which our own country presented to them, and searched in strange lands for a foreign princess, from whose womb the line of our future rulers were to derive their title to govern millions of men through a series of ages?

The Princess Sophia[53] was named in the act of settlement[N] of the 12th and 13th of King William, for a *stock* and root of *inheritance* to our kings, and not for her merits as a temporary administratrix of a power, which she might not, and in fact did not, herself ever exercise. She was adopted for one reason, and for one only, because, says the act, 'the most excellent Princess Sophia, Electress and Dutchess Dowager of Hanover, is *daughter* of the most excellent Princess Elizabeth, late Queen of Bohemia, *daughter* of our late *sovereign lord* King James the First, of happy memory, and is hereby declared to be the next in *succession* in the Protestant line,' &c. &c.; 'and the crown shall continue to the *heirs* of her body, being Protestants.' This limitation was made by parliament,

---

[53] See n. 32 above.

that through the Princess Sophia an inheritable line, not only was to be continued in future but (what they thought very material) that through her it was to be connected with the old stock of inheritance in King James the First; in order that the monarchy might preserve an unbroken unity through all ages, and might be preserved (with safety to our religion) in the old approved mode by descent, in which, if our liberties had been once endangered, they had often, through all storms and struggles of prerogative and privilege, been preserved. They did well. No experience has taught us, that in any other course or method than that of an *hereditary crown*, our liberties can be regularly perpetuated and preserved sacred as our *hereditary right*. An irregular, convulsive movement may be necessary to throw off an irregular, convulsive disease. But the course of succession is the healthy habit of the British constitution. Was it that the legislature wanted, at the act for the limitation of the crown in the Hanoverian line, drawn through the female descendants of James the First, a due sense of the inconveniencies of having two or three, or possibly more, foreigners in succession to the British throne? No! They had a due sense of the evils which might happen from such foreign rule, and more than a due sense of them. But a more decisive proof cannot be given of the full conviction of the British nation, that the principles of the Revolution did not authorize them to elect kings at their pleasure, and without any attention to the antient fundamental principles of our government, than their continuing to adopt a plan of hereditary Protestant succession in the old line, with all the dangers and all the inconveniencies of its being a foreign line full before their eyes, and operating with the utmost force upon their minds.

A few years ago I should be ashamed to overload a matter, so capable of supporting itself, by the then unnecessary support of any argument; but this seditious, unconstitutional doctrine is now publicly taught, avowed, and printed. The dislike I feel to revolutions, the signals for which have so often been given from pulpits; the spirit of change that is gone abroad; the total contempt which prevails with you, and may come to prevail with us, of all ancient institutions, when set in opposition to a present sense of convenience, or to the bent of a present inclination: all these considerations make it not unadviseable, in my opinion, to call back our attention to the true principles of our own domestic laws; that you, my French friend, should begin to know, and that we should continue to cherish them. We ought not, on either side of the water, to suffer ourselves to be imposed upon by the counterfeit wares which some persons, by a double fraud, export to you in illicit bottoms[54] as raw commodities of British growth though wholly alien to our soil, in order afterwards to smuggle them back again into this country, manufactured after the newest Paris fashion of an improved liberty.

The people of England will not ape the fashions they have never tried; nor go back to those which they have found mischievous on trial. They look upon the legal hereditary succession of their crown as among their rights, not as among their wrongs; as a benefit, not as a grievance; as a security for their liberty, not as a badge of servitude. They look on the frame of their commonwealth, *such as it stands*, to be of inestimable value; and they conceive the undisturbed succession of the crown to be a pledge of the stability and perpetuity of all the other members of our constitution.

I shall beg leave, before I go any further, to take notice of some paltry artifices, which the abettors of election as the only lawful title to the crown, are ready to employ, in order to render the support of the just principles of our constitution a task somewhat invidious. These sophisters substitute a fictitious cause, and feigned personages, in whose favour they suppose you engaged, whenever you defend the inheritable nature of the crown. It is common with them to dispute as if they were in a conflict with some of those exploded fanatics of slavery, who formerly maintained, what I believe no creature now maintains, 'that the crown is held by divine, hereditary, and indefeasible right.' These old fanatics of single arbitrary power dogmatized as if hereditary royalty was the only lawful government in the world, just as our new fanatics of popular arbitrary power maintain that a popular election is the sole lawful source of authority. The old prerogative enthusiasts, it is true, did speculate foolishly, and perhaps impiously too, as if monarchy had more of a divine sanction than any other mode of government; and as if a right to govern by inheritance were in strictness *indefeasible* in every person, who should be found in the succession to a throne, and under every circumstance, which no civil or political right can be. But an absurd opinion concerning the king's hereditary right to the crown does not prejudice one that is rational, and bottomed upon solid principles of law and policy. If all the absurd theories of lawyers and divines were to vitiate the objects in which they are conversant, we should have no law, and no religion, left in the world.

---

[54] *Illicit bottoms*: the hulls of smugglers' or otherwise illegally trading ships. The attempt to monopolise trade for indigenous vessels was a major aim of British commercial empire.

But an absurd theory on one side of a question forms no justification for alledging a false fact, or promulgating mischievous maxims on the other.

The second claim of the Revolution Society[N] is 'a right of cashiering their governors for *misconduct*.' Perhaps the apprehensions our ancestors entertained of forming such a precedent as that 'of cashiering for misconduct,' was the cause that the declaration of the act which implied the abdication of King James, was, if it had any fault, rather too guarded, and too circumstantial.[vi] But all this guard, and all this accumulation of circumstances, serves to shew the spirit of caution which predominated in the national councils, in a situation in which men irritated by oppression, and elevated by a triumph over it, are apt to abandon themselves to violent and extreme courses: it shews the anxiety of the great men who influenced the conduct of affairs at that great event, to make the Revolution a parent of settlement, and not a nursery of future revolutions.

No government could stand a moment, if it could be blown down with anything so loose and indefinite as an opinion of '*misconduct*.' They who led at the Revolution, grounded the virtual abdication of King James upon no such light and uncertain principle. They charged him with nothing less than a design, confirmed by a multitude of illegal overt acts, to *subvert the Protestant church and state*, and their *fundamental*, unquestionable laws and liberties: they charged him with having broken the *original contract* between king and people. This was more than *misconduct*. A grave and over-ruling necessity obliged them to take the step they took, and took with infinite reluctance, as under that most rigorous of all laws. Their trust for the future preservation of the constitution was not in future revolutions. The grand policy of all their regulations was to render it almost impracticable for any future sovereign to compel the states of the kingdom to have again recourse to those violent remedies. They left the crown what, in the eye and estimation of law, it had ever been, perfectly irresponsible. In order to lighten the crown still further, they aggravated responsibility on ministers of state. By the statute of the 1st of king William, sess. 2nd, called '*the act for declaring the rights and liberties of the*

---

vi 'That King James the second, having endeavoured to *subvert the constitution* of the kingdom, by breaking the *original contract* between king and people, and by the advice of jesuits, and other wicked persons, having violated the *fundamental* laws, and *having withdrawn himself out of the kingdom*, hath *abdicated* the government, and the throne is thereby *vacant*.'[55]

55 Resolution of the House of Commons, 28 Jan. 1689. Similar forms of words were incorporated into the Bill of Rights[N] (1689); see *C18C*, pp. 26ff.

*subject, and for settling the succession of the crown*,'[56] they enacted, that the ministers should serve the crown on the terms of that declaration. They secured soon after the *frequent meetings of parliament*, by which the whole government would be under the constant inspection and active controul of the popular representative and of the magnates of the kingdom. In the next great constitutional act, that of the 12th and 13th of King William, for the further limitation of the crown, and *better* securing the rights and liberties of the subject, they provided, 'that no pardon under the great seal of England should be pleadable to impeachment by the commons in parliament.' The rule laid down for government in the Declaration of Right,[N] the constant inspection of parliament, the practical claim of impeachment, they thought infinitely a better security not only for their constitutional liberty, but against the vices of administration, than the reservation of a right so difficult in the practice, so uncertain in the issue, and often so mischievous in the consequences, as that of 'cashiering their governors.'

Dr. Price,[N] in this sermon,[vii,57] condemns very properly the practice of gross, adulatory addresses to kings. Instead of this fulsome style, he proposes that his majesty should be told, on occasions of congratulation, that 'he is to consider himself as more properly the servant than the sovereign of his people.' For a compliment, this new form of address does not seem to be very soothing. Those who are servants, in name, as well as in effect, do not like to be told of their situation, their duty, and their obligations. The slave, in the old play, tells his master, '*Haec commemoratio est quasi exprobratio*.'[58] It is not pleasant as compliment; it is not wholesome as instruction. After all, if the king were to bring himself to echo this new kind of address, to adopt it in terms, and even to take the appellation of Servant of the People as his royal style, how either he or we should be much mended by it, I cannot imagine. I have seen very assuming letters, signed, 'Your most obedient, humble servant.' The

---

[vii] P. 22, 23, 24.

[56] The 'Declaration of Right'.

[57] Price, *Discourse*, ed. Thomas, pp. 185–7: 'Adulation is always odious when offered to men in power'; 'The disposition in mankind to this kind of idolatry is indeed a mortifying subject of reflexion,' etc.

[58] Terence, *Andria*, 1.1.45–6. Original reads: *nam istaec commemoratio quasi exprobratio est inmemoris benefici* ['for this remembrance is almost a reproach, as though forgetful of a kindness']. Spoken by the freed slave Sosia to his master Simo, who had reminded Sosia of his generosity in freeing him, and thereby of Sosia's lowly origins.

proudest domination that ever was endured on earth took a title of still greater humility than that which is now proposed for sovereigns by the Apostle of Liberty. Kings and nations were trampled upon by the foot of one calling himself 'the Servant of Servants'; and mandates for deposing sovereigns were sealed with the signet of 'the Fisherman.'[59]

I should have considered all this as no more than a sort of flippant vain discourse, in which, as in an unsavoury fume,[60] several persons suffer the spirit of liberty to evaporate, if it were not plainly in support of the idea, and a part of the scheme, of 'cashiering kings for misconduct.' In that light it is worth some observation.

Kings, in one sense, are undoubtedly the servants of the people, because their power has no other rational end than that of the general advantage; but it is not true that they are, in the ordinary sense (by our constitution, at least) any thing like servants; the essence of whose situation is to obey the commands of some other, and to be removeable at pleasure. But the king of Great Britain obeys no other person; all other persons are individually, and collectively too, under him, and owe to him a legal obedience. The law, which knows neither to flatter nor to insult, calls this high magistrate, not our servant, as this humble Divine calls him, but '*our sovereign Lord the King;*' and we, on our parts, have learned to speak only the primitive language of the law, and not the confused jargon of their Babylonian pulpits.[61]

As he is not to obey us, but as we are to obey the law in him, our constitution has made no sort of provision towards rendering him, as a servant, in any degree responsible. Our constitution knows nothing of a magistrate like the *Justicia* of Arragon;[62] nor of any court legally appointed, nor of any process legally settled for submitting the king to the responsibility belonging to all servants. In this he is not distinguished from the commons and the lords; who, in their several public capacities, can never be called to an account for their conduct; although the Revolution Society chooses to assert, in direct opposition to one of the wisest and

---

[59] The 'one' is the Pope, whose bulls were signed *servus servorum Dei* and carried the seal of a fish as a claim to bear the authority of St Peter, the fisherman, the first Pope.

[60] *Unsavoury fume*: literally, a powerful and unpleasant smoke; figuratively, a kind of rage or temper.

[61] *Babylonian*: Babylon, where the Jews were held in exile, becomes an emblem of paganism and slavery. Burke implies that the Dissenters' politics and theology are such.

[62] *Arragon (sc.* Aragon): one of the kingdoms of the composite monarchy of Spain. Aragon, unlike other Spanish kingdoms, was famously a constitutionally limited one. The *justicia* had competence to settle disputes between the King and his subjects.

most beautiful parts of our constitution, that 'a king is no more than the first servant of the public, created by it, *and responsible to it.*'

Ill would our ancestors at the Revolution have deserved their fame for wisdom, if they had found no security for their freedom, but in rendering their government feeble in its operations, and precarious in its tenure; if they had been able to contrive no better remedy against arbitrary power than civil confusion. Let these gentlemen state who that *representative* public is to whom they will affirm the king, as a servant, to be responsible. It will be then time enough for me to produce to them the positive statute law which affirms that he is not.[63]

The ceremony of cashiering kings, of which these gentlemen talk so much at their ease, can rarely, if ever, be performed without force. It then becomes a case of war, and not of constitution. Laws are commanded to hold their tongues amongst arms;[64] and tribunals fall to the ground with the peace they are no longer able to uphold. The Revolution of 1688[N] was obtained by a just war, in the only case in which any war, and much more a civil war, can be just. 'Justa bella quibus *necessaria.*'[65] The question of dethroning, or, if these gentlemen like the phrase better, 'cashiering' kings, will always be, as it has always been, an extraordinary question of state, and wholly out of the law; a question (like all other questions of state) of dispositions, and of means, and of probable consequences, rather than of positive rights. As it was not made for common abuses, so it is not to be agitated by common minds. The speculative line of demarcation, where obedience ought to end, and resistance must begin, is faint, obscure, and not easily definable. It is not a single act, or a single event, which determines it. Governments must be abused and deranged indeed, before it can be thought of; and the prospect of the future must be as bad as the experience of the past. When things are in that lamentable condition, the nature of the disease is to indicate the remedy to those whom nature

---

[63] *Positive Statute*: The statute Burke threatens to produce would presumably have been the Attainder of Regicides Act 1660 (12 Car. II. cap. 30), which in its preamble (§7) 'declared, that by the undoubted and fundamental Laws of this Kingdom, neither the Peers of this Realm, nor the Commons, nor both together in Parliament or out of Parliament, nor the People collectively or representatively, nor any other Persons whatsoever, ever had, have, hath or ought to have, any coercive Power over the Persons of the Kings of this Realm.'

[64] Cicero, *Pro Milone*, 4.11. A famous tag: *silent enim leges inter arma* ['laws are silent in the presence of arms'].

[65] 'That war is just which is *necessary.*' An approximate quotation from Livy, *History*, 9.1.10: *Justa piaque sunt arma, quibus necessaria* ['recourse to arms is just and honest when it is necessary']. The more general claim becomes part of just war theory – to be justified in resorting to war, all other means have to have been exhausted.

has qualified to administer in extremities this critical, ambiguous, bitter portion to a distempered state. Times and occasions, and provocations, will teach their own lessons. The wise will determine from the gravity of the case; the irritable from sensibility to oppression; the high-minded from disdain and indignation at abusive power in unworthy hands; the brave and bold from the love of honourable danger in a generous cause: but, with or without right, a revolution will be the very last resource of the thinking and the good.

The third head of right, asserted by the pulpit of the Old Jewry,[N] namely, the 'right to form a government for ourselves,' has, at least, as little countenance from any thing done at the Revolution, either in precedent or principle, as the two first of their claims. The Revolution[66] was made to preserve our *antient* indisputable laws and liberties, and that *antient* constitution of government which is our only security for law and liberty. If you are desirous of knowing the spirit of our constitution, and the policy which predominated in that great period which has secured it to this hour, pray look for both in our histories, in our records, in our acts of parliament, and journals of parliament, and not in the sermons of the Old Jewry, and the after-dinner toasts of the Revolution Society. In the former you will find other ideas and another language. Such a claim is as ill-suited to our temper and wishes as it is unsupported by any appearance of authority. The very idea of the fabrication of a new government is enough to fill us with disgust and horror. We wished at the period of the Revolution, and do now wish, to derive all we possess as *an inheritance from our forefathers*. Upon that body and stock of inheritance we have taken care not to inoculate any cyon[67] alien to the nature of the original plant. All the reformations we have hitherto made, have proceeded upon the principle of reference to antiquity; and I hope, nay I am persuaded, that all those which possibly may be made hereafter, will be carefully formed upon analogical precedent, authority, and example.

Our oldest reformation is that of Magna Charta.[N] You will see that Sir Edward Coke,[N] that great oracle of our law, and indeed all the great men who follow him, to Blackstone[viii],[N] are industrious to prove the pedigree of our liberties. They endeavour to prove, that the antient charter, the

---

[viii] See Blackstone's Magna Charta, printed at Oxford, 1759.

[66] *The Revolution:* the Glorious Revolution of 1688.[N]

[67] *Cyon* (sc. scion): a twig or off-cut from a tree or shrub prepared for grafting onto another stock.

Magna Charta of King John, was connected with another positive charter from Henry I.[68] and that both the one and the other were nothing more than a re-affirmance of the still more antient standing law of the kingdom. In the matter of fact, for the greater part, these authors appear to be in the right; perhaps not always: but if the lawyers mistake in some particulars, it proves my position still the more strongly; because it demonstrates the powerful prepossession towards antiquity, with which the minds of all our lawyers and legislators, and of all the people whom they wish to influence, have been always filled; and the stationary policy of this kingdom in considering their most sacred rights and franchises as an inheritance.

In the famous law of the 3rd of Charles I. called the *Petition of Right*,[N] the parliament says to the king, 'Your subjects have *inherited* this freedom,' claiming their franchises, not on abstract principles as the 'rights of men,' but as the rights of Englishmen, and as a patrimony derived from their forefathers. Selden,[69] and the other profoundly learned men, who drew this petition of right, were as well acquainted, at least, with all the general theories concerning the 'rights of men,' as any of the discoursers in our pulpits, or on your tribune; full as well as Dr. Price,[N] or as the Abbé Seyes.[N] But, for reasons worthy of that practical wisdom which superseded their theoretic science, they preferred this positive, recorded, *hereditary* title to all which can be dear to the man and the citizen, to that vague speculative right, which exposed their sure inheritance to be scrambled for and torn to pieces by every wild litigious spirit.

The same policy pervades all the laws which have since been made for the preservation of our liberties. In the 1st of William and Mary, in the famous statute, called the Declaration of Right,[N] the two houses utter not a syllable of 'a right to frame a government for themselves.' You will see, that their whole care was to secure the religion, laws, and liberties, that had been long possessed, and had been lately endangered.

---

[68] *Henry I*, English King (1068–1135), fourth son of William the Conqueror. His coronation charter in 1100 acknowledged certain rights to his barons across the whole kingdom, and is often mentioned along with Magna Carta in the 'pedigree of English Liberties'.

[69] [John] *Selden* (1584–1654), lawyer and MP for Oxford. Jurist and political controversialist, typically grounding claims in historical usage and practice. Selden drew up the *Petition of Right*.[N] He propounded a political theory which combined ideas of social contract with a version of ancient constitutionalism. See Richard Tuck, *Natural Rights Theories* (Cambridge, 1979), Ch. 4.

'Taking[ix] into their most serious consideration the *best* means for making such an establishment, that their religion, laws, and liberties might not be in danger of being again subverted,' they auspicate all their proceedings, by stating as some of those *best* means, 'in the *first place*' to do 'as their *ancestors in like cases have usually* done for vindicating their *antient* rights and liberties, to *declare*'; – and then they pray the king and queen, 'that it may be *declared* and enacted, that *all and singular* the rights and liberties *asserted and declared* are the true *antient* and indubitable rights and liberties of the people of this kingdom.'

You will observe, that from Magna Charta[N] to the Declaration of Right,[N] it has been the uniform policy of our constitution to claim and assert our liberties, as an *entailed inheritance*[70] derived to us from our forefathers, and to be transmitted to our posterity; as an estate specially belonging to the people of this kingdom without any reference whatever to any other more general or prior right. By this means our constitution preserves an unity in so great a diversity of its parts. We have an inheritable crown; an inheritable peerage; and an house of commons and a people inheriting privileges, franchises, and liberties, from a long line of ancestors.

This policy appears to me to be the result of profound reflection; or rather the happy effect of following nature, which is wisdom without reflection, and above it. A spirit of innovation is generally the result of a selfish temper and confined views. People will not look forward to posterity, who never look backward to their ancestors. Besides, the people of England well know, that the idea of inheritance furnishes a sure principle of conservation, and a sure principle of transmission; without at all excluding a principle of improvement. It leaves acquisition free; but it secures what it acquires. Whatever advantages are obtained by a state proceeding on these maxims, are locked fast as in a sort of family settlement; grasped as in a kind of mortmain[71] for ever. By a constitutional policy, working after the pattern of nature, we receive, we hold, we

---

[ix] I W. and M.

[70] *Entailed inheritance*: a heritable landed property, the right to which is fixed by descent within a particular family: the current possessor having no right to sell off parts of, or otherwise diminish the property.

[71] *Mortmain*: Norman French, literally 'dead hand', a kind of feudal property right which could not be sold or alienated at will (so related to entailment). A way of establishing a persisting property right in a corporation or other legally fictive person for the same purpose.

34

transmit our government and our privileges, in the same manner in which we enjoy and transmit our property and our lives. The institutions of policy, the goods of fortune, the gifts of Providence, are handed down, to us and from us, in the same course and order. Our political system is placed in a just correspondence and symmetry with the order of the world, and with the mode of existence decreed to a permanent body composed of transitory parts; wherein, by the disposition of a stupendous wisdom, moulding together the great mysterious incorporation of the human race, the whole, at one time, is never old, or middle-aged, or young, but in a condition of unchangeable constancy, moves on through the varied tenour of perpetual decay, fall, renovation, and progression. Thus, by preserving the method of nature in the conduct of the state, in what we improve we are never wholly new; in what we retain we are never wholly obsolete.[72] By adhering in this manner and on those principles to our forefathers, we are guided not by the superstition of antiquarians, but by the spirit of philosophic analogy. In this choice of inheritance we have given to our frame of polity the image of a relation in blood; binding up the constitution of our country with our dearest domestic ties; adopting our fundamental laws into the bosom of our family affections; keeping inseparable, and cherishing with the warmth of all their combined and mutually reflected charities, our state, our hearths, our sepulchres, and our altars.

Through the same plan of a conformity to nature in our artificial institutions, and by calling in the aid of her unerring and powerful instincts, to fortify the fallible and feeble contrivances of our reason, we have derived several other, and those no small benefits, from considering our liberties in the light of an inheritance. Always acting as if in the presence of canonized forefathers, the spirit of freedom, leading in itself to misrule and excess, is tempered with an awful gravity. This idea of a liberal descent inspires us with a sense of habitual native dignity, which prevents that upstart insolence almost inevitably adhering to and disgracing those who are the first acquirers of any distinction. By this means our liberty becomes a noble freedom. It carries an imposing and majestic aspect. It has a pedigree and

---

[72] Burke's argument and language surely draws here, as so often, from one of his favourite authors, Francis Bacon: 'what is settled by custom, though it be not good, yet at least it is fit; and those things which have long gone together, are as it were confederate within themselves; whereas new things piece not so well . . . It were good therefore that men in their innovations would follow the example of time itself; which innovateth greatly, but quietly, and by degrees scarce to be perceived.' *Essays*, XXIV 'Of Innovations'.

illustrating ancestors. It has its bearings and its ensigns armorial.[73] It has its gallery of portraits; its monumental inscriptions; its records, evidences, and titles. We procure reverence to our civil institutions on the principle upon which nature teaches us to revere individual men; on account of their age; and on account of those from whom they are descended. All your sophisters[74] cannot produce any thing better adapted to preserve a rational and manly freedom than the course that we have pursued, who have chosen our nature rather than our speculations, our breasts rather than our inventions, for the great conservatories and magazines of our rights and privileges.[75]

You might, if you pleased, have profited of our example, and have given to your recovered freedom a correspondent dignity. Your privileges, though discontinued, were not lost to memory. Your constitution, it is true, whilst you were out of possession, suffered waste and dilapidation; but you possessed in some parts the walls, and in all the foundations, of a noble and venerable castle. You might have repaired those walls; you might have built on those old foundations.[76] Your constitution was suspended before it was perfected; but you had the elements of a constitution very nearly as good as could be wished. In your old states you possessed that variety of parts corresponding with the various descriptions of which your community was happily composed; you had all that combination, and all that opposition of interests, you had that action and counteraction which, in the natural and in the political world, from the reciprocal struggle of discordant powers, draws out the harmony of the universe.[77] These opposed and conflicting interests, which you considered as so great a blemish in your old and in our present constitution, interpose a salutary check to all precipitate resolutions; They render deliberation a matter not

---

73 *Armorial ensign*: an arrangement of heraldic symbols or devices identifying an ennobled family.

74 *Sophist[er]s*: a group of teachers in ancient Greece who taught skills of rhetorical argument for a fee, conventionally opposed to philosophers such as Socrates, and derided for their supposed moral irresponsibility.

75 *Magazines*: here in the sense of a storehouse of weapons or military supplies.

76 Burke's claim that France might have restored, rather than revolutionised, her constitution was a view held by some French moderates led by the Marquis de Lally-Tollendal.[N] It was directly contested by others, notably J.-J. Mounier.[N] In England, both Burke's friend Philip Francis (to Burke 3, 4 November 1790, *Corr.* vi) and even moderate opponents, such as James Mackintosh, denied this: *Vindiciae Gallicae* (1791), p. 105.

77 Burke here alludes to the principle of the balanced or mixed constitution, according to which the competition between different constitutional elements safeguarded liberty by preventing the complete dominance of any one.

of choice, but of necessity; they make all change a subject of *compromise*, which naturally begets moderation; they produce *temperaments*, preventing the sore evil of harsh, crude, unqualified reformations; and rendering all the headlong exertions of arbitrary power, in the few or in the many, for ever impracticable. Through that diversity of members and interests, general liberty had as many securities as there were separate views in the several orders; whilst by pressing down the whole by the weight of a real monarchy, the separate parts would have been prevented from warping and starting from their allotted places.

You had all these advantages in your antient states; but you chose to act as if you had never been moulded into civil society, and had everything to begin anew. You began ill, because you began by despising everything that belonged to you. You set up your trade without a capital. If the last generations of your country appeared without much lustre in your eyes, you might have passed them by, and derived your claims from a more early race of ancestors. Under a pious predilection for those ancestors, your imaginations would have realized in them a standard of virtue and wisdom, beyond the vulgar practice of the hour: and you would have risen with the example to whose imitation you aspired. Respecting your forefathers, you would have been taught to respect yourselves. You would not have chosen to consider the French as a people of yesterday, as a nation of low-born servile wretches until the emancipating year of 1789. In order to furnish, at the expence of your honour, an excuse to your apologists here for several enormities of yours, you would not have been content to be represented as a gang of Maroon slaves,[78] suddenly broke loose from the house of bondage, and therefore to be pardoned for your abuse of the liberty to which you were not accustomed and ill fitted. Would it not, my worthy friend, have been wiser to have you thought, what I, for one, always thought you, a generous and gallant nation, long misled to your disadvantage by your high and romantic sentiments of fidelity, honour, and loyalty; that events had been unfavourable to you, but that you were not enslaved through any illiberal or servile disposition; that in your most devoted submission, you were actuated by a principle of public spirit, and that it was your country you worshipped, in the person of your king? Had you made it to be understood, that in the delusion of this amiable error you had gone further than your wise ancestors; that you were resolved to resume your ancient privileges, whilst you preserved the

---

[78] *Maroon slaves*: armed communities of escaped slaves in the Caribbean.

spirit of your ancient and your recent loyalty and honour; or, if diffident of yourselves, and not clearly discerning the almost obliterated constitution of your ancestors, you had looked to your neighbours in this land, who had kept alive the ancient principles and models of the old common law of Europe meliorated and adapted to its present state – by following wise examples you would have given new examples of wisdom to the world. You would have rendered the cause of liberty venerable in the eyes of every worthy mind in every nation. You would have shamed despotism from the earth, by showing that freedom was not only reconcileable, but as, when well disciplined it is, auxiliary to law. You would have had an unoppressive but a productive revenue. You would have had a flourishing commerce to feed it. You would have had a free constitution; a potent monarchy; a disciplined army; a reformed and venerated clergy; a mitigated but spirited nobility, to lead your virtue, not to overlay it; you would have had a liberal order of commons, to emulate and to recruit that nobility; you would have had a protected, satisfied, laborious, and obedient people, taught to seek and to recognize the happiness that is to be found by virtue in all conditions; in which consists the true moral equality of mankind, and not in that monstrous fiction, which, by inspiring false ideas and vain expectations into men destined to travel in the obscure walk of laborious life, serves only to aggravate and imbitter that real inequality, which it never can remove; and which the order of civil life establishes as much for the benefit of those whom it must leave in an humble state, as those whom it is able to exalt to a condition more splendid, but not more happy. You had a smooth and easy career of felicity and glory laid open to you, beyond anything recorded in the history of the world; but you have shewn that difficulty is good for man.

Compute your gains: see what is got by those extravagant and presumptuous speculations which have taught your leaders to despise all their predecessors, and all their contemporaries, and even to despise themselves, until the moment in which they became truly despicable. By following those false lights, France has bought undisguised calamities at a higher price than any nation has purchased the most unequivocal blessings! France has bought poverty by crime! France has not sacrificed her virtue to her interest; but she has abandoned her interest, that she might prostitute her virtue. All other nations have begun the fabric of a new government, or the reformation of an old, by establishing originally, or by enforcing with greater exactness some rites or other of religion.[79] All other people have laid the foundations of civil freedom in severer manners, and a system of a more austere and masculine morality. France, when she let loose the reins of regal authority, doubled the licence, of a ferocious dissoluteness in manners, and of an insolent irreligion in opinions and practices; and has extended through all ranks of life, as if she were communicating some privilege, or laying open some secluded benefit, all the unhappy corruptions that usually were the disease of wealth and power. This is one of the new principles of equality in France.

France, by the perfidy of her leaders, has utterly disgraced the tone of lenient council in the cabinets of princes, and disarmed it of its most potent topics. She has sanctified the dark suspicious maxims of tyrannous distrust; and taught kings to tremble at (what will hereafter be called) the delusive plausibilities, of moral politicians. Sovereigns will consider those who advise them to place an unlimited confidence in their people, as subverters of their thrones; as traitors who aim at their destruction, by leading their easy good-nature, under specious pretences, to admit combinations of bold and faithless men into a participation of their power. This alone (if there were nothing else) is an irreparable calamity to you and to mankind. Remember that your parliament of Paris told your king, that in calling the states together, he had nothing to fear but the prodigal excess of their zeal in providing for the support of the throne. It is right that these men should hide their heads. It is right that they should bear their part in the ruin which their counsel has brought on their sovereign and their country. Such sanguine declarations tend to lull authority asleep; to encourage it rashly to engage in perilous adventures of untried policy; to neglect those provisions, preparations, and precautions, which distinguish benevolence from imbecillity; and without which no man can answer for the salutary effect of any abstract plan of government or of freedom. For want of these, they have seen the medicine of the state corrupted into its poison. They have seen the French rebel against a mild and lawful monarch, with more fury, outrage, and insult, than ever any people has been known to rise against the most illegal usurper, or the most sanguinary tyrant. Their resistance was made to concession; their revolt was from protection; their blow was aimed at an hand holding out graces, favours, and immunities.

[79] Burke refers to the classical notion that the act of foundation requires the imposition of some code of discipline – in laws or religion – marking off the new political community from the old. Thus Moses, Lycurgus, Solon.

This was unnatural. The rest is in order. They have found their punishment in their success. Laws overturned; tribunals subverted; industry without vigour; commerce expiring; the revenue unpaid, yet the people impoverished; a church pillaged, and a state not relieved; civil and military anarchy made the constitution of the kingdom; every thing human and divine sacrificed to the idol of public credit, and national bankruptcy the consequence; and to crown all, the paper securities of new, precarious, tottering power, the discredited paper securities of impoverished fraud,[80] and beggared rapine, held out as a currency for the support of an empire, in lieu of the two great recognised species that represent the lasting conventional credit of mankind,[81] which disappeared and hid themselves in the earth from whence they came, when the principle of property, whose creatures and representatives they are, was systematically subverted.

Were all these dreadful things necessary? Were they the inevitable results of the desperate struggle of determined patriots, compelled to wade through blood and tumult, to the quiet shore of a tranquil and prosperous liberty? No! nothing like it. The fresh ruins of France, which shock our feelings wherever we can turn our eyes, are not the devastation of civil war; they are the sad but instructive monuments of rash and ignorant counsel in time of profound peace. They are the display of inconsiderate and presumptuous, because unresisted and irresistible authority. The persons who have thus squandered away the precious treasure of their crimes, the persons who have made this prodigal and wild waste of public evils (the last stake reserved for the ultimate ransom of the state) have met in their progress with little, or rather with no opposition at all. Their whole march was more like a triumphal procession than the progress of a war. Their pioneers have gone before them, and demolished and laid every thing level at their feet. Not one drop of *their* blood have they shed in the cause of the country they have ruined. They have made no sacrifices to their projects of greater consequence than their shoebuckles,[82] whilst they were imprisoning their king, murdering their fellow citizens, and bathing in tears, and plunging in poverty and distress, thousands of worthy men and worthy families. Their cruelty has not even been the base result of fear. It has been the effect of their sense of perfect safety,

---

[80] *Paper securities*: the *assignats*,[N] paper currency backed by expropriated Church lands which will form the basis of an extended critique by Burke; see below, pp. 193–99; 235–42.

[81] *Two great recognised species*: gold and silver.

[82] *Shoebuckles*: Precious metal shoe-buckles featured amongst the objects donated by the wealthy in support of the revolution in 'patriotic collections'.

in authorizing treasons, robberies, rapes, assassinations, slaughters, and burnings throughout their harrassed land.[83] But the cause of all was plain from the beginning.

This unforced choice, this fond election of evil, would appear perfectly unaccountable, if we did not consider the composition of the National Assembly;[N] I do not mean its formal constitution, which, as it now stands, is exceptionable enough, but the materials of which in a great measure it is composed, which is of ten thousand times greater consequence than all the formalities in the world. If we were to know nothing of this Assembly but by its title and function, no colours could paint to the imagination any thing more venerable. In that light the mind of an enquirer, subdued by such an awful image as that of the virtue and wisdom of a whole people collected into a focus, would pause and hesitate in condemning things even of the very worst aspect. Instead of blameable, they would appear only mysterious. But no name, no power, no function, no artificial institution whatsoever, can make the men of whom any system of authority is composed, any other than God, and nature, and education, and their habits of life have made them. Capacities beyond these the people have not to give. Virtue and wisdom may be the objects of their choice; but their choice confers neither the one nor the other on those upon whom they lay their ordaining hands. They have not the engagement of nature, they have not the promise of revelation for any such powers.

After I had read over the list of the persons and descriptions elected into the *Tiers Etat*,[N] nothing which they afterwards did could appear astonishing. Among them, indeed, I saw some of known rank; some of shining talents; but of any practical experience in the state, not one man was to be found. The best were only men of theory. But whatever the distinguished few may have been, it is the substance and mass of the body which constitutes its character, and must finally determine its direction. In all bodies, those who will lead, must also, in a considerable degree, follow. They must conform their propositions to the taste, talent, and disposition of those whom they wish to conduct: therefore, if an Assembly is viciously or feebly composed in a very great part of it, nothing but such a supreme degree of virtue as very rarely appears in the world, and for that reason cannot enter into calculation, will prevent the men of talents

---

[83] Fear of counter-revolution had provoked violence and looting in the countryside and some provincial cities in the autumn of 1789, reported to Burke's son by a family friend in Auxerre, Mme Parisot (14 September 1789, *Corr.* vi, pp. 16ff.), and analysed in Georges Lefèbvre's study *The Great Fear of 1789* (trs. London, 1973).

disseminated through it from becoming only the expert instruments of absurd projects! If what is the more likely event, instead of that unusual degree of virtue, they should be actuated by sinister ambition and a lust of meretricious glory, then the feeble part of the Assembly, to whom at first they conform, becomes in its turn the dupe and instrument of their designs. In this political traffick the leaders will be obliged to bow to the ignorance of their followers, and the followers to become subservient to the worst designs of their leaders.

To secure any degree of sobriety in the propositions made by the leaders in any public assembly, they ought to respect, in some degree perhaps to fear, those whom they conduct. To be led any otherwise than blindly, the followers must be qualified, if not for actors, at least for judges; they must also be judges of natural weight and authority. Nothing can secure a steady and moderate conduct in such assemblies, but that the body of them should be respectably composed, in point of condition in life, of permanent property, of education, and of such habits as enlarge and liberalize the understanding.

In the calling of the states general<sup>N</sup> of France, the first thing which struck me, was a great departure from the antient course. I found the representation for the Third Estate<sup>N</sup> composed of six hundred persons. They were equal in number to the representatives of both of the other orders. If the orders were to act separately, the number would not, beyond the consideration of the expence, be of much moment. But when it became apparent that the three orders were to be melted down into one, the policy and necessary effect of this numerous representation became obvious. A very small desertion from either of the other two orders must throw the power of both into the hands of the third. In fact, the whole power of the state was soon resolved into that body. Its due composition became therefore of infinitely the greater importance.

Judge, Sir, of my surprize, when I found that a very great proportion of the Assembly (a majority, I believe, of the members who attended) was composed of practitioners in the law.[84] It was composed not of distinguished magistrates, who had given pledges to their country of

---

[84] Burke was broadly correct: A modern analyst identifies 53% of the Third Estate as practising lawyers or members of the judiciary (Harriet B. Applewhite, *Political Alignment in the French National Assembly, 1789–1791* (Baton Rouge, 1993), p. 42.), although it is not clear that they were predominantly as lowly as Burke goes on to imply. The higher, ennobled, judiciary would not in any case have been represented in the Third Estate. For similar if slightly lower figures see E. H. Lemay, 'La composition de l'Assemblée nationale constituante', *Revue d'histoire moderne et contemporaine* 26(3) (1977), pp. 341–63.

their science, prudence, and integrity; not of leading advocates, the glory of the bar; not of renowned professors in universities; – but for the far greater part, as it must in such a number, of the inferior, unlearned, mechanical, merely instrumental members of the profession. There were distinguished exceptions; but the general composition was of obscure provincial advocates, of stewards of petty local jurisdictions, country attornies, notaries, and the whole train of the ministers of municipal litigation, the fomenters and conductors of the petty war of village vexation. From the moment I read the list I saw distinctly, and very nearly as it has happened, all that was to follow.

The degree of estimation in which any profession is held becomes the standard of the estimation in which the professors hold themselves. Whatever the personal merits of many individual lawyers might have been, and in many it was undoubtedly very considerable, in that military kingdom, no part of the profession had been much regarded, except the highest of all, who often united to their professional offices great family splendour, and were invested with great power and authority. These certainly were highly respected, and even with no small degree of awe. The next rank was not much esteemed; the mechanical part was in a very low degree of repute.

Whenever the supreme authority is invested in a body so composed, it must evidently produce the consequences of supreme authority placed in the hands of men not taught habitually to respect themselves; who had no previous fortune in character at stake; who could not be expected to bear with moderation, or to conduct with discretion, a power which they themselves, more than any others, must be surprized to find in their hands. Who could flatter himself that these men, suddenly, and, as it were, by enchantment, snatched from the humblest rank of sub-ordination, would not be intoxicated with their unprepared greatness? Who could conceive, that men who are habitually meddling, daring, sub-tle, active, of litigious dispositions and unquiet minds, would easily fall back into their old condition of obscure contention, and laborious, low, unprofitable chicane? Who could doubt but that, at any expence to the state, of which they understood nothing, they must pursue their private interests, which they understood but too well? It was not an event depending on chance or contingency. It was inevitable; it was necessary; it was planted in the nature of things. They must *join* (if their capacity did not permit them to *lead*) in any project which could procure to them a *litigious constitution*; which could lay open to them those innumerable

43

lucrative jobs which follow in the train of all great convulsions and revolutions in the state, and particularly in all great and violent permutations of property. Was it to be expected that they would attend to the stability of property, whose existence had always depended upon whatever rendered property questionable, ambiguous, and insecure? Their objects would be enlarged with their elevation, but their disposition and habits, and mode of accomplishing their designs, must remain the same.

Well! but these men were to be tempered and restrained by other descriptions, of more sober minds, and more enlarged understandings. Were they then to be awed by the super-eminent authority and awful dignity of an handful of country clowns who have seats in that Assembly, some of whom are said not to be able to read and write? and by not a greater number of traders, who, though somewhat more instructed, and more conspicuous in the order of society, had never known any thing beyond their counting-house? No! both these descriptions were more formed to be overborne and swayed by the intrigues and artifices of lawyers, than to become their counterpoise. With such a dangerous disproportion, the whole must needs be governed by them. To the faculty of law was joined a pretty considerable proportion of the faculty of medicine.[85] This faculty had not, any more than that of the law, possessed in France its just estimation. Its professors therefore must have the qualities of men not habituated to sentiments of dignity. But supposing they had ranked as they ought to do, and as with us they do actually, the sides of sick beds are not the academies for forming statesmen and legislators. Then came the dealers in stocks and funds, who must be eager, at any expence, to change their ideal paper wealth for the more solid substance of land. To these were joined men of other descriptions, from whom as little knowledge of or attention to the interests of a great state was to be expected, and as little regard to the stability of any institution; men formed to be instruments, not controls. Such in general was the composition of the *Tiers Etat*[N] in the National Assembly;[N] in which was scarcely to be perceived the slightest traces of what we call the natural landed interest of the country.[86]

We know that the British house of commons, without shutting its doors to any merit in any class, is, by the sure operation of adequate causes,

---

85 Doctors formed only 3%, merchants and 'bourgeois' 14% of the initial membership. (Applewhite, *Political Alignment*, p. 42). Raynaud reports that estimates of the number of doctors vary between 12 and 15 (*Réflexions*, p. 631).

86 Landed aristocrats would not, in any case, have been represented in the *Tiers Etat*.

filled with every thing illustrious in rank, in descent, in hereditary and in acquired opulence, in cultivated talents, in military, civil, naval, and politic distinction, that the country can afford.[87] But supposing, what hardly can be supposed as a case, that the house of commons should be composed in the same manner with the Tiers Etat in France, would this dominion of chicane be borne with patience, or even conceived without horror? God forbid I should insinuate any thing derogatory to that profession, which is another priesthood, administering the rites of sacred justice. But whilst I revere men in the functions which belong to them, and would do, as much as one man can do, to prevent their exclusion from any, I cannot, to flatter them, give the lye to nature. They are good and useful in the composition; they must be mischievous if they preponderate so as virtually to become the whole. Their very excellence in their peculiar functions may be far from a qualification for others. It cannot escape observation, that when men are too much confined to professional and faculty habits, and, as it were, inveterate in the recurrent employment of that narrow circle, they are rather disabled than qualified for whatever depends on the knowledge of mankind, on experience in mixed affairs, on a comprehensive connected view of the various complicated external and internal interests which go to the formation of that multifarious thing called a state.

After all, if the house of commons were to have an wholly professional and faculty composition, what is the power of the house of commons, circumscribed and shut in by the immoveable barriers of laws, usages, positive rules of doctrine and practice, counterpoized by the house of lords, and every moment of its existence at the discretion of the crown to continue, prorogue, or dissolve us?[88] The power of the house of commons, direct or indirect, is indeed great; and long may it be able to preserve its greatness, and the spirit belonging to true greatness, at the full; and it will

---

[87] The House of Commons was certainly representative of 'acquired opulence'. In the 1790s more than half of MPs were substantial landowners, and more than half were themselves sons of MPs or married to daughters of MPs. The most represented professional classes were military officers, followed by lawyers and bankers. As for 'cultivated talents', although the academic standing of Oxford and Cambridge in the later eighteenth century was not generally high, nearly half had taken degrees there (*History of Parliament: The House of Commons 1790–1820*, ed. R. G. Thorne, 5 vols. (London, 1986), vol. 1, pp. 202ff. (education), 306ff. (army officers)).

[88] The Bill of Rights[N] had declared that 'Parliaments ought to be held frequently.' But the maximum length had been increased from three to seven years by the *Septennial Act* of 1716, although it was constitutionally within the prerogative of the monarch to dissolve it at any time.

do so, as long as it can keep the breakers of law in India from becoming the makers of law for England.[89] The power, however, of the house of commons, when least diminished, is as a drop of water in the ocean, compared to that residing in a settled majority of your National Assembly.[N] That Assembly, since the destruction of the orders, has no fundamental law, no strict convention, no respected usage to restrain it. Instead of finding themselves obliged to conform to a fixed constitution, they have a power to make a constitution which shall conform to their designs. Nothing in heaven or upon earth can serve as a control on them. What ought to be the heads, the hearts, the dispositions, that are qualified, or that dare, not only to make laws under a fixed constitution, but at one heat to strike out a totally new constitution for a great kingdom, and in every part of it, from the monarch on the throne to the vestry of a parish? But – '*Fools rush in where angels fear to tread.*'[90] In such a state of unbounded power, for undefined and undefinable purposes, the evil of a moral and almost physical inaptitude of the man to the function must be the greatest we can conceive to happen in the management of human affairs.

Having considered the composition of the third estate[N] as it stood in its original frame, I took a view of the representatives of the clergy. There too it appeared, that full as little regard was had to the general security of property, or to the aptitude of the deputies for their public purposes, in the principles of their election. That election was so contrived as to send a very large proportion of mere country curates[91] to the great and arduous work of new-modelling a state;[92] men who never had seen the state so

---

[89] Burke's worries about the plunderers of India ('Nabobs') returning to purchase parliamentary seats go back to the early 1770s. In 1783 he had warned that 'If we are not able to contrive some method of governing India well, which will not, of necessity become the means of governing Great Britain ill, a ground is laid for their eternal separation' ('Speech on Fox's India Bill', *W&S*, v, p. 383).

[90] The line is from Alexander Pope's *An Essay on Criticism* (1711), l. 625. Pope refers to arrogant scriptural critics willing to pronounce definitively on difficult theological issues.

[91] *Curates*: In the eighteenth-century Anglican Church a curate was a priest holding parish services as deputy for the incumbent and for a fraction of the income from the living: the proverbially meanest clerical office. A rhetorical flourish to emphasise the lowly status of the officeholders. Confusingly, in the French Church, the curé was the parish priest, whilst the equivalent of the English curate was the 'vicaire'. The *Clergé pastoral* were not necessarily 'curates' in the English sense.

[92] Burke was right. So long was it since the Estates General[N] had met (1614) that a royal commission considered the means of election no longer appropriate, although any plan of reform was highly political since it would affect the relative powers of the different groups. Necker[N] had drawn up procedures ('Regulation for the Execution of the Letters of Convocation' (24 Jan. 1789) arts. 11–19. in *DocS*, pp. 31ff.) – which were enthusiastically used – allowing representatives of parish priests to predominate over those from

much as in a picture; men who knew nothing of the world beyond the bounds of an obscure village; who, immersed in hopeless poverty, could regard all property, whether secular or ecclesiastical, with no other eye than that of envy; among whom must be many, who, for the smallest hope of the meanest dividend in plunder, would readily join in any attempts upon a body of wealth, in which they could hardly look to have any share, except in a general scramble. Instead of balancing the power of the active chicaners in the other assembly, these curates must necessarily become the active coadjutors, or at best the passive instruments of those by whom they had been habitually guided in their petty village concerns. They too could hardly be the most conscientious of their kind, who, presuming upon their incompetent understanding, could intrigue for a trust which led them from their natural relation to their flocks, and their natural spheres of action, to undertake the regeneration of kingdoms. This preponderating weight being added to the force of the body of chicane in the Tiers Etat, compleated that momentum of ignorance, rashness, presumption, and lust of plunder, which nothing has been able to resist.

To observing men it must have appeared from the beginning, that the majority of the Third Estate, in conjunction with such a deputation from the clergy as I have described, whilst it pursued the destruction of the nobility, would inevitably become subservient to the worst designs of individuals in that class. In the spoil and humiliation of their own order these individuals would possess a sure fund for the pay of their new followers. To squander away the objects which made the happiness of their fellows, would be to them no sacrifice at all. Turbulent, discontented men of quality, in proportion as they are puffed up with personal pride and arrogance, generally despise their own order. One of the first symptoms they discover of a selfish and mischievous ambition, is a profligate disregard of a dignity which they partake with others. To be attached to the subdivision, to love the little platoon we belong to in society,[93] is the first principle (the germ as it were) of public affections. It is the first link in the series by which we proceed towards a love to our country and to

Cathedral or monastic posts. See N. Aston, *Religion and Revolution in France 1780–1804* (Houndmills, 2000), pp. 110–16. In the event, of 296 elected to the Clerical Estate, 208 were 'Clergé pastoral' and only 46 Bishops (John McManners, *French Revolution and the Church* (London, 1969), p. 18).

[93] *Platoon*: a small company of people, here not in a military, but a social sense. The origins of the thought have been ascribed both to Cicero, *De Officiis*, 1.17 and to Pope, *Essay On Man*, iv, ll. 360–72.

mankind. The interests of that portion of social arrangement is a trust in the hands of all those who compose it; and as none but bad men would justify it in abuse, none but traitors would barter it away for their own personal advantage.

There were, in the time of our civil troubles in England (I do not know whether you have any such in your Assembly in France) several persons, like the then Earl of Holland,[94] who by themselves or their families had brought an odium on the throne, by the prodigal dispensation of its bounties towards them, who afterwards joined in the rebellions arising from the discontents of which they were themselves the cause; men who helped to subvert that throne to which they owed, some of them, their existence, others all that power which they employed to ruin their benefactor. If any bounds are set to the rapacious demands of that sort of people, or that others are permitted to partake in the objects they would engross, revenge and envy soon fill up the craving void that is left in their avarice. Confounded by the complication of distempered passions, their reason is disturbed; their views become vast and perplexed; to others inexplicable; to themselves uncertain. They find, on all sides, bounds to their unprincipled ambition in any fixed order of things. But in the fog and haze of confusion all is enlarged, and appears without any limit.

When men of rank sacrifice all ideas of dignity to an ambition without a distinct object, and work with low instruments and for low ends, the whole composition becomes low and base. Does not something like this now appear in France? Does it not produce something ignoble and inglorious? a kind of meanness in all the prevalent policy? a tendency in all that is done to lower along with individuals all the dignity and importance of the state? Other revolutions have been conducted by persons, who whilst they attempted or effected changes in the commonwealth, sanctified their ambition by advancing the dignity of the people whose peace they troubled. They had long views. They aimed at the rule, not at the destruction of their country. They were men of great civil, and great military talents, and if the terror, the ornament of their age. They were not like Jew brokers[95] contending with each other who could best remedy

---

94  *1st Earl of Holland* (1590–1649): a notorious political turncoat. A favourite of James I, he later fought on both sides in the Civil War. Beheaded in 1649. Here the epitome of the opportunist, unprincipled politician.

95  *Broker*: dealer in financial securities. *Jew*: despite his wide sympathies when considering other religions directly, Burke displayed the virtually universal, casual anti-Semitism of his age.

with fraudulent circulation and depreciated paper the wretchedness and ruin brought on their country by their degenerate councils. The compliment made to one of the great bad men of the old stamp (Cromwell[N]) by his kinsman, a favourite poet of that time, shews what it was he proposed, and what indeed to a great degree he accomplished in the success of his ambition:

> Still as *you* rise, the *state*, exalted too,
> Finds no distemper whilst 'tis changed by *you*;
> Chang'd like the world's great scene, when without noise
> The rising sun night's *vulgar* lights destroys.[96]

These disturbers were not so much like men usurping power, as asserting their natural place in society. Their rising was to illuminate and beautify the world. Their conquest over their competitors was by outshining them. The hand that, like a destroying angel, smote the country, communicated to it the force and energy under which it suffered. I do not say, (God forbid) I do not say, that the virtues of such men were to be taken as a balance to their crimes; but they were some corrective to their effects. Such was, as I said, our Cromwell. Such were your whole race of Guises,[N] Condés,[N] and Colignis.[N] Such the Richlieus,[N] who in more quiet times acted in the spirit of a civil war. Such, as better men, and in a less dubious cause, were your Henry the 4th[N] and your Sully,[N] though nursed in civil confusions, and not wholly without some of their taint. It is a thing to be wondered at, to see how very soon France, when she had a moment to respire, recovered and emerged from the longest and most dreadful civil war that ever was known in any nation. Why? Because, among all their massacres, they had not slain the *mind* in their country. A conscious dignity, a noble pride, a generous sense of glory and emulation, was not extinguished. On the contrary, it was kindled and inflamed. The organs also of the state, however shattered, existed. All the prizes of honour and virtue, all the rewards, all the distinctions, remained. But your present confusion, like a palsy,[97] has attacked the fountain of life itself. Every person in your country, in a situation to be actuated by a principle of honour, is disgraced and degraded, and can entertain no sensation of life, except in a mortified and humiliated indignation. But this generation will

---

96 Edmund Waller, *Panegyric to My Lord Protector* (London, 1655). *Kinsman* because Waller was related by marriage to Cromwell.

97 *Palsy*: a disease of the nervous system which affects the sufferer's sensation and ability to control their limbs.

quickly pass away. The next generation of the nobility will resemble the artificers and clowns, and money-jobbers,[98] usurers, and Jews, who will be always their fellows, sometimes their masters. Believe me, Sir, those who attempt to level, never equalize. In all societies, consisting of various descriptions of citizens, some description must be uppermost. The levellers therefore only change and pervert the natural order of things; they load the edifice of society, by setting up in the air what the solidity of the structure requires to be on the ground. The associations of taylors and carpenters, of which the republic (of Paris, for instance) is composed, cannot be equal to the situation, into which, by the worst of usurpations, an usurpation on the prerogatives of nature, you attempt to force them.

The chancellor of France at the opening of the states, said, in a tone of oratorial flourish, that all occupations were honourable. If he meant only, that no honest employment was disgraceful, he would not have gone beyond the truth. But in asserting, that any thing is honourable, we imply some distinction in its favour. The occupation of an hair-dresser, or of a working tallow-chandler,[99] cannot be a matter of honour to any person – to say nothing of a number of other more servile employments. Such descriptions of men ought not to suffer oppression from the state; but the state suffers oppression, if such as they, either individually or collectively, are permitted to rule. In this you think you are combating prejudice, but you are at war with nature[x].

---

[x]  Ecclesiasticus, chap. xxxviii, verse 24, 25. 'The wisdom of a learned man cometh by opportunity of leisure: and he that hath little business shall become wise.' – 'How can he get wisdom that holdeth the plough, and that glorieth in the goad; that driveth oxen; and is occupied with their labours; and whose talk is of bullocks?"

Ver. 27. 'So every carpenter and work-master that laboureth night and day.' &c.

Ver. 33. 'They shall not be sought for in public counsel, nor sit high in the congregation: They shall not sit on the judges seat, nor understand the sentence of judgment: they cannot declare justice and judgment, and shall not be found where parables are spoken.'

Ver. 34 'But they will maintain the state of the world.'

I do not determine whether this book be canonical, as the Gallican church (till lately) has considered it, or apocryphal as it is here taken.[100] I am sure it contains a great deal of sense, and truth.

---

[98]  *Money jobbers*: traders in financial instruments.

[99]  *Tallow chandler*: a processor and vendor of rendered animal fat products such as candle and soap; a proverbially lowly activity, not least because it involved exposure to pervasive and unpleasant smells.

[100]  *Apocryphal*: a religious text not accorded full scriptural authority. Which these were differed from Church to Church. *Ecclesiasticus* (not to be confused with *Ecclesiastes*) was not included in the canonical texts of the Jewish Torah, or of the Protestant (Lutheran) version of the Old Testament, nor, consequently, in the King James Bible. However, it

I do not, my dear Sir, conceive you to be of that sophistical captious spirit, or of that uncandid dulness, as to require, for every general observation or sentiment, an explicit detail of the correctives and exceptions, which reason will presume to be included in all the general propositions which come from reasonable men. You do not imagine, that I wish to confine power, authority, and distinction to blood, and names, and titles. No, Sir. There is no qualification for government, but virtue and wisdom, actual or presumptive. Wherever they are actually found, they have, in whatever state, condition, profession or trade, the passport of Heaven to human place and honour. Woe to the country which would madly and impiously reject the service of the talents and virtues, civil, military, or religious, that are given to grace and to serve it; and would condemn to obscurity every thing formed to diffuse lustre and glory around a state. Woe to that country too, that passing into the opposite extreme, considers a low education, a mean contracted view of things, a sordid mercenary occupation, as a preferable title to command. Every thing ought to be open; but not indifferently to every man. No rotation; no appointment by lot; no mode of election operating in the spirit of sortition or rotation,[101] can be generally good in a government conversant in extensive objects. [Because they have no tendency, direct or indirect, to select the man with a view to the duty, or to accommodate the one to the other.][102] I do not hesitate to say, that the road to eminence and power, from obscure condition, ought not to be made too easy, nor a thing too much of course. If rare merit be the rarest of all rare things, it ought to pass through some sort of probation. The temple of honour ought to be seated on an eminence. If it be open through virtue, let it be remembered too, that virtue is never tried but by some difficulty, and some struggle.

Nothing is a due and adequate representation of a state, that does not represent its ability, as well as its property. But as ability is a vigorous and active principle, and as property is sluggish, inert, and timid, it never can

had been included in the Latin Vulgate – the Catholic Bible – the Old Testament of which derived from the Septuagint, a pre-Christian translation into Greek of Jewish scriptures. In acknowledging its apocryphal rather than its canonical status Burke is being careful here not to give hostages to fortune by endorsing Catholic claims. It was a recurrent slur on him that he was a closet Catholic.

101 *Lot, sortition*: selection for office by some chance-based or routinised procedure, irrespective of merit, such as was practised in Athenian democracy, and suggested for England by Harrington in the seventeenth century.

102 1st edn reads: 'Because they have no tendency, direct or indirect, to fit the man to the duty.'

be safe from the invasions of ability, unless it be, out of all proportion, predominant in the representation. It must be represented too in great masses of accumulation, or it is not rightly protected. The characteristic essence of property, formed out of the combined principles of its acquisition and conservation, is to be *unequal*. The great masses therefore which excite envy, and tempt rapacity, must be put out of the possibility of danger. Then they form a natural rampart about the lesser properties in all their gradations. The same quantity of property, which is by the natural course of things divided among many, has not the same operation. Its defensive power is weakened as it is diffused. In this diffusion each man's portion is less than what, in the eagerness of his desires, he may flatter himself to obtain by dissipating the accumulations of others. The plunder of the few would indeed give but a share inconceivably small in the distribution to the many. But the many are not capable of making this calculation; and those who lead them to rapine, never intend this distribution.

[The power of perpetuating our property in our families is one of the most valuable and interesting circumstances belonging to it, and that which tends the most to the perpetuation of society itself.[103] It makes our weakness subservient to our virtue; it grafts benevolence even upon avarice.][104] The possessors of family wealth, and of the distinction which attends hereditary possession (as most concerned in it) are the natural securities for this transmission. With us, the house of peers is formed upon this principle. It is wholly composed of hereditary property and hereditary distinction; and made therefore the third of the legislature; and in the last event, the sole judge of all property in all its subdivisions. The house of commons too, though not necessarily, yet in fact, is always so composed in the far greater part. Let those large proprietors be what

---

[103] The centrality of property rights to social stability was a classical theme, famously advocated by Cicero. However, in Burke's century the Scottish historians of civil society had elaborated a social typology and an understanding of social change grounded in changes in property rights. Such a view began to be elaborated by Henry Home, Lord Kames as early as the 1730s, culminating in his *Sketches of the History of Man* (1776). As Professor of Moral Philosophy at the University of Glasgow, Adam Smith's *Lectures on Jurisprudence* elaborated a similar scheme. Although unpublished at the time, they influenced generations of students and the schema forms a conceptual presupposition to his famous *Wealth of Nations* (1776).

[104] 1st edn reads: 'The perpetuation of property in our families is the most valuable and most interesting circumstance attending it, that which demonstrates most of a benevolent disposition in its owners, and that which tends most to the perpetuation of society itself.'

they will, and they have their chance of being amongst the best, they are at the very worst, the ballast in the vessel of the commonwealth. For though hereditary wealth, and the rank which goes with it, are too much idolized by creeping sycophants, and the blind abject admirers of power, they are too rashly slighted in shallow speculations of the petulant, assuming, short-sighted coxcombs of philosophy.[105] Some decent regulated pre-eminence, some preference (not exclusive appropriation) <u>given to birth,</u> is neither unnatural, nor unjust, nor impolitic.

It is said, that twenty-four millions ought to prevail over two hundred thousand. True; if the constitution of a kingdom be a problem of arithmetic. This sort of discourse does well enough with the lamp-post for its second:[106] to men who *may* reason calmly, it is ridiculous. The will of the many, and their interest, must very often differ; and great will be the difference when they make an evil choice. A government of five hundred country attornies and obscure curates is not good for twenty-four millions of men, though it were chosen by eight and forty millions; nor is it the better for being guided by a dozen of persons of quality, who have betrayed their trust in order to obtain that power. At present, you seem in everything to have strayed out of the high road of nature. The property of France does not govern it. Of course property is destroyed, and rational liberty has no existence. All you have got for the present is a paper circulation, and a stock-jobbing constitution: and as to the future, do you seriously think that the territory of France, upon the republican system of eighty-three independent municipalities,[107] (to say nothing of the parts that compose them) can ever be governed as one body, or can ever be set in motion by the impulse of one mind? When the National Assembly[N] has completed its work, it will have accomplished its ruin. These commonwealths will not long bear a state of subjection to the republic of Paris. They will not bear that this one body should monopolize the captivity of the king, and the dominion over the assembly calling itself National. Each will keep its own portion of the spoil of the church to itself; and it will not suffer either that spoil, or the more just

---

[105] *Coxcomb*: the horned and quartered cap worn by a jester, hence a foolish, shallow or inconsequential person.

[106] I.e. arguments which are seconded (backed up) with the threat of hanging opponents from the lamp-posts. (See, below, p. 75.)

[107] The *ancien régime*'s rambling administrative structure had been replaced by 83 *Departments* further subdivided into *Districts* by the Decree of 26 February 1790 (t. II) (pp. 139–40 in *DocS*, pp. 137–41).

fruits of their industry, or the natural produce of their soil, to be sent to swell the insolence, or pamper the luxury of the mechanics of Paris. In this they will see none of the equality, under the pretence of which they have been tempted to throw off their allegiance to their sovereign, as well as the antient constitution of their country. There can be no capital city in such a constitution as they have lately made. They have forgot, that when they framed democratic governments, they had virtually dismembered their country. The person whom they persevere in calling king, has not power left to him by the hundredth part sufficient to hold together this collection of republics.[108] The republic of Paris will endeavour indeed to compleat the debauchery of the army, and illegally to perpetuate the assembly, without resort to its constituents, as the means of continuing its despotism. It will make efforts, by becoming the heart of a boundless paper circulation, to draw every thing to itself; but in vain. All this policy in the end will appear as feeble as it is now violent.

If this be your actual situation, compared to the situation to which you were called, as it were by the voice of God and man, I cannot find it in my heart to congratulate you on the choice you have made, or the success which has attended your endeavours. I can as little recommend to any other nation a conduct grounded on such principles, and productive of such effects. That I must leave to those who can see further into your affairs than I am able to do, and who best know how far your actions are favourable to their designs. The gentlemen of the Revolution Society,[N] who were so early in their congratulations, appear to be strongly of opinion that there is some scheme of politics relative to this country, in which your proceedings may, in some way, be useful. For your Dr. Price,[N] who seems to have speculated himself into no small degree of fervour upon this subject, addresses his auditory in the following very remarkable words: 'I cannot conclude without recalling *particularly* to your recollection a consideration which I have *more than once alluded to*, and which probably your thoughts have *been all along anticipating*; a consideration with which my *mind is impressed more than I can express.* I mean the consideration of the *favourableness of the present times to all exertions in the cause of liberty.*'

---

[108] The view that republican government – being active and direct – had to be small, and in a large modern state would therefore have to be federal, was an eighteenth-century commonplace – extensively rehearsed at the American founding, and in the *Federalist Papers*. In the French Revolution such views initially provoked worries – and criticisms – that the creation of the *Departments* effectively divided, and would lead to the break-up of, the state, despite Sièyes' insistence on the indivisibility of the 'nation'.

It is plain that the mind of this *political* Preacher was at the time big with some extraordinary design; and it is very probable, that the thoughts of his audience, who understood him better than I do, did all along run before him in his reflection, and in the whole train of consequences to which it led.

Before I read that sermon, I really thought I had lived in a free country; and it was an error I cherished, because it gave me a greater liking to the country I lived in. I was indeed aware, that a jealous, ever-waking vigilance, to guard the treasure of our liberty, not only from invasion, but from decay and corruption, was our best wisdom and our first duty. However, I considered that treasure rather as a possession to be secured than as a prize to be contended for. I did not discern how the present time came to be so very favourable to all *exertions* in the cause of freedom. The present time differs from any other only by the circumstance of what is doing in France. If the example of that nation is to have an influence on this, I can easily conceive why some of their proceedings which have an unpleasant aspect, and are not quite reconcileable to humanity, generosity, good faith, and justice, are palliated with so much milky good-nature towards the actors, and borne with so much heroic fortitude towards the sufferers. It is certainly not prudent to discredit the authority of an example we mean to follow. But allowing this, we are led to a very natural question; – What is that cause of liberty, and what are those exertions in its favour, to which the example of France is so singularly auspicious? Is our monarchy to be annihilated, with all the laws, all the tribunals, and all the antient corporations of the kingdom? Is every land-mark of the country to be done away in favour of a geometrical and arithmetical constitution? Is the house of lords to be voted useless? Is episcopacy to be abolished?[109] Are the church lands to be sold to Jews and jobbers; or given to bribe new-invented municipal republics into a participation in sacrilege? Are all the taxes to be voted grievances, and the revenue reduced to a patriotic contribution, or patriotic presents? Are silver shoe-buckles to be substituted in the place of the land tax and the malt tax, for the support of the naval strength of this kingdom?[110] Are all orders, ranks,

---

[109] *Episcopacy*: the governance of Church by Bishops. Both Lords and Bishops were abolished in England under the Commonwealth, the former in terms to which Burke's prose here alludes: 'That the House of Peers in Parliament is useless and dangerous, and ought to be abolished' (Resolution of the House of Commons, 6 Feb. 1649).

[110] Taxes on land and malt (used in brewing beer) in England were introduced in the 1690s to fund the army and navy. On shoe-buckles see above fn. 82.

and distinctions, to be confounded, that out of universal anarchy, joined to national bankruptcy, three or four thousand democracies should be formed into eighty-three, and that they may all, by some sort of unknown attractive power, be organized into one? For this great end, is the army to be seduced from its discipline and its fidelity, first, by every kind of debauchery, and then by the terrible precedent of a donative in the encrease of pay? Are the curates to be seduced from their bishops, by holding out to them the delusive hope of a dole out of the spoils of their own order? Are the citizens of London to be drawn from their allegiance, by feeding them at the expence of their fellow-subjects? [Is a compulsory paper currency to be substituted in the place of the legal coin of this kingdom?][111] Is what remains of the plundered stock of public revenue to be employed in the wild project of maintaining two armies to watch over and to fight with each other?[112] – If these are the ends and means of the Revolution Society,[N] [I admit they are well assorted;][113] and France may furnish them for both with precedents in point.

I see that your example is held out to shame us. I know that we are supposed a dull sluggish race, rendered passive by finding our situation tolerable; and prevented by a mediocrity of freedom from ever attaining to its full perfection. Your leaders in France began by affecting to admire, almost to adore, the British constitution; but as they advanced they came to look upon it with a sovereign contempt. The friends of your National Assembly[N] amongst us have full as mean an opinion of what was formerly thought the glory of their country. The Revolution Society has discovered that the English nation is not free. They are convinced that the inequality in our representation is a 'defect in our constitution so *gross and palpable*, as to make it excellent chiefly in *form* and *theory*[xi].' That a representation in the legislature of a kingdom is not only the basis of all constitutional liberty in it, but of '*all legitimate government*; that without it a *government* is nothing but an *usurpation*;' – that 'when the representation is *partial*, the kingdom possesses liberty only *partially*; and if extremely partial it

---

[xi] Discourse on the Love of our Country, 3d edit. P. 39.

---

[111] 1st edn reads: 'Are all the public revenues levied in their city to be put under their administration?'

[112] A Decree of 10 August 1789 (*DocS*, p. 110) had required municipal authorities to establish local militias to assist in keeping order (which some had already done). Their oath of loyalty was 'to the nation, to the King and to the Law'. These forces existed independently of the royal troops, whose loyalty was to the King personally.

[113] 1st edn reads: 'I admit they are well adapted to each other.'

gives only a *semblance*; and if not only extremely partial, but corruptly chosen, it becomes a *nuisance*.' Dr. Price[N] considers this inadequacy of representation as our *fundamental grievance*; and though, as to the corruption of this semblance of representation, he hopes it is not yet arrived to its full perfection of depravity; he fears that 'nothing will be done towards gaining for us this *essential blessing*, until some *great abuse of power* again provokes our resentment, or some *great calamity* again alarms our fears, or perhaps till the acquisition of a *pure and equal representation by other countries*, whilst we are *mocked* with the *shadow*, kindles our shame.'[114] To this he subjoins a note in these words. 'A representation, chosen chiefly by the Treasury, and a *few* thousands of the *dregs* of the people, who are generally paid for their votes.'

You will smile here at the consistency of those democratists, who, when they are not on their guard, treat the humbler part of the community with the greatest contempt, whilst, at the same time, they pretend to make them the depositories of all power. It would require a long discourse to point out to you the many fallacies that lurk in the generality and equivocal nature of the terms 'inadequate representation.' I shall only say here, in justice to that old-fashioned constitution, under which we have long prospered, that our representation has been found perfectly adequate to all the purposes for which a representation of the people can be desired or devised. I defy the enemies of our constitution to show the contrary. To detail the particulars in which it is found so well to promote its ends, would demand a treatise on our practical constitution. I state here the doctrine of the Revolutionists, only that you and others may see, what an opinion these gentlemen entertain of the constitution of their country, and why they seem to think that some great abuse of power, or some great calamity, as giving a chance for the blessing of a constitution according to their ideas, would be much palliated to their feelings; you see *why they* are so much enamoured of your fair and equal representation, which being once obtained, the same effects might follow. You see they consider our house of commons as only 'a semblance,' 'a form,' 'a theory,' 'a shadow,' 'a mockery,' perhaps 'a nuisance.'

These gentlemen value themselves on being systematic; and not without reason. They must therefore look on this gross and palpable defect of representation, this fundamental grievance (so they call it) as a thing not only vicious in itself, but as rendering our whole government absolutely

---

[114] Price, *Discourse*, ed. Thomas, p. 192.

*illegitimate*, and not at all better than a downright *usurpation*. Another revolution, to get rid of this illegitimate and usurped government, would of course be perfectly justifiable, if not absolutely necessary. Indeed their principle, if you observe it with any attention, goes much further than to an alteration in the election of the house of commons; for, if popular representation, or choice, is necessary to the *legitimacy* of all government, the house of lords is, at one stroke, bastardized and corrupted in blood. That house is no representative of the people at all, even in 'semblance' or in 'form.' The case of the crown is altogether as bad.[115] In vain the crown may endeavour to screen itself against these gentlemen by the authority of the establishment made on the Revolution. The Revolution which is resorted to for a title, on their system, wants a title itself. The Revolution is built, according to their theory, upon a basis not more solid than our present formalities, as it was made by an house of lords not representing any one but themselves; and by an house of commons exactly such as the present, that is, as they term it, by a mere 'shadow and mockery' of representation.

[Something they must destroy, or they seem to themselves to exist for no purpose. One set is for destroying the civil power through the ecclesiastical; another for demolishing the ecclesiastick through the civil. They are aware that the worst consequences might happen to the public in accomplishing this double ruin of church and state; but they are so heated with their theories, that they give more than hints, that this ruin, with all the mischiefs that must lead to it and attend it, and which to themselves appear quite certain,][116] would not be unacceptable to them, or very remote from their wishes. A man amongst them[117] of great authority, and certainly of great talents, speaking of a supposed alliance between church and state, says, 'perhaps *we must wait for the fall of the civil powers* before this most unnatural alliance be broken. Calamitous no doubt will that time be. But what convulsion in the political world ought to be a subject of lamentation, if it be attended with so desirable an effect?'[118] You see

---

[115] Burke's view was not, at the time, so eccentric as it now appears. 'Representation' did not then have the modern sense of having to proportionally mimic properties of the whole. The King, could plausibly be thought to 'represent' the nation, in the way we still talk about ambassadors 'representing' their states.

[116] 1st edn reads: 'Some of them are so heated with their particular religious theories, that they give more than hints that the fall of the civil powers, with all the dreadful consequences of that fall, provided they might be of service to their theories.'

[117] I.e. Joseph Priestley.[N]

[118] Priestley, *An History of the Corruptions of Christianity*, 2 vols. (Birmingham, 1782), p. 484. The *Alliance between Church and State* (1736) was a famous work by William Warburton,

with what a steady eye these gentlemen are prepared to view the greatest calamities which can befall their country!

It is no wonder therefore, that with these ideas of every thing in their constitution and government at home, either in church or state, as illegitimate and usurped, or, at best as a vain mockery, they look abroad with an eager and passionate enthusiasm. Whilst they are possessed by these notions, it is vain to talk to them of the practice of their ancestors, the fundamental laws of their country, the fixed form of a constitution, whose merits are confirmed by the solid test of long experience, and an increasing public strength and national prosperity. They despise experience as the wisdom of unlettered men; and as for the rest, they have wrought under-ground a mine that will blow up at one grand explosion all examples of antiquity, all precedents, charters, and acts of parliament. They have 'the rights of men.' Against these there can be no prescription; against these no agreement is binding: these admit no temperament, and no compromise: any thing withheld from their full demand is so much of fraud and injustice. Against these their rights of men let no government look for security in the length of its continuance, or in the justice and lenity of its administration. The objections of these speculatists, if its forms do not quadrate with their theories, are as valid against such an old and beneficent government as against the most violent tyranny, or the greenest usurpation. They are always at issue with governments, not on a question of abuse, but a question of competency, and a question of title. I have nothing to say to the clumsy subtilty of their political metaphysics. Let them be their amusement in the schools. – 'Illa *se jactet in aula – Æolus, et clauso ventorum carcere regnet.*'[119] But let them not break prison to burst like a *Levanter,*[120] to sweep the earth with their hurricane, and to break up the fountains of the great deep to overwhelm us.

Far am I from denying in theory; full as far is my heart from withholding in practice, (if I were of power to give or to withhold,) the *real* rights of men. In denying their false claims of right, I do not mean to injure those which are real, and are such as their pretended rights would

---

defending an established Church and the operation of religious tests for membership of it as a condition of holding state office. Nonconformists such as Priestly not only rejected the idea of an established Church but thought the use of religious tests for political purposes immoral since it provided a secular incentive to compromise one's spiritual integrity.

[119] Virgil, *Aeneid*, 1.140–1: 'Let Aeolus blow about in his Hall, and rule in the winds' closed prison.' Aeolus was the god of the winds.

[120] *Levanter*: a strong Mediterranean wind blowing from the East.

totally destroy. If civil society be made for the advantage of man, all the advantages for which it is made become his right. It is an institution of beneficence; and law itself is only beneficence acting by a rule. Men have a right to live by that rule; they have a right to justice; as between their fellows, whether their fellows are in politic function or in ordinary occupation. They have a right to the fruits of their industry; and to the means of making their industry fruitful. They have a right to the acquisitions of their parents; to the nourishment and improvement of their offspring; to instruction in life, and to consolation in death. Whatever each man can separately do, without trespassing upon others, he has a right to do for himself; and he has a right to a fair portion of all which society, with all its combinations of skill and force, can do in his favour. [In this partnership all men have equal rights; but not to equal things. He that has but five shillings in the partnership, has as good a right to it, as he that has five hundred pound has to his larger proportion. But he has not a right to an equal dividend in the product of the joint stock; and][121] as to the share of power, authority, and direction which each individual ought to have in the management of the state, that I must deny to be amongst the direct original rights of man in civil society; for I have in my contemplation the civil social man, and no other. It is a thing to be settled by convention.

If civil society be the offspring of convention, that convention must be its law. That convention must limit and modify all the descriptions of constitution which are formed under it. Every sort of legislative, judicial, or executory power are its creatures. They can have no being in any other state of things; and how can any man claim, under the conventions of civil society, rights which do not so much as suppose its existence? Rights which are absolutely repugnant to it?[122] One of the first motives to civil society, and which becomes one of its fundamental rules, is, *that no man should be judge in his own cause*. By this each person has at once divested himself of the first fundamental right of uncovenanted man, that is, to judge for himself, and to assert his own cause. He abdicates all right to be his own governor. He inclusively, in a great measure, abandons the right of self-defence, the first law of nature. Men cannot enjoy the rights of an

---

[121] Not in 1st edn. Next sentence there begins 'But . . . '

[122] Natural rights theories could be used either to argue (as with the Levellers, Locke and Paine) that at least some natural rights were *retained* and constituted a continuing standard against which government behaviour could be measured; or (as with Grotius, Selden, Hobbes – and here Burke) to emphasise that the establishment of government involved the *giving up* of natural right.

uncivil and of a civil state together. That he may obtain justice he gives up his right of determining what it is in points the most essential to him. That he may secure some liberty, he makes a surrender in trust of the whole of it.

Government is not made in virtue of natural rights, which may and do exist in total independence of it; and exist in much greater clearness, and in a much greater degree of abstract perfection: but their abstract perfection is their practical defect. By having a right to every thing they want every thing. Government is a contrivance of human wisdom to provide for human *wants*. Men have a right that these wants should be provided for by this wisdom. Among these wants is to be reckoned the want, out of civil society, of a sufficient restraint upon their passions. Society requires not only that the passions of individuals should be subjected, but that even in the mass and body as well as in the individuals, the inclinations of men should frequently be thwarted, their will controlled, and their passions brought into subjection. This can only be done *by a power out of themselves*; and not, in the exercise of its function, subject to that will and to those passions which it is its office to bridle and subdue. In this sense the restraints on men, as well as their liberties, are to be reckoned among their rights. But as the liberties and the restrictions vary with times and circumstances, and admit of infinite modifications, they cannot be settled upon any abstract rule; and nothing is so foolish as to discuss them upon that principle.

The moment you abate any thing from the full rights of men, each to govern himself, and suffer any artificial positive limitation upon those rights, from that moment the whole organization of government becomes a consideration of convenience. This it is which makes the constitution of a state, and the due distribution of its powers, a matter of the most delicate and complicated skill. It requires a deep knowledge of human nature and human necessities, and of the things which facilitate or obstruct the various ends which are to be pursued by the mechanism of civil institutions. The state is to have recruits to its strength, and remedies to its distempers. What is the use of discussing a man's abstract right to food or to medicine? The question is upon the method of procuring and administering them. In that deliberation I shall always advise to call in the aid of the farmer and the physician, rather than the professor of metaphysics.[123]

---

[123]  1st edn: no paragraph break.

The science of constructing a commonwealth, or renovating it, or reforming it, is, like every other experimental science, not to be taught *à priori*. Nor is it a short experience that can instruct us in that practical science; because the real effects of moral causes are not always immediate;[124] but that which in the first instance is prejudicial may be excellent in its remoter operation; and its excellence may arise even from the ill effects it produces in the beginning. The reverse also happens; and very plausible schemes, with very pleasing commencements, have often shameful and lamentable conclusions. In states there are often some obscure and almost latent causes, things which appear at first view of little moment, on which a very great part of its prosperity or adversity may most essentially depend. The science of government being therefore so practical in itself, and intended for such practical purposes, a matter which requires experience, and even more experience than any person can gain in his whole life, however sagacious and observing he may be, it is with infinite caution that any man ought to venture upon pulling down an edifice which has answered in any tolerable degree for ages the common purposes of society, or on building it up again, without having models and patterns of approved utility before his eyes.

These metaphysic rights entering into common life, like rays of light which pierce into a dense medium, are, by the laws of nature, refracted from their straight line. Indeed in the gross and complicated mass of human passions and concerns, the primitive rights of men undergo such a variety of refractions and reflections, that it becomes absurd to talk of them as if they continued in the simplicity of their original direction. The nature of man is intricate; the objects of society are of the greatest possible complexity; and therefore no simple disposition or direction of power can be suitable either to man's nature, or to the quality of his affairs. When I hear the simplicity of contrivance aimed at and boasted of in any new political constitutions, I am at no loss to decide that the artificers are grossly ignorant of their trade, or totally negligent of their duty. The simple governments are fundamentally defective, to say no worse of them. If you were to contemplate society in but one point of view, all these simple modes of polity are infinitely captivating. In effect each would answer its single end much more perfectly than the more complex is able to attain all its complex purposes. But it is better that the

---

[124] *Moral*: here, not in the sense of ethical but in the common eighteenth-century sense of 'to do with humans' social/psychological nature', not physical.

whole should be imperfectly and anomalously answered, than that, while some parts are provided for with great exactness, others might be totally neglected, or perhaps materially injured, by the overcare of a favourite member.

The pretended rights of these theorists are all extremes; and in proportion as they are metaphysically true, they are morally and politically false. The rights of men are in a sort of *middle*, incapable of definition, but not impossible to be discerned. The rights of men in governments are their advantages; and these are often in balances between differences of good; in compromises sometimes between good and evil, and sometimes, between evil and evil. Political reason is a computing principle; adding, subtracting, multiplying, and dividing, morally and not metaphysically or mathematically, true moral denominations.

By these theorists the right of the people is almost always sophistically confounded with their power. The body of the community, whenever it can come to act, can meet with no effectual resistance; but till power and right are the same, the whole body of them has no right inconsistent with virtue, and the first of all virtues, prudence. Men have no right to what is not reasonable, and to what is not for their benefit; for though a pleasant writer said, *Liceat perire poetis*, when one of them, in cold blood, is said to have leaped into the flames of a volcanic revolution, *Ardentem frigidus Ætnam insiluit*,[125] I consider such a frolic rather as an unjustifiable poetic licence, than as one of the franchises of Parnassus;[126] and whether he were poet, or divine, or politician, that chose to exercise this kind of right, I think that more wise, because more charitable thoughts would urge me rather to save the man, than to preserve his brazen slippers as the monuments of his folly.

The kind of anniversary sermons, to which a great part of what I write refers, if men are not shamed out of their present course, in commemorating the fact, will cheat many out of the principles, and deprive them of the benefits of the Revolution they commemorate. I confess to you, Sir, I never liked this continual talk of resistance and revolution, or

---

[125] Horace, *On the Art of Poetry*, l. 466: 'Poets must be allowed to die' ... 'He coolly leapt into burning Etna.' The poet in question was Empedocles[N] (490–430 BC), a pre-Socratic philosopher who wrote in verse and formulated the view – which persisted to early modernity – that the world comprises the four elements – earth, air, fire and water. One legend has him jumping into Mt. Etna, the Sicilian volcano, in order to join the gods.

[126] *Parnassus*: mountain in Greece, legendary home of the muses who inspired human artistic creativity.

the practice of making the extreme medicine of the constitution its daily bread. It renders the habit of society dangerously valetudinary: it is taking periodical doses of mercury sublimate,[127] and swallowing down repeated provocatives of cantharides[128] to our love of liberty.

This distemper of remedy, grown habitual, relaxes and wears out, by a vulgar and prostituted use, the spring of that spirit which is to be exerted on great occasions. It was in the most patient period of Roman servitude that themes of tyrannicide made the ordinary exercise of boys at school – *cum perimit saevos classis numerosa tyrannos*.[129] In the ordinary state of things, it produces in a country like ours the worst effects, even on the cause of that liberty which it abuses with the dissoluteness of an extravagant speculation. Almost all the high-bred republicans of my time have, after a short space, become the most decided, thorough-paced courtiers; they soon left the business of a tedious, moderate, but practical resistance, to those of us whom, in the pride and intoxication of their theories, they have slighted, as not much better than tories. Hypocrisy, of course, delights in the most sublime speculations; for, never intending to go beyond speculation, it costs nothing to have it magnificent. But even in cases where rather levity than fraud was to be suspected in these ranting speculations, the issue has been much the same. These professors, finding their extreme principles not applicable to cases which call only for a qualified, or, as I may say, civil and legal resistance, in such cases employ no resistance at all. It is with them a war or a revolution, or it is nothing. Finding their schemes of politics not adapted to the state of the world in which they live, they often come to think lightly of all public principle; and are ready, on their part, to abandon for a very trivial interest what they find of very trivial value. Some indeed are of more steady and persevering natures; but these are eager politicians out of parliament, who have little to tempt them to abandon their favourite projects. They have some change in the church or state, or both, constantly in their view. When that is the case, they are always bad citizens, and perfectly unsure connexions. For, considering their speculative designs as of infinite value,

---

[127] *Mercury sublimate*: mercury chloride. Historically considered a cure for syphilis, but so toxic that it was often fatal and produced mental deterioration.

[128] *Cantharides*: 'spanish fly', a species of beetle, the crushed bodies of which had been used since antiquity as an inflammatory and aphrodisiac, but which was also poisonous, the dosage being critical.

[129] Juvenal, *Satires*, 7.151: 'When our squadron of scholars destroys the cruel tyrant.' Burke is echoing Juvenal's irony that the rhetoric of republican tyrannicide was being ineffectually rehearsed by scholars at a time of entrenched tyranny.

and the actual arrangement of the state as of no estimation, they are at best indifferent about it. They see no merit in the good, and no fault in the vicious management of public affairs; they rather rejoice in the latter, as more propitious to revolution. They see no merit or demerit in any man, or any action, or any political principle, any further than as they may forward or retard their design of change: they therefore take up, one day, the most violent and stretched prerogative, and another time the wildest democratic ideas of freedom, and pass from the one to the other without any sort of regard to cause, to person, or to party.

In France you are now in the crisis of a revolution, and in the transit from one form of government to another – you cannot see that character of men exactly in the same situation in which we see it in this country. With us it is militant; with you it is triumphant; and you know how it can act when its power is commensurate to its will. I would not be supposed to confine those observations to any description of men, or to comprehend all men of any description within them – No! far from it. I am as incapable of that injustice, as I am of keeping terms with those who profess principles of extremes; and who under the name of religion teach little else than wild and dangerous politics. The worst of these politics of revolution is this; they temper and harden the breast, in order to prepare it for the desperate strokes which are sometimes used in extreme occasions. But as these occasions may never arrive, the mind receives a gratuitous taint; and the moral sentiments suffer not a little, when no political purpose is served by the depravation. This sort of people are so taken up with their theories about the rights of man, that they have totally forgot his nature. Without opening one new avenue to the understanding, they have succeeded in stopping up those that lead to the heart. They have perverted in themselves, and in those that attend to them, all the well-placed sympathies of the human breast.

This famous sermon of the Old Jewry[N] breathes nothing but this spirit through all the political part. Plots, massacres, assassinations, seem to some people a trivial price for obtaining a revolution. A cheap, bloodless reformation, a guiltless liberty, appear flat and vapid to their taste. There must be a great change of scene; there must be a magnificent stage effect; there must be a grand spectacle to rouze the imagination, grown torpid with the lazy enjoyment of sixty years security, and the still unanimating repose of public prosperity. The Preacher found them all in the French revolution. This inspires a juvenile warmth through his whole frame. His enthusiasm kindles as he advances; and when he arrives at his peroration, it is in a full blaze. Then viewing, from the Pisgah[130] of his pulpit, the free, moral, happy, flourishing, and glorious state of France, as in a bird-eye landscape of a promised land, he breaks out into the following rapture:

> 'What an eventful period is this! I am *thankful* that I have lived to it; I could almost say, *Lord, now lettest thou thy servant depart in peace, for mine eyes have seen thy salvation.* – I have lived to see a *diffusion* of knowledge, which has undermined superstition and error. – I have lived to see *the rights of men* better understood than ever; and nations panting for liberty which seemed to have lost the idea of it. – I have lived to see *Thirty Millions of People*, indignant and resolute, spurning at slavery, and demanding liberty with an irresistible voice. *Their King led in triumph, and an arbitrary monarch surrendering himself to his subjects*[xii].'

Before I proceed further, I have to remark, that Dr. Price[N] seems rather to over-value the great acquisitions of light which he has obtained and diffused in this age. The last century appears to me to have been quite as much enlightened. It had, though in a different place, a triumph as memorable as that of Dr. Price; and some of the great preachers of that period partook of it as eagerly as he has done in the triumph of France. On the trial of the Rev. Hugh Peters[N] for high treason, it was deposed, that when King Charles was brought to London for his trial, the Apostle of Liberty in that day conducted the *triumph*. 'I saw,' says the witness, 'his majesty in the coach with six horses, and Peters riding before the king *triumphing*.' Dr. Price, when he talks as if he had made a discovery, only follows a precedent; for, after the commencement of the king's trial, this precursor, the same Dr. Peters, concluding a long prayer at the royal chapel at Whitehall, (he had very triumphantly chosen his place) said, 'I have prayed and preached these twenty years; and now I may say with old Simeon,[131] *Lord, now lettest thou thy servant depart in peace,*

---

[xii] Another of these reverend gentlemen, who was witness to some of the spectacles which Paris has lately exhibited – expresses himself thus, '*A King dragged in submissive triumph by his conquering subjects* is one of those appearances of grandeur which seldom rise in the prospect of human affairs, and which, during the remainder of my life, I shall think of with wonder and gratification.' These gentlemen agree marvellously in their feelings.

[130] *Pisgah:* (Hebrew) meaning 'a high place'; referring especially to the mountain (Mt. Nebo) from which Moses supposedly viewed the promised land before his death (Deuteronomy 34:1).

[131] *Old Simeon:* In the Gospel according to Luke (2:25), Simeon the elder, having been promised he should not die until he had seen the saviour of Israel, utters this prayer after having received the infant Jesus into the Temple.

*for mine eyes have seen thy salvation*[xiii].' Peters had not the fruits of his prayer; for he neither departed so soon as he wished, nor in peace. He became (what I heartily hope none of his followers may be in this country) himself a sacrifice to the triumph which he led as Pontiff. They dealt at the Restoration, perhaps, too hardly with this poor good man.[132] But we owe it to his memory and his sufferings, that he had as much illumination, and as much zeal, and had as effectually undermined all *the superstition and error* which might impede the great business he was engaged in, as any who follow and repeat after him, in this age, which would assume to itself an exclusive title to the knowledge of the rights of men, and all the glorious consequences of that knowledge.

After this sally of the preacher of the Old Jewry,[N] which differs only in place and time, but agrees perfectly with the spirit and letter of the rapture of 1648, the Revolution Society,[N] the fabricators of governments, the heroic band of *cashierers* of *monarchs*, electors of sovereigns, and leaders of kings in triumph, strutting with a proud consciousness of the diffusion of knowledge, of which every member had obtained so large a share in the donative, were in haste to make a generous diffusion of the knowledge they had thus gratuitously received. To make this bountiful communication, they adjourned from the church in the Old Jewry, to the London Tavern; where the famous Dr. Price, in whom the fumes of his oracular tripod were not entirely evaporated, moved and carried the resolution, or address of congratulation, transmitted by Lord Stanhope[N] to the National Assembly[N] of France.[133]

I find a preacher of the gospel prophaning the beautiful and prophetic ejaculation, commonly called '*nunc dimittis*,'[134] made on the first presentation of our Saviour in the Temple, and applying it, with an inhuman and unnatural rapture, to the most horrid, atrocious, and afflicting spectacle, that perhaps ever was exhibited to the pity and indignation of mankind. This '*leading in triumph*,' a thing in its best form unmanly and irreligious, which fills our Preacher with such unhallowed transports, must shock, I

---

[xiii] State Trials, vol. ii. p. 363.

[132] Along with the other regicides who had signed Charles I's death warrant, Hugh Peter received the statutory penalty for commoners convicted of treason: to be hung, brought down whilst still alive, cut open and have his entrails burnt before his eyes. His body was then cut into pieces which were exhibited in public places.

[133] The Letter sent from the Revolution Society to the National Assembly was printed in the Appendix, p. 13 of Price's *Discourse* (not in *Political Writings*).

[134] *Nunc dimitis*: the prayer uttered by Simeon, above fn. 131.

believe, the moral taste of every well-born mind. Several English were the stupified and indignant spectators of that triumph. It was (unless we have been strangely deceived) a spectacle more resembling a procession of American savages, entering into Onondaga,[135] after some of their murders called victories, and leading into hovels hung round with scalps, their captives, overpowered with the scoffs and buffets of women as ferocious as themselves, much more than it resembled the triumphal pomp of a civilized martial nation; – if a civilized nation, or any men who had a sense of generosity, were capable of a personal triumph over the fallen and afflicted.

This, my dear Sir, was not the triumph of France. I must believe that, as a nation, it overwhelmed you with shame and horror. I must believe that the National Assembly find themselves in a state of the greatest humiliation, in not being able to punish the authors of this triumph, or the actors in it; and that they are in a situation in which any enquiry they may make upon the subject, must be destitute even of the appearance of liberty or impartiality. The apology of that Assembly is found in their situation; but when we approve what they *must* bear, it is in us the degenerate choice of a vitiated mind.

With a compelled appearance of deliberation, they vote under the dominion of a stern necessity. They sit in the heart, as it were, of a foreign republic: they have their residence in a city whose constitution has emanated neither from the charter of their king, nor from their legislative power. There they are surrounded by an army not raised either by the authority of their crown, or by their command;[136] and which, if they should order to dissolve itself, would instantly dissolve them. [There they sit, after a gang of assassins had driven away some hundreds of the members;[137] whilst those who held the same moderate principles, with more patience or better hope, continued every day exposed to outrageous insults and murderous threats. There a majority, sometimes

---

[135] *Onondaga*: a group of the Iroquois tribe inhabiting the Canadian/US border in upstate New York, and hence their main settlement, where the Iroquois federation met. Notoriously bloody wars were fought between the Onondaga and the Hurons in the seventeenth and eighteenth centuries. Onondaga sided with the British in the American War of Independence. Burke had luridly described the Amerindian return from warfare in an earlier collaborative work: *An Account of the European Settlements in America*, 2 vols. (London, 1757), pt. II, ch 4, pp. 187ff.

[136] The revolutionary National Guard. See fn. 112 above.

[137] *Driven away*: Several hundred moderate deputies withdrew from the *Assemblée* and from Paris; many, including Mounier,[N] Lally-Tollendal[N] and the Bishop of Langres, emigrated to England.

real, sometimes pretended, captive itself, compels a captive king to issue as royal edicts, at third hand, the polluted nonsense of their most licentious and giddy coffee-houses.]'[138] It is notorious, that all their measures are decided before they are debated. It is beyond doubt, that under the terror of the bayonet, and the lamp-post, and the torch to their houses, they are obliged to adopt all the crude and desperate measures suggested by clubs composed of a monstrous medley of all conditions, tongues, and nations. Among these are found persons, in comparison of whom Catiline[139] would be thought scrupulous, and Cethegus[140] a man of sobriety and moderation. Nor is it in these clubs alone that the publick measures are deformed into monsters. They undergo a previous distortion in academies, intended as so many seminaries for these clubs, which are set up in all the places of publick resort. In these meetings of all sorts, every counsel, in proportion as it is daring, and violent, and perfidious, is taken for the mark of superior genius. Humanity and compassion are ridiculed as the fruits of superstition and ignorance. Tenderness to individuals is considered as treason to the public. Liberty is always to be estimated perfect as property is rendered insecure. Amidst assassination, massacre, and confiscation, perpetrated or meditated, they are forming plans for the good order of future society. Embracing in their arms the carcases of base criminals, and promoting their relations on the title of their offences, they drive hundreds of virtuous persons to the same end, by forcing them to subsist by beggary or by crime.

The Assembly,[N] their organ, acts before them the farce of deliberation with as little decency as liberty. They act like the comedians of a fair before a riotous audience; they act amidst the tumultuous cries of a mixed mob

[138] 1st edn reads: 'There they sit, after a gang of assassins had driven away all the men of moderate minds and moderating authority amongst them, and left them as a sort of dregs and refuse, under the apparent lead of those in whom they do not so much as pretend to have any confidence. There they sit, in mockery of legislation, repeating in resolutions the words of those whom they detest and despise. Captives themselves, they compel a captive king to issue as royal edicts, at third hand, the polluted nonsense of their most licentious and giddy coffee-houses.'

[139] *Catiline*: L. Sergius Catilina, notoriously corrupt and unscrupulous Roman politician who conspired to overthrow the Roman republic and was famously denounced and accused by Cicero. Having twice failed to gain the consulship he plotted a coup but was forced into exile and eventually killed at the battle of Pistoria in 62 BC. His name becomes synonymous with political untrustworthiness and disloyalty.

[140] *Cethegus*, Gaius Cornelius, *fl.* first century BC. Roman Consul, an ally of Catiline in his conspiracy. When Catiline left Rome following Cicero's exposure of his treason, Cethegus remained, planning to assassinate Cicero and set fire to Rome. He was executed in 63 BC, having been shown to have plotted with the Gauls to overthrow the Republic.

of ferocious men, and of women lost to shame, who, according to their insolent fancies, direct, control, applaud, explode them; and sometimes mix and take their seats amongst them; domineering over them with a strange mixture of servile petulance and proud presumptuous authority. As they have inverted order in all things, the gallery is in the place of the house.[141] This Assembly, which overthrows kings and kingdoms, has not even the physiognomy and aspect of a grave legislative body – *nec color imperii, nec frons erat ulla senatus.*[142] They have a power given to them, like that of the evil principle, to subvert and destroy; but none to construct, except such machines as may be fitted for further subversion and further destruction.

Who is it that admires, and from the heart is attached to national representative assemblies, but must turn with horror and disgust from such a profane burlesque, and abominable perversion of that sacred institute? Lovers of monarchy, lovers of republicks, must alike abhor it. The members of your Assembly must themselves groan under the tyranny of which they have all the shame, none of the direction, and little of the profit. I am sure many of the members who compose even the majority of that body, must feel as I do, notwithstanding the applauses of the Revolution Society. Miserable king! miserable Assembly! How must that assembly be silently scandalized with those of their members, who could call a day which seemed to blot the sun out of Heaven, '*Un beau jour*[xiv]!'[143] How must they be inwardly indignant at hearing others, who thought fit to declare to them, 'that the vessel of the state would fly forward in her course towards regeneration with more speed than ever,' from the stiff gale of treason and murder, which preceded our Preacher's triumph! What must they have felt, whilst with outward patience and inward indignation they heard of the slaughter of innocent gentlemen in their houses, that 'the blood spilled was not the most pure?' What must they have felt, when they were besieged by complaints of disorders which shook their

---

xiv   6th of October, 1789.

---

141   *Gallery... the house*: In the English House of Commons the Gallery was for visitors – Burke implies that in France the common people have usurped the arena and role of the statesmen.

142   Lucan, *Pharsalia*, 9.206–7 (After the death of Pompey): *Non iam regnare pudebit: Nec color imperii, nec frons erit ulla senatus.* ['Now no one will be ashamed to rule [as King], there will be no pretence about military power, no need for the senate as a front.']

143   Bailly, the mayor of Paris, called 6 October, on which the royal family were forced back to Paris, a 'beautiful day'. In fact it rained – Burke, indulging in pathetic fallacy, points out the sun was, appropriately, obscured.

country to its foundations, at being compelled coolly to tell the complainants, that they were under the protection of the law, and that they would address the king (the captive king) to cause the laws to be enforced for their protection; when the enslaved ministers of that captive king had formally notified to them, that there were neither law, nor authority, nor power left to protect? What must they have felt at being obliged, as a felicitation on the present new year, to request their captive king to forget the stormy period of the last, on account of the great good which *he* was likely to produce to his people; to the complete attainment of which good they adjourned the practical demonstrations of their loyalty, assuring him of their obedience, when he should no longer possess any authority to command?

This address was made with much good-nature and affection, to be sure. But among the revolutions in France, must be reckoned a considerable revolution in their ideas of politeness. In England we are said to learn manners at second-hand from your side of the water, and that we dress our behaviour in the frippery of France.[144] If so, we are still in the old cut; and have not so far conformed to the new Parisian mode of good-breeding, as to think it quite in the most refined strain of delicate compliment (whether in condolence or congratulation) to say to the most humiliated creature that crawls upon the earth, that great public benefits are derived from the murder of his servants, the attempted assassination of himself and of his wife, and the mortification, disgrace, and degradation, that he has personally suffered. It is a topic of consolation which our ordinary of Newgate[145] would be too humane to use to a criminal at the foot of the gallows. I should have thought that the hangman of Paris, now that he is liberalized by the vote of the National Assembly, and is allowed his rank and arms in the Herald's College[146] of the rights of men, would be too generous, too gallant a man, too full of the sense of his new dignity, to employ that cutting consolation to any of the persons whom

---

[144] Burke is playing not only on the still-obvious ambiguity between manners and politeness as, on the one hand, 'frippery' – cheap and passing finery – and on the other as a deeper-seated cultural repertoire of values and predispositions explored by Enlightenment thinkers, but also exploiting the original, and now lost, meaning of 'frippery' as items of second-hand clothing, recycled and presented as new. Paris was already the leader and source of innovations in fashion in the former sense, hence England was merely taking up French cast-offs.

[145] *Ordinary of Newgate*: the duty-priest officiating at public executions.

[146] *Herald's College*: The body in England responsible for regulating titles of honour, coats of arms etc.

the *leze nation*[147] might bring under the administration of his *executive powers*.

A man is fallen indeed, when he is thus flattered. The anodyne draught of oblivion, thus drugged, is well calculated to preserve a galling wakefulness, and to feed the living ulcer of a corroding memory. Thus to administer the opiate potion of amnesty, powdered with all the ingredients of scorn and contempt, is to hold to his lips, instead of 'the balm of hurt minds,' the cup of human misery full to the brim, and to force him to drink it to the dregs.

Yielding to reasons, at least as forcible as those which were so delicately urged in the compliment on the new year, the king of France will probably endeavour to forget these events, and that compliment. But history, who keeps a durable record of all our acts, and exercises her awful censure over the proceedings of all sorts of sovereigns, will not forget either those events or the aera of this liberal refinement in the intercourse of mankind. History will record, that on the morning of the 6th of October 1789, the king and queen of France, after a day of confusion, alarm, dismay, and slaughter, lay down, under the pledged security of public faith, to indulge nature in a few hours of respite, and troubled melancholy repose. From this sleep the queen was first startled by the voice of the centinel at her door, who cried out to her, to save herself by flight – that this was the last proof of fidelity he could give – that they were upon him, and he was dead. Instantly he was cut down. A band of cruel ruffians and assassins, reeking with his blood, rushed into the chamber of the queen, and pierced with an hundred strokes of bayonets and poniards the bed, from whence this persecuted woman had but just had time to fly almost naked, and through ways unknown to the murderers had escaped to seek refuge at the feet of a king and husband, not secure of his own life for a moment.

This king, to say no more of him, and this queen, and their infant children (who once would have been the pride and hope of a great and generous people) were then forced to abandon the sanctuary of the most splendid palace in the world, which they left swimming in blood, polluted

---

[147] *Leze nation*: In dynastic monarchies (including Britain) the crime of *lèse majesté* involved an attempt to injure the dignity of the monarch, and could constitute treason. In August 1789 a member of the Assembly (M. de Créniere) proposed that contravening the rights of man should be considered a crime of *lèse nation*. The Assembly redefined treason in this way the following month.

by massacre, and strewed with scattered limbs and mutilated carcases.[148] Thence they were conducted into the capital of their kingdom. Two had been selected from the unprovoked, unresisted, promiscuous slaughter, which was made of the gentlemen of birth and family who composed the king's body guard. These two gentlemen, with all the parade of an execution of justice, were cruelly and publickly dragged to the block, and beheaded in the great court of the palace. Their heads were stuck upon spears, and led the procession; whilst the royal captives who followed in the train were slowly moved along, amidst the horrid yells, and shrilling screams, and frantic dances, and infamous contumelies,[149] and all the unutterable abominations of the furies of hell, in the abused shape of the vilest of women. After they had been made to taste, drop by drop, more than the bitterness of death, in the slow torture of a journey of twelve miles, protracted to six hours, they were, under a guard, composed of those very soldiers who had thus conducted them through this famous triumph, lodged in one of the old palaces of Paris, now converted into a Bastile[150] for kings.

Is this a triumph to be consecrated at altars? to be commemorated with grateful thanksgiving? to be offered to the divine humanity with fervent prayer and enthusiastick ejaculation? – These Theban and Thracian Orgies,[151] acted in France, and applauded only in the Old Jewry,[N] I assure you, kindle prophetic enthusiasm in the minds but of very few people in this kingdom; although a saint and apostle, who may have revelations of his own, and who has so completely vanquished all the mean superstitions of the heart, may incline to think it pious and decorous to compare it with the entrance into the world of the Prince of Peace, proclaimed in an holy temple by a venerable sage, and not long before not worse announced by the voice of angels to the quiet innocence of shepherds.

At first I was at a loss to account for this fit of unguarded transport. I knew, indeed, that the sufferings of monarchs make a delicious repast to some sort of palates. There were reflexions which might serve to keep this appetite within some bounds of temperance. But when I took one

---

[148] *The Times* (17 Oct. 1789) reckoned that 'about [!]106' had been killed in the episode.
[149] *Contumelies*: acts of offensive insolence, expressive of contempt.
[150] *Bastille*: a fortress used as a prison. The storming, on 14 July 1789, of *The Bastille* (de Saint Antoine), which had become a prison for common criminals, was one of the emblematic events of the Revolution. The 'old Palace' where the royal family were kept was the Tuileries, near the Louvre. Only the Gardens remain.
[151] *Theban and Thracian Orgies*: ancient Greek religious festivals associated with the cult of Dionysus, the god associated with wine, intoxication and ecstatic possession.

circumstance into my consideration, I was obliged to confess, that much allowance ought to be made for the Society, and that the temptation was too strong for common discretion; I mean, the circumstance of the Io Pæan[152] of the triumph, the animating cry which called 'for *all* the BISH-OPS to be hanged on the lamp-posts[xv],' might well have brought forth a burst of enthusiasm on the foreseen consequences of this happy day. I allow to so much enthusiasm some little deviation from prudence. I allow this prophet to break forth into hymns of joy and thanksgiving on an event which appears like the precursor of the Millennium, and the projected fifth monarchy,[153] in the destruction of all church establishments. There was, however (as in all human affairs there is) in the midst of this joy something to exercise the patience of these worthy gentlemen, and to try the long-suffering of their faith. The actual murder of the king and queen, and their child, was wanting to the other auspicious circumstances of this '*beautiful day*.' The actual murder of the bishops, though called for by so many holy ejaculations, was also wanting. A groupe of regicide and sacrilegious slaughter, was indeed boldly sketched, but it was only sketched. It unhappily was left unfinished, in this great history-piece of the massacre of innocents. What hardy pencil of a great master, from the school of the rights of men, will finish it, is to be seen hereafter. The age has not yet the compleat benefit of that diffusion of knowledge that has undermined superstition and error; and the king of France wants another object or two, to consign to oblivion, in consideration of all the good which is to arise from his own sufferings, and the patriotic crimes of an enlightened age[xvi].

---

[xv]  Tous les Eveques à la lanterne.

[xvi]  It is proper here to refer to a letter written upon this subject by an eye-witness. That eye-witness was one of the most honest, intelligent, and eloquent members of the National Assembly[N], one of the most active and zealous reformers of the state. He was obliged to secede from the assembly; and he afterwards became a voluntary exile, on account of the horrors of this pious triumph, and the dispositions of men, who, profiting of crimes, if not causing them, have taken the lead in public affairs.

EXTRACT of M. de Lally Tollendal's[N] Second Letter to a Friend.

---

[152]  *Io Paean*: hymn of praise.

[153]  *Fifth monarchy*: foretold in the Book of Daniel (2:44), the supposed millennial epoch in which Christ returns for a thousand-year rule with his saints, forming a fifth and final monarchy following those of Assyria, Persia, Greece and Rome. The belief recurs in western Christian history and is typically associated with the overthrow of secular powers. One episode involved the radical religious sect – the Fifth Monarchy Men – during the English Civil War and Commonwealth, who believed the troubles of the time presaged the imminence of Christ's return.

Although this work of our new light and knowledge, did not go to the length, that in all probability it was intended it should be carried; yet I

"Parlons du parti que j'ai pris; il est bien justifié dans ma conscience. – Ni cette ville coupable, ni cette assemblée plus coupable encore, ne meritoient que je me justifie; mais j'ai à coeur que vous, et les personnes qui pensent comme vous, ne me condamnent pas. – Ma santé, je vous jure, me rendoit mes fonctions impossibles; mais meme en les mettant de coté il a eté au-dessus de mes forces de supporter plus long-tems l'horreur que me causoit ce sang, – ces têtes, – cette reine *presque egorgée*, – ce roi, – amené *esclave*, entrant à Paris, au milieu de ses assassins, et precedé des tetes de ces malheureux gardes. – Ces perfides jannissaires, ces assassins, ces femmes canibales, ce cri de, TOUS LES EVEQUES A LA LANTERNE, dans le moment ou le roi entre sa capitale avec deux eveques de son conseil dans sa voiture. Un *coup de fusil*, que j'ai vu tirer dans un *des carosses de la reine*. M Bailley appellant cela *un beau jour*. L'assemblée ayant declaré froidement le matin, qu'il n'étoit pas de sa dignité d'aller tout entier environner le roi. M. Mirabeau disant impunement dans cette assemblée, que le vaisseau de l'état, loins d'etre arrêté dans sa course, s'élanceroit avec plus de rapidité que jamais vers sa régenération. M. Barnave, riant avec lui, quand des flots de sang couloient autour de nous. Le vertueux Mounier* echappant par miracle à vingt assassins, que avoient voulu faire de sa tete un trophée de plus.

"Voila ce qui me fit jurer de ne plus mettre le pied *dans cette caverne d'Antropophages* [the National Assembly] où je n'avois plus de force d'élever la voix, ou depuis six semaines je l'avois elevée en vain. Moi, Mounier, et tous les honnêtes gens, ont le dernier effort à faire pour le bien étoit d'en sortir. Aucune idée de crainte ne s'est approchée de moi. Je rougirois de m'en defendre. J'avois encore reçû sur la route de la part de ce peuple, moins coupable que ceux qui l'ont enivré de fureur, des acclamations, et des applaudissements, dont d'autres auroient été flattés, et qui m'ont fait fremir. C'est à l'indignation, c'est à l'horreur, c'est aux convulsions physiques, que se seul aspect du sang me fait eprouver que j'ai cédé. On brave une seule mort; on la brave plusieurs fois, quand elle peut être utile. Mais aucune puissance sous le Ciel, mais aucune opinion publique ou privée n'ont le droit de me condamner à souffrir inutilement mille supplices par minute, et à perir de désespoir, de rage, au milieu des *triomphes*, du crime que je n'ai pu arrêter. Ils me proscriront, ils confisqueront mes biens. Je labourerai la terre, et je ne les verrai plus. – Voila ma justification. Vous pourez la lire, la montrer, la laisser copier; tant pis pour ceux qui ne la comprendront pas; ce ne sera alors moi qui auroit eu tort de la leur donner."[154]

This military man had not so good nerves as the peacable gentleman of the Old Jewry[N]. – See Mons. Mounier's narrative of these transactions; a man also of honour and virtue, and talents, and therefore a fugitive.

\*N.B. Mr. Mounier[N] was then speaker of the National Assembly. He has since been obliged to live in exile, though one of the firmest assertors of liberty.

---

[154] 'Speaking of the position I have taken, it is well justified in my conscience. – Neither this culpable town, nor this even more guilty assembly are worthy of my having to justify myself; but I am very concerned that you and people who think like you, should not condemn me. – My health, I swear, made my duties impossible; but even putting them aside it has been beyond my strength to bear any longer the horror caused me by this blood, – these heads, – this queen *with her throat almost cut*, this king, – led *as a slave*, – entering Paris, in the midst of his assassins, and preceded by the heads of these unhappy guards. – These traitorous jannisaries [Palace guards], these assassins, these cannibal women, this cry of, ALL THE BISHOPS TO THE LAMP-POST at the very moment when the king enters his capital with two bishops from his council in his carriage. A *gunshot*, which I saw fired into one *of the queen's carriages*. M. Bailley

must think, that such treatment of any human creatures must be shocking to any but those who are made for accomplishing Revolutions. But
I cannot stop here. Influenced by the inborn feelings of my nature, and
not being illuminated by a single ray of this new-sprung modern light,
I confess to you, Sir, that the exalted rank of the persons suffering, and
particularly the sex, the beauty, and the amiable qualities of the descendant of so many kings and emperors, with the tender age of royal infants,
insensible only through infancy and innocence of the cruel outrages to
which their parents were exposed, instead of being a subject of exultation,
adds not a little to my sensibility on that most melancholy occasion.

I hear that the august person, who was the principal object of our
preacher's triumph, though he supported himself, felt much on that
shameful occasion. As a man, it became him to feel for his wife and his
children, and the faithful guards of his person, that were massacred in
cold blood about him; as a prince, it became him to feel for the strange and
frightful transformation of his civilized subjects, and to be more grieved
for them, than solicitous for himself. It derogates little from his fortitude,
while it adds infinitely to the honour of his humanity. I am very sorry to
say it, very sorry indeed, that such personages are in a situation in which
it is not unbecoming in us to praise the virtues of the great.

---

calling that *a beautiful day*. The assembly having coldly declared that morning, that it was
not consistent with their dignity to gather around the King. M. Mirabeau saying – and
getting away with it – in this assembly, that the vessel of state, far from being held up in
its course, was speeding more swiftly than before towards its regeneration. M. Barnave,
laughing with him, whilst the streams of blood flowed about us. The virtuous Mounier[N]
escaping by a miracle from twenty assassins who had wanted to make of his head yet
another trophy.

'This is what made me swear never again to set *foot in this cave of cannibals* [the National
Assembly[N]], where I did not have not the strength to raise my voice, where for six weeks I
had raised it in vain. I, Mounier, and all men of honour have a last effort to make for [some
good outcome from it *or* to make a good escape from it??]. The thought of fear never even
occurred to me. I would blush to defend myself from it. I had again received on the way,
from those people, less blameworthy than those who had intoxicated them with rage,
cheering, and applause, with which others would have been flattered and which made me
shudder. It is to the indignation, it is to the horror, it is to the physical convulsions, which
the sight alone of blood raises in me, that I have given way. One braves death once; one
braves it several times, when it can be useful. But no power under Heaven, no opinion,
public or private, has the right to condemn me to suffer uselessly a thousand tortures a
minute, and to die of despair and of rage in the midst of *triumphs*, of crime which I have
been unable to stop. They will banish me, they will confiscate my possessions. I shall
work the land, and shall never see them again. That is my justification. You will be able
to read it, display it, allow it to be copied; too bad for those who will not understand it,
it will not, then, be I who will have been wrong to have given it to them.'

I hear, and I rejoice to hear, that the great lady,[155] the other object of the triumph, has borne that day (one is interested that beings made for suffering should suffer well) and that she bears all the succeeding days, that she bears the imprisonment of her husband, and her own captivity, and the exile of her friends, and the insulting adulation of addresses, and the whole weight of her accumulated wrongs, with a serene patience, in a manner suited to her rank and race, and becoming the offspring of a sovereign distinguished for her piety and her courage; that like her she has lofty sentiments; that she feels with the dignity of a Roman matron; that in the last extremity she will save herself from the last disgrace, and that if she must fall, she will fall by no ignoble hand.[156]

It is now sixteen or seventeen years since I saw the queen of France, then the dauphiness, at Versailles;[157] and surely never lighted on this orb, which she hardly seemed to touch, a more delightful vision. I saw her just above the horizon, decorating and cheering the elevated sphere she just began to move in, – glittering like the morning-star, full of life, and splendor, and joy. Oh! what a revolution! and what an heart must I have, to contemplate without emotion that elevation and that fall! Little did I dream when she added titles of veneration to those of enthusiastic, distant, respectful love, that she should ever be obliged to carry the sharp antidote against disgrace concealed in that bosom; little did I dream that I should have lived to see such disasters fallen upon her in a nation of gallant men, in a nation of men of honour and of cavaliers. I thought ten thousand swords must have leaped from their scabbards

[155] Marie Antoinette, whose moral character had been persistently attacked in the pro-revolutionary press, both in France and in England.

[156] *By no ignoble hand*: i.e. by her own. Burke expresses the hope that like Lucretia, the model for the virtuous Roman mother, she would prefer suicide to the dishonour of violation.

[157] Burke had visited France early in 1773, but had not then recorded this impression. This famous and sentimental passage aroused much controversy. Burke's friend Philip Francis read it in draft and thought it 'pure foppery' and asked his friend: 'are you such a determined Champion of Beauty as to draw your sword in defense of any Jade [tart] upon earth provided she be handsome?' Given 'the opinion of the world about her', he urged him to rewrite it. Burke protested vigorously that his feelings were genuine and deeply felt, and that the composition of the passage had so affected him that it 'did draw Tears from me and wetted my paper' (Francis to EB, 19 Feb. 1790, *Corr.* vi, pp. 86–7; EB to Francis, 20 Feb. 1790, *Corr.* vi, p. 91). Cf. Paine's comment on it as evidence of Burke's subscription to the inauthenticity of the aristocratic regime: 'Accustomed to kiss the aristocratical hand that hath purloined him from himself, he degenerates into a composition of art, and the genuine soul of nature forsakes him. His hero or heroine must be a tragedy-victim expiring in show, not the real prisoner of misery, sliding into death in the silence of a dungeon.' (*Rights of Man*, p. 73)

to avenge even a look that threatened her with insult. – But the age of chivalry is gone. – That of sophisters, œconomists, and calculators, has succeeded; and the glory of Europe is extinguished for ever. Never, never more, shall we behold that generous loyalty to rank and sex, that proud submission, that dignified obedience, that subordination of the heart, which kept alive, even in servitude itself, the spirit of an exalted freedom. The unbought grace of life, the cheap defence of nations, the nurse of manly sentiment and heroic enterprize, is gone! It is gone, that sensibility of principle, that chastity of honour, which felt a stain like a wound, which inspired courage whilst it mitigated ferocity, which ennobled whatever it touched, and under which vice itself lost half its evil, by losing all its grossness.

This mixed system of opinion and sentiment had its origin in the antient chivalry; and the principle, though varied in its appearance by the varying state of human affairs, subsisted and influenced through a long succession of generations, even to the time we live in.[158] If it should ever

[158] Modern scholarship has revealed the importance of this passage in drawing on claims by the Scottish historians of civil society about the role of chivalry in forming modern sensibilities. Adam Ferguson claimed it was this which distinguished modern 'civilised or polished' nations (*History of Civil Society*, ed. F. Oz-Salzburger (Cambridge, 1995), pp. 190ff.). John Millar pointed out that feudalism had given rise to 'a set of customs and institutions of which we have no [other] example' through which 'sentiments of military honour, and the love and gallantry so universally diffused... were displayed in all the amusements and diversions of the people'. Consequently 'the manners introduced by chivalry... may still be observed to have a good deal of influence upon the taste and sentiments even of the present age' (John Millar, *Origin of the Distinction of Ranks* (1771), pp. 72–84). But it is William Robertson's *Progress of Society in Europe*, prefixed to his *History of the Reign of Charles V* (1769), which most clearly reverses the notion of Chivalry as belonging to a more violent social epoch, by making, as does Burke, its morals and manners a condition, and not the antithesis, of modern civility:

> sentiments more liberal and generous had begun to animate the nobles. These were inspired by the spirit of Chivalry, which though considered, commonly, as a wild institution... had a very serious influence in refining the manners of the European nations... The wild exploits of those romantic knights who sallied forth in quest of adventures, are well known, and have been treated with proper ridicule. The political and permanent effects... have been less observed... the humanity which accompanies all the operations of war, the refinements of gallantry, and the point of honour... may be ascribed in great measure to this whimsical institution, seemingly of so little benefit to mankind... [and] continued to operate after the vigour and reputation of the institution itself began to decline. (William Robertson *The Progress of Society in Europe*, ed. Felix Gilbert (Chicago and London, 1972), pp. 57–9)

be totally extinguished, the loss I fear will be great. It is this which has given its character to modern Europe. It is this which has distinguished it under all its forms of government, and distinguished it to its advantage, from the states of Asia, and possibly from those states which flourished in the most brilliant periods of the antique world. It was this, which, without confounding ranks, had produced a noble equality, and handed it down through all the gradations of social life. It was this opinion which mitigated kings into companions, and raised private men to be fellows with kings. Without force, or opposition, it subdued the fierceness of pride and power; it obliged sovereigns to submit to the soft collar of social esteem, compelled stern authority to submit to elegance, and gave a domination vanquisher of laws, to be subdued by manners.

But now all is to be changed. All the pleasing illusions, which made power gentle, and obedience liberal, which harmonized the different shades of life, and which, by a bland assimilation, incorporated into politics the sentiments which beautify and soften private society, are to be dissolved by this new conquering empire of light and reason. All the decent drapery of life is to be rudely torn off. All the superadded ideas, furnished from the wardrobe of a moral imagination, which the heart owns, and the understanding ratifies, as necessary to cover the defects of our naked shivering nature, and to raise it to dignity in our own estimation, are to be exploded as a ridiculous, absurd, and antiquated fashion.

On this scheme of things, a king is but a man; a queen is but a woman; a woman is but an animal; and an animal not of the highest order. All homage paid to the sex in general as such, and without distinct views, is to be regarded as romance and folly. Regicide, and parricide, and sacrilege, are but fictions of superstition, corrupting jurisprudence by destroying its simplicity. The murder of a king, or a queen, or a bishop, or a father, are only common homicide; and if the people are by any chance, or in any way gainers by it, a sort of homicide much the most pardonable, and into which we ought not to make too severe a scrutiny.

On the scheme of this barbarous philosophy, which is the offspring of cold hearts and muddy understandings, and which is as void of solid wisdom, as it is destitute of all taste and elegance, laws are to be supported only by their own terrors, and by the concern which each individual may find in them from his own private speculations, or can spare to them from his own private interests. In the groves of *their* academy, at the end of every visto, you see nothing but the gallows. Nothing is left which engages the affections on the part of the commonwealth. On the principles of this mechanic philosophy, our institutions can never be embodied, if I may use the expression, in persons; so as to create in us love, veneration, admiration, or attachment. But that sort of reason which banishes the affections is incapable of filling their place. These public affections, combined with manners, are required sometimes as supplements, sometimes as correctives, always as aids to law. The precept given by a wise man, as well as a great critic, for the construction of poems, is equally true as to states. *Non satis est pulchra esse poemata, dulcia sunto.*[159] There ought to be a system of manners in every nation which a well-formed mind would be disposed to relish. To make us love our country, our country ought to be lovely.

But power, of some kind or other, will survive the shock in which manners and opinions perish; and it will find other and worse means for its support. The usurpation which, in order to subvert antient institutions, has destroyed antient principles, will hold power by arts similar to those by which it has acquired it. When the old feudal and chivalrous spirit of *Fealty,*[160] which, by freeing kings from fear, freed both kings and subjects from the precautions of tyranny, shall be extinct in the minds of men, plots and assassinations will be anticipated by preventive murder and preventive confiscation, and that long roll of grim and bloody maxims, which form the political code of all power, not standing on its own honour, and the honour of those who are to obey it. Kings will be tyrants from policy when subjects are rebels from principle.

When antient opinions and rules of life are taken away, the loss cannot possibly be estimated. From that moment we have no compass to govern us; nor can we know distinctly to what port we steer. Europe undoubtedly, taken in a mass, was in a flourishing condition the day on which your Revolution was compleated. How much of that prosperous state was owing to the spirit of our old manners and opinions is not easy to say; but as such causes cannot be indifferent in their operation, we must presume, that, on the whole, their operation was beneficial.

We are but too apt to consider things in the state in which we find them, without sufficiently adverting to the causes by which they have been produced, and possibly may be upheld. Nothing is more certain, than that our manners, our civilization, and all the good things which are

---

[159] Horace, *On the Art of Poetry*, l. 99: 'It is not enough for poems to be beautiful, they must charm and delight.'

[160] *Fealty*: the oath of loyalty sworn by a feudal vassal to his lord.

connected with manners, and with civilization, have, in this European world of ours, depended for ages upon two principles; and were indeed the result of both combined; I mean the spirit of a gentleman, and the spirit of religion. The nobility and the clergy, the one by profession, the other by patronage, kept learning in existence, even in the midst of arms and confusions, and whilst governments were rather in their causes than formed. Learning paid back what it received to nobility and to priesthood; and paid it with usury, by enlarging their ideas, and by furnishing their minds. Happy if they had all continued to know their indissoluble union, and their proper place! Happy if learning, not debauched by ambition, had been satisfied to continue the instructor, and not aspired to be the master! Along with its natural protectors and guardians, learning will be cast into the mire, and trodden down under the hoofs of a swinish multitude[xvii].[161]

If, as I suspect, modern letters owe more than they are always willing to own to antient manners, so do other interests which we value full as much as they are worth. Even commerce, and trade, and manufacture, the gods of our œconomical politicians, are themselves perhaps but creatures; are themselves but effects, which, as first causes, we choose to worship. They certainly grew under the same shade in which learning flourished. They too may decay with their natural protecting principles. With you, for the present at least, they all threaten to disappear together.[163] Where trade and manufactures are wanting to a people, and the spirit of nobility and religion remains, sentiment supplies, and not always ill supplies their place; but if commerce and the arts should be lost in an experiment to try how well a state may stand without these old fundamental principles, what sort of a thing must be a nation of gross, stupid, ferocious, and at

---

[xvii] [See the fate of Bailly[N] and Condorcet, supposed to be here particularly alluded to. Compare the circumstances of the trial, and execution of the former with this prediction.][162]

---

[161] *Swinish multitude*: the phrase was taken up and used as a badge of honour by radical pamphleteers such as Daniel Isaac Eaton in his periodical *Politics for the People, or a Salamagundy for Swine* (1794–5) and Thomas Spence, *Pig's Meat, or lessons for the swinish multitude* (1793–5).

[162] This footnote added in the 1803 edition of Burke's collected *Works*, presumed to have been sanctioned by Burke before his death. *Condorcet*: Nicolas de Caritat (1743–94), philosopher and mathematician, had applied mathematical theory to voting processes. He was elected to, and presided over, the Constituent Assembly but despite his championship of liberal causes – universal education, the abolition of slavery and enfranchisement of women – was arrested in 1794 and died suspiciously in prison.

[163] See above fn. 158.

the same time, poor and sordid barbarians, destitute of religion, honour, or manly pride, possessing nothing at present, and hoping for nothing hereafter?

I wish you may not be going fast, and by the shortest cut, to that horrible and disgustful situation. Already there appears a poverty of conception, a coarseness and vulgarity in all the proceedings of the assembly and of all their instructors. Their liberty is not liberal.[164] Their science is presumptuous ignorance. Their humanity is savage and brutal.

It is not clear, whether in England we learned those grand and decorous principles, and manners, of which considerable traces yet remain, from you, or whether you took them from us. But to you, I think, we trace them best. You seem to me to be – *"gentis incunabula nostrae."*[165] France has always more or less influenced manners in England; and when your fountain is choaked up and polluted, the stream will not run long, or not run clear with us, or perhaps with any nation. This gives all Europe, in my opinion, but too close and connected a concern in what is done in France. Excuse me, therefore, if I have dwelt too long on the atrocious spectacle of the sixth of October 1789, or have given too much scope to the reflections which have arisen in my mind on occasion of the most important of all revolutions, which may be dated from that day, I mean a revolution in sentiments, manners, and moral opinions. As things now stand, with every thing respectable destroyed without us, and an attempt to destroy within us every principle of respect, one is almost forced to apologize for harbouring the common feelings of men.

Why do I feel so differently from the Reverend Dr. Price,[N] and those of his lay flock, who will choose to adopt the sentiments of his discourse? – For this plain reason – because it is *natural* I should; because we are so made as to be affected at such spectacles with melancholy sentiments upon the unstable condition of mortal prosperity, and the tremendous uncertainty of human greatness; because in those natural feelings we learn great lessons; because in events like these our passions instruct our reason; because when kings are hurl'd from their thrones by the Supreme Director of this great drama, and become the objects of insult to the base, and of pity to the good, we behold such disasters in the moral, as we should behold a miracle in the physical order of things. We are alarmed

---

[164] *Liberal*: here in the sense of generous-spirited; the word did not yet have specifically political connotations.

[165] Virgil, *Aeneid*, 3.105: 'the cradle of our people'.

into reflexion; our minds (as it has long since been observed) are purified by terror and pity;[166] our weak unthinking pride is humbled, under the dispensations of a mysterious wisdom. – Some tears might be drawn from me, if such a spectacle were exhibited on the stage. I should be truly ashamed of finding in myself that superficial, theatric sense of painted distress, whilst I could exult over it in real life. With such a perverted mind, I could never venture to shew my face at a tragedy. People would think the tears that Garrick formerly, or that Siddons not long since,[167] have extorted from me, were the tears of hypocrisy; I should know them to be the tears of folly.

Indeed the theatre is a better school of moral sentiments than churches, where the feelings of humanity are thus outraged. Poets, who have to deal with an audience not yet graduated in the school of the rights of men, and who must apply themselves to the moral constitution of the heart, would not dare to produce such a triumph as a matter of exultation. There, where men follow their natural impulses, they would not bear the odious maxims of a Machiavelian[N] policy, whether applied to the attainment of monarchical or democratic tyranny. They would reject them on the modern, as they once did on the antient stage, where they could not bear even the hypothetical proposition of such wickedness in the mouth of a personated tyrant, though suitable to the character he sustained. No theatric audience in Athens would bear what has been borne, in the midst of the real tragedy of this triumphal day; a principal actor weighing, as it were in scales hung in a shop of horrors, – so much actual crime against so much contingent advantage, – and after putting in and out weights, declaring that the balance was on the side of the advantages. They would not bear to see the crimes of new democracy posted as in a ledger against the crimes of old despotism, and the book-keepers

---

[166] *Purified by terror and pity*: Aristotle had identified the cathartic or emotionally purgative effect of tragedy:

> Tragedy, then, is the imitation of action that is serious, complete, and with a kind of greatness; in language embellished with each kind of artistic ornament, the several kinds being found in separate parts of the play; in the form of action, not of narrative; through pity and fear effecting the proper purgation of these emotions. (*Poetics*, 1449b20)

[167] *Garrick . . . Siddons*: the two pre-eminent actors of the time. David Garrick (1717–79), actor, playwright and Director of the Theatre Royal, Drury Lane in London, was noted for his introduction of a more naturalistic style of acting. Sarah Siddons (1755–1831) was leading lady at Garrick's theatre. Both were acquaintances of Burke.

of politics finding democracy still in debt, but by no means unable or unwilling to pay the balance. In the theatre, the first intuitive glance, without any elaborate process of reasoning, would shew, that this method of political computation, would justify every extent of crime. They would see, that on these principles, even where the very worst acts were not perpetrated, it was owing rather to the fortune of the conspirators than to their parsimony in the expenditure of treachery and blood. They would soon see, that criminal means once tolerated are soon preferred. They present a shorter cut to the object than through the highway of the moral virtues. Justifying perfidy[168] and murder for public benefit, public benefit would soon become the pretext, and perfidy and murder the end; until rapacity, malice, revenge, and fear more dreadful than revenge, could satiate their insatiable appetites. Such must be the consequences of losing in the splendour of these triumphs of the rights of men, all natural sense of wrong and right.

But the Reverend Pastor exults in this 'leading in triumph,' because truly Louis the XVIth was 'an arbitrary monarch'; that is, in other words, neither more nor less, than because he was Louis the XVIth, and because he had the misfortune to be born king of France, with the prerogatives of which, a long line of ancestors, and a long acquiescence of the people, without any act of his, had put him in possession. A misfortune it has indeed turned out to him, that he was born king of France. But misfortune is not crime, nor is indiscretion always the greatest guilt. I shall never think that a prince, the acts of whose whole reign were a series of concessions to his subjects, who was willing to relax his authority, to remit his prerogatives, to call his people to a share of freedom, not known, perhaps not desired, by their ancestors; such a prince, though he should be subject to the common frailties attached to men and to princes, though he should have once thought it necessary to provide force against the desperate designs manifestly carrying on against his person, and the remnants of his authority; though all this should be taken into consideration, I shall be led with great difficulty to think he deserves the cruel and insulting triumph of Paris, and of Dr. Price.[N] I tremble for the cause of liberty, from such an example to kings. I tremble for the cause of humanity, in the unpunished outrages of the most wicked of mankind. But there are some people of that low and degenerate fashion of mind, that they look up with a sort of complacent awe and admiration to kings, who

---

[168] *Perfidy*: betrayal of trust.

know to keep firm in their seat, to hold a strict hand over their subjects, to assert their prerogative, and by the awakened vigilance of a severe despotism, to guard against the very first approaches of freedom. Against such as these they never elevate their voice. Deserters from principle, listed with fortune, they never see any good in suffering virtue, nor any crime in prosperous usurpation.

If it could have been made clear to me, that the king and queen of France (those I mean who were such before the triumph) were inexorable and cruel tyrants, that they had formed a deliberate scheme for massacring the National Assembly (I think I have seen something like the latter insinuated in certain publications) I should think their captivity just. If this be true, much more ought to have been done, but done, in my opinion, in another manner. The punishment of real tyrants is a noble and awful act of justice; and it has with truth been said to be consolatory to the human mind. But if I were to punish a wicked king, I should regard the dignity in avenging the crime. Justice is grave and decorous, and in its punishments rather seems to submit to a necessity, than to make a choice. Had Nero, or Agrippina, or Louis the Eleventh, or Charles the Ninth, been the subject;[169] if Charles the Twelfth of Sweden, after the murder of Patkul,[170] or his predecessor Christina, after the murder of

---

[169] *Nero* (d. AD 68): Roman Emperor notorious for his cruelty and the immorality of his private life. He was thought to have murdered his first wife Octavia and his mother Agrippina. He publicly tortured and killed Christians, including the disciples Peter and Paul, as scapegoats for the fire that destroyed much of Rome in AD 64 and subsequently instituted a reign of terror against the Senate following an attempted coup against him in 65. His notoriously ambitious, sexually outrageous and unscrupulous mother Agrippina supposedly poisoned her second husband (her brother-in-law) and married then poisoned her uncle, the Emperor Claudius, to advance Nero's succession, with whom she was rumoured to have had a sexual liaison, before herself being murdered by him.

*Louis XI* (1423–83): French King who, rebelling twice against his father before succeeding to the throne, became notorious for his duplicity and treacherous behaviour.

*Charles IX* of France (1550–74) presided over the St Bartholomew's Day massacre of Protestants in 1572.

[170] *Charles XII of Sweden* (1682–1718) onducted the bloody 'Great Northern War' against Saxony, Poland, Norway-Denmark and Russia. Resolved never to end a just war except by the defeat of his enemies, but his defeat by Peter the Great at Poltava (1709) marked the end of the Swedish empire.

Johann Rheinhold *Patkul*/Patkin (1660–1707) was banished from Sweden for protesting at the cruelty of Charles in his home province of Livonia. Patkin became a diplomat working for Peter the Great of Russia. In defiance of diplomatic immunity he was imprisoned in Saxony whilst on a mission there and handed over to Charles, who had him executed for treason.

Monaldeschi,[171] had fallen into your hands, Sir, or into mine, I am sure our conduct would have been different.

If the French King, or King of the French, (or by whatever name he is known in the new vocabulary of your constitution)[172] has in his own person, and that of his Queen, really deserved these unavowed but unavenged murderous attempts, and those subsequent indignities more cruel than murder, such a person would ill deserve even that subordinate executory trust, which I understand is to be placed in him; nor is he fit to be called chief of a nation which he has outraged and oppressed. A worse choice for such an office in a new commonwealth, than that of a deposed tyrant, could not possibly be made. But to degrade and insult a man as the worst of criminals, and afterwards to trust him in your highest concerns, as a faithful, honest, and zealous servant, is not consistent in reasoning, nor prudent in policy, nor safe in practice. Those who could make such an appointment must be guilty of a more flagrant breach of trust than any they have yet committed against the people. As this is the only crime in which your leading politicians could have acted inconsistently, I conclude that there is no sort of ground for these horrid insinuations. I think no better of all the other calumnies.[173]

In England, we give no credit to them. We are generous enemies: We are faithful allies. We spurn from us with disgust and indignation the slanders of those who bring us their anecdotes with the attestation of the flower-de-luce on their shoulder.[174] We have Lord George Gordon fast in

---

[171] *Christina*: Queen of Sweden (1626–89). Succeeded her father, Gustavus Adolphus, aged 6. A great scholar and determined spinster, after ruling as a model monarch she abdicated in 1654 and converted to Catholicism. She subsequently sought the throne of Naples.

*Monaldeschi*: Gian Rinaldo, Marchese de Monaldeschi, descended from a powerful family in Orvieto, in Umbria, central Italy, was a courtier of Queen Christina of Sweden, who had him 'executed' in her presence at Fontainebleau, officially for having revealed to the Spanish her plan to acquire the crown of Naples, but allegedly for rejecting her advances.

[172] The National Constituent Assembly had decreed in October 1789 that the King's title should be changed from 'Louis by the grace of God, King of France and Navarre' to 'Louis, by the grace of God and the constitutional law of the State, King of the French' (*DocS*, p. 115).

[173] *Calumnies*: false and derogatory misrepresentation of another's views or behaviour.

[174] *Flower de luce*: The fleur-de-lys was the heraldic device of the French royal family. Jeanne Valois de la Motte, an adventuress, had been branded with the fleur-de-lys on the shoulders as part of her punishment for a fraudulent conspiracy involving an attempt to impersonate the Queen in order to steal a diamond necklace. Though imprisoned she had subsequently sought refuge in England.

Newgate;[N,175] and neither his being a public proselyte to Judaism,[176] nor his having, in his zeal against Catholic priests and all sort of ecclesiastics, raised a mob (excuse the term, it is still in use here) which pulled down all our prisons, have preserved to him a liberty, of which he did not render himself worthy by a virtuous use of it. We have rebuilt Newgate, and tenanted the mansion. We have prisons almost as strong as the Bastile, for those who dare to libel the queens of France. In this spiritual retreat, let the noble libeller remain. Let him there meditate on his Thalmud,[177] until he learns a conduct more becoming his birth and parts, and not so disgraceful to the antient religion to which he has become a proselyte; or until some persons from your side of the water, to please your new Hebrew brethren,[178] shall ransom him. He may then be enabled to purchase, with the old hoards of the synagogue, and a very small poundage, on the long compound interest of the thirty pieces of silver (Dr. Price has shewn us what miracles compound interest will perform in 1790 years[179]) the lands which are lately discovered to have been usurped by the Gallican church. Send us your popish Archbishop of Paris, and we will send you our protestant Rabbin. We shall treat the person you send us in exchange like a gentleman and an honest man, as he is; but pray let him bring with him the fund of his hospitality, bounty, and charity; and, depend upon it, we shall never confiscate a shilling of that honourable and pious fund, nor think of enriching the treasury with the spoils of the poor-box.

To tell you the truth, my dear Sir, I think the honour of our nation to be somewhat concerned in the disclaimer of the proceedings of this society of the Old Jewry[N] and the London Tavern. I have no man's proxy. I speak only from myself; when I disclaim, as I do with all possible earnestness,

[175] *Lord George Gordon* (1751–93): MP for Luggershall. He led 'protestant associations' to oppose the Catholic Relief Act of 1778, and later instigated the sectarian anti-Catholic Gordon Riots (1780) in which Burke's house was attacked and Newgate Prison destroyed. In 1787 Gordon converted to Judaism, apparently intending to bring the Jews over to Christianity – a sign of the imminence of Christ's second coming, which he thereby hoped to hasten. He was committed in 1788, for libellous attacks on the French Queen and ambassador, to the rebuilt Newgate Prison, where he died of cholera in 1793.

[176] *Proselyte*: a convert, one who has changed religious or doctrinal allegiance.

[177] *Thalmud*: *Talmud*, the corpus of Jewish religious law and commentary.

[178] *New Hebrew brethren*: The National Assembly, having originally excluded Jews from the abolition of religious tests for citizenship, had voted to include them on 28 Jan. 1790.

[179] Richard Price was a statistician of some eminence, and friend of the probability theorist, Thomas Bayes, whose work he applied to the creation of actuarial tables relating to life expectancies. This enabled the poor to organise life insurance, through mutual and friendly societies, to pay their funeral expenses. Price was elected fellow of the Royal Society in recognition of this work.

all communion with the actors in that triumph, or with the admirers of it. When I assert anything else, as concerning the people of England, I speak from observation, not from authority; but I speak from the experience I have had in a pretty extensive and mixed communication with the inhabitants of this kingdom, of all descriptions and ranks, and after a course of attentive observation, began early in life, and continued for near forty years. I have often been astonished, considering that we are divided from you but by a slender dyke of about twenty-four miles, and that the mutual intercourse between the two countries has lately been very great, to find how little you seem to know of us. I suspect that this is owing to your forming a judgment of this nation from certain publications, which do very erroneously, if they do at all, represent the opinions and dispositions generally prevalent in England. The vanity, restlessness, petulance, and spirit of intrigue of several petty cabals,[180] who attempt to hide their total want of consequence in bustle and noise, and puffing, and mutual quotation of each other, makes you imagine that our contemptuous neglect of their abilities is a mark of general acquiescence in their opinions. No such thing, I assure you. Because half a dozen grashoppers under a fern make the field ring with their importunate chink, whilst thousands of great cattle, reposed beneath the shadow of the British oak, chew the cud and are silent, pray do not imagine, that those who make the noise are the only inhabitants of the field; that, of course, they are many in number; or that, after all, they are other than the little shrivelled, meagre, hopping, though loud and troublesome insects of the hour.[181]

I almost venture to affirm, that not one in a hundred amongst us participates in the 'triumph' of the Revolution Society.[N] If the king and queen of France, and their children, were to fall into our hands by the chance of war, in the most acrimonious of all hostilities (I deprecate such an event, I deprecate such hostility) they would be treated with another sort of triumphal entry into London. We formerly have had a king of France in that situation; you have read how he was treated by the victor in the field; and in what manner he was afterwards received in England.[182] Four hundred years have gone over us; but I believe we are

---

[180] *Cabal*: a small and secretive political clique.
[181] A well known image from Virgil, *Georgics*, 3.327ff.
[182] Jean II – 'le Bon' – was captured by Edward, the Black Prince, at the battle of Poitiers in 1356 and brought back to London, where he held a full royal court. A ransom of 3 million crowns was agreed but when his son – held by the English as surety – escaped, and payments fell short, Jean dutifully returned and was feted in great honour. He died

not materially changed since that period. Thanks to our sullen resistance to innovation, thanks to the cold sluggishness of our national character, we still bear the stamp of our forefathers. We have not (as I conceive) lost the generosity and dignity of thinking of the fourteenth century; nor as yet have we subtilized ourselves into savages. We are not the converts of Rousseau;[N] we are not the disciples of Voltaire;[N] Helvetius[N] has made no progress amongst us. Atheists are not our preachers; madmen are not our lawgivers. We know that *we* have made no discoveries, and we think that no discoveries are to be made, in morality; nor many in the great principles of government, nor in the ideas of liberty, which were understood long before we were born, altogether as well as they will be after the grave has heaped its mould upon our presumption, and the silent tomb shall have imposed its law on our pert loquacity. In England we have not yet been completely embowelled of our natural entrails; we still feel within us, and we cherish and cultivate, those inbred sentiments which are the faithful guardians, the active monitors of our duty, the true supporters of all liberal and manly morals. We have not been drawn and trussed, in order that we may be filled, like stuffed birds in a museum, with chaff and rags, and paltry, blurred shreds of paper about the rights of man. We preserve the whole of our feelings still native and entire, unsophisticated by pedantry and infidelity. We have real hearts of flesh and blood beating in our bosoms. We fear God; we look up with awe to kings; with affection to parliaments; with duty to magistrates; with reverence to priests; and with respect to nobility[xviii]. Why? Because when such ideas are brought before our minds, it is *natural* to be so affected; because all other feelings are false and spurious, and tend to corrupt our minds, to vitiate our primary morals, to render us unfit for rational liberty; and by teaching us a servile, licentious, and abandoned insolence, to be our low sport for a

---

[xviii] The English are, I conceive, misrepresented in a Letter published in one of the papers, by a gentleman thought to be a dissenting minister. – When writing to Dr. Price, of the spirit which prevails at Paris, he says, 'The spirit of the people in this place has abolished all the proud *distinctions* which the *king* and *nobles* had usurped in their minds; whether talk of *the king, the noble, or the priest*, their whole language is that of the most *enlightened and liberal amongst the English.*' If this gentleman means to confine the terms *enlightened and liberal* to one set of men in England, it may be true. It is not generally so.[183]

in London in 1364. 'You have read' – the story is told in Froissart's famous contemporary *Chronicles* (14th century), a major source of chivalrous stories and values.

[183] The '*gentleman in Paris*' identified as Price's nephew, George Cadogan Morgan (1754– 98), a dissenting minister and assistant to Price at his meeting house in Stoke Newington.

few holidays, to make us perfectly fit for, and justly deserving of slavery, through the whole course of our lives.

You see, Sir, that in this enlightened age I am bold enough to confess, that we are generally men of untaught feelings; that instead of casting away all our old prejudices, we cherish them to a very considerable degree, and, to take more shame to ourselves, we cherish them because they are prejudices;[184] and the longer they have lasted, and the more generally they have prevailed, the more we cherish them. We are afraid to put men to live and trade each on his own private stock of reason; because we suspect that this stock in each man is small, and that the individuals would do better to avail themselves of the general bank and capital of nations, and of ages. Many of our men of speculation, instead of exploding general prejudices, employ their sagacity to discover the latent wisdom which prevails in them.[185] If they find what they seek, and they seldom fail, they think it more wise to continue the prejudice, with the reason involved, than to cast away the coat of prejudice, and to leave nothing but the naked reason; because prejudice, with its reason, has a motive to give action to that reason, and an affection which will give it permanence. Prejudice is of ready application in the emergency; it previously engages the mind in a steady course of wisdom and virtue, and does not leave the man hesitating in the moment of decision, sceptical, puzzled, and unresolved. Prejudice renders a man's virtue his habit; and not a series of unconnected acts. Through just prejudice, his duty becomes a part of his nature.[186]

[184] *Prejudice*: 'a preconceived opinion' (OED, 3) To the modern reader, one of Burke's most striking and outrageous claims. Prejudice is originally and etymologically simply a position held prior to any formal or quasi-technical process of appraisal – literally *pre-* 'before', *judex* 'a judge'. Burke's claim might have been less striking in his day, when prejudice did not necessarily possess the modern connotation of bigotry or political incorrectness – indeed possession of the *appropriate* prejudices could be thought desirable. Johnson's entry on the word in his *Dictionary of the English Language* (1755–6) cautions against what was obviously an emerging usage in which the negative view of the content of prejudice overpowered the strict sense of it as a 'prepossession'. Burke's stress here, too, is on the way beliefs are held rather than on the content of them, and is of a piece with his attack on rationalist politics.

[185] The poet Alexander Pope, essayists Addison, Johnson and Lord Chesterfield all cautioned against the overconfident rationalist dismissal of customary moral belief. It formed the main target of Burke's satirical imitation of Bolingbroke's philosophy in his *Vindication of Natural Society* (1756).

[186] The idea that habituation to good actions is the foundation of a virtuous character is crucial to Aristotle's ethical theory (*Nicomachean Ethics* 2.4; 1105a–b) and now revived as 'virtue ethics'.

Your literary men, and your politicians, and so do the whole clan of the enlightened among us, essentially differ in these points. They have no respect for the wisdom of others; but they pay it off by a very full measure of confidence in their own. With them it is a sufficient motive to destroy an old scheme of things, because it is an old one. As to the new, they are in no sort of fear with regard to the duration of a building run up in haste; because duration is no object to those who think little or nothing has been done before their time, and who place all their hopes in discovery. They conceive, very systematically, that all things which give perpetuity are mischievous, and therefore they are at inexpiable[187] war with all establishments. They think that government may vary like modes of dress, and with as little ill effect. That there needs no principle of attachment, except a sense of present conveniency, to any constitution of the state. They always speak as if they were of opinion that there is a singular species of compact between them and their magistrates,[188] which binds the magistrate, but which has nothing reciprocal in it, but that the majesty of the people has a right to dissolve it without any reason, but its will. Their attachment to their country itself, is only so far as it agrees with some of their fleeting projects; it begins and ends with that scheme of polity which falls in with their momentary opinion.

These doctrines, or rather sentiments, seem prevalent with your new statesmen. But they are wholly different from those on which we have always acted in this country.

I hear it is sometimes given out in France, that what is doing among you is after the example of England. I beg leave to affirm, that scarcely any thing done with you has originated from the practice or the prevalent opinions of this people, either in the act or in the spirit of the proceeding. Let me add, that we are as unwilling to learn these lessons from France, as we are sure that we never taught them to that nation. The cabals here who take a sort of share in your transactions as yet consist but of an handful of people. If unfortunately by their intrigues, their sermons, their publications, and by a confidence derived from an expected union with the counsels and forces of the French nation, they should draw considerable numbers into their faction, and in consequence should seriously attempt

---

[187] *Inexpiable*: implacable, incapable of fulfilling its aims or being brought to satisfactory conclusion.

[188] *Singular species of contract*: a *particular* version of the social contract, but also here with overtones of the contract working only 'one way' – that is, the ruler promises to be bound by its terms, whilst the ruled reserve the right not to.

any thing here in imitation of what has been done with you, the event, I dare venture to prophesy, will be, that, with some trouble to their country, they will soon accomplish their own destruction. This people refused to change their law in remote ages from respect to the infallibility of popes;[189] and they will not now alter it from a pious implicit faith in the dogmatism of philosophers; though the former was armed with the anathema and crusade, and though the latter should act with the libel and the lamp-iron.[190]

Formerly your affairs were your own concern only. We felt for them as men; but we kept aloof from them, because we were not citizens of France. But when we see the model held up to ourselves, we must feel as Englishmen, and feeling, we must provide as Englishmen. Your affairs, in spite of us, are made a part of our interest; so far at least as to keep at a distance your panacea,[191] or your plague. If it be a panacea, we do not want it. We know the consequences of unnecessary physic. If it be a plague, it is such a plague; that the precautions of the most severe quarantine ought to be established against it.

I hear on all hands that a cabal, calling itself philosophic, receives the glory of many of the late proceedings; and that their opinions and systems are the true actuating spirit of the whole of them. I have heard of no party in England, literary or political, at any time, known by such a description. It is not with you composed of those men, is it? whom the vulgar, in their blunt, homely style, commonly call Atheists and Infidels? If it be, I admit that we too have had writers of that description, who made some noise in their day. At present they repose in lasting oblivion. Who, born within the last forty years, has read one word of Collins, and Toland, and Tindal, and Chubb, and Morgan,[192] and that whole race who called

---

[189] *Refuse . . . infallibility of popes*: Attempts by successive popes to appoint their nominees to bishoprics in England (which entailed control of lands, and potential remission of income to the Holy See) were an ongoing medieval controversy. Famous statutes under Edward I (1306) and Edward III (1350) resisted this, using the phrase found in the Statute of Merton (1235) by which the Barons sought to restrain the powers of Henry III: *nolemus leges angliae mutari* ['we do not wish the laws of England to be changed']. The phrase becomes a famous constitutional formula used by Charles I in his response to Parliament's attempt to constrain *him* in the *Nineteen Propositions* (1642).

[190] *Lamp-iron*: a possible reference to the street lamp-posts from which the Parisian revolutionary mob had sought to hang their enemies.

[191] *Panacea*: a cure-all.

[192] All names of prominent deists, freethinkers who subjected religious dogma and scripture to rational scrutiny and often questioned the divinity of Christ. Worries about such views

themselves Freethinkers? Who now reads Bolingbroke?[N] Who ever read him through? Ask the booksellers of London what is become of all these lights of the world. In as few years their few successors will go to the family vault of "all the Capulets". But whatever they were, or are, with us, they were and are wholly unconnected individuals. With us they kept the common nature of their kind, and were not gregarious. They never acted in corps, nor were known as a faction in the state, nor presumed to influence, in that name or character, or for the purposes of such a faction, on any of our public concerns. Whether they ought so to exist, and so be permitted to act, is another question. As such cabals have not existed in England, so neither has the spirit of them had any influence in establishing the original frame of our constitution, or in any one of the several reparations and improvements it has undergone. The whole

constituted an ongoing controversial nexus in the eighteenth century and are a major context for Burke's response to the French Revolution.

*Anthony Collins* (1676–1729) opposed Samuel Clarke in a famous controversy over the materiality of the soul; his subsequent *A Discourse of Free-Thinking* (1713), burnt by the hangman, asserted the universal right and religious duty of withholding assent from any propositions which are not clear and true on the balance of evidence or probability.

*John Toland* (1670–1722): Irish philosopher and freethinker. Toland scandalised Irish society in 1695 with the publication of *Christianity not Mysterious* – a radical application of Locke's *Reasonableness of Christianity* – arguing that the principle of reason, Locke's 'comparison of clear and distinct ideas', should be used to rid religion of irrational claims, such as the Trinity and the virgin birth. He left Ireland to escape arrest, and a subsequent career as a radical Whig pamphleteer re-enforced associations between religious free-thinking and political radicalism.

*Matthew Tindal* (1657–1733): lawyer and notorious religious controversialist. His anticlerical *The rights of the Christian church asserted*... (1706), an attack on the Catholic Church, was widely perceived to be a veiled attack on the Church of England and provoked a long-lasting pamphlet war. His last work, *Christianity as Old as the Creation* (1731), sought to assimilate Christian revelation to 'natural religion', a set of moral principles available to any human being.

*Thomas Chubb* (1679–1747): a poor, largely self-taught, religious controversialist, who accepted the divinity of Christ's message but not that of his person. His *A Discourse... (showing that) Reason is, or else that it ought to be, a Sufficient Guide in Matters of Religion* (1731) champions the view satirised in Burke's *Vindication of Natural Society* (1756), whilst his *A Discourse on Miracles* (1741) adopted a mildly sceptical attitude. Mild and sincere in his faith, he completely lacked the acerbity of the more combative deists.

*Thomas Morgan* (d. 1743): freethinker and deist. From a poor background, Morgan was ordained a Nonconformist minister, but was dismissed for his anti-Trinitarian views assembled in *A Collection of Tracts* (1726). His major work, in three volumes, was *The Moral Philosopher* (1737, 1739, 1740), in which he subjected religious tenets to independent moral criteria. Morgan was also notorious for subjecting scriptural writings to historical and textual criticism.

has been done under the auspices, and is confirmed by the sanctions of religion and piety. The whole has emanated from the simplicity of our national character, and from a sort of native plainness and directness of understanding, which for a long time characterized those men who have successively obtained authority amongst us. This disposition still remains, at least in the great body of the people.

We know, and what is better, we feel inwardly, that religion is the basis of civil society, and the source of all good and of all comfort[xix]. In England we are so convinced of this, that there is no rust of superstition, with which the accumulated absurdity of the human mind might have crusted it over in the course of ages, that ninety-nine in an hundred of the people of England would not prefer to impiety. We shall never be such fools as to call in an enemy to the substance of any system to remove its corruptions, to supply its defects, or to perfect its construction. If our religious tenets should ever want a further elucidation, we shall not call on atheism to explain them. We shall not light up our temple from that unhallowed fire. It will be illuminated with other lights. It will be perfumed with other incense, than the infectious stuff which is imported by the smugglers of adulterated metaphysics. If our ecclesiastical establishment should want a revision, it is not avarice or rapacity, public or private, that we shall employ for the audit, or receipt, or application, of its consecrated revenue. – Violently condemning neither the Greek nor the Armenian, nor, since heats are subsided, the Roman system of religion, we prefer the Protestant;[194] not because we

---

[xix] Sic igitur hoc ab initio persuasum civibus, dominos esse omnium rerum ac moderatores, deos; eaque, quae gerantur, eorum geri vi, ditione, ac numine; eosdemque optime de genere hominum mereri; qualis quisque sit, quid agat, quid in se admittat, qua mente, qua pietate colat religiones intueri: piorum et impiorum habere rationem. His enim rebus imbutae mentes haud sane abhorrebunt ab utili et a vera sententia. Cic. de Legibus, 1.2.[193]

[193] Burke quotes imprecisely from Cicero's work *De Legibus* ['On the Laws'], 2.7.15 (not 1.2 as claimed): 'So from the outset, citizens must be persuaded of this, that the Gods are the masters and managers of all things, and all that is done is done through their judgement and divinity, and they deserve the very best treatment from humankind; and what each man is, what he does, what he allows, what his disposition, with what piety he tends (and) cultivates his religious duties, of the pious and impious, they take account. For certainly, minds that are imbued with such things can hardly reject true and useful sentiments.'

[194] *Greek...Armenian...Roman...Protestant:* the four major divisions of the Christian Church which accepted the Nicean Creed (AD 325) asserting Trinitarianism. This did not include the Unitarianism espoused by Price[N] and Priestley,[N] concerning which Burke was far less indulgent.

think it has less of the Christian religion in it, but because, in our judgment, it has more. We are protestants, not from indifference, but from zeal.

We know, and it is our pride to know, that man is by his constitution a religious animal;[195] that atheism is against, not only our reason, but our instincts; and that it cannot prevail long. But if, in the moment of riot, and in a drunken delirium from the hot spirit drawn out of the alembick[196] of hell, which in France is now so furiously boiling, we should uncover our nakedness by throwing off that Christian religion which has hitherto been our boast and comfort, and one great source of civilization amongst us, and among many other nations, we are apprehensive (being well aware that the mind will not endure a void) that some uncouth, pernicious, and degrading superstition, might take place of it.

For that reason, before we take from our establishment the natural human means of estimation, and give it up to contempt, as you have done, and in doing it have incurred the penalties you well deserve to suffer, we desire that some other may be presented to us in the place of it. We shall then form our judgment.

On these ideas, instead of quarrelling with establishments, as some do, who have made a philosophy and a religion of their hostility to such institutions, we cleave closely to them. We are resolved to keep an established church, an established monarchy, an established aristocracy, and an established democracy, each in the degree it exists, and in no greater. I shall shew you presently how much of each of these we possess.

It has been the misfortune (not as these gentlemen think it, the glory) of this age, that every thing is to be discussed; as if the constitution of our country were to be always a subject rather of altercation than enjoyment. For this reason, as well as for the satisfaction of those among you (if any such you have among you) who may wish to profit of examples, I venture to trouble you with a few thoughts upon each of these establishments. I do not think they were unwise in antient Rome, who, when they wished to

---

[195] Possibly echoing and contrasting Aristotle's claim made at the start of his *Politics* that 'Man is by nature a political animal' (1253a3), and in contrast to the French, who were indeed prioritising man's political, over his religious, nature.

[196] *Alembic*: an early kind of distillation vessel. Burke persistently insinuates a relationship between alchemy – an occult and unchristian science – and the social experiments taking place in France.

new-model their laws, sent commissioners to examine the best constituted republics within their reach.[197]

First, I beg leave to speak of our church establishment, which is the first of our prejudices; not a prejudice destitute of reason, but involving in it profound and extensive wisdom. I speak of it first. It is first, and last, and midst in our minds. For, taking ground on that religious system, of which we are now in possession, we continue to act on the early received and uniformly continued sense of mankind. That sense not only, like a wise architect, hath built up the august fabric of states, but like a provident proprietor, to preserve the structure from prophanation and ruin, as a sacred temple, purged from all the impurities of fraud, and violence, and injustice, and tyranny, hath solemnly and for ever consecrated the commonwealth, and all that officiate in it. This consecration is made, that all who administer in the government of men, in which they stand in the person of God himself, should have high and worthy notions of their function and destination; that their hope should be full of immortality; that they should not look to the paltry pelf[198] of the moment, nor to the temporary and transient praise of the vulgar, but to a solid, permanent existence, in the permanent part of their nature, and to a permanent fame and glory, in the example they leave as a rich inheritance to the world.

Such sublime principles ought to be infused into persons of exalted situations; and religious establishments provided, that may continually revive and enforce them. Every sort of moral, every sort of civil, every sort of politic institution, aiding the rational and natural ties that connect the human understanding and affections to the divine, are not more than necessary, in order to build up that wonderful structure, Man; whose prerogative it is, to be in a great degree a creature of his own making; and who when made as he ought to be made, is destined to hold no trivial place in the creation. But whenever man is put over men, as the better nature ought ever to preside, in that case more particularly, he should as nearly as possible be approximated to his perfection.

This consecration of the state, by a state religious establishment, is necessary also to operate with an wholesome awe upon free citizens; because,

---

[197] According to Livy, following a long-standing constitutional dispute about the right of the Tribunes of the Plebs to prosecute the Consuls, a delegation was sent to Athens to report on the famous laws of Solon in force there (Livy, *History of Rome*, 3.31).

[198] *Paltry pelf*: paltry – worthless, insignificant; pelf – booty, spoils of crime; hence, small gains made from criminal acts.

in order to secure their freedom, they must enjoy some determinate portion of power. To them therefore a religion connected with the state, and with their duty towards it, becomes even more necessary than in such societies, where the people by the terms of their subjection are confined to private sentiments, and the management of their own family concerns. All persons possessing any portion of power ought to be strongly and awefully impressed with an idea that they act in trust; and that they are to account for their conduct in that trust to the one great master, author and founder of society.

This principle ought even to be more strongly impressed upon the minds of those who compose the collective sovreignty than upon those of single princes. Without instruments, these princes can do nothing. Whoever uses instruments, in finding helps, finds also impediments. Their power is therefore by no means compleat; nor are they safe in extreme abuse. Such persons, however elevated by flattery, arrogance, and self-opinion, must be sensible that, whether covered or not by positive law, in some way or other they are accountable even here for the abuse of their trust. If they are not cut off by a rebellion of their people, they may be strangled by the very Janissaries[199] kept for their security against all other rebellion. Thus we have seen the king of France sold by his soldiers for an encrease of pay. But where popular authority is absolute and unrestrained, the people have an infinitely greater, because a far better founded confidence in their own power. They are themselves, in a great measure, their own instruments. They are nearer to their objects. Besides, they are less under responsibility to one of the greatest controlling powers on earth, the sense of fame and estimation. The share of infamy that is likely to fall to the lot of each individual in public acts, is small indeed; the operation of opinion being in the inverse ratio to the number of those who abuse power. Their own approbation of their own acts has to them the appearance of a public judgment in their favour. A perfect democracy is therefore the most shameless thing in the world. As it is the most shameless, it is also the most fearless. No man apprehends in his person he can be made subject to punishment. Certainly the people at large never ought: for as all punishments are for example towards the conservation of the people at large, the people at large can never become the subject of

---

[199] *Janissaries*: the elite palace guard of the Ottoman Emperor; so also the Praetorian Guard of the Roman Emperor. In both cases the Emperor, although absolute in his power over his polity, was vulnerable to assassination by the guard that protected his person.

punishment by any human hand[xx]. It is therefore of infinite importance that they should not be suffered to imagine that their will, any more than that of kings, is the standard of right and wrong. They ought to be persuaded that they are full as little entitled, and far less qualified, with safety to themselves, to use any arbitrary power whatsoever; that therefore they are not, under a false shew of liberty, but, in truth, to exercise an unnatural inverted domination, tyrannically to exact, from those who officiate in the state, not an entire devotion to their interest, which is their right, but an abject submission to their occasional will; extinguishing thereby, in all those who serve them, all moral principle, all sense of dignity, all use of judgment, and all consistency of character, whilst by the very same process they give themselves up a proper, a suitable, but a most contemptible prey to the servile ambition of popular sycophants or courtly flatterers.

When the people have emptied themselves of all the lust of selfish will, which without religion it is utterly impossible they ever should, when they are conscious that they exercise, and exercise perhaps in an higher link of the order of delegation, the power, which to be legitimate must be according to that eternal immutable law, in which will and reason are the same,[201] they will be more careful how they place power in base and incapable hands. In their nomination to office, they will not appoint to the exercise of authority, as to a pitiful job, but as to an holy function; not according to their sordid selfish interest, nor to their wanton caprice, nor to their arbitrary will; but they will confer that power (which any man may well tremble to give or to receive) on those only, in whom they may discern that predominant proportion of active virtue and wisdom, taken together and fitted to the charge, such, as in the great and inevitable mixed mass of human imperfections and infirmities, is to be found.

When they are habitually convinced that no evil can be acceptable, either in the act or the permission, to him whose essence is good, they will be better able to extirpate out of the minds of all magistrates, civil,

---

[xx] Quicquid multis peccatur inultum.[200]

[200] Lucan, *Pharsalia*, 5.260: 'Whatever wrongs the many do go unpunished.' Burke later (p. 247) describes reading Lucan with pleasure. Nicholas Rowe's 1718 translation, possessed by Burke, renders the passage as a memorable couplet:

> For laws in great rebellions lose their end
> And all go free when multitudes offend.

[201] *Will and reason are the same*: a reference to the theological claim that it is only God whose will is invariably reasonable.

ecclesiastical, or military, any thing that bears the least resemblance to a proud and lawless domination.

But one of the first and most leading principles on which the commonwealth and the laws are consecrated, is lest the temporary possessors and life-renters[202] in it, unmindful of what they have received from their ancestors, or of what is due to their posterity, should act as if they were the entire masters; that they should not think it amongst their rights to cut off the entail,[203] or commit waste on the inheritance,[204] by destroying at their pleasure the whole original fabric of their society; hazarding to leave to those who come after them, a ruin instead of an habitation – and teaching these successors as little to respect their contrivances, as they had themselves respected the institutions of their forefathers. By this unprincipled facility of changing the state as often, and as much, and in as many ways as there are floating fancies or fashions, the whole chain and continuity of the commonwealth would be broken. No one generation could link with the other. Men would become little better than the flies of a summer.

And first of all, the science of jurisprudence, the pride of the human intellect, which, with all its defects, redundancies, and errors, is the collected reason of ages,[205] combining the principles of original justice with the infinite variety of human concerns, as a heap of old exploded errors, would be no longer studied. Personal self-sufficiency and arrogance (the certain attendants upon all those who have never experienced a wisdom greater than their own) would usurp the tribunal. Of course, no certain laws, establishing invariable grounds of hope and fear, would keep the actions of men in a certain course, or direct them to a certain end. Nothing stable in the modes of holding property, or exercising function, could form a solid ground on which any parent could speculate in the education of his offspring, or in a choice for their future establishment in the world.

---

[202] *Life-renter*: a tenant whose lease lasts only during his lifetime, the property then reverting to the landlord. Such tenure was thought to provide less incentive (than freehold) to improve or even maintain the property in good order. Burke is reminding his readers that a polity is not at the disposal of any one generation.

[203] *Cut off the entail*: to deprive those entitled to inherit. See above, fn. 70.

[204] *Commit waste*: in English Law refers to 'the unauthorized act of a tenant . . . which tends to the destruction . . . or injury of the inheritance' (OED).

[205] Theorists of English common law such as Coke and Hale argued that common law – through its continual adjustment of precedent to changing social circumstance – was a kind of impersonal and 'collected reason'. On this see in particular Pocock, 'Burke and the Ancient Constitution . . . ', *Historical Journal* 3 (1960), pp. 125–43, and in his *Politics, Language and Time* (New York and London, 1971).

No principles would be early worked into the habits. As soon as the most able instructor had completed his laborious course of institution, instead of sending forth his pupil, accomplished in a virtuous discipline, fitted to procure him attention and respect, in his place in society, he would find everything altered; and that he had turned out a poor creature to the contempt and derision of the world, ignorant of the true grounds of estimation. Who would insure a tender and delicate sense of honour to beat almost with the first pulses of the heart, when no man could know what would be the test of honour in a nation, continually varying the standard of its coin? No part of life would retain its acquisitions. Barbarism with regard to science and literature, unskilfulness with regard to arts and manufactures, would infallibly succeed to the want of a steady education and settled principle; and thus the commonwealth itself would, in a few generations, crumble away, be disconnected into the dust and powder of individuality, and at length dispersed to all the winds of heaven.

To avoid therefore the evils of inconstancy and versatility, ten thousand times worse than those of obstinacy and the blindest prejudice, we have consecrated the state, that no man should approach to look into its defects or corruptions but with due caution; that he should never dream of beginning its reformation by its subversion; that he should approach to the faults of the state as to the wounds of a father, with pious awe and trembling sollicitude. By this wise prejudice we are taught to look with horror on those children of their country who are prompt rashly to hack that aged parent in pieces, and put him into the kettle of magicians, in hopes that by their poisonous weeds, and wild incantations, they may regenerate the paternal constitution, and renovate their father's life.[206]

Society is indeed a contract. Subordinate contracts for objects of mere occasional interest, may be dissolved at pleasure – but the state ought not to be considered as nothing better than a partnership agreement in a trade of pepper and coffee, callico[207] or tobacco, or some other such low concern, to be taken up for a little temporary interest, and to be dissolved by the fancy of the parties. It is to be looked on with other reverence; because it is

---

[206] According to myth, Medea, brought back by Jason as wife from his expedition to find the Golden Fleece, tricked the daughters of Pelias (who had usurped Jason's throne in his absence) into cutting their father up and boiling him with magic herbs to rejuvenate him. For a version: Ovid, *Metamorphoses*, 7. The application of the image had been used in a similar way by Hobbes in his *De Corpore Politico* (*Hobbes on the Citizen*, ed. Tuck and Silverthorn (Cambridge, 1997), p. 140).

[207] *Callico*: coarse, cotton cloth, originally from Calcutta, from which the word derives.

not a partnership in things subservient only to the gross animal existence of a temporary and perishable nature. It is a partnership in all science; a partnership in all art; a partnership in every virtue, and in all perfection. As the ends of such a partnership cannot be obtained in many generations, it becomes a partnership not only between those who are living, but between those who are living, those who are dead, and those who are to be born. Each contract of each particular state is but a clause in the great primæval contract of eternal society, linking the lower with the higher natures, connecting the visible and invisible world, according to a fixed compact sanctioned by the inviolable oath which holds all physical and all moral natures, each in their appointed place.[208] This law is not subject to the will of those, who by an obligation above them, and infinitely superior, are bound to submit their will to that law. The municipal corporations of that universal kingdom are not morally at liberty at their pleasure, and on their speculations of a contingent improvement, wholly to separate and tear asunder the bands of their subordinate community, and to dissolve it into an unsocial, uncivil, unconnected chaos of elementary principles. It is the first and supreme necessity only, a necessity that is not chosen but chooses, a necessity paramount to deliberation, that admits no discussion, and demands no evidence, which alone can justify a resort to anarchy. This necessity is no exception to the rule; because this necessity itself is a part too of that moral and physical disposition of things to which man must be obedient by consent or force, but if that which is only submission to necessity should be made the object of choice, the law is broken, nature is disobeyed: and the rebellious are outlawed, cast forth, and exiled, from this world of reason, and order, and peace, and virtue, and fruitful penitence, into the antagonist world of madness, discord, vice, confusion, and unavailing sorrow.

These, my dear Sir, are, were, and I think long will be the sentiments of not the least learned and reflecting part of this kingdom. They who are included in this description, form their opinions on such grounds as such persons ought to form them. The less enquiring receive them from an authority which those whom Providence dooms to live on trust need not be ashamed to rely on. These two sorts of men move in the same

[208] Whig ideology was in a sense burdened with the notion of the social contract, which had potentially embarrassingly radical implications. Burke's 'extension' of the social contract to include past and future generations' expectations was an important subversion of the radical notion urged by Paine that the present generation's rights held against those of the past. See Introduction, p. xx.

direction, tho' in a different place. They both move with the order of
the universe. They all know or feel this great antient truth: 'Quod illi
principi et præpotenti Deo qui omnem hunc mundum regit, nihil eorum
quæ quidem fiant in terris acceptius quam concilia et cætus hominum
jure sociati quæ civitates appellantur.'[209] They take this tenet of the head
and heart, not from the great name which it immediately bears, nor from
the greater from whence it is derived;[210] but from that which alone can
give true weight and sanction to any learned opinion, the common nature
and common relation of men. Persuaded that all things ought to be done
with reference, and referring all to the point of reference to which all
should be directed, they think themselves bound, not only as individuals
in the sanctuary of the heart, or as congregated in that personal capacity,
to renew the memory of their high origin and cast; but also in their
corporate character to perform their national homage to the institutor,
and author and protector of civil society; without which civil society man
could not by any possibility arrive at the perfection of which his nature is
capable, nor even make a remote and faint approach to it. They conceive
that He who gave our nature to be perfected by our virtue, willed also
the necessary means of its perfection – He willed therefore the state –
He willed its connexion with the source and original archetype of all
perfection. They who are convinced of this his will, which is the law
of laws and the sovereign of sovereigns, cannot think it reprehensible,
that this our corporate fealty and homage, that this our recognition of a
signiory paramount,[211] I had almost said this oblation of the state itself,[212]
as a worthy offering on the high altar of universal praise, should be
performed, as all publick solemn acts are performed, in buildings, in
musick, in decoration, in speech, in the dignity of persons, according
to the customs of mankind, taught by their nature; that is, with modest
splendour, with unassuming state, with mild majesty and sober pomp.
For those purposes they think some part of the wealth of the country is

---

[209] Cicero, *De Re Publica*, 6.13: 'For of all things done on earth nothing is more pleasing to
that God who rules over all this world, than those assemblies and comings-together of
human beings associated in justice called states.' Cicero's *De Re Publica* was not available
as a complete text in Burke's time, but the section from which this quotation is drawn,
known as 'Scipio's dream', had survived independently, being the subject of an important
commentary by Macrobius (*fl.* AD 430), *Somnium Scipionis*, §5.
[210] *Great name . . . greater*: the first is Scipio Aemilianus, the conqueror of Carthage, into
whose mouth the words are put; the greater, who wrote them, is Cicero.
[211] *Signiory paramount*: the highest authority.
[212] *Oblation*: an offering or dedication to god.

as usefully employed as it can be, in fomenting the luxury of individuals. It is the publick ornament. It is the publick consolation. It nourishes the publick hope. The poorest man finds his own importance and dignity in it, whilst the wealth and pride of individuals at every moment makes the man of humble rank and fortune sensible of his inferiority, and degrades and vilifies his condition. It is for the man in humble life, and to raise his nature, and to put him in mind of a state in which the privileges of opulence will cease, when he will be equal by nature, and may be more than equal by virtue, that this portion of the general wealth of his country is employed and sanctified.

I assure you I do not aim at singularity. I give you opinions which have been accepted amongst us, from very early times to this moment, with a continued and general approbation; and which indeed are so worked into my mind, that I am unable to distinguish what I have learned from others from the results of my own meditation.[213]

It is on some such principles that the majority of the people of England, far from thinking a religious, national establishment unlawful, hardly think it lawful to be without one. In France you are wholly mistaken if you do not believe us above all other things attached to it, and beyond all other nations; and when this people has acted unwisely and unjustifiably in its favour (as in some instances they have done most certainly) in their very errors you will at least discover their zeal.

This principle runs through the whole system of their polity. They do not consider their church establishment as convenient, but as essential to their state; not as a thing heterogeneous and separable; something added for accommodation; what they may either keep up or lay aside, according to their temporary ideas of convenience. They consider it as the foundation of their whole constitution, with which, and with every part of which, it holds an indissoluble union. Church and state are ideas inseparable in their minds, and scarcely is the one ever mentioned without mentioning the other.

Our education is so formed as to confirm and fix this impression. Our education is in a manner wholly in the hands of ecclesiastics, and in all stages from infancy to manhood. Even when our youth, leaving schools and universities, enter that most important period of life which begins

---

[213] Burke later claimed that his intention had merely been 'to convey to a foreign people...the prevalent opinions and sentiments of a nation' (Burke, *Appeal* (1791), p. 3 (*Further Reflections*, ed. Ritchie, p. 56)).

to link experience and study together, and when with that view they visit other countries, instead of old domestics whom we have seen as governors to principal men from other parts, three-fourths of those who go abroad with our young nobility and gentlemen are ecclesiastics; not as austere masters, nor as mere followers; but as friends and companions of a graver character, and not seldom persons as well born as themselves. With them, as relations, they most commonly keep up a close connexion through life. By this connexion we conceive that we attach our gentlemen to the church; and we liberalize the church by an intercourse with the leading characters of the country.

So tenacious are we of the old ecclesiastical modes and fashions of institution, that very little alteration has been made in them since the fourteenth or fifteenth century; adhering in this particular, as in all things else, to our old settled maxim, never entirely nor at once to depart from antiquity. We found these old institutions, on the whole, favourable to morality and discipline; and we thought they were susceptible of amendment, without altering the ground.[214] We thought that they were capable of receiving and meliorating, and above all of preserving the accessions of science and literature, as the order of Providence should successively produce them. And after all, with this Gothic and monkish education (for such it is in the ground-work) we may put in our claim to as ample and as early a share in all the improvements in science, in arts, and in literature, which have illuminated and adorned the modern world, as any other nation in Europe; we think one main cause of this improvement was our not despising the patrimony of knowledge which was left us by our forefathers.

It is from our attachment to a church establishment that the English nation did not think it wise to entrust that great fundamental interest of the whole to what they trust no part of their civil or military public service, that is, to the unsteady and precarious contribution of individuals. They go further. They certainly never have suffered and never will suffer the fixed estate of the church to be converted into a pension, to depend on the treasury, and to be delayed, withheld, or perhaps to be extinguished by fiscal difficulties; which difficulties may sometimes be pretended for political purposes, and are in fact often brought on by the extravagance,

---

[214] *Without altering the ground*: Burke's controversial claim is that the English Reformation – like the Revolution of 1688[N] – preserved continuity with the past, rather than constituting a break.

negligence, and rapacity of politicians. The people of England think that they have constitutional motives, as well as religious, against any project of turning their independent clergy into ecclesiastical pensioners of state.[215] They tremble for their liberty, from the influence of a clergy dependent on the crown; they tremble for the public tranquillity from the disorders of a factious clergy, if it were made to depend upon any other than the crown. They therefore made their church, like their king and their nobility, independent.

From the united considerations of religion and constitutional policy, from their opinion of a duty to make a sure provision for the consolation of the feeble and the instruction of the ignorant, they have incorporated and identified the estate of the church with the mass of *private property*, of which the state is not the proprietor, either for use or dominion, but the guardian only and the regulator. They have ordained that the provision of this establishment might be as stable as the earth on which it stands, and should not fluctuate with the Euripus of funds and actions.[216]

The men of England, the men, I mean, of light and leading in England, whose wisdom (if they have any) is open and direct, would be ashamed, as of a silly deceitful trick, to profess any religion in name, which by their proceedings they appeared to contemn. If by their conduct (the only language that rarely lies) they seemed to regard the great ruling principle of the moral and the natural world, as a mere invention to keep the vulgar in obedience,[217] they apprehend that by such a conduct they would defeat the politic purpose they have in view. They would find it difficult to make others to believe in a system to which they manifestly gave no credit themselves. The Christian statesmen of this land would indeed first provide for the *multitude*; because it is the *multitude*; and is

[215] The Decree of 2 November 1789 had announced that 'all ecclesiastical property is at the disposal of the nation'; that of the 12 July 1790 established the Civil Constitution of the Clergy, making all ecclesiastical appointments elective and establishing a regular salary scale, all subject to the secular power (*DocS*, p. 169). Burke implicitly contrasts this state of affairs with the English practice whereby the Church of England was a landowner in its own right, funding its activities independently, from its own income.

[216] *Euripus*: the very narrow strait between Euboea and mainland Boeotia, Greece. It became a byword for instability on account of its complex and violent tides, which were very slight elsewhere in the Mediterranean (e.g. Plato, *Phaedo*, 90c). Hence anything unstable and unpredictable.

*Funds and actions*: money lent out at interest and shares in a joint stock company, and so subject to market fluctuation.

[217] As infamously suggested by one of Burke's *bêtes noires*, Voltaire: 'Si Dieu n'existait pas, il faudrait l'inventer' ['if God did not exist he would have to be invented'] (*Letter to the Author of the Book of the Three Imposters*, 1770).

therefore, as such, the first object in the ecclesiastical institution, and in all institutions. They have been taught, that the circumstance of the gospel's being preached to the poor was one of the great tests of its true mission. They think, therefore, that those do not believe it, who do not take care it should be preached to the poor. But as they know that charity is not confined to any one description, but ought to apply itself to all men who have wants, they are not deprived of a due and anxious sensation of pity to the distresses of the miserable great. They are not repelled through a fastidious delicacy, at the stench of their arrogance and presumption, from a medicinal attention to their mental blotches and running sores. They are sensible, that religious instruction is of more consequence to them than to any others; from the greatness of the temptation to which they are exposed; from the important consequences that attend their faults; from the contagion of their ill example; from the necessity of bowing down the stubborn neck of their pride and ambition to the yoke of moderation and virtue; from a consideration of the fat stupidity and gross ignorance concerning what imports men most to know, which prevails at courts, and at the head of armies, and in senates, as much as at the loom and in the field.

The English people are satisfied, that to the great the consolations of religion are as necessary as its instructions. They too are among the unhappy. They feel personal pain and domestic sorrow. In these they have no privilege, but are subject to pay their full contingent to the contributions levied on mortality. They want this sovereign balm under their gnawing cares and anxieties, which being less conversant about the limited wants of animal life, range without limit, and are diversified by infinite combinations in the wild and unbounded regions of imagination. Some charitable dole is wanting to these, our often very unhappy brethren, to fill the gloomy void that reigns in minds which have nothing on earth to hope or fear; something to relieve in the killing languor and over-laboured lassitude of those who have nothing to do; something to excite an appetite to existence in the palled satiety which attends on all pleasures which may be bought, where nature is not left to her own process, where even desire is anticipated, and therefore fruition defeated by meditated schemes and contrivances of delight; and no interval, no obstacle, is interposed between the wish and the accomplishment.

The people of England know how little influence the teachers of religion are likely to have with the wealthy and powerful of long standing, and how much less with the newly fortunate, if they appear in a manner no way assorted to those with whom they must associate, and over whom they must even exercise, in some cases, something like an authority. What must they think of that body of teachers, if they see it in no part above the establishment of their domestic servants? If the poverty were voluntary, there might be some difference. Strong instances of self-denial operate powerfully on our minds; and a man who has no wants has obtained great freedom and firmness, and even dignity. But as the mass of any description of men are but men, and their poverty cannot be voluntary, that disrespect which attends upon all Lay poverty, will not depart from the Ecclesiastical. Our provident constitution has therefore taken care that those who are to instruct presumptuous ignorance, those who are to be censors over insolent vice, should neither incur their contempt, nor live upon their alms; nor will it tempt the rich to a neglect of the true medicine of their minds. For these reasons, whilst we provide first for the poor, and with a parental solicitude, we have not relegated religion (like something we were ashamed to shew) to obscure municipalities or rustic villages. No! We will have her to exalt her mitred front in courts and parliaments.[218] We will have her mixed throughout the whole mass of life, and blended with all the classes of society. The people of England will shew to the haughty potentates of the world, and to their talking sophisters, that a free, a generous, an informed nation, honours the high magistrates of its church; that it will not suffer the insolence of wealth and titles, or any other species of proud pretension, to look down with scorn upon what they look up to with reverence; nor presume to trample on that acquired personal nobility, which they intend always to be, and which often is the fruit, not the reward, (for what can be the reward?) of learning, piety, and virtue. They can see, without pain or grudging, an Archbishop precede a Duke. They can see a Bishop of Durham, or a Bishop of Winchester, in possession of ten thousand pounds a year; and cannot conceive why it is in worse hands than estates to the like amount in the hands of this Earl, or that Squire; although it may be true, that so many dogs and horses are not kept by the former, and fed with the victuals which ought to nourish the children of the people. It is true, the whole church revenue is not always employed, and to every shilling, in charity; nor perhaps ought it; but something is generally so employed. It is better to cherish virtue and humanity, by leaving much to free will,

---

[218] *Mitre*: the distinctive headdress of a bishop. Senior bishops of the Church of England sat, by right, in the House of Lords and were thus part of Parliament.

even with some loss to the object, than to attempt to make men mere machines and instruments of a political benevolence. The world on the whole will gain by a liberty, without which virtue cannot exist.[219]

When once the commonwealth has established the estates of the church as property, it can, consistently, hear nothing of the more or the less. Too much and too little are treason against property. What evil can arise from the quantity in any hand, whilst the supreme authority has the full, sovereign superintendance over this, as over all property, to prevent every species of abuse; and, whenever it notably deviates, to give to it a direction agreeable to the purposes of its institution.

In England most of us conceive that it is envy and malignity towards those who are often the beginners of their own fortune, and not a love of the self-denial and mortification of the antient church, that makes some look askance at the distinctions, and honours, and revenues, which, taken from no person, are set apart for virtue. The ears of the people of England are distinguishing. They hear these men speak broad. Their tongue betrays them. Their language is in the *patois* of fraud; in the cant and gibberish of hypocrisy.[220] The people of England must think so, when these praters affect to carry back the clergy to that primitive evangelic poverty which, in the spirit, ought always to exist in them, (and in us too, however we may like it) but in the thing must be varied, when the relation of that body to the state is altered; when manners, when modes of life, when indeed the whole order of human affairs has undergone a total revolution. We shall believe those reformers to be then honest enthusiasts, not as now we think them, cheats and deceivers, when we see them throwing their own goods into common, and submitting their own persons to the austere discipline of the early church.

With these ideas rooted in their minds, the commons of Great Britain, in the national emergencies, will never seek their resource from the confiscation of the estates of the church and poor. Sacrilege and proscription are not among the ways and means in our committee of supply. The Jews in Change Alley have not yet dared to hint their hopes of a mortgage on the revenues belonging to the see of Canterbury. I am not afraid that I shall be disavowed, when I assure you that there is not *one* public man in this kingdom, whom you would wish to quote; no not one of any party or

---

[219] Aristotle had made it an argument against state administration of property that the virtues of generosity and liberality can only be practised where there is private property (*Politics*, 1263b).

[220] *Patois* (Fr.): any localised dialect. *Cant*: slang, street-speech.

description, who does not reprobate the dishonest, perfidious, and cruel confiscation which the national assembly has been compelled to make of that property which it was their first duty to protect.

It is with the exultation of a little national pride I tell you, that those amongst us who have wished to pledge the societies of Paris in the cup of their abominations, have been disappointed. The robbery of your church has proved a security to the possessions of ours. It has roused the people. They see with horror and alarm that enormous and shameless act of proscription. It has opened, and will more and more open their eyes upon the selfish enlargement of mind, and the narrow liberality of sentiment of insidious men, which commencing in close hypocrisy and fraud have ended in open violence and rapine. At home we behold similar beginnings. We are on our guard against similar conclusions.

I hope we shall never be so totally lost to all sense of the duties imposed upon us by the law of social union, as, upon any pretext of public service, to confiscate the goods of a single unoffending citizen. Who but a tyrant (a name expressive of every thing which can vitiate and degrade human nature) could think of seizing on the property of men, unaccused, unheard, untried, by whole descriptions, by hundreds and thousands together? who that had not lost every trace of humanity could think of casting down men of exalted rank and sacred function, some of them of an age to call at once for reverence and compassion, of casting them down from the highest situation in the commonwealth, wherein they were maintained by their own landed property, to a state of indigence, depression and contempt?

The confiscators truly have made some allowance to their victims from the scraps and fragments of their own tables from which they have been so harshly driven, and which have been so bountifully spread for a feast to the harpies of usury.[221] But to drive men from independence to live on alms is itself great cruelty. That which might be a tolerable condition to men in one state of life, and not habituated to other things, may, when all these circumstances are altered, be a dreadful revolution; and one to which a virtuous mind would feel pain in condemning any guilt except that which would demand the life of the offender. But to many minds this punishment of *degradation* and *infamy* is worse than death. Undoubtedly

---

[221] *Harpies*: mythical, winged, female creatures who seized food from others. In a famous episode in the *Aeneid* they attacked a feast which the escaping Trojans had set out on the Ionian isles of the Strophades, unaware that this was where the harpies lived.

it is an infinite aggravation of this cruel suffering, that the persons who were taught a double prejudice in favour of religion, by education and by the place they held in the administration of its functions, are to receive the remnants of their property as alms from the profane and impious hands of those who had plundered them of all the rest; to receive [(if they are at all to receive)]²²² not from the charitable contributions of the faithful, but from the insolent tenderness of known and avowed Atheism, the maintenance of religion, measured out to them on the standard of the contempt in which it is held; and for the purpose of rendering those who receive the allowance vile and of no estimation in the eyes of mankind.

But this act of seizure of property, it seems, is a judgment in law, and not a confiscation. They have, it seems, found out in the academies of the *Palais Royal*,²²³ and the *Jacobins*,ᴺ that certain men had no right to the possessions which they held under law, usage, the decisions of courts, and the accumulated prescription of a thousand years. They say that ecclesiastics are fictitious persons, creatures of the state; whom at pleasure they may destroy, and of course limit and modify in every particular; that the goods they possess are not properly theirs, but belong to the state which created the fiction; and we are therefore not to trouble ourselves with what they may suffer in their natural feelings and natural persons, on account of what is done towards them in this their constructive character.²²⁴ Of what import is it, under what names you injure men, and deprive them of the just emoluments of a profession, in which they were not only permitted but encouraged by the state to engage; and upon the supposed certainty of which emoluments they had formed the plan of their lives, contracted debts, and led multitudes to an entire dependence upon them?

---

²²² Absent from 1st edn.
²²³ *Palais Royal*: residence of the Ducs d'Orléans, the foremost noble family in France. The courtyard was a well-known forum for political discussions, here ironised as 'academies'. This was encouraged by Duc Louis Philippe II (1747–93), who led those of the Nobility who left the Estates Generalᴺ to join with the Third Estate.ᴺ He was to be elected to the Constituent Assembly and the National Convention and vote for the execution of the King, his cousin. He was guillotined in the Terror.
²²⁴ The Assembly's argument had been that legal corporations such as the Church, since they existed only as creations of the politico-legal system, could be broken up and their property might be appropriated without injustice. The National Assembly duly declared the property of the Church was 'at the disposal of the nation' (Decree of 2 November 1789, *DocS*, p. 158). The Clergy was abolished as a distinct social and political order the following month.

You do not imagine, Sir, that I am going to compliment this miserable distinction of persons with any long discussion. The arguments of tyranny are as contemptible as its force is dreadful. Had not your confiscators by their early crimes obtained a power which secures indemnity to all the crimes of which they have since been guilty, or that they can commit, it is not the syllogism of the logician but the lash of the executioner that would have refuted a sophistry which becomes an accomplice of theft and murder. The sophistick tyrants of Paris are loud in their declamations against the departed regal tyrants who in former ages have vexed the world. They are thus bold, because they are safe from the dungeons and iron cages of their old masters. Shall we be more tender of the tyrants of our own time, when we see them acting worse tragedies under our eyes? shall we not use the same liberty that they do, when we can use it with the same safety? when to speak honest truth only requires a contempt of the opinions of those whose actions we abhor?

. This outrage on all the rights of property was at first covered with what, on the system of their conduct, was the most astonishing of all pretexts – a regard to national faith. The enemies to property at first pretended a most tender, delicate, and scrupulous anxiety for keeping the king's engagements with the public creditor. These professors of the rights of men are so busy in teaching others, that they have not leisure to learn any thing themselves; otherwise they would have known that it is to the property of the citizen, and not to the demands of the creditor of the state, that the first and original faith of civil society is pledged. The claim of the citizen is prior in time, paramount in title, superior in equity. The fortunes of individuals, whether possessed by acquisition, or by descent, or in virtue of a participation in the goods of some community, were no part of the creditor's security, expressed or implied. They never so much as entered into his head when he made his bargain. He well knew that the public, whether represented by a monarch, or by a senate, can pledge nothing but the public estate; and it can have no public estate, except in what it derives from a just and proportioned imposition upon the citizens at large. This was engaged, and nothing else could be engaged, to the public creditor. No man can mortgage his injustice as a pawn for his fidelity.[225]

---

[225] The Assembly pledged the Church estates as security against the state's debts to avoid declaring a bankruptcy, and so claimed it was keeping faith with creditors. Burke argues that the state has a prior duty to protect the private property of citizens (or corporations)

It is impossible to avoid some observation on the contradictions caused by the extreme rigour and the extreme laxity of the new public faith, which influenced in this transaction, and which influenced not according to the nature of the obligation, but to the description of the persons to whom it was engaged.[226] No acts of the old government of the kings of France are held valid in the National Assembly, except its pecuniary engagements; acts of all others of the most ambiguous legality. The rest of the acts of that royal government are considered in so odious a light, that to have a claim under its authority is looked on as a sort of crime. A pension, given as a reward for service to the state, is surely as good a ground of property as any security for money advanced to the state. It is a better; for money is paid, and well paid, to obtain that service. We have however seen multitudes of people under this description in France, who never had been deprived of their allowances by the most arbitrary ministers, in the most arbitrary times, by this assembly of the rights of men, robbed without mercy. They were told, in answer to their claim to the bread earned with their blood, that their services had not been rendered to the country that now exists.

This laxity of public faith is not confined to those unfortunate persons. The assembly, with perfect consistency it must be owned, is engaged in a respectable deliberation how far it is bound by the treaties made with other nations under the former government, and their Committee is to report which of them they ought to ratify, and which not. By this means they have put the external fidelity of this virgin state on a par with its internal.[227]

It is not easy to conceive upon what rational principle the royal government should not, of the two, rather have possessed the power of

and such private property cannot be held or delivered as security for debts incurred by a government.

[226] Burke here insinuates what he goes on to articulate at length in discussing the 'great monied interest' below (pp. 113ff.), namely, that the real explanation as to which of the *ancien régime*'s obligations were being honoured and which not, was to be found not in the character of the obligations but in the interests of those who were deciding – namely, the interests that Assembly members had, many of whom were debt-holders, in ensuring the debt was honoured.

[227] Burke is here being savagely ironic. Although the Assembly had nationalised the Church's estates to be able to 'keep faith' with the state's creditors (many of whom were deputies), it had clearly broken faith with the Church. The Assembly was much more fastidious about honouring these debts than it was about honouring some long-standing institutions. It was now assessing which of its international debts it would acknowledge – thus, he points out, keeping its external (un)trustworthiness on a par with its internal.

rewarding service, and making treaties, in virtue of its prerogative, than that of pledging to creditors the revenue of the state actual and possible. The treasure of the nation, of all things, has been the least allowed to the prerogative of the king of France, or to the prerogative of any king in Europe. To mortgage the public revenue implies the sovereign dominion, in the fullest sense, over the public purse. It goes far beyond the trust even of a temporary and occasional taxation. The acts however of that dangerous power (the distinctive mark of a boundless despotism) have been alone held sacred. Whence arose this preference given by a democratic assembly to a body of property deriving its title from the most critical and obnoxious of all the exertions of monarchical authority? Reason can furnish nothing to reconcile inconsistency; nor can partial favour be accounted for upon equitable principles. But the contradiction and partiality which admit no justification, are not the less without an adequate cause; and that cause I do not think it difficult to discover.[228]

By the vast debt of France a great monied interest had insensibly grown up, and with it a great power. By the antient usages which prevailed in that kingdom, the general circulation of property, and in particular the mutual convertibility of land into money, and of money into land, had always been a matter of difficulty. Family settlements,[229] rather more general and more strict than they are in England, the *jus retractus*,[230] the great mass of landed property held by the crown, and by a maxim of the French law held unalienably,[231] the vast estates of the ecclesiastic corporations, – all these had kept the landed and monied interests more separated in France, less miscible, and the owners of the two distinct species of property not so well disposed to each other as they are in this country.

---

[228] Burke's following analysis of the political economy of the Revolution is classically analysed by J. G. A. Pocock, 'The Political Economy of Burke's Analysis of the French Revolution', *Historical Journal* 25 (1982), pp. 331–49; also in his *Virtue, Commerce and History* (Cambridge, 1985).

[229] *Family settlements*: property acquired as dowries or marriage portions could, in *ancien régime* France, come with restrictions binding future generations over their use or alienation.

[230] *Jus retractus:* The right of a feudal superior to recover title to a property held by a tenant. In France those inheriting feudal estates retained the right to compulsorily reacquire from the current owner any lands that had previously formed part of the estate.

[231] *Unalienably*: rights incapable of being given up. A specific version of the *jus retractus* made all property once held by the Crown – even if sold to another party – vulnerable to repossession.

The monied property was long looked on with rather an evil eye by the people. They saw it connected with their distresses, and aggravating them. It was no less envied by the old landed interests, partly for the same reasons that rendered it obnoxious to the people, but much more so as it eclipsed, by the splendour of an ostentatious luxury, the unendowed pedigrees and naked titles of several among the nobility. Even when the nobility, which represented the more permanent landed interest, united themselves by marriage (which sometimes was the case) with the other description, the wealth which saved the family from ruin, was supposed to contaminate and degrade it. Thus the enmities and heart-burnings of these parties were encreased even by the usual means by which discord is made to cease, and quarrels are turned into friendship. In the mean time, the pride of the wealthy men, not noble or newly noble, encreased with its cause. They felt with resentment an inferiority, the grounds of which they did not acknowledge. There was no measure to which they were not willing to lend themselves, in order to be revenged of the outrages of this rival pride, and to exalt their wealth to what they considered as its natural rank and estimation. They struck at the nobility through the crown and the church. They attacked them particularly on the side on which they thought them the most vulnerable, that is, the possessions of the church, which, through the patronage of the crown, generally devolved upon the nobility. The bishopricks, and the great commendatory abbies, were, with few exceptions, held by that order.

In this state of real, though not always perceived warfare between the noble antient landed interest, and the new monied interest, the greatest because the most applicable strength was in the hands of the latter. The monied interest is in its nature more ready for any adventure; and its possessors more disposed to new enterprizes of any kind. Being of a recent acquisition, it falls in more naturally with any novelties. It is therefore the kind of wealth which will be resorted to by all who wish for change.[232]

Along with the monied interest, a new description of men had grown up, with whom that interest soon formed a close and marked union; I mean the political Men of Letters. Men of Letters, fond of distinguishing

---

[232] The idea that the representation of landed property provided a constitution with stability was an old one. However, the Scottish Enlightenment thinkers, especially Hume, in his *Essays*, and Adam Smith, had developed a kind of social psychology of property, showing how different forms of property developed different predispositions in their holders – long-term views amongst landed proprietors, shorter-term calculation of interest amongst traders, speculative risk-taking amongst financiers.

themselves, are rarely averse to innovation. Since the decline of the life and greatness of Lewis the XIVth,[N] they were not so much cultivated either by him, or by the regent, or the successors to the crown; nor were they engaged to the court by favours and emoluments so systematically as during the splendid period of that ostentatious and not impolitic reign. What they lost in the old court protection, they endeavoured to make up by joining in a sort of incorporation of their own; to which the two academies of France,[233] and afterwards the vast undertaking of the Encyclopaedia,[234] carried on by a society of these gentlemen, did not a little contribute.

The literary cabal had some years ago formed something like a regular plan for the destruction of the Christian religion. This object they pursued with a degree of zeal which hitherto had been discovered only in the propagators of some system of piety. They were possessed with a spirit of proselytism in the most fanatical degree; and from thence by an easy progress, with the spirit of persecution according to their means[xxi]. What was not to be done towards their great end by any direct or immediate act, might be wrought by a longer process through the medium of opinion. To command that opinion, the first step is to establish a dominion over those who direct it. They contrived to possess themselves, with great method and perseverance, of all the avenues to literary fame. Many of them indeed stood high in the ranks of literature and science. The world had done them justice; and in favour of general talents forgave the evil tendency of their peculiar principles. This was true liberality; which they returned by endeavouring to confine the reputation of sense, learning, and taste to themselves or their followers. I will venture to say that this narrow, exclusive spirit has not been less prejudicial to literature and

---

[xxi] [This, (down to the end of the first sentence in the next paragraph) and some other parts here and there, were inserted, on his reading the manuscript, by my lost son.][235]

---

[233] *Academies:* There were several; the most prominent literary ones being the Académie Française, established 1635 to provide authoritative guidance on the correct use of the French language, and the Académie des inscriptions et belles lettres (est. 1663). Others extant at the time were those for painting and sculpture, architecture, and music. They were disbanded in 1793 but re-emerged as Academies within the *Institut de France* set up in 1795.

[234] *L'Encyclopédie ou Dictionnaire Raisonné*, ed. Jean d'Alembert[N] and Denis Diderot,[N] 35 vols. (1751–72), often seen as a manifesto of the Revolution, was intended to provide a compendium of contemporary knowledge, much of it practical, agricultural and scientific. However, it offended religious sensibilities by its tone of philosophic detachment – theology, for example, was classified in the table of knowledge as a branch of philosophy.

[235] This footnote added from the 1803 text. Burke's son Richard had died in 1794. The Burkes had lost their younger son, Christopher (d. 1762), in childhood.

to taste, than to morals and true philosophy. These Atheistical fathers have a bigotry of their own; and they have learnt to talk against monks with the spirit of a monk. But in some things they are men of the world. The resources of intrigue are called in to supply the defects of argument and wit. To this system of literary monopoly was joined an unremitting industry to blacken and discredit in every way, and by every means, all those who did not hold to their faction. To those who have observed the spirit of their conduct, it has long been clear that nothing was wanted but the power of carrying the intolerance of the tongue and of the pen into a persecution which would strike at property, liberty, and life.

The desultory and faint persecution carried on against them,[236] more from compliance with form and decency than with serious resentment, neither weakened their strength, nor relaxed their efforts. The issue of the whole was, that what with opposition, and what with success, a violent and malignant zeal, of a kind hitherto unknown in the world, had taken an entire possession of their minds, and rendered their whole conversation, which otherwise would have been pleasing and instructive, perfectly disgusting. A spirit of cabal, intrigue, and proselytism, pervaded all their thoughts, words, and actions. And, as controversial zeal soon turns its thoughts on force, they began to insinuate themselves into a correspondence with foreign princes; in hopes, through their authority, which at first they flattered, they might bring about the changes they had in view. To them it was indifferent whether these changes were to be accomplished by the thunderbolt of despotism, or by the earthquake of popular commotion. The correspondence between this cabal, and the late king of Prussia,[237] will throw no small light upon the spirit of all their proceedings[xxii]. For the same purpose for which they intrigued with princes, they cultivated, in a distinguished manner, the monied interest of France; and partly through the means furnished by those whose peculiar offices gave them the most extensive and certain means of communication, they carefully occupied all the avenues to opinion.

---

[xxii] [I do not choose to shock the feeling of the moral reader with any quotation of their vulgar, base and prophane language.][238]

---

[236] The publication of *L'Encyclopedie* had been suppressed by the royal censor between 1759 and 1775.

[237] *The late king of Prussia* was Frederick the Great (1712–86), a famous patron of philosophy and the arts.

[238] Footnote absent from 1st edn.

Writers, especially when they act in a body, and with one direction, have great influence on the publick mind; the alliance therefore of these writers with the monied interest[xxiii] had no small effect in removing the popular odium and envy which attended that species of wealth. These writers, like the propagators of all novelties, pretended to a great zeal for the poor, and the lower orders, whilst in their satires they rendered hateful, by every exaggeration, the faults of courts, of nobility, and of priesthood. They became a sort of demagogues. They served as a link to unite, in favour of one object, obnoxious wealth to restless and desperate poverty.

As these two kinds of men appear principal leaders in all the late transactions, their junction and politics will serve to account, not upon any principles of law or of policy, but as a *cause*, for the general fury with which all the landed property of ecclesiastical corporations has been attacked; and the great care which, contrary to their pretended principles, has been taken, of a monied interest originating from the authority of the crown. All the envy against wealth and power, was artificially directed against other descriptions of riches. On what other principle than that which I have stated can we account for an appearance so extraordinary and unnatural as that of the ecclesiastical possessions, which had stood so many successions of ages and shocks of civil violences, and were guarded at once by justice, and by prejudice, being applied to the payment of debts, comparatively recent, invidious, and contracted by a decried and subverted government?

Was the public estate a sufficient stake for the publick debts? Assume that it was not, and that a loss *must* be incurred somewhere – When the only estate lawfully possessed, and which the contracting parties had in contemplation at the time in which their bargain was made, happens to fail, who, according to the principles of natural and legal equity, ought to be the sufferer? Certainly it ought to be either the party who trusted; or the party who persuaded him to trust; or both; and not third parties who had no concern with the transaction. Upon any insolvency they ought to suffer who were weak enough to lend upon bad security, or they who fraudulently held out a security that was not valid. Laws are acquainted with no other rules of decision. But by the new institute of the rights of

---

[xxiii] [Their connection with Turgot and almost all the people of the finance.][239]

[239] Footnote added from 1803 edition. *A. R. Jacques Turgot* (1727–81), economic theorist and Controller-General of Finances 1774–6, under Louis XVI, when he attempted to rein in expenditure and bring debt under control.

men, the only persons, who in equity ought to suffer, are the only persons who are to be saved harmless: those are to answer the debt who neither were lenders or borrowers, mortgagers or mortgagees.

What had the clergy to do with these transactions? What had they to do with any publick engagement further than the extent of their own debt? To that, to be sure, their estates were bound to the last acre. Nothing can lead more to the true spirit of the assembly, which sits for publick confiscation, with its new equity and its new morality, than an attention to their proceeding with regard to this debt of the clergy. The body of confiscators, true to that monied interest for which they were false to every other, have found the clergy competent to incur a legal debt. Of course they declared them legally entitled to the property which their power of incurring the debt and mortgaging the estate implied; recognising the rights of those persecuted citizens, in the very act in which they were thus grossly violated.

If, as I said, any persons are to make good deficiencies to the publick creditor, besides the publick at large, they must be those who managed the agreement. Why therefore are not the estates of all the comptrollers general confiscated[xxiv]? Why not those of the long succession of ministers, financiers, and bankers who have been enriched whilst the nation was impoverished by their dealings and their counsels? Why is not the estate of Mr. Laborde declared forfeited rather than of the archbishop of Paris,[241] who has had nothing to do in the creation or in the jobbing of the publick funds? Or, if you must confiscate old landed estates in favour of the money-jobbers, why is the penalty confined to one description? I do not know whether the expences of the duke de Choiseul[242] have left any thing of the infinite sums which he had derived from the bounty of his master, during the transactions of a reign which contributed largely, by every species of prodigality in war and peace, to the present debt of France. If any such remains, why is not this confiscated? I remember to have been in Paris during the time of the old government. I was there

---

[xxiv] [All have been confiscated in their turn.][240]

---

[240] Footnote added from 1803 edn.

[241] *Mr. Laborde*: Jean-Joseph Laborde (1724–94): Keeper of the French Royal Treasury, and so by implication more responsible for the French economic plight than the Archbishop. Laborde, although noble, had, like Mirabeau, joined the Tiers Etat.[N] He would be guillotined in 1794.

[242] *Choiseul*: Etienne-Francois, Duc de Choiseul (1719–85), prominent courtier and First Minister under Louis XV.

just after the duke d'Aiguillon had been snatched (as it was generally thought) from the block by the hand of a protecting despotism.[243] He was a minister, and had some concern in the affairs of that prodigal period. Why do I not see his estate delivered up to the municipalities in which it is situated? The noble family of Noailles have long been servants (meritorious servants I admit) to the crown of France, and have had of course some share in its bounties.[244] Why do I hear nothing of the application of their estates to the publick debt? Why is the estate of the duke de Rochefoucault[N] more sacred than that of the cardinal de Rochefoucault? The former is, I doubt not, a worthy person; and (if it were not a sort of profaneness to talk of the use, as affecting the title to property) he makes a good use of his revenues; but it is no disrespect to him to say, what authentic information well warrants me in saying, that the use made of a property equally valid, by his brother[xxv] the cardinal archbishop of Rouen, was far more laudable and far more publick-spirited. Can one hear of the proscription of such persons, and the confiscation of their effects, without indignation and horror? He is not a man who does not feel such emotions on such occasions. He does not deserve the name of a free man who will not express them.

Few barbarous conquerors have ever made so terrible a revolution in property. None of the heads of the Roman factions, when they established '*crudelem illam hastam*'[246] in all their auctions of rapine, have ever set up to sale the goods of the conquered citizen to such an enormous amount. It must be allowed in favour of those tyrants of antiquity, that what was done by them could hardly be said to be done in cold blood. Their passions were inflamed, their tempers soured, their understandings confused, with the spirit of revenge, with the innumerable reciprocated and recent inflictions and retaliations of blood and rapine. They were driven beyond all bounds

---

[xxv] [Not his brother, nor any near relation; but this mistake does not affect the argument.][245]

[243] *Duke d'Aiguillon*: Emanuel-Armand de Vignoret du Plessis-Richelieu, duc d' Aiguillon (1720–88). His trial for corruption in 1770 had been stopped on the orders of Louis XV, after the intervention of Madame du Barry. His son had joined the Revolution.

[244] *Noailles*: The family, created Dukes of Noailles in 1663, had, by the time of the Revolution, provided three Marshals of France (2nd, 3rd and 4th dukes), an admiral, an archbishop and a number of prominent soldiers.

[245] Footnote added from 1803 edition. The Archbishop, Dominique de la Rochefoucauld, was only distantly related. He was President of the Order of the Clergy in the Estates General[N] of 1789.

[246] *Crudelem illam hastam*: 'that cruel spear'. Roman auctions – originally of the goods of a defeated enemy – were conducted around a spear plunged into the ground.

of moderation by the apprehension of the return to power with the return of property to the families of those they had injured beyond all hope of forgiveness.

These Roman confiscators, who were yet only in the elements of tyranny, and were not instructed in the rights of men to exercise all sorts of cruelties on each other without provocation, thought it necessary to spread a sort of colour over their injustice. They considered the vanquished party as composed of traitors who had borne arms, or otherwise had acted with hostility against the commonwealth. They regarded them as persons who had forfeited their property by their crimes. With you, in your improved state of the human mind, there was no such formality. You seized upon five millions sterling of annual rent, and turned forty or fifty thousand human creatures out of their houses, because 'such was your pleasure.' The tyrant, Harry the Eighth of England,[247] as he was not better enlightened than the Roman Marius's and Sylla's,[248] and had not studied in your new schools, did not know what an effectual instrument of despotism was to be found in that grand magazine of offensive weapons, the rights of men. When he resolved to rob the abbies, as the club of the Jacobins have robbed all the ecclesiastics, he began by setting on foot a commission to examine into the crimes and abuses which prevailed in those communities. As it might be expected, his commission reported truths, exaggerations, and falsehoods. But, truly or falsely, it reported abuses and offences. However, as abuses might be corrected, as every crime of persons does not infer a forfeiture with regard to communities, and as property, in that dark age, was not discovered to be a creature of prejudice, all those abuses (and there were enough of them)

[247] *Harry* [Henry] *the Eighth* (1491–1547): autocratic King of England, notorious for his six wives and increasingly bloodthirsty suppression of opposition. After separating the Church of England from the Catholic Church he broke up the monastic foundations and appropriated their lands.

[248] *Marius*: Gaius Marius (155–86 BC), extraordinarily successful Roman General, Tribune of the Plebs and seven times Consul. Marius created Rome's first professional army. His use of soldiers within Rome to enforce the decrees awarding land to military veterans in 100 BC and eventual sack of Rome in 87 over the same issue constituted a militarisation of Rome's politics.

*Sylla*: Lucius Cornelius Sulla (138–78 BC), Roman General, Consul and Dictator, returned from Middle Eastern campaigns to fight the battle of the Colline Gate against senatorial forces and occupied the city, becoming Dictator. He massacred 8,000 prisoners and assassinated and dispossessed opponents. He concentrated power in the Senate, emasculating other political bodies such as the Tribunes of the Plebs and the *Comitia Centuriata*. His career, with that of Marius, marks the political collapse of Rome's republican institutions.

were hardly thought sufficient ground for such a confiscation as it was for his purposes to make. He therefore procured the formal surrender of these estates. All these operose proceedings were adopted by one of the most decided tyrants in the rolls of history, as necessary preliminaries, before he could venture, by bribing the members of his two servile houses with a share of the spoil, and holding out to them an eternal immunity from taxation, to demand a confirmation of his iniquitous proceedings by an act of parliament. Had fate reserved him to our times, four technical terms would have done his business, and saved him all this trouble; he needed nothing more than one short form of incantation – '*Philosophy, Light, Liberality, the Rights of Men.*'

I can say nothing in praise of those acts of tyranny, which no voice has hitherto ever commended under any of their false colours; yet in these false colours an homage was paid by despotism to justice. The power which was above all fear and all remorse was not set above all shame. Whilst Shame keeps its watch, Virtue is not wholly extinguished in the heart; nor will Moderation be utterly exiled from the minds of tyrants.[249]

I believe every honest man sympathizes in his reflections with our political poet on that occasion, and will pray to avert the omen whenever these acts of rapacious despotism present themselves to his view or his imagination:

'———— May no such storm
Fall on our times, where ruin must reform.
Tell me (my muse) what monstrous, dire offence,
What crimes could any Christian king incense
To such a rage? Was't luxury, or lust?
Was *he* so temperate, so chaste, so just?
Were these their crimes? they were his own much more;
But wealth is crime enough to him that's poor[xxvi].'[250]

xxvi The rest of the passage is this –

'Who having spent the treasures of his crown,
Condemns their luxury to feed his own.
And yet this act, to varnish o'er the shame
Of sacrilege, must bear devotion's name.
No crime so bold, but would be understood
A real, or at least a seeming good,
Who fears not to do ill, yet fears the name;

249 Shame – whilst it still exists – acts as a restraint on immorality even amongst the most powerful tyrants.
250 Sir John Denham, *Cooper's Hill*, ll. 115–22.

This same wealth, which is at all times treason and *lese nation* to indigent and rapacious despotism, under all modes of polity, was your temptation to violate property, law, and religion, united in one object. But was the state of France so wretched and undone, that no other resource but rapine remained to preserve its existence? On this point I wish to receive some information. When the states met, was the condition of the finances of France such, that, after œconomising on principles of justice and mercy through all departments, no fair repartition of burthens upon all the orders could possibly restore them? If such an equal imposition would have been sufficient, you well know it might easily have been made. Mr. Necker,[N] in the budget which he laid before the Orders assembled at Versailles, made a detailed exposition of the state of the French nation.[xxvii,251]

> And, free from conscience is a slave to fame.
> Thus he the church at once protects and spoils:
> But princes' swords are sharper than their styles.
> And thus to th'ages past he makes amends,
> Their charity destroys, their faith defends.
> Then did religion in a lazy cell,
> In empty aëry contemplations dwell;
> And, like the block, unmoved he lay: but ours,
> As much too active, like the storm devours.
> Is there no temp'rate region can be known,
> Betwixt the frigid, and our torrid zone?
> Could we not wake from that lethargic dream,
> But to be restless in a worse extreme?
> And for that lethargy was there no cure,
> But to be cast into a calenture?
> Can knowledge have no bound, but must advance
> So far, to make us wish for ignorance?
> And rather in the dark to grope our way,
> Than, led by a false guide, to err by day?
> Who sees these dismal heaps, but would demand,
> What barbarous invader sack'd the land?
> But when he hears, no Goth, no Turk did bring
> This desolation but a Christian king;
> When nothing, but the name of zeal, appears
> 'Twixt our best actions, and the worst of theirs,
> What does he think our sacrilege would spare,
> When such th'effects of our Devotion are?'
> COOPER'S HILL, by Sir JOHN DENHAM.

xxvii   Rapport de Mons. Le Directeur general des finances, fait par ordre du Roi à Versailles. Mai 5, 1789.

251  'Report by the Director-general of Finances, made by order of the King at Versailles, 5 May 1789'. The opening of the title of the work Burke refers to is *Ouverture des États-Généraux . . .* (Paris, 1789).

If we give credit to him, it was not necessary to have recourse to any new impositions whatsoever, to put the receipts of France on a balance with its expences. He stated the permanent charges of all descriptions, including the interest of a new loan of four hundred millions, at 531,444,000 livres; the fixed revenue at 475,294,000, making the deficiency 56,150,000, or short of 2,200,000 sterling. But to balance it, he brought forward savings and improvements of revenue (considered as entirely certain) to rather more than the amount of that deficiency; and he concludes with these emphatical words (p. 39) 'Quel pays, Messieurs, que celui, ou, *sans impôts* et avec de simples objêts *inapperçus*, on peut faire disparoitre un deficit qui a fait tant de bruit en Europe.'[252] As to the re-imbursement, the sinking of debt, and the other great objects of public credit and political arrangement indicated in Mons. Necker's speech, no doubt could be entertained, but that a very moderate and proportioned assessment on the citizens without distinction would have provided for all of them to the fullest extent of their demand.

If this representation of Mons. Necker was false, then the assembly are in the highest degree culpable for having forced the king to accept as his minister, and since the king's deposition, for having employed as *their* minister, a man who had been capable of abusing so notoriously the confidence of his master and their own; in a matter too of the highest moment, and directly appertaining to his particular office. But if the representation was exact (as, having always, along with you, conceived a high degree of respect for Mr. Necker, I make no doubt it was) then what can be said in favour of those, who, instead of moderate, reasonable, and general contribution, have in cold blood, and impelled by no necessity, had recourse to a partial and cruel confiscation?

Was that contribution refused on a pretext of privilege, either on the part of the clergy or on that of the nobility? No certainly. As to the clergy, they even ran before the wishes of the third order. Previous to the meeting of the states, they had in all their instructions expressly directed their deputies to renounce every immunity, which put them upon a footing distinct from the condition of their fellow-subjects. In this renunciation the clergy were even more explicit than the nobility.

---

[252] 'In what country, Gentlemen, but this one, could one *without taxes*, and with merely *imperceptible* objects [of duty], get rid of a deficit which has made such an impact in Europe.'

But let us suppose that the deficiency had remained at the 56 millions, (or £. 2,200,000 sterling) as at first stated by Mr. Necker.<sup>N</sup> Let us allow that all the resources he opposed to that deficiency were impudent and groundless fictions; and that the assembly (or their lords of articles<sup>xxviii</sup> at the Jacobins<sup>N</sup>[253]) were from thence justified in laying the whole burthen of that deficiency on the clergy, – yet allowing all this, a necessity of £. 2,200,000 sterling will not support a confiscation to the amount of five millions. The imposition of £. 2,200,000 on the clergy, as partial, would have been oppressive and unjust, but it would not have been altogether ruinous to those on whom it was imposed; and therefore it would not have answered the real purpose of the managers.

Perhaps persons, unacquainted with the state of France, on hearing the clergy and the noblesse were privileged in point of taxation, may be led to imagine, that previous to the revolution these bodies had contributed nothing to the state. This is a great mistake. They certainly did not contribute equally with each other, nor either of them equally with the commons. They both however contributed largely. Neither nobility nor clergy enjoyed any exemption from the excise on consumable commodities, from duties of custom, or from any of the other numerous *indirect* impositions, which in France as well as here, make so very large a proportion of all payments to the public. The noblesse paid the capitation. They paid also a land-tax, called the twentieth penny, to the height sometimes of three, sometimes of four shillings in the pound; both of them *direct* impositions of no light nature, and no trivial produce. The clergy of the provinces annexed by conquest to France (which in extent make about an eighth part of the whole but in wealth a much larger proportion) paid likewise to the capitation and the twentieth penny, at the rate paid by the nobility. The clergy in the old provinces did not pay the capitation; but they had redeemed themselves at the expence of about 24 millions, or a little more than a million sterling. They were exempted from the twentieths; but then they made free gifts; they contracted debts for the

---

<sup>xxviii</sup>  In the constitution of Scotland during the Stuart reigns, a committee sat for preparing bills; and none could pass, but those previously approved by them. The committee was called lords of articles.

---

[253] *Lords of articles*: a legislative committee of the Scottish parliament abolished in 1690. Widely believed to comprise royal placemen and to have supplanted the legislature itself (although this is now disputed). Burke here sees it as epitomising the subversion of representative chambers and implies that the Jacobins<sup>N</sup> are controlling the activities of the Assembly.

state; and they were subject to some other charges, the whole computed at about a thirteenth part of their clear income. They ought to have paid annually about forty thousand pounds more, to put them on a par with the contribution of the nobility.

When the terrors of this tremendous proscription hung over the clergy, they made an offer of a contribution, through the archbishop of Aix, which, for its extravagance, ought not to have been accepted.[254] But it was evidently and obviously more advantageous to the public creditor, than any thing which could rationally be promised by the confiscation. Why was it not accepted? The reason is plain – There was no desire that the church should be brought to serve the state. The service of the state was made a pretext to destroy the church. [In their way to the destruction of the church they would not scruple to destroy their country: and they have destroyed it.] One great end in the project would have been defeated, if the plan of extortion had been adopted in lieu of the scheme of confiscation. The new landed interest connected with the new republic, and connected with it for its very being, could not have been created. This was [among] the reason[s] why that extravagant ransom was not accepted.[255]

The madness of the project of confiscation, on the plan that was first pretended, soon became apparent. To bring this unwieldly mass of landed property, enlarged by the confiscation of all the vast landed domain of the crown, at once into market, was obviously to defeat the profits proposed by the confiscation, by depreciating the value of those lands, and indeed of all the landed estates throughout France. Such a sudden diversion of all its circulating money from trade to land, must be an additional mischief. What step was taken? Did the assembly, on becoming sensible of the inevitable ill effects of their projected sale, revert to the offers of the clergy? No distress could oblige them to travel in a course which was disgraced by any appearance of justice. Giving over all hopes from a general immediate sale, another project seems to have succeeded. They proposed to take stock in exchange for the church lands. In that project great difficulties arose in equalizing the objects to be exchanged. Other obstacles also presented themselves, which threw them back again upon some project

---

[254] The offer was for a loan of 400 million *livres* if the Church were allowed to retain their estates and the income from tithes. The Archbishop had opposed the Civil Constitution of the Clergy and made this offer as a compromise. Burke wrote him a letter admiring his conduct (15 July 1791, *Corr.* vi, p. 293).

[255] Bracketed text absent from 1st edn.

of sale. The municipalities had taken an alarm. They would not hear of transferring the whole plunder of the kingdom to the stock-holders in Paris. Many of those municipalities had been (upon system) reduced to the most deplorable indigence. Money was no where to be seen. They were therefore led to the point that was so ardently desired. They panted for a currency of any kind which might revive their perishing industry. The municipalities were then to be admitted to a share in the spoil, which evidently rendered the first scheme (if ever it had been seriously entertained) altogether impracticable. Publick exigencies pressed upon all sides. The minister of finance reiterated his call for supply with a most urgent, anxious, and boding voice. Thus pressed on all sides, instead of the first plan of converting their bankers into bishops and abbots, instead of paying the old debt, they contracted a new debt, at 3 per cent. creating a new paper currency, founded on an eventual sale of the church lands. They issued this paper currency to satisfy in the first instance chiefly the demands made upon them by the *Bank of discount*,[256] the great machine, or paper-mill, of their fictitious wealth.

The spoil of the church was now become the only resource of all their operations in finance; the vital principle of all their politics; the sole security for the existence of their power. It was necessary by all, even the most violent means, to put every individual on the same bottom, and to bind the nation in one guilty interest to uphold this act, and the authority of those by whom it was done. In order to force the most reluctant into a participation of their pillage, they rendered their paper circulation compulsory in all payments. Those who consider the general tendency of their schemes to this one object as a centre; and a centre from which afterwards all their measures radiate, will not think that I dwell too long upon this part of the proceedings of the national assembly.[N]

To cut off all appearance of connection between the crown and publick justice, and to bring the whole under implicit obedience to the dictators in Paris, the old independent judicature of the parliaments, with all its merits, and all its faults, was wholly abolished.[257] Whilst the parliaments

---

[256] The *Caisse d'Escompte*[N] was a bank set up by Turgot, the finance minister in 1775. Burke may be referring here to the *Caisse de l'Extraordinaire*, which was set up to administer the controversial *assignat*[N] paper money established in decrees of 19 and 21 December 1789, and which was gradually to convert bills issued by the *Caisse d'Escompte* into *assignats* (Decree on *Assignats*, 17 April 1790, §11, *DocS*, p. 161).

[257] *Parliaments*: sometimes used by Burke for *parlements*.[N] They were abolished by the decree of 6 September 1790; their operation having been suspended in November 1789.

existed, it was evident that the people might some time or other come
to resort to them, and rally under the standard of their antient laws.
It became however a matter of consideration that the magistrates and
officers, in the courts now abolished, *had purchased their places* at a very
high rate, for which, as well as for the duty they performed, they received
but a very low return of interest. Simple confiscation is a boon only
for the clergy; – to the lawyers some appearances of equity are to be
observed; and they are to receive compensation to an immense amount.
Their compensation becomes part of the national debt, for the liquidation
of which there is the one exhaustless fund. The lawyers are to obtain their
compensation in the new church paper, which is to march with the new
principles of judicature and legislature. The dismissed magistrates are to
take their share of martyrdom with the ecclesiastics, or to receive their
own property from such a fund and in such a manner, as all those, who
have been seasoned with the antient principles of jurisprudence, and had
been the sworn guardians of property, must look upon with horror. Even
the clergy are to receive their miserable allowance out of the depreciated
paper which is stamped with the indelible character of sacrilege, and with
the symbols of their own ruin, or they must starve. So violent an outrage
upon credit, property, and liberty, as this compulsory paper currency,
has seldom been exhibited by the alliance of bankruptcy and tyranny, at
any time, or in any nation.

In the course of all these operations, at length comes out the grand
*arcanum*;[258] – that in reality, and in a fair sense, the lands of the church
(so far as any thing certain can be gathered from their proceedings) are
not to be sold at all. By the late resolutions of the national assembly[N], they
are indeed to be delivered to the highest bidder. But it is to be observed,
that *a certain portion only of the purchase money is to be laid down.* A period
of twelve years is to be given for the payment of the rest. The philosophic
purchasers are therefore, on payment of a sort of fine,[259] to be put instantly
into possession of the estate. It becomes in some respects a sort of gift to
them; to be held on the feudal tenure of zeal to the new establishment.
This project is evidently to let in a body of purchasers without money.
The consequence will be, that these purchasers, or rather grantees, will
pay, not only from the rents as they accrue, which might as well be

---

[258] *Arcanum*: something hidden, secret, mysterious and often of great power.
[259] *Fine*: not in the modern sense of a monetary penalty for wrongdoing, but in the old sense
of a fee paid on entering into ownership of a feudal possession.

received by the state, but from the spoil of the materials of buildings, from waste in woods, and from whatever money, by hands habituated to the gripings of usury, they can wring from the miserable peasant. He is to be delivered over to the mercenary and arbitrary discretion of men, who will be stimulated to every species of extortion by the growing demands on the growing profits of an estate held under the precarious settlement of a new political system.

When all the frauds, impostures, violences, rapines, burnings, murders, confiscations, compulsory paper currencies, and every description of tyranny and cruelty employed to bring about and to uphold this revolution, have their natural effect, that is, to shock the moral sentiments of all virtuous and sober minds, the abettors of this philosophic system immediately strain their throats in a declamation against the old monarchical government of France. When they have rendered that deposed power sufficiently black, they then proceed in argument, as if all those who disapprove of their new abuses, must of course be partizans of the old; that those who reprobate their crude and violent schemes of liberty ought to be treated as advocates for servitude. I admit that their necessities do compel them to this base and contemptible fraud. Nothing can reconcile men to their proceedings and projects but the supposition that there is no third option between them, and some tyranny as odious as can be furnished by the records of history, or by the invention of poets. This prattling of theirs hardly deserves the name of sophistry. It is nothing but plain impudence. Have these gentlemen never heard, in the whole circle of the worlds of theory and practice, of any thing between the despotism of the monarch and the despotism of the multitude? Have they never heard of a monarchy directed by laws, controlled and balanced by the great hereditary wealth and hereditary dignity of a nation; and both again controlled by a judicious check from the reason and feeling of the people at large acting by a suitable and permanent organ? Is it then impossible that a man may be found who, without criminal ill intention, or pitiable absurdity, shall prefer such a mixed and tempered government to either of the extremes; and who may repute that nation to be destitute of all wisdom and of all virtue, which, having in its choice to obtain such a government with ease, *or rather to confirm it when actually possessed*, thought proper to commit a thousand crimes, and to subject their country to a thousand evils, in order to avoid it? Is it then a truth so universally acknowledged, that a pure democracy is the only tolerable form into which human society can be thrown, that a man is not permitted to hesitate about its merits, without the suspicion of being a friend to tyranny, that is, of being a foe to mankind?

I do not know under what description to class the present ruling authority in France. It affects to be a pure democracy, though I think it in a direct train of becoming shortly a mischievous and ignoble oligarchy. But for the present I admit it to be a contrivance of the nature and effect of what it pretends to. I reprobate no form of government merely upon abstract principles. There may be situations in which the purely democratic form will become necessary. There may be some (very few, and very particularly circumstanced) where it would be clearly desireable. This I do not take to be the case of France, or of any other great country.[260] Until now, we have seen no examples of considerable democracies.[261] The antients were better acquainted with them. Not being wholly unread in the authors, who had seen the most of those constitutions, and who best understood them, I cannot help concurring with their opinion, that an absolute democracy, no more than absolute monarchy, is to be reckoned among the legitimate forms of government. They think it rather the corruption and degeneracy, than the sound constitution of a republic.[262] If I recollect rightly, Aristotle observes, that a democracy has many striking points of resemblance with a tyranny[xxix]. Of this I am certain, that in a democracy, the majority of

---

[xxix] When I wrote this I quoted from memory, after many years had elapsed from my reading the passage. A learned friend has found it, and it is as follows:

> τὸ ἦθος τὸ αὐτό, καὶ ἄμφω δεσποτικὰ τῶν βελτιόνων, καὶ τὰ ψηφίσματα, ὥσπερ ἐκεῖ τὰ ἐπιτάγματα· καὶ ὁ δημαγωγὸς καὶ ὁ κόλαξ, οἱ αὐτοὶ καὶ ἀνάλογον· καὶ μάλιστα ἑκάτεροι παρ᾽ ἑκατέροις ἰσχύουσιν, οἱ μὲν κόλακες παρὰ τυράννοις, οἱ δὲ δημαγωγοὶ παρὰ τοῖς δήμοις τοῖς τοιούτοις. –

> 'The ethical character is the same; both exercise despotism over the better class of citizens; and decrees are in the one, what ordinances and arrêts are in the other: the demagogue too, and the court favourite, are not unfrequently

---

[260] *Great* here meaning geographically extensive. Democracy (and republican government more generally) was considered only practicable for small states. See Montesquieu, *De l'Esprit des Lois*, Bk VII, ch. 16: 'It is of the nature of a republic that it should only have a small territory, without that it can hardly subsist.' The possibility of the Federated American states sustaining republican government had been intensely discussed in 1786.

[261] *Considerable*: again, meaning large. Democratic states were all city-state republics.

[262] Classical authors, following Aristotle, classified states according to two criteria: the number of the ruling body – the one, the few, the many – and according to whether that body ruled for the good of the whole or in its own sectional interest. Aristotle suggests that the respect for or departure from constitutional rules is a good proxy for the latter. Thus constitutional democracy would be a legitimate constitution but an unconstrained – here 'absolute' – democracy would be a form of tyranny – of the many poor, over the rest.

the citizens is capable of exercising the most cruel oppressions upon the minority, whenever strong divisions prevail in that kind of polity, as they often must; and that oppression of the minority will extend to far greater numbers, and will be carried on with much greater fury, than can almost ever be apprehended from the dominion of a single sceptre. In such a popular persecution, individual sufferers are in a much more deplorable condition than in any other. Under a cruel prince they have the balmy compassion of mankind to assuage the smart of their wounds; they have the plaudits of the people to animate their generous constancy under their sufferings: but those who are subjected to wrong under multitudes, are deprived of all external consolation. They seem deserted by mankind; overpowered by a conspiracy of their whole species.

But admitting democracy not to have that inevitable tendency to party tyranny, which I suppose it to have, and admitting it to possess as much good in it when unmixed, as I am sure it possesses when compounded with other forms; does monarchy, on its part, contain nothing at all to recommend it? I do not often quote Bolingbroke,[N] nor have his works in general, left any permanent impression on my mind.[263] He is a presumptuous and a superficial writer. But he has one observation, which, in my opinion, is not without depth and solidity. He says, that he prefers a monarchy to other governments; because you can better ingraft any description of republic on a monarchy than any thing of monarchy upon the republican forms.[264] I think him perfectly in the right. The fact is so historically; and it agrees well with the speculation.

I know how easy a topic it is to dwell on the faults of departed greatness. By a revolution in the state, the fawning sycophant of yesterday, is

the same identical men, and always bear a close analogy; and these have the principal power, each in their respective forms of government, favourites with the absolute monarch, and demagogues with the people such as I have described.' Arist. Politic. lib.iv. cap. 4.[265]

[263] Burke is here being more than slightly disingenuous. His first published work, *A Vindication of Natural Society* (1756), had been devoted to satirising Bolingbroke's sceptical philosophy.

[264] 'When monarchy is the essential form, it may be more easily and more usefully *tempered* with *aristocracy*, or *democracy*, or both, than either of them, when they are the essential forms, can be *tempered* with *monarchy*' (Bolingbroke, 'Idea of a Patriot King' [1749] in *Works*, ed. Mallet, vol. 3 (1754), pp. 51–2; and in *Bolingbroke's Political Writings*, ed. B. Cottret (Basingstoke and New York, 1997) (same pagination)).

[265] Evidently Burke's slightly free translation, although he possessed that by William Ellis (1774). The passage is at 1292a.

converted into the austere critic of the present hour. But steady independant minds, when they have an object of so serious a concern to mankind
as government, under their contemplation, will disdain to assume the part
of satirists and declaimers. They will judge of human institutions as they
do of human characters. They will sort out the good from the evil, which
is mixed in mortal institutions as it is in mortal men.

Your government in France, though usually, and I think justly, reputed
the best of the unqualified or ill-qualified monarchies, was still full of
abuses. These abuses accumulated in a length of time, as they must
accumulate in every monarchy not under the constant inspection of a
popular representative. I am no stranger to the faults and defects of
the subverted government of France; and I think I am not inclined by
nature or policy to make a panegyric upon any thing which is a just and
natural object of censure. But the question is not now of the vices of that
monarchy, but of its existence. Is it then true, that the French government
was such as to be incapable or undeserving of reform; so that it was of
absolute necessity the whole fabric should be at once pulled down, and
the area cleared for the erection of a theoretic experimental edifice in its
place?[266] All France was of a different opinion in the beginning of the
year 1789. The instructions to the representatives to the states-general,[N]
from every district in that kingdom, were filled with projects for the
reformation of that government, without the remotest suggestion of a
design to destroy it.[267] Had such a design been then even insinuated, I
believe there would have been but one voice, and that voice for rejecting
it with scorn and horror. Men have been sometimes led by degrees,
sometimes hurried into things, [of which, if they could have seen the
whole together,][268] they never would have permitted the most remote
approach. When those instructions were given, there was no question
but that abuses existed, and that they demanded a reform; nor is there

---

[266] One of the few major British replies to Burke to take this question seriously was James
Mackintosh's *Vindiciae Gallicae* (1791). He insisted the answer to Burke's questions was
'yes'.

[267] The local bodies electing to the Estates General also compiled instructions to their
representatives, known as the *Cahiers des Doléances*; these were published as *Résumé
général... des Cahiers de Pouvoirs, Instructions, Demandes et Doléances*, 3 vols., ed. L. M.
Proudhomme and F. S. Laurent de Mezières (Paris, 1789). This, or another compendium,
was sent by William Windham from Paris to Burke in September 1789 (Windham to
Burke, 15 Sept. 1789, *Corr.* vi, p. 21) and by January 1790 Burke refers to having read
them 'with some attention' (Burke to Unknown, Jan. 1790, *Corr.* v, p. 79).

[268] Replaces 'the whole of which, if they could have seen together' in 1st edn.

now. In the interval between the instructions and the revolution, things changed their shape; and in consequence of that change, the true question at present is, Whether those who would have reformed, or those who have destroyed, are in the right?

To hear some men speak of the late monarchy of France, you would imagine that they were talking of Persia bleeding under the ferocious sword of Tæhmas Kouli Khân;[269] or at least describing the barbarous anarchic despotism of Turkey, where the finest countries in the most genial climates in the world are wasted by peace more than any countries have been worried by war; where arts are unknown, where manufactures languish, where science is extinguished, where agriculture decays, where the human race itself melts away and perishes under the eye of the observer. Was this the case of France? I have no way of determining the question but by a reference to facts. Facts do not support this resemblance. Along with much evil, there is some good in monarchy itself; and some corrective to its evil, from religion, from laws, from manners, from opinions, the French monarchy must have received; which rendered it (though by no means a free, and therefore by no means a good constitution) a despotism rather in appearance than in reality.

Among the standards upon which the effects of government on any country are to be estimated, I must consider the state of its population as not the least certain. No country in which population flourishes, and is in progressive improvement, can be under a *very* mischievous government. About sixty years ago, the Intendants of the generalities of France made, with other matters, a report of the population of their several districts.[270] I have not the books, which are very voluminous, by me, nor do I know where to procure them (I am obliged to speak by memory, and therefore the less positively) but I think the population of France was by them, even at that period, estimated at twenty-two millions of souls. At the end of the last century it had been generally calculated at eighteen. On either of these estimations France was not ill-peopled. Mr. Necker[N] who

---

[269] *Tæhmas Kouli Khan*: Tahmasp Kuli Kan, alias Nadir Shah (1688–1747), Shah of Iran (1736–42), founder of Afsharid dynasty, the 'Napoleon of Persia', reunited Persia, expelled the Russians and Ottomans, and conquered modern Pakistan. In later life he became gratuitously cruel and paranoid and was eventually assassinated by his personal guard. He was well known in Europe, the English Oriental scholar Sir William Jones having translated a Persian-language biography of him into French, published in 1770 as *Histoire de Nadir Chah*.

[270] *Generality*: an administrative district of the *ancien régime* under the direction of an Intendant.

is an authority for his own time at least equal to the Intendants for theirs, reckons, and upon apparently sure principles, the people of France, in the year 1780, at twenty-four millions six hundred and seventy thousand. But was this the probable ultimate term under the old establishment? Dr. Price[N] is of opinion, that the growth of population in France was by no means at its *acmé* in that year. I certainly defer to Dr. Price's authority a good deal more in these speculations, than I do in his general politics.[271] This gentleman, taking ground on Mr. Necker's data, is very confident, that since the period of that minister's calculation, the French population has encreased rapidly; so rapidly that in the year 1789 he will not consent to rate the people of that kingdom at a lower number than thirty millions. After abating much (and much I think ought to be abated) from the sanguine calculation of Dr. Price, I have no doubt that the population of France did encrease considerably during this later period: but supposing that it encreased to nothing more than will be sufficient to compleat the 24,670,000 to 25 millions, still a population of 25 millions, and that in an encreasing progress, on a space of about twenty-seven thousand square leagues, is immense. It is, for instance, a good deal more than the proportional population of this island, or even than that of England, the best-peopled part of the united kingdom.

It is not universally true, that France is a fertile country. Considerable tracts of it are barren, and labour under other natural disadvantages. In the portions of that territory, where things are more favourable, as far as I am able to discover, the numbers of the people correspond to the indulgence of nature[xxx]. The Generality of Lisle (this I admit is the strongest example) upon an extent of 404½ leagues, about ten years ago, contained 734,600 souls, which is 1772 inhabitants to each square league. The middle term for the rest of France is about 900 inhabitants to the same admeasurement.

I do not attribute this population to the deposed government; because I do not like to compliment the contrivances of men, with what is due in a great degree to the bounty of Providence. But that decried government could not have obstructed, most probably it favoured, the operation of

[xxx] De l'Adminstration des Finances de la France, par Mons. Necker, vol. i. p. 288.[272]

[271] *Defer to Dr Price:* Price was an impressive statistician, as Burke here acknowledges. His work on the population of London was published in the *Philosophical Transactions* of the Royal Society, and his early actuarial tables formed the basis of modern life insurance.

[272] J. Necker, *De l'Administration des Finances de la France* ['On the administration of the French finances'], 3 vols. (Paris, 1988).

those causes (whatever they were) whether of nature in the soil, or in habits of industry among the people, which has produced so large a number of the species throughout that whole kingdom, and exhibited in some particular places such prodigies of population. I never will suppose that fabrick of a state to be the worst of all political institutions, which, by experience, is found to contain a principle favourable (however latent it may be) to the encrease of mankind.

The wealth of a country is another, and no contemptible standard, by which we may judge whether, on the whole, a government be protecting or destructive. France far exceeds England in the multitude of her people; but I apprehend that her comparative wealth is much inferior to ours; that it is not so equal in the distribution, nor so ready in the circulation. I believe the difference in the form of the two governments to be amongst the causes of this advantage on the side of England. I speak of England, not of the whole British dominions; which, if compared with those of France, will, in some degree, weaken the comparative rate of wealth upon our side. But that wealth, which will not endure a comparison with the riches of England, may constitute a very respectable degree of opulence. Mr. Necker's book published in 1785,[xxxi] contains an accurate and interesting collection of facts relative to public œconomy and to political arithmetic; and his speculations on the subject are in general wise and liberal. In that work he gives an idea of the state of France, very remote from the portrait of a country whose government was a perfect grievance, an absolute evil, admitting no cure but through the violent and uncertain remedy of a total revolution. He affirms, that from the year 1726 to the year 1784, there was coined at the mint of France, in the species of gold and silver, to the amount of about one hundred millions of pounds sterling.[xxxii]

It is impossible that Mr. Necker should be mistaken in the amount of the bullion which has been coined in the mint. It is a matter of official record. The reasonings of this able financier, concerning the quantity of gold and silver which remained for circulation, when he wrote in 1785, that is about four years before the deposition and imprisonment of the French King, are not of equal certainty; but they are laid on grounds so apparently solid, that it is not easy to refuse a considerable degree of assent to his calculation. He calculates the *numéraire*, or what we call *specie*, then actually existing in France, at about eighty-eight millions of the same English money. A great accumulation of wealth for one country, large

---

xxxi   De L'Administration des Finances de la France, par M. Necker.
xxxii  Vol. iii. chap. 8. and chap. 9.

as that country is! Mr. Necker was so far from considering this influx of
wealth as likely to cease, when he wrote in 1785, that he presumes upon
a future annual increase of two per cent. upon the money brought into
France during the periods from which he computed.

Some adequate cause must have originally introduced all the money
coined at its mint into that kingdom; and some cause as operative must
have kept at home, or returned into its bosom, such a vast flood of treasure
as Mr. Necker calculates to remain for domestic circulation. Suppose any
reasonable deductions from Mr. Necker's computation: the remainder
must still amount to an immense sum. Causes thus powerful to acquire and
to retain, cannot be found in discouraged industry, insecure property, and
a positively destructive government. Indeed, when I consider the face of
the kingdom of France; the multitude and opulence of her cities; the useful
magnificence of her spacious high roads and bridges; the opportunity of
her artificial canals and navigations opening the conveniences of maritime
communication through a solid continent of so immense an extent;[273]
when I turn my eyes to the stupendous works of her ports and harbours,
and to her whole naval apparatus, whether for war or trade; when I bring
before my view the number of her fortifications, constructed with so bold
and masterly a skill, and made and maintained at so prodigious a charge,
presenting an armed front and impenetrable barrier to her enemies upon
every side; when I recollect how very small a part of that extensive region
is without cultivation, and to what complete perfection the culture of
many of the best productions of the earth have been brought in France;
when I reflect on the excellence of her manufactures and fabrics, second
to none but ours, and in some particulars not second; when I contemplate the grand foundations of charity, public and private; when I survey
the state of all the arts that beautify and polish life; when I reckon the
men she has bred for extending her fame in war, her able statesmen, the
multitude of her profound lawyers and theologians, her philosophers, her
critics, her historians and antiquaries, her poets, and her orators sacred
and profane, I behold in all this something which awes and commands the
imagination, which checks the mind on the brink of precipitate and indis-
criminate censure, and which demands, that we should very seriously
examine, what and how great are the latent vices that could authorise us

[273] *Maritime communication through a solid continent*: Under Louis XIV's[N] minister Colbert,
Pierre-Paul Ricquet constructed a canal – *Le canal royale de Languedoc*, now the *Canal
du Midi* – from the river Garonne at Narbonne to Toulouse, thereby connecting the
Atlantic to the Mediterranean.

at once to level so spacious a fabric with the ground. I do not recognize, in this view of things, the despotism of Turkey. Nor do I discern the character of a government, that has been, on the whole, so oppressive, or so corrupt, or so negligent, as to be utterly unfit *for all reformation.* I must think such a government well deserved to have its excellencies heightened; its faults corrected; and its capacities improved into a British constitution.

Whoever has examined into the proceedings of that deposed government for several years back, cannot fail to have observed, amidst the inconstancy and fluctuation natural to courts, an earnest endeavour towards the prosperity and improvement of the country; he must admit, that it had long been employed, in some instances, wholly to remove, in many considerably to correct, the abusive practices and usages that had prevailed in the state; and that even the unlimited power of the sovereign over the persons of his subjects, inconsistent, as undoubtedly it was, with law and liberty, had yet been every day growing more mitigated in the exercise. So far from refusing itself to reformation, that government was open, with a censurable degree of facility, to all sorts of projects and projectors on the subject. Rather too much countenance was given to the spirit of innovation, which soon was turned against those who fostered it, and ended in their ruin. It is but cold, and no very flattering justice to that fallen monarchy, to say, that, for many years, it trespassed more by levity and want of judgment in several of its schemes, than from any defect in diligence or in public spirit. To compare the government of France for the last fifteen or sixteen years with wise and well-constituted establishments, during that, or during any period, is not to act with fairness. But if in point of prodigality in the expenditure of money, or in point of rigour in the exercise of power, it be compared with any of the former reigns, I believe candid judges will give little credit to the good intentions of those who dwell perpetually on the donations to favourites, or on the expences of the court, or on the horrors of the Bastile in the reign of Louis the XVIth[xxxiii].

---

[xxxiii] [The world is obliged to Mr. de Calonne[N] for the pains he has taken to refute the scandalous exaggerations relative to some of the royal expences, and to detect the fallacious account given of pensions, for the wicked purpose of provoking the populace to all sorts of crimes.][274]

---

[274] Footnote absent from 1st edn. The contents of the *Livre Rouge*, an account book of secret expenditures of the French King, had been published by a committee of the Constituent Assembly and used by critics to discredit the monarchy. Calonne had written a defence.

Whether the system, if it deserves such a name, now built on the ruins of that antient monarchy, will be able to give a better account of the population and wealth of the country, which it has taken under its care, is a matter very doubtful. Instead of improving by the change, I apprehend that a long series of years must be told before it can recover in any degree the effects of this philosophic revolution, and before the nation can be replaced on its former footing. If Dr. Price[N] should think fit, a few years hence, to favour us with an estimate of the population of France, he will hardly be able to make up his tale of thirty millions of souls, as computed in 1789, or the assembly's computation of twenty-six millions of that year; or even Mr. Necker's twenty-five millions in 1780. I hear that there are considerable emigrations from France; and that many, quitting that voluptuous climate, and that seductive *Circean* liberty,[275] have taken refuge in the frozen regions, and under the British despotism, of Canada.

In the present disappearance of coin, no person could think it the same country, in which the present minister of the finances has been able to discover fourscore millions sterling in specie. From its general aspect one would conclude that it had been for some time past under the special direction of the learned academicians of Laputa and Balnibarbi[xxxiv].[276] Already the population of Paris has so declined, that Mr. Necker[N] stated to the national assembly the provision to be made for its subsistence at a fifth less than what had formerly been found requisite[xxxv]. It is said (and I have never heard it contradicted) that an hundred thousand people are out of employment in that city, though it is become the seat of the imprisoned

---

[xxxiv]  See Gulliver's Travels for the idea of countries governed by philosophers.
[xxxv]  Mr. de Calonne states the falling off of the population of Paris as far more considerable; and it may be so, since the period of Mr. Necker's calculation.

[275]  *Circean*: pertaining to *Circe*, the mythical enchantress who, in Homer's epic, bewitched Odysseus' companions into staying on her island and turned them into pigs. Burke is being ironic: *Circean* liberty is no liberty at all.
[276]  *Laputa and Balnibarbi*: two countries visited by Gulliver in his famous travels. There the 'professors contrive new rules and methods of agriculture and building, and new instruments, and tools for all trades and manufactures; whereby, as they undertake, one man shall do the work of ten; a palace may be built in a week, of materials so durable as to last for ever without repairing. All the fruits of the earth shall come to maturity at whatever season we think fit to choose, and increase a hundred fold more than they do at present; with innumerable other happy proposals. The only inconvenience is, that none of these projects are yet brought to perfection; and in the mean time, the whole country lies miserably waste, the houses in ruins, and the people without food or clothes' (Jonathan Swift, *Gulliver's Travels*; pt. III: *A Voyage to Laputa, Balnibarbi etc.*, 1726 ch. 4).

court and national assembly.<sup>N</sup> Nothing, I am credibly informed, can exceed the shocking and disgusting spectacle of mendicancy displayed in that capital. Indeed, the votes of the national assembly leave no doubt of the fact. They have lately appointed a standing committee of mendicancy. They are contriving at once a vigorous police on this subject, and, for the first time, the imposition of a tax to maintain the poor, for whose present relief great sums appear on the face of the public accounts of the year[xxxvi] . In the mean time, the leaders of the legislative clubs and coffee-houses are intoxicated with admiration at their own wisdom and ability. They speak with the most sovereign contempt of the rest of the world. They tell the people, to comfort them in the rags with which they have cloathed them,

| [xxxvi] Travaux de charité pour subvenir au | Liv. | | $\pounds$. | s. | d |
|---|---|---|---|---|---|
| manque de travail à Paris et dans les provinces | 3,886,920 | Stg | 161,121 | 13 | 4 |
| Destruction de vagbondage et de la mendicité | 1,671,417 | – | 69,642 | 7 | 6 |
| Primes pour l'importation de grains | 5,671,907 | – | 236,329 | 9 | 2[277] |
| Dépenses relatives aux subsistances, deduction | 39,871,790 | – | 1,661,324 | 11 | 8 |
| fait des récouveremens qui ont eu lieu[278] | | | | | |
| Total – Liv. | 51,082,034 | Stg | 2,128,418 | 1 | 8 |

[When I sent this book to the press I entertained some doubt concerning the nature and extent of the last article in the above accounts, which is only under a general head, without any detail. Since then I have seen M. de Calonne's work. I must think it a great loss to me that I had not that advantage earlier. Mr de Calonne thinks this article to be on account of general subsistence: but as he is not able to comprehend how so great a loss as upwards of $\pounds$.1,661,000 sterling could be sustained on the difference between the price and sale of grain, he seems to attribute this enormous head of charge to secret expenses of the revolution. I cannot say any thing positively on that subject. The reader is capable of judging, by the aggregate of these immense charges, on the state and condition of France; and the system of public œconomy adopted in that nation. These articles of account produced no enquiry or discussion in the National Assembly.][279]

---

[277] In the first edition Burke inserted a line of subtotals at this point, followed by a remark, followed, as here, by the next heading, 'Dépenses relatives', which he later removed. The removed text reads:

    Liv        11,210,244         Stg      467,093     10    0

    As I am not quite satisfied with the nature and extent of the annexed article in the public accounts, I do not insert it in the above reference; but if it be understood of the purchase of provisions for the poor, it is immense indeed, and swells the total to a formidable bulk.

[278] Headings for the expenditures read:

Works of charity to make up for the lack of work in Paris and the Provinces
Eradication of vagabondage and begging
Subsidies for the importation of grain
Expenditure related to subsistence, deduction made for recovery that had taken place.

[279] Absent from 1st edn.

that they are a nation of philosophers; and, sometimes, by all the arts of quackish parade, by shew, tumult, and bustle, sometimes by the alarms of plots and invasions, they attempt to drown the cries of indigence, and to divert the eyes of the observer from the ruin and wretchedness of the state. A brave people will certainly prefer liberty, accompanied with a virtuous poverty, to a depraved and wealthy servitude. But before the price of comfort and opulence is paid, one ought to be pretty sure it is real liberty which is purchased, and that she is to be purchased at no other price. I shall always, however, consider that liberty as very equivocal in her appearance, which has not wisdom and justice for her companions; and does not lead prosperity and plenty in her train.

The advocates for this revolution, not satisfied with exaggerating the vices of their antient government, strike at the fame of their country itself, by painting almost all that could have attracted the attention of strangers, I mean their nobility and their clergy, as objects of horror. If this were only a libel, there had not been much in it. But it has practical consequences. Had your nobility and gentry, who formed the great body of your landed men, and the whole of your military officers, resembled those of Germany, at the period when the Hanse-towns[280] were necessitated to confederate against the nobles in defence of their property – had they been like the *Orsini* and *Vitelli* in Italy,[281] who used to sally from their fortified dens to rob the trader and traveller – had they been such as the *Mamalukes* in Egypt, or the *Nayrs* on the coast of Malabar,[282] I do admit, that too critical an enquiry might not be adviseable into the means of freeing the world from such a nuisance. The statues of Equity and Mercy might be veiled for a moment. The tenderest minds, confounded with the dreadful exigence in which morality submits to the suspension of its own

---

[280] *Hanse-town*s: towns on the Baltic and North Seas belonging to the Hanseatic League, a medieval trading and – in the case of German free cities – defence association.

[281] *Orsini*: a prominent Roman family that provided many Popes. In the turbulent conditions of Renaissance Italy such powerful families often operated without any legal constraints and Burke refers to the propensity of such families to engage in feuds, fighting from the safety of their own castles.
  *Vitelli*: the brothers Vitellozzo and Paolo Vitelli were famous *condottieri* - mercenary soldiers – in the fifteenth-century power struggles of central Italy.

[282] *Mamalukes* were warrior-slaves imported from outside their domains by Muslim rulers to avoid reliance on local lords. In Egypt those imported by Saladin's descendants had seized power in their own right and had ruled there since the thirteenth century, latterly under the Turkish Sultan.
  *Nayrs* (Nayar): a warrior caste of Kerala, southern India, known since antiquity for their ferocity.

rules in favour of its own principles, might turn aside whilst fraud and violence were accomplishing the destruction of a pretended nobility which disgraced whilst it persecuted human nature. The persons most abhorrent from blood, and treason, and arbitrary confiscation, might remain silent spectators of this civil war between the vices.

But did the privileged nobility who met under the king's precept at Versailles, in 1789, or their constituents, deserve to be looked on as the *Nayres* or *Mamalukes* of this age, or as the *Orsini* and *Vitelli* of ancient times? If I had then asked the question, I should have passed for a madman. What have they since done that they were to be driven into exile, that their persons should be hunted about, mangled, and tortured, their families dispersed, their houses laid in ashes, that their order should be abolished, and the memory of it, if possible, extinguished, by ordaining them to change the very names by which they were usually known? Read their instructions to their representatives. They breathe the spirit of liberty as warmly, and they recommend reformation as strongly, as any other order. Their privileges relative to contribution were voluntarily surrendered; as the king, from the beginning, surrendered all pretence to a right of taxation. Upon a free constitution there was but one opinion in France. The absolute monarchy was at an end. It breathed its last, without a groan, without struggle, without convulsion. All the struggle, all the dissension arose afterwards upon the preference of a despotic democracy to a government of reciprocal controul. The triumph of the victorious party was over the principles of a British constitution.[283]

I have observed the affectation, which, for many years past, has prevailed in Paris even to a degree perfectly childish, of idolizing the memory of your Henry the Fourth.[N] If any thing could put one out of humour with that ornament to the kingly character, it would be this overdone style of insidious panegyric. The persons who have worked this engine the most busily, are those who have ended their panegyrics in dethroning his successor and descendant; a man, as good-natured at the least, as Henry the Fourth; altogether as fond of his people; and who has done infinitely more to correct the antient vices of the state than that great monarch did, or we are sure he ever meant to do. Well it is for his panegyrists that they

---

[283] *All the struggle . . . arose afterwards*: Burke's claim is that the acceptance of a constitutional monarchy on the English model was agreed on all sides from the very start of the Estates General;[N] subsequent criticism was therefore motivated by a desire to institute an 'absolute democracy'. This insistence is directed to those of his English audience, who still saw in the French Revolution an attempt to emulate the Revolution of 1688.[N]

have not him to deal with. For Henry of Navarre was a resolute, active, and politic prince. He possessed indeed great humanity and mildness; but an humanity and mildness that never stood in the way of his interests. He never sought to be loved without putting himself first in a condition to be feared.[284] He used soft language with determined conduct. He asserted and maintained his authority in the gross, and distributed his acts of concession only in the detail. He spent the income of his prerogatives nobly; but he took care not to break in upon the capital; never abandoning for a moment any of the claims, which he made under the fundamental laws, nor sparing to shed the blood of those who opposed him, often in the field, sometimes upon the scaffold. Because he knew how to make his virtues respected by the ungrateful, he has merited the praises of those whom, if they had lived in his time, he would have shut up in the Bastile, and brought to punishment along with the regicides whom he hanged after he had famished Paris into a surrender.

If these panegyrists are in earnest in their admiration of Henry the Fourth[N], they must remember, that they cannot think more highly of him, than he did of the noblesse of France; whose virtue, honour, courage, patriotism, and loyalty were his constant theme.

But the nobility of France are degenerated since the days of Henry the Fourth. – This is possible. But it is more than I can believe to be true in any great degree. I do not pretend to know France as correctly as some others; but I have endeavoured through my whole life to make myself acquainted with human nature: otherwise I should be unfit to take even my humble part in the service of mankind. In that study I could not pass by a vast portion of our nature, as it appeared modified in a country but twenty-four miles from the shore of this island. On my best observation, compared with my best enquiries, I found your nobility for the greater part composed of men of an high spirit, and of a delicate sense of honour, both with regard to themselves individually, and with regard to their whole corps, over whom they kept, beyond what is common in other countries, a censorial eye. They were tolerably well bred; very officious, humane, and hospitable; in their conversation frank and open; with a good military tone; and reasonably tinctured with literature, particularly of the authors in their own language. Many had pretensions far above this description. I speak of those who were generally met with.

[284] *Loved . . . feared*: an echo of Machiavelli's advice to a ruler that if one has to choose between the two 'it is much safer to be feared than loved' (Machiavelli, *The Prince*, ed. Skinner and Price (Cambridge, 1988), ch. 17, p. 59).

As to their behaviour to the inferior classes, they appeared to me to comport themselves towards them with good-nature, and with something more nearly approaching to familiarity, than is generally practised with us in the intercourse between the higher and lower ranks of life. To strike any person, even in the most abject condition, was a thing in a manner unknown, and would be highly disgraceful. Instances of other ill-treatment of the humble part of the community were rare; and as to attacks made upon the property or the personal liberty of the commons, I never heard of any whatsoever from *them*; nor, whilst the laws were in vigour under the antient government, would such tyranny in subjects have been permitted. As men of landed estates, I had no fault to find with their conduct, though much to reprehend, and much to wish changed, in many of the old tenures. Where the letting of their land was by rent, I could not discover that their agreements with their farmers were oppressive; nor when they were in partnership with the farmer, as often was the case, have I heard that they had taken the lion's share. The proportions seemed not inequitable. There might be exceptions; but certainly they were exceptions only. I have no reason to believe that in these respects the landed noblesse of France were worse than the landed gentry of this country; certainly in no respect more vexatious than the landholders, not noble, of their own nation. In cities the nobility had no manner of power; in the country very little. You know, Sir, that much of the civil government, and the police in the most essential parts, was not in the hands of that nobility which presents itself first to our consideration. The revenue, the system and collection of which were the most grievous parts of the French Government, was not administered by the men of the sword; nor were they answerable for the vices of its principle, or the vexations, where any such existed, in its management.

Denying, as I am well warranted to do, that the nobility had any considerable share in the oppression of the people, in cases in which real oppression existed, I am ready to admit that they were not without considerable faults and errors. A foolish imitation of the worst part of the manners of England, which impaired their natural character without substituting in its place what perhaps they meant [to copy][285], has certainly rendered them worse than formerly they were. Habitual dissoluteness of manners continued beyond the pardonable period of life, was more common amongst them than it is with us; and it reigned with the less hope

[285] Absent from 1st edn.

of remedy, though possibly with something of less mischief, by being covered with more exterior decorum. They countenanced too much that licentious philosophy which has helped to bring on their ruin. There was another error amongst them more fatal. Those of the commons, who approached to or exceeded many of the nobility in point of wealth, were not fully admitted to the rank and estimation which wealth, in reason and good policy, ought to bestow in every country; though I think not equally with that of other nobility. The two kinds of aristocracy[286] were too punctiliously kept asunder; less so, however, than in Germany and some other nations.[287]

This separation, as I have already taken the liberty of suggesting to you, I conceive to be one principal cause of the destruction of the old nobility. The military, particularly, was too exclusively reserved for men of family. But after all, this was an error of opinion, which a conflicting opinion would have rectified. A permanent assembly, in which the commons had their share of power, would soon abolish whatever was too invidious and insulting in these distinctions; and even the faults in the morals of the nobility would have been probably corrected by the greater varieties of occupation and pursuit to which a constitution by orders would have given rise.

All this violent cry against the nobility I take to be a mere work of art. To be honoured and even privileged by the laws, opinions, and inveterate usages of our country, growing out of the prejudice of ages, has nothing to provoke horror and indignation in any man. Even to be too tenacious of those privileges, is not absolutely a crime. The strong struggle in every individual to preserve possession of what he has found to belong to him and to distinguish him, is one of the securities against injustice and despotism implanted in our nature. It operates as an instinct to secure property, and to preserve communities in a settled state. What is there to shock in this? Nobility is a graceful ornament to the civil order. It is the Corinthian capital[288] of polished society. *Omnes boni nobilitati semper favemus*, was the saying of a wise and good man.[289] It is indeed one sign of a liberal and benevolent mind to incline to it with some sort of

---

[286] *Two kinds of aristocracy*: the aristocracy of birth and the aristocracy of wealth.

[287] No paragraph break in 1st edn.

[288] *Corinthian capital*: The Corinthian had the most elaborately decorated capital (top) of the three orders of columns in classical architecture: Doric, Ionic and Corinthian.

[289] *Wise and good man*: Cicero: 'we good men always support those nobly born' (*Pro Sestio* 9.21).

partial propensity. He feels no ennobling principle in his own heart who wishes to level all the artificial institutions which have been adopted for giving a body to opinion, and permanence to fugitive esteem. It is a sour, malignant, envious disposition, without taste for the reality, or for any image or representation of virtue, that sees with joy the unmerited fall of what had long flourished in splendour and in honour. I do not like to see any thing destroyed; any void produced in society; any ruin on the face of the land. It was therefore with no disappointment or dissatisfaction that my enquiries and observation did not present to me any incorrigible vices in the noblesse of France, or any abuse which could not be removed by a reform very short of abolition. Your noblesse did not deserve punishment; but to degrade is to punish.

It was with the same satisfaction I found that the result of my enquiry concerning your clergy was not dissimilar. It is no soothing news to my ears, that great bodies of men are incurably corrupt. It is not with much credulity I listen to any, when they speak evil of those whom they are going to plunder. I rather suspect that vices are feigned or exaggerated, when profit is looked for in their punishment. An enemy is a bad witness: a robber is a worse. Vices and abuses there were undoubtedly in that order, and must be. It was an old establishment, and not frequently revised. But I saw no crimes in the individuals that merited confiscation of their substance, nor those cruel insults and degradations, and that unnatural persecution which has been substituted in the place of meliorating regulation.

If there had been any just cause for this new religious persecution, the atheistic libellers, who act as trumpeters to animate the populace to plunder, do not love any body so much as not to dwell with complacence on the vices of the existing clergy. This they have not done. They find themselves obliged to rake into the histories of former ages (which they have ransacked with a malignant and profligate industry) for every instance of oppression and persecution which has been made by that body or in its favour, in order to justify, upon very iniquitous, because very illogical principles of retaliation, their own persecutions, and their own cruelties. After destroying all other genealogies and family distinctions, they invent a sort of pedigree of crimes. It is not very just to chastise men for the offences of their natural ancestors; but to take the fiction of ancestry in a corporate succession, as a ground for punishing men who have no relation to guilty acts, except in names and general descriptions, is a sort of refinement in injustice belonging to the philosophy of this enlightened age. The assembly punishes men, many, if not most, of whom abhor the violent conduct of ecclesiastics in former times as much as their present persecutors can do, and who would be as loud and as strong in the expression of that sense, if they were not well aware of the purposes for which all this declamation is employed.

Corporate bodies are immortal for the good of the members, but not for their punishment. Nations themselves are such corporations. As well might we in England think of waging inexpiable war upon all Frenchmen for the evils which they have brought upon us in the several periods of our mutual hostilities. You might, on your part, think yourselves justified in falling upon all Englishmen on account of the unparalleled calamities brought upon the people of France by the unjust invasions of our Henries and our Edwards. Indeed we should be mutually justified in this exterminatory war upon each other, full as much as you are in the unprovoked persecution of your present countrymen, on account of the conduct of men of the same name in other times.

We do not draw the moral lessons we might from history. On the contrary, without care it may be used to vitiate our minds and to destroy our happiness. In history a great volume is unrolled for our instruction, drawing the materials of future wisdom from the past errors and infirmities of mankind. It may, in the perversion, serve for a magazine, furnishing offensive and defensive weapons for parties in church and state, and supply the means of keeping alive, or reviving dissensions and animosities, and adding fuel to civil fury. History consists, for the greater part, of the miseries brought upon the world by pride, ambition, avarice, revenge, lust, sedition, hypocrisy, ungoverned zeal, and all the train of disorderly appetites, which shake the public with the same

> '————troublous storms that toss
> The private state, and render life unsweet.'[290]

These vices are the *causes* of those storms. Religion, morals, laws, prerogatives, privileges, liberties, rights of men, are the *pretexts*. The pretexts are always found in some specious appearance of a real good. You would not secure men from tyranny and sedition, by rooting out of the mind the principles to which these fraudulent pretexts apply? If you did, you would root out every thing that is valuable in the human breast. As these are the pretexts, so the ordinary actors and instruments in great public

[290] Edmund Spenser, *The Faerie Queen* (1590), Bk II, canto vii, xiv, p. 275.

evils are kings, priests, magistrates, senates, parliaments, national assemblies, judges, and captains. You would not cure the evil by resolving,
that there should be no more monarchs, nor ministers of state, nor of
the gospel; no interpreters of law; no general officers; no public councils.
You might change the names. The things in some shape must remain. A
certain *quantum* of power must always exist in the community, in some
hands, and under some appellation. Wise men will apply their remedies to
vices, not to names; to the causes of evil which are permanent, not to the
occasional organs by which they act, and the transitory modes in which
they appear. Otherwise you will be wise historically, a fool in practice.
Seldom have two ages the same fashion in their pretexts and the same
modes of mischief. Wickedness is a little more inventive. Whilst you are
discussing fashion, the fashion is gone by. The very same vice assumes
a new body. The spirit transmigrates; and, far from losing its principle
of life by the change of its appearance, it is renovated in its new organs
with the fresh vigour of a juvenile activity. It walks abroad; it continues
its ravages; whilst you are gibbeting the carcass, or demolishing the tomb.
You are terrifying yourself with ghosts and apparitions, whilst your house
is the haunt of robbers. It is thus with all those, who, attending only to
the shell and husk of history, think they are waging war with intolerance,
pride, and cruelty, whilst, under colour of abhorring the ill principles of
antiquated parties, they are authorizing and feeding the same odious vices
in different factions, and perhaps in worse.

Your citizens of Paris formerly had lent themselves as the ready instruments to slaughter the followers of Calvin, at the infamous massacre of
St. Bartholomew.[N] What should we say to those who could think of retal-
iating on the Parisians of this day the abominations and horrors of that
time? They are indeed brought to abhor *that* massacre. Ferocious as they
are, it is not difficult to make them dislike it; because the politicians and
fashionable teachers have no interest in giving their passions exactly the
same direction. Still however they find it their interest to keep the same
savage dispositions alive. It was but the other day that they caused this
very massacre to be acted on the stage for the diversion of the descendants
of those who committed it. In this tragic farce they produced the Cardinal
of Lorraine[N] in his robes of function, ordering general slaughter. Was
this spectacle intended to make the Parisians abhor persecution, and loath
the effusion of blood? – No, it was to teach them to persecute their own
pastors; it was to excite them, by raising a disgust and horror of their
clergy, to an alacrity in hunting down to destruction an order, which, if it

ought to exist at all, ought to exist not only in safety, but in reverence. It was to stimulate their cannibal appetites (which one would think had been gorged sufficiently) by variety and seasoning; and to quicken them to an alertness in new murders and massacres, if it should suit the purpose of the Guises[N] of the day. An assembly, in which sat a multitude of priests and prelates, was obliged to suffer this indignity at its door. The author was not sent to the gallies, nor the players to the house of correction. Not long after this exhibition, those players came forward to the assembly to claim the rites of that very religion which they had dared to expose, and to shew their prostituted faces in the senate, whilst the archbishop of Paris, whose function was known to his people only by his prayers and benedictions, and his wealth only by his alms, is forced to abandon his house, and to fly from his flock (as from ravenous wolves) because, truly, in the sixteenth century, the Cardinal of Lorraine[N] was a rebel and a murderer[xxxvii].

Such is the effect of the perversion of history, by those, who, for the same nefarious purposes, have perverted every other part of learning. But those who will stand upon that elevation of reason, which places centuries under our eye, and brings things to the true point of comparison, which obscures little names, and effaces the colours of little parties, and to which nothing can ascend but the spirit and moral quality of human actions, will say to the teachers of the Palais Royal, – the Cardinal of Lorraine[N] was the murderer of the sixteenth century, you have the glory of being the murderers in the eighteenth; and this is the only difference between you. But history, in the nineteenth century, better understood, and better employed, will, I trust, teach a civilized posterity to abhor the misdeeds of both these barbarous ages. It will teach future priests and magistrates not to retaliate upon the speculative and inactive atheists of future times, the enormities committed by the present practical zealots and furious fanatics of that wretched error, which, in its quiescent state, is more than punished, whenever it is embraced. It will teach posterity not to make war upon either religion or philosophy, for the abuse which the hypocrites of both have made of the two most valuable blessings conferred upon us by the bounty of the universal Patron, who in all things eminently favours and protects the race of man.

---

[xxxvii] [This is on a supposition of the truth of this story; but he was not in France at the time. One name serves as well as another.][291]

---

[291] Footnote added from 1803 edn.

If your clergy, or any clergy, should shew themselves vicious beyond the fair bounds allowed to human infirmity, and to those professional faults which can hardly be separated from professional virtues, though their vices never can countenance the exercise of oppression, I do admit, that they would naturally have the effect of abating very much of our indignation against the tyrants who exceed measure and justice in their punishment. I can allow in clergymen, through all their divisions, some tenaciousness of their own opinion; some overflowings of zeal for its prop-agation; some predilection to their own state and office; some attachment to the interest of their own corps; some preference to those who listen with docility to their doctrines, beyond those who scorn and deride them. I allow all this, because I am a man who have to deal with men, and who would not, through a violence of toleration, run into the greatest of all intolerance. I must bear with infirmities until they fester into crimes.

Undoubtedly, the natural progress of the passions, from frailty to vice, ought to be prevented by a watchful eye and a firm hand. But is it true that the body of your clergy had past those limits of a just allowance? From the general style of your late publications of all sorts, one would be led to believe that your clergy in France were a sort of monsters; an horrible composition of superstition, ignorance, sloth, fraud, avarice, and tyranny. But is this true? Is it true, that the lapse of time, the cessation of conflicting interests, the woeful experience of the evils resulting from party rage, have had no sort of influence gradually to meliorate their minds? Is it true, that they were daily renewing invasions on the civil power, troubling the domestic quiet of their country, and rendering the operations of its government feeble and precarious? Is it true, that the clergy of our times have pressed down the laity with an iron hand, and were in all places, lighting up the fires of a savage persecution? Did they by every fraud endeavour to encrease their estates? Did they use to exceed the due demands on estates that were their own? Or, rigidly screwing up right into wrong, did they convert a legal claim into a vexatious extortion? When not possessed of power, were they filled with the vices of those who envy it? Were they enflamed with a violent litigious spirit of controversy? Goaded on with the ambition of intellectual sovereignty, were they ready to fly in the face of all magistracy, to fire churches, to massacre the priests of other descriptions, to pull down altars, and to make their way over the ruins of subverted governments to an empire of doctrine, sometimes flattering, sometimes forcing the consciences of men from the jurisdiction of public institutions into a submission to their personal authority, beginning with a claim of liberty and ending with an abuse of power?

These, or some of these, were the vices objected, and not wholly without foundation, to several of the churchmen of former times, who belonged to the two great parties which then divided and distracted Europe.[292]

If there was in France, as in other countries there visibly is, a great abatement, rather than any increase of these vices, instead of loading the present clergy with the crimes of other men, and the odious character of other times, in common equity they ought to be praised, encouraged, and supported, in their departure from a spirit which disgraced their predecessors, and for having assumed a temper of mind and manners more suitable to their sacred function.

When my occasions took me into France, towards the close of the late reign, the clergy, under all their forms, engaged a considerable part of my curiosity. So far from finding (except from one set of men, not then very numerous though very active) the complaints and discontents against that body, which some publications had given me reason to expect, I perceived little or no public or private uneasiness on their account. On further examination, I found the clergy in general, persons of moderate minds and decorous manners; I include the seculars, and the regulars of both sexes. I had not the good fortune to know a great many of the parochial clergy; but in general I received a perfectly good account of their morals, and of their attention to their duties. With some of the higher clergy I had a personal acquaintance; and of the rest in that class, very good means of information. They were, almost all of them, persons of noble birth. They resembled others of their own rank; and where there was any difference, it was in their favour. They were more fully educated than the military noblesse; so as by no means to disgrace their profession by ignorance, or by want of fitness for the exercise of their authority. They seemed to me, beyond the clerical character, liberal and open; with the hearts of gentlemen, and men of honour; neither insolent nor servile in their manners and conduct. They seemed to me rather a superior class; a set of men, amongst whom you would not be surprised to find a *Fénelon*.[293] I saw among the clergy in Paris (many of the description are

---

[292] *Two great parties*: i.e. Catholics and Protestants.
[293] *Fénelon*: François de Salignac de la Mothe-Fénelon (1651–1715), Archbishop of Cambrai, tutor to the grandson of Louis XIV[N], and author of the universally read *Telemachus*. Fénelon was extraordinarily famous in the eighteenth century and had an unimpeachable reputation as a virtuous man.

not to be met with any where) men of great learning and candour; and I had reason to believe, that this description was not confined to Paris. What I found in other places, I know was accidental; and therefore to be presumed a fair sample. I spent a few days in a provincial town,[294] where, in the absence of the bishop, I passed my evenings with three clergymen, his vicars-general, persons who would have done honour to any church. They were all well informed; two of them of deep, general, and extensive erudition, antient and modern, oriental and western; particularly in their own profession. They had a more extensive knowledge of our English divines than I expected; and they entered into the genius of those writers with a critical accuracy. One of these gentlemen is since dead, the Abbé *Morangis*.[295] I pay this tribute, without reluctance, to the memory of that noble, reverend, learned, and excellent person; and I should do the same, with equal cheerfulness, to the merits of the others, who I believe are still living, if I did not fear to hurt those whom I am unable to serve.

Some of these ecclesiastics of rank, are, by all titles, persons deserving of general respect. They are deserving of gratitude from me, and from many English. If this letter should ever come into their hands, I hope they will believe there are those of our nation who feel for their unmerited fall, and for the cruel confiscation of their fortunes, with no common sensibility. What I say of them is a testimony, as far as one feeble voice can go, which I owe to truth. Whenever the question of this unnatural persecution is concerned, I will pay it. No one shall prevent me from being just and grateful. The time is fitted for the duty; and it is particularly becoming to shew our justice and gratitude, when those who have deserved well of us and of mankind are labouring under popular obloquy and the persecutions of oppressive power.

You had before your revolution about an hundred and twenty bishops.[296] A few of them were men of eminent sanctity, and charity without limit. When we talk of the heroic, of course we talk of rare, virtue. I believe the instances of eminent depravity may be as rare amongst them as those of transcendent goodness. Examples of avarice and of

---

[294] *A provincial town*: Auxerre, a town in northern Burgundy. Burke had stayed there in 1773.

[295] *Morangis*: the abbé is unknown. Morangis is the name of two small communes in north-eastern France.

[296] Payne (*Select Works*) gives a figure of 131, Raynaud, 117 (135 including archbishops). The National Assembly[N] reduced the number to one for each of the 83 Departments, as well as providing for their election (*Civil Constitution of the Clergy* (12 June 1790), *DocS*, p. 169).

licentiousness may be picked out, I do not question it, by those who delight in the investigation which leads to such discoveries. A man, as old as I am, will not be astonished that several, in every description, do not lead that perfect life of self-denial, with regard to wealth or to pleasure, which is wished for by all, by some expected, but by none exacted with more rigour, than by those who are the most attentive to their own interests, or the most indulgent to their own passions. When I was in France, I am certain that the number of vicious prelates was not great. Certain individuals among them not distinguishable for the regularity of their lives, made some amends for their want of the severe virtues, in their possession of the liberal; and were endowed with qualities which made them useful in the church and state. I am told, that with few exceptions, Louis the Sixteenth had been more attentive to character, in his promotions to that rank, than his immediate predecessor; and I believe, (as some spirit of reform has prevailed through the whole reign) that it may be true. But the present ruling power has shewn a disposition only to plunder the church. It has punished *all* prelates; which is to favour the vicious, at least in point of reputation. It has made a degrading pensionary[297] establishment, to which no man of liberal ideas or liberal condition will destine his children. It must settle into the lowest classes of the people. As with you the inferior clergy are not numerous enough for their duties; as these duties are, beyond measure, minute and toilsome; as you have left no middle classes of clergy at their ease, in future nothing of science or erudition can exist in the Gallican church. To complete the project, without the least attention to the rights of patrons, the assembly has provided in future an elective clergy; an arrangement which will drive out of the clerical profession all men of sobriety; all who can pretend to independence in their function or their conduct; and which will throw the whole direction of the public mind into the hands of a set of licentious, bold, crafty, factious, flattering wretches, of such condition and such habits of life as will make their contemptible pensions (in comparison of which the stipend of an exciseman is lucrative and honourable) an object of low and illiberal intrigue. Those officers, whom they still call bishops, are to be elected to a provision comparatively mean, through the same arts, (that is, electioneering arts) by men of all religious tenets that are known

---

[297] *Pensionary*: one dependant on a fixed wage or salary. The church's property, from which its livings were derived, having been appropriated by the state, the clergy would be paid as civil servants.

or can be invented. The new lawgivers have not ascertained any thing whatsoever concerning their qualifications, relative either to doctrine or to morals; no more than they have done with regard to the subordinate clergy; nor does it appear but that both the higher and the lower may, at their discretion, practise or preach any mode of religion or irreligion that they please. I do not yet see what the jurisdiction of bishops over their subordinates is to be; or whether they are to have any jurisdiction at all.

In short, Sir, it seems to me, that this new ecclesiastical establishment is intended only to be temporary, and preparatory to the utter abolition, under any of its forms, of the Christian religion, whenever the minds of men are prepared for this last stroke against it, by the accomplishment of the plan for bringing its ministers into universal contempt. They who will not believe, that the philosophical fanatics who guide in these matters, have long entertained such a design, are utterly ignorant of their character and proceedings. These enthusiasts do not scruple to avow their opinion, that a state can subsist without any religion better than with one; and that they are able to supply the place of any good which may be in it, by a project of their own – namely, by a sort of education they have imagined, founded in a knowledge of the physical wants of men; progressively carried to an enlightened self-interest, which, when well understood, they tell us will identify with an interest more enlarged and public. The scheme of this education has been long known. Of late they distinguish it (as they have got an entire new nomenclature of technical terms) by the name of a *Civic Education*.

I hope their partizans in England, (to whom I rather attribute very inconsiderate conduct than the ultimate object in this detestable design) will succeed neither in the pillage of the ecclesiastics, nor in the introduction of a principle of popular election to our bishoprics and parochial cures. This, in the present condition of the world, would be the last corruption of the church; the utter ruin of the clerical character; the most dangerous shock that the state ever received through a misunderstood arrangement of religion. I know well enough that the bishoprics and cures, under kingly and seignoral patronage, as now they are in England, and as they have been lately in France, are sometimes acquired by unworthy methods; but the other mode of ecclesiastical canvas subjects them infinitely more surely and more generally to all the evil arts of low ambition, which, operating on and through greater numbers, will produce mischief in proportion.

Those of you who have robbed the clergy, think that they shall easily reconcile their conduct to all protestant nations; because the clergy, whom they have thus plundered, degraded, and given over to mockery and scorn, are of the Roman Catholic, that is, of *their own* pretended persuasion. I have no doubt that some miserable bigots will be found here as well as elsewhere, who hate sects and parties different from their own, more than they love the substance of religion; and who are more angry with those who differ from them in their particular plans and systems, than displeased with those who attack the foundation of our common hope. These men will write and speak on the subject in the manner that is to be expected from their temper and character. Burnet[298] says, that when he was in France, in the year 1683, 'the method which carried over the men of the finest parts to popery was this – – they brought themselves to doubt of the whole Christian religion. When that was once done, it seemed a more indifferent thing of what side or form they continued outwardly.' If this was then the ecclesiastic policy of France, it is what they have since but too much reason to repent of. They preferred atheism to a form of religion not agreeable to their ideas. They succeeded in destroying that form; and atheism has succeeded in destroying them. I can readily give credit to Burnet's story; because I have observed too much of a similar spirit (for a little of it is 'much too much') amongst ourselves. The humour, however, is not general.

The teachers who reformed our religion in England bore no sort of resemblance to your present reforming doctors in Paris. Perhaps they were (like those whom they opposed) rather more than could be wished under the influence of a party spirit; but they were most sincere believers; men of the most fervent and exalted piety; ready to die (as some of them did die) like true heroes in defence of their particular ideas of Christianity; as they would with equal fortitude, and more chearfully, for that stock of general truth, for the branches of which they contended with their blood. These men would have disavowed with horror those wretches who claimed a fellowship with them upon no other titles than those of their having pillaged the persons with whom they maintained controversies, and their having despised the common religion, for the purity of which they exerted themselves with a zeal, which unequivocally bespoke their highest reverence for the substance of that system which they wished

---

[298] *Burnet*: Gilbert Burnet (1643–1715), Whig theologian, Bishop of Salisbury, religious controversialist and author of the widely read *History of my Own Time* (1683–1715).

to reform. Many of their descendants have retained the same zeal; but, (as less engaged in conflict) with more moderation. They do not forget that justice and mercy are substantial parts of religion. Impious men do not recommend themselves to their communion by iniquity and cruelty towards any description of their fellow creatures.

We hear these new teachers continually boasting of their spirit of toleration. That those persons should tolerate all opinions, who think none to be of estimation, is a matter of small merit. Equal neglect is not impartial kindness. The species of benevolence, which arises from contempt, is no true charity. There are in England abundance of men who tolerate in the true spirit of toleration. They think the dogmas of religion, though in different degrees, are all of moment; and that amongst them there is, as amongst all things of value, a just ground of preference. They favour, therefore, and they tolerate. They tolerate, not because they despise opinions, but because they respect justice. They would reverently and affectionately protect all religions, because they love and venerate the great principle upon which all agree, and the great object to which they are all directed. They begin more and more plainly to discern, that we have all a common cause, as against a common enemy. They will not be so misled by the spirit of faction, as not to distinguish what is done in favour of their subdivision, from those acts of hostility, which, through some particular description, are aimed at the whole corps, in which they themselves, under another denomination, are included. It is impossible for me to say what may be the character of every description of men amongst us. But I speak for the greater part; and for them, I must tell you, that sacrilege is no part of their doctrine of good works; that, so far from calling you into their fellowship on such title, if your professors are admitted to their communion, they must carefully conceal their doctrine of the lawfulness of the proscription of innocent men; and that they must make restitution of all stolen goods whatsoever. Till then they are none of ours.

You may suppose that we do not approve your confiscation of the revenues of bishops, and deans, and chapters, and parochial clergy possessing independent estates arising from land, because we have the same sort of establishment in England. That objection, you will say, cannot hold as to the confiscation of the goods of monks and nuns, and the abolition of their order. It is true, that this particular part of your general confiscation does not affect England, as a precedent in point: but the reason applies; and it goes a great way. The long parliament confiscated the lands of deans and chapters in England on the same ideas upon which your assembly set to sale the lands of the monastic orders.[299] But it is in the principle of injustice that the danger lies, and not in the description of persons on whom it is first exercised. I see, in a country very near us, a course of policy pursued, which sets justice, the common concern of mankind, at defiance. With the national assembly[N] of France, possession is nothing; law and usage are nothing. I see the national assembly openly reprobate the doctrine of prescription,[300] which[xxxviii] one of the greatest of their own lawyers tells us, with great truth, is a part of the law of nature. He tells us, that the positive ascertainment of its limits, and its security from invasion, were among the causes for which civil society itself has been instituted. If prescription be once shaken, no species of property is secure, when it once becomes an object large enough to tempt the cupidity of indigent power. I see a practice perfectly correspondent to their contempt of this great fundamental part of natural law. I see the confiscators begin with bishops, and chapters, and monasteries; but I do not see them end there. I see the princes of the blood, who, by the oldest usages of that kingdom, held large landed estates, (hardly with the compliment of a debate) deprived of their possessions, and in lieu of their stable independent property, reduced to the hope of some precarious, charitable pension, at the pleasure of an assembly, which of course will pay little regard to the rights of pensioners at pleasure, when it despises those of legal proprietors. Flushed with the insolence of their first inglorious victories, and pressed by the distresses caused by their lust of unhallowed lucre, disappointed but not discouraged, they have at length ventured completely to subvert all property of all descriptions throughout the extent of a great kingdom. They have compelled all men, in all transactions of commerce, in the disposal of lands, in civil dealing, and through the whole communion of life, to accept as perfect payment and good and lawful tender, the symbols of their

---

xxxviii   Domat.[301]

[299]   *Confiscated the lands*: During the English Civil War, the Long Parliament passed an ordinance (6 Oct. 1646) abolishing government of the Church by bishops and handed over their lands to trustees; the land was later used as security for a loan, and some later sold.

[300]   *Prescription*: a legal title to property derived from long usage or possession, acknowledged by both Common and Roman Law.

[301]   *Domat*: Jean Domat (1625–96), legal philosopher, author of *Les lois civiles dans leur ordre naturel* (1689), a major attempt to synthesise traditional French law on the organisational principles of Roman law. Burke owned a copy.

speculations on a projected sale of their plunder. What vestiges of liberty or property have they left? The tenant-right of a cabbage-garden, a year's interest in a hovel, the good-will of an alehouse, or a baker's shop, the very shadow of a constructive property, are more ceremoniously treated in our parliament than with you the oldest and most valuable landed possessions, in the hands of the most respectable personages, or than the whole body of the monied and commercial interest of your country. We entertain an high opinion of the legislative authority; but we have never dreamt that parliaments had any right whatever to violate property, to overrule prescription, or to force a currency of their own fiction in the place of that which is real, and recognized by the law of nations. But you, who began with refusing to submit to the most moderate restraints, have ended by establishing an unheard of despotism. I find the ground upon which your confiscators go is this; that indeed their proceedings could not be supported in a court of justice; but that the rules of prescription cannot bind a legislative assembly[xxxix]. So that this legislative assembly of a free nation sits, not for the security, but for the destruction of property, and not of property only, but of every rule and maxim which can give it stability, and of those instruments which can alone give it circulation.

When the Anabaptists of Münster,[302] in the sixteenth century, had filled Germany with confusion by their system of levelling and their wild opinions concerning property, to what country in Europe did not the progress of their fury furnish just cause of alarm? Of all things, wisdom is the most terrified with epidemical fanaticism, because of all enemies it is that against which she is the least able to furnish any kind of resource. We cannot be ignorant of the spirit of atheistical fanaticism, that is inspired by a multitude of writings, dispersed with incredible assiduity and expence, and by sermons delivered in all the streets and places of public resort in Paris. These writings and sermons have filled the populace with a black and savage atrocity of mind, which supersedes in them the common feelings of nature, as well as all sentiments of morality and religion;

---

[xxxix] Speech of Mr. Camus, published by order of the National Assembly.

[302] *Anabaptists of Münster*: Anabaptists were so called because they rejected the idea of infant baptism on the grounds that only conscious commitment could make one a Christian. But this was a symbol of their wider rejection of the sacraments or (according to their opponents) any formal morality. Anabaptists took over the city of Münster in February 1534. Under John of Leiden they legalised polygamy and the communal ownership of goods. The city was retaken and the leaders tortured, executed and their bodies exposed in cages, in June 1535.

insomuch that these wretches are induced to bear with a sullen patience the intolerable distresses brought upon them by the violent convulsions and permutations that have been made in property[xl]? The spirit of proselytism attends this spirit of fanaticism. They have societies to cabal and correspond at home and abroad for the propagation of their tenets. The republic of Berne,[303] one of the happiest, the most prosperous, and the best governed countries upon earth, is one of the great objects, at the destruction of which they aim. I am told they have in some measure succeeded in sowing there the seeds of discontent. They are busy throughout Germany. Spain and Italy have not been untried. England is not left out of the comprehensive scheme of their malignant charity; and in England we find those who stretch out their arms to them, who recommend their examples from more than one pulpit, and who choose, in more than one periodical meeting, publicly to correspond with them, to applaud them,

[xl] Whether the following description is strictly true I know not; but it is what the publishers would have pass for true, in order to animate others. In a letter from Toul, given in one of their papers, is the following passage concerning the people of that district: 'Dans la Révolution actuelle, ils ont résisté à toutes les *séductions du bigotisme, aux persécutions et aux tracasseries* des Ennemis de la Révolution. *Oubliant leurs plus grands intérêts* pour rendre hommage aux vues d'ordre général qui ont determiné l'Assemblée Nationale, ils voient, *sans se plaindre*, supprimer cette foule d'établissemens ecclésiastiques par lesquels *ils subsistoient*; et même, en perdant leur siège épiscopal, la seule de toutes ces ressources qui pouvoit, ou plutôt *qui devoit, en tout équité,* leur être conservée; condamnés *à la plus effrayante misère,* sans avoir *été ni pu être entendus, ils ne murmurent point,* ils restent fidèles aux principes du plus pur patriotisme; ils sont encore prêts à *verser leur sang* pour le maintien de la Constitution, qui va reduire leur Ville *à la plus déplorable nullité.'* These people are not supposed to have endured those sufferings and injustices in a struggle for liberty, for the same account states truly that they had been always free; their patience in beggary and ruin, and their suffering, without remonstrance, the most flagrant and confessed injustice, if strictly true, can be nothing but the effect of this dire fanaticism. A great multitude all over France is in the same condition and the same temper.[304]

[303] *Berne*: One of the Cantons of the Swiss Confederation, it was one of a number of small states bordering France in which movements sympathetic to the Revolution emerged (and were encouraged by the French).

[304] 'In the present Revolution, they have resisted all the *seductions of bigotry, the persecutions and harassments* of the enemies of the Revolution. *Forgetting their own greatest interests* in order to render obedience to the considerations of a general nature which have guided the National Assembly, they see, *without complaint,* the suppression of a crowd of church establishments by means of which *they were gaining their living*; and even in losing their episcopal seat, the only one of all these resources which could have, or rather *which should have, in all equity,* been preserved for them; condemned to the most dreadful privation *without being – or being able to be – heard, they uttered not a word of protest,* they remained faithful to the principles of the purest patriotism; they are still ready to *spill their blood* for the preservation of the constitution that will reduce their town *to a most deplorable non-entity.'*

and to hold them up as objects for imitation; who receive from them tokens of confraternity, and standards consecrated amidst their rites and mysteries[xli]; who suggest to them leagues of perpetual amity, at the very time when the power, to which our constitution has exclusively delegated the federative capacity of this kingdom, may find it expedient to make war upon them.

It is not[305] the confiscation of our church property from this example in France that I dread, though I think this would be no trifling evil. The great source of my solicitude is, lest it should ever be considered in England as the policy of a state, to seek a resource in confiscations of any kind; or that any one description of citizens should be brought to regard any of the others as their proper prey[xlii]. Nations are wading deeper and deeper into an ocean of boundless debt. Public debts, which at first were

---

[xli] See the proceedings of the confederation of *Nantz*.[306]

[xlii] 'Si Plures sunt ii quibus improbe datum est, quam illi quibus injuste ademptum est, idcirco plus etiam valent? Non enim numero hæc judicantur sed pondere. Quam autem habet æquitatem, ut agrum multis annis, aut etiam sæculis ante possessum, qui nullum habuit habeat; qui autem habuit amittat. Ac, propter hoc injuriæ genus, Lacedæmonii Lysandrum Ephorum expulerunt: Agin regem (quod nunquam antea apud eos acciderat) necaverunt: exque eo tempore tantæ discordiæ secutæ sunt, ut et tyranni exsisterint, et optimates exterminarentur, et preclarissime constituta republica dilaberetur. Nec vero solum ipsa cecidit, sed etiam reliquam Græciam evertit contagionibus malorum, quæ a Lacedæmoniis profectæ manarunt latius.' – After speaking of the conduct of the model of true patriots, Aratus of Sycion, which was in a very different spirit, he says, 'Sic par est agere cum civibus; non ut bis jam vidimus, hastam in foro ponere et bona civium voci subjicere præconis. At ille Græcus (id quod fuit sapientis præstantis viri) omnibus consulendum esse putavit: eaque est summa ratio et sapientia boni civis, commode civium non divellere, sed omnes eadem æquitate continere.' Cic. Off. I.2.[307]

---

[305] 1st edn has: 'It is not my fear of . . .'.
[306] *Proceedings of the confederation of Nantz*: The Jacobin[N] society of Nantes had entered into correspondence with and visited the members of the Revolution Society[N] in London. See Goodwin, *The Friends of Liberty*, p. 127.
[307] 'Thus even if those to whom property has been wrongfully given are more numerous than those from whom it has been unjustly taken, should they for that reason prevail? For in such matters influence is measured not by numbers but by weight [of reason]. And how is it fair that a man who never had any property should take possession of lands that had been occupied for many years or even generations, and that he who had them before should lose possession of them? Now, it was on account of just this sort of wrong-doing that the Spartans banished their ephor Lysander, and put their King Agis to death – an act without precedent in the history of Sparta. From that time on dissensions so serious ensued that tyrants arose, the nobles were sent into exile, and the state, although most admirably constituted, crumbled to pieces. Nor did it fall alone, but by the contagion of the ills that, starting in Lacedaemon, spread more widely, it dragged the rest of Greece down to ruin.'

. . .

a security to governments, by interesting many in the public tranquillity, are likely in their excess to become the means of their subversion. If governments provide for these debts by heavy impositions, they perish by becoming odious to the people. If they do not provide for them, they will be undone by the efforts of the most dangerous of all parties; I mean an extensive discontented monied interest, injured and not destroyed. The men who compose this interest look for their security, in the first instance, to the fidelity of government; in the second, to its power. If they find the old governments effete, worn out, and with their springs relaxed, so as not to be of sufficient vigour for their purposes, they may seek new ones that shall be possessed of more energy; and this energy will be derived, not from an acquisition of resources, but from a contempt of justice. Revolutions are favourable to confiscation; and it is impossible to know under what obnoxious names the next confiscations will be authorised. I am sure that the principles predominant in France extend to very many persons and descriptions of persons in all countries who think their innoxious indolence their security. This kind of innocence in proprietors may be argued into inutility; and inutility into an unfitness for their estates. Many parts of Europe are in open disorder. In many others there is a hollow murmuring under ground; a confused movement is felt, that threatens a general earthquake in the political world. Already confederacies and correspondences of the most extraordinary nature are forming, in several countries[xliii]. In such a state of things we ought to

---

[xliii] See two books intitled, Enige Originalenschriften des Illuminatenordens. – System und Folgen des Illuminatenordens. Munchen 1787.[308]

'That is the way to deal with one's fellow citizens, and not, as we have already witnessed on two occasions, to plant the spear in the forum and knock down citizens' property under the auctioneer's hammer. But that Greek, who was a wise and excellent man, thought that he must look out for the welfare of all. And this is the highest statesmanship and the soundest wisdom on the part of a good citizen, not to divide the interests of the citizens, but to unite all on the basis of impartial justice.' (Cicero, *De Officiis*, 2.22.79–23.80, and 2.23.83)

[308] The Illuminati were a quasi-secret society of rationalists founded in Bavaria in 1776 by Adam Weishaupt, a Professor of Law at Ingolstadt. The two titles Burke mentions (*Einige Originalschriften des Illuminatenordens* (Munich, 1787) and the *System und Folgen des Illuminatenordens . . . in Briefen* (Munich, 1786)) were compilations of papers seized from the order and published to expose it as a conspiracy against organised religion by the Elector of Bavaria. The order fuelled wider fears of an intellectual conspiracy against religion and the existing social order to which Burke may also have been prey. The Abbé Barruel, and a Scot, John Robison, both published books very shortly after Burke's death claiming the influence of the Illuminati on the French Revolution.

hold ourselves upon our guard. In all mutations (if mutations must be) the circumstance which will serve most to blunt the edge of their mischief, and to promote what good may be in them, is, that they should find us with our minds tenacious of justice, and tender of property.

But it will be argued, that this confiscation in France ought not to alarm other nations. They say it is not made from wanton rapacity; that it is a great measure of national policy, adopted to remove an extensive, inveterate, superstitious mischief. It is with the greatest difficulty that I am able to separate policy from justice. Justice is itself the great standing policy of civil society; and any eminent departure from it, under any circumstances, lies under the suspicion of being no policy at all.

When men are encouraged to go into a certain mode of life by the existing laws, and protected in that mode as in a lawful occupation – when they have accommodated all their ideas, and all their habits to it – when the law had long made their adherence to its rules a ground of reputation, and their departure from them a ground of disgrace and even of penalty – I am sure it is unjust in legislature, by an arbitrary act, to offer a sudden violence to their minds and their feelings; forcibly to degrade them from their state and condition, and to stigmatize with shame and infamy that character and those customs which before had been made the measure of their happiness and honour. If to this be added an expulsion from their habitations, and a confiscation of all their goods, I am not sagacious enough to discover how this despotic sport, made of the feelings, consciences, prejudices, and properties of men, can be discriminated from the rankest tyranny.

If the injustice of the course pursued in France be clear, the policy of the measure, that is, the public benefit to be expected from it, ought to be at least as evident, and at least as important. To a man who acts under the influence of no passion, who has nothing in view in his projects but the public good, a great difference will immediately strike him, between what policy would dictate on the original introduction of such institutions, and on a question of their total abolition, where they have cast their roots wide and deep, and where by long habit things more valuable than themselves are so adapted to them, and in a manner interwoven with them, that the one cannot be destroyed without notably impairing the other. He might be embarrassed, if the case were really such as sophisters represent it in their paltry style of debating. But in this, as in most questions of state, there is a middle. There is something else than the mere alternative of absolute destruction, or unreformed existence. *Spartam nactus es; hanc exorna.*[309] This is, in my opinion, a rule of profound sense, and ought never to depart from the mind of an honest reformer. I cannot conceive how any man can have brought himself to that pitch of presumption, to consider his country as nothing but *carte blanche*, upon which he may scribble whatever he pleases. A man full of warm speculative benevolence may wish his society otherwise constituted than he finds it; but a good patriot, and a true politician, always considers how he shall make the most of the existing materials of his country. A disposition to preserve, and an ability to improve, taken together, would be my standard of a statesman. Every thing else is vulgar in the conception, perilous in the execution.

There are moments in the fortune of states when particular men are called to make improvements by great mental exertion. In those moments, even when they seem to enjoy the confidence of their prince and country, and to be invested with full authority, they have not always apt instruments. A politician, to do great things, looks for a *power*, what our workmen call a *purchase*;[310] and if he finds that power, in politics as in mechanics he cannot be at a loss to apply it. In the monastic institutions, in my opinion, was found a great *power* for the mechanism of politic benevolence. There were revenues with a public direction; there were men wholly set apart and dedicated to public purposes, without any other than public ties and public principles; men without the possibility of converting the estate of the community into a private fortune; men denied to self-interests, whose avarice is for some community; men to whom personal poverty is honour, and implicit obedience stands in the place of freedom. In vain shall a man look to the possibility of making such things when he wants them. The winds blow as they list. These institutions are the products of enthusiasm; they are the instruments of wisdom. Wisdom cannot create materials; they are the gifts of nature or of chance; her pride is in the use. The perennial existence of bodies corporate and their fortunes, are things particularly suited to a man who has long views; who meditates designs that require time in fashioning; and which propose duration when they are accomplished. He is not deserving

---

[309] Cicero, *Letters to Atticus*, 4.6, quoting Agamemnon to Menelaus, King of Sparta, in a fragment from *Telephos*, a play by Euripides: 'Your lot is Sparta – embellish it.' Sparta being proverbially austere and simple, it was not a great prize. Agamemnon is telling Menelaus to make the best of what he has got.

[310] *Purchase*: here any feature of a material or body by which it may be worked or a force applied to it – as for example the grain of a piece of wood or stone with which a carpenter or mason may work or a crack or roughness in rock which a climber may exploit as a foot- or handhold.

to rank high, or even to be mentioned in the order of great statesmen, who, having obtained the command and direction of such a power as existed in the wealth, the discipline, and the habits of such corporations, as those which you have rashly destroyed, cannot find any way of converting it to the great and lasting benefit of his country. On the view of this subject a thousand uses suggest themselves to a contriving mind. To destroy any power, growing wild from the rank productive force of the human mind, is almost tantamount, in the moral world, to the destruction of the apparently active properties of bodies in the material. It would be like the attempt to destroy (if it were in our competence to destroy) the expansive force of fixed air in nitre,[311] or the power of steam, or of electricity, or of magnetism.[312] These energies always existed in nature, and they were always discernible. They seemed, some of them unserviceable, some noxious, some no better than a sport to children; until contemplative ability, combining with practic skill, tamed their wild nature, subdued them to use, and rendered them at once the most powerful and the most tractable agents, in subservience to the great views and designs of men. Did fifty thousand persons, whose mental and whose bodily labour you might direct, and so many hundred thousand a year of a revenue, which was neither lazy nor superstitious, appear too big for your abilities to wield? Had you no way of using the men but by converting monks into pensioners? Had you no way of turning the revenue to account, but through the improvident resource of a spendthrift sale? If you were thus destitute of mental funds, the proceeding is in its natural course. Your politicians do not understand their trade; and therefore they sell their tools.

But the institutions savour of superstition in their very principle; and they nourish it by a permanent and standing influence. This I do not mean to dispute; but this ought not to hinder you from deriving from superstition itself any resources which may thence be furnished for the public advantage. You derive benefits from many dispositions and many passions of the human mind, which are of as doubtful a colour in the moral eye, as superstition itself. It was your business to correct and mitigate every thing which was noxious in this passion, as in all the passions. But is superstition the greatest of all possible vices? In its possible excess I

---

[311] *Nitre*: saltpetre or potassium nitrate, an ingredient of gunpowder. On fixed air see above, fn. 9.

[312] More than a little prescient in the case of electricity and magnetism. Primitive steam engines designed by Thomas Newcomen (d. 1729) had been in use throughout the century for pumping water out of mines.

think it becomes a very great evil. It is, however, a moral subject; and of course admits of all degrees and all modifications. Superstition is the religion of feeble minds; and they must be tolerated in an intermixture of it, in some trifling or some enthusiastic shape or other, else you will deprive weak minds of a resource found necessary to the strongest. The body of all true religion consists, to be sure, in obedience to the will of the sovereign of the world; in a confidence in his declarations; and an imitation of his perfections. The rest is our own. It may be prejudicial to the great end; it may be auxiliary. Wise men, who as such are not *admirers*, (not admirers at least of the *Munera Terrae*[313]) are not violently attached to these things, nor do they violently hate them. Wisdom is not the most severe corrector of folly. They are the rival follies, which mutually wage so unrelenting a war; and which make so cruel a use of their advantages, as they can happen to engage the immoderate vulgar on the one side or the other in their quarrels. Prudence would be neuter; but if, in the contention between fond attachment and fierce antipathy concerning things in their nature not made to produce such heats, a prudent man were obliged to make a choice of what errors and excesses of enthusiasm he would condemn or bear, perhaps he would think the superstition which builds, to be more tolerable than that which demolishes – that which adorns a country, than that which deforms it – that which endows, than that which plunders – that which disposes to mistaken beneficence, than that which stimulates to real injustice – that which leads a man to refuse to himself lawful pleasures, than that which snatches from others the scanty subsistence of their self-denial. Such, I think, is very nearly the state of the question between the ancient founders of monkish superstition, and the superstition of the pretended philosophers of the hour.

For the present I postpone all considerations of the supposed public profit of the sale, which however I conceive to be perfectly delusive. I shall here only consider it as a transfer of property. On the policy of that transfer I shall trouble you with a few thoughts.

In every prosperous community something more is produced than goes to the immediate support of the producer. This surplus forms the income of the landed capitalist. It will be spent by a proprietor who does not labour. But this idleness is itself the spring of labour; this repose the spur to industry. The only concern of the state is, that the capital taken in rent from the land, should be returned again to the industry from whence it

---

[313] *Munera Terrae*: 'gifts of the earth'; the things provided by nature (Horace, *Odes*, 2.14.10).

came; and that its expenditure should be with the least possible detriment to the morals of those who expend it, and to those of the people to whom it is returned.

In all the views of receipt, expenditure, and personal employment, a sober legislator would carefully compare the possessor whom he has recommended to expel, with the stranger who was proposed to fill his place. Before the inconveniences are incurred which *must* attend all violent revolutions in property through extensive confiscation, we ought to have some rational assurance that the purchasers of the confiscated property will be in a considerable degree more laborious, more virtuous, more sober, less disposed to extort an unreasonable proportion of the gains of the labourer, or to consume on themselves a larger share than is fit for the measure of an individual, or that they should be qualified to dispense the surplus in a more steady and equal mode, so as to answer the purposes of a politic expenditure, than the old possessors, call those possessors, bishops, or canons, or commendatory abbots, or monks, or what you please. The monks are lazy. Be it so. Suppose them no otherwise employed than by singing in the choir. They are as usefully employed as those who neither sing nor say. As usefully even as those who sing upon the stage. They are as usefully employed as if they worked from dawn to dark in the innumerable servile, degrading, unseemly, unmanly, and often most unwholesome and pestiferous occupations, to which by the social œconomy so many wretches are inevitably doomed. If it were not generally pernicious to disturb the natural course of things, and to impede, in any degree, the great wheel of circulation which is turned by the strangely directed labour of these unhappy people, I should be infinitely more inclined forcibly to rescue them from their miserable industry, than violently to disturb the tranquil repose of monastic quietude. Humanity, and perhaps policy, might better justify me in the one than in the other. It is a subject on which I have often reflected, and never reflected without feeling from it. I am sure that no consideration, except the necessity of submitting to the yoke of luxury, and the despotism of fancy, who in their own imperious way will distribute the surplus product of the soil, can justify the toleration of such trades and employments in a well-regulated state. But, for this purpose of distribution, it seems to me, that the idle expences of monks are quite as well directed as the idle expences of us lay-loiterers.

When the advantages of the possession, and of the project, are on a par, there is no motive for a change. But in the present case, perhaps they are not upon a par, and the difference is in favour of the possession. It does not appear to me, that the expences of those whom you are going to expel, do, in fact, take a course so directly and so generally leading to vitiate and degrade and render miserable those through whom they pass, as the expences of those favourites whom you are intruding into their houses. Why should the expenditure of a great landed property, which is a dispersion of the surplus product of the soil, appear intolerable to you or to me, when it takes its course through the accumulation of vast libraries, which are the history of the force and weakness of the human mind; through great collections of antient records, medals, and coins, which attest and explain laws and customs; through paintings and statues, that, by imitating nature, seem to extend the limits of creation; through grand monuments of the dead, which continue the regards and connexions of life beyond the grave; through collections of the specimens of nature, which become a representative assembly of all the classes and families of the world, that by disposition facilitate, and, by exciting curiosity, open the avenues to science? If, by great permanent establishments, all these objects of expence are better secured from the inconstant sport of personal caprice and personal extravagance, are they worse than if the same tastes prevailed in scattered individuals? Does not the sweat of the mason and carpenter, who toil in order to partake the sweat of the peasant, flow as pleasantly and as salubriously, in the construction and repair of the majestic edifices of religion, as in the painted booths and sordid sties of vice and luxury; as honourably and as profitably in repairing those sacred works, which grow hoary with innumerable years, as on the momentary receptacles of transient voluptuousness; in opera-houses, and brothels, and gaming-houses, and club-houses, and obelisks in the Champ de Mars?[314] Is the surplus product of the olive and the vine worse employed in the frugal sustenance of persons, whom the fictions of a pious imagination raise to dignity by construing in the service of God, than in pampering the innumerable multitude of those who are degraded by being made useless domestics subservient to the pride of man? Are the decorations of temples an expenditure less worthy a wise man than ribbons, and laces, and national cockades, and petits maisons, and petit

[314] *Champ de Mars*: The field of Mars (the Roman god of war) – a military parade ground in Paris, also used in the Revolution for public displays and ceremonies such as the *Fête de la Fédération* on the first anniversary of the storming of the Bastille, designed by the revolutionary artist David, to celebrate national unity.

soupers, and all the innumerable fopperies and follies in which opulence sports away the burthen of its superfluity?

We tolerate even these; not from love of them, but for fear of worse. We tolerate them, because property and liberty, to a degree, require that toleration. But why proscribe the other, and surely, in every point of view, the more laudable use of estates? Why, through the violation of all property, through an outrage upon every principle of liberty, forcibly carry them from the better to the worse?

This comparison between the new individuals and the old corps is made upon a supposition that no reform could be made in the latter. But in a question of reformation, I always consider corporate bodies, whether sole or consisting of many,[315] to be much more susceptible of a public direction by the power of the state, in the use of their property, and in the regulation of modes and habits of life in their members, than private citizens ever can be, or perhaps ought to be; and this seems to me a very material consideration for those who undertake any thing which merits the name of a politic enterprize. – So far as to the estates of monasteries.

With regard to the estates possessed by bishops and canons, and commendatory abbots, I cannot find out for what reason some landed estates may not be held otherwise than by inheritance. Can any philosophic spoiler undertake to demonstrate the positive or the comparative evil, of having a certain, and that too a large portion of landed property, passing in succession thro' persons whose title to it is, always in theory, and often in fact, an eminent degree of piety, morals, and learning; a property which, by its destination, in their turn, and on the score of merit, gives to the noblest families renovation and support, to the lowest the means of dignity and elevation; a property, the tenure of which is the performance of some duty, (whatever value you may choose to set upon that duty) and the character of whose proprietors demands at least an exterior decorum and gravity of manners; who are to exercise a generous but temperate hospitality; part of whose income they are to consider as a trust for charity; and who, even when they fail in their trust, when they slide from their character, and degenerate into a mere common secular nobleman or gentleman, are in no respect worse than those who may succeed them in their forfeited possessions? Is it better that estates should be held by

---

[315] *Corporate bodies... whether sole*: A corporation is a body established by law to exercise certain defined rights. Normally these are collective bodies, but they could be constitutive of a post or office occupied by an individual – a corporation sole – such as a bishop.

those who have no duty than by those who have one? – by those whose character and destination point to virtues, than by those who have no rule and direction in the expenditure of their estates but their own will and appetite? Nor are these estates held altogether in the character or with the evils supposed inherent in mortmain. They pass from hand to hand with a more rapid circulation than any other. No excess is good; and therefore too great a proportion of landed property may be held officially for life; but it does not seem to me of material injury to any commonwealth, that there should exist some estates that have a chance of being acquired by other means than the previous acquisition of money.

This letter is grown to a great length,[316] though it is indeed short with regard to the infinite extent of the subject. Various avocations have from time to time called my mind from the subject. I was not sorry to give myself leisure to observe whether, in the proceedings of the national assembly,[N] I might not find reasons to change or to qualify some of my first sentiments. Every thing has confirmed me more strongly in my first opinions. It was my original purpose to take a view of the principles of the national assembly with regard to the great and fundamental establishments; and to compare the whole of what you have substituted in the place of what you have destroyed, with the several members of our British constitution. But this plan is of greater extent than at first I computed, and I find that you have little desire to take the advantage of any examples. At present I must content myself with some remarks upon your establishments; reserving for another time what I proposed to say concerning the spirit of our British monarchy, aristocracy, and democracy, as practically they exist.

I have taken a review of what has been done by the governing power in France. I have certainly spoke of it with freedom. Those whose principle it is to despise the antient permanent sense of mankind, and to set up a scheme of society on new principles, must naturally expect that such of us who think better of the judgment of the human race than of theirs, should consider both them and their devices, as men and schemes upon their trial. They must take it for granted that we attend much to their reason, but not at all to their authority. They have not one of the great influencing prejudices of mankind in their favour. They avow their hostility

---

[316] Previous editors have remarked that this break in the flow of Burke's argument may indicate a resumption of writing following interruption during his attendance at the House of Commons during the parliamentary session, e.g. Clark (ed. *Reflections*, p. 334n.) The impeachment of Warren Hastings was also suspended between the end of February and late April 1790.

to opinion. Of course they must expect no support from that influence, which, with every other authority, they have deposed from the seat of its jurisdiction.

I can never consider this assembly as any thing else than a voluntary association of men, who have availed themselves of circumstances, to seize upon the power of the state. They have not the sanction and authority of the character under which they first met. They have assumed another of a very different nature; and have completely altered and inverted all the relations in which they originally stood. They do not hold the authority they exercise under any constitutional law of the state. They have departed from the instructions of the people by whom they were sent; which instructions, as the assembly did not act in virtue of any antient usage or settled law, were the sole source of their authority. The most considerable of their acts have not been done by great majorities; and in this sort of near divisions, which carry only the constructive authority of the whole, strangers will consider reasons as well as resolutions.[317]

If they had set up this new experimental government as a necessary substitute for an expelled tyranny, mankind would anticipate the time of prescription,[318] which, through long usage, mellows into legality governments that were violent in their commencement. All those who have affections which lead them to the conservation of civil order would recognize, even in its cradle, the child as legitimate, which has been produced from those principles of cogent expediency to which all just governments owe their birth, and on which they justify their continuance. But they will be late and reluctant in giving any sort of countenance to the operations of a power, which has derived its birth from no law and no necessity;

---

[317] Burke was to considerably sharpen this criticism in his *Appeal from the New to the Old Whigs*, pointing out that majority decision-making is itself a convention, and cannot be resorted to by those who seek to overthrow existing conventions as though it were a presumptively legitimate default position:

> We are so little affected by things which are habitual, that we consider this idea of the decision of a majority as if it were a law of our original nature: But such constructive whole, residing in a part only, is one of the most violent fictions of positive law, that ever has been or can be made on the principles of artificial incorporation. Out of civil society nature knows nothing of it; nor are men, even when arranged according to civil order, otherwise than by very long training, brought at all to submit to it.
>
> (*Appeal* (1791), p. 216 (*Further Reflections*, ed. Ritchie, p. 105))

[318] *Anticipate the time of prescription*: That is – if the new government had been necessitated by a previously tyrannical one, we could have indulged the presumption that in time it would acquire the legitimacy with which prescription (long usage) would endow it.

but which on the contrary has had its origin in those vices and sinister practices by which the social union is often disturbed and sometimes destroyed. This assembly has hardly a year's prescription. We have their own word for it that they have made a revolution. To make a revolution is a measure which, *prima fronte*,[319] requires an apology. To make a revolution is to subvert the antient state of our country; and no common reasons are called for to justify so violent a proceeding. The sense of mankind authorizes us to examine into the mode of acquiring new power, and to criticise on the use that is made of it with less awe and reverence than that which is usually conceded to a settled and recognized authority.

In obtaining and securing their power, the assembly proceeds upon principles the most opposite from those which appear to direct them in the use of it. An observation on this difference will let us into the true spirit of their conduct. Every thing which they have done, or continue to do, in order to obtain and keep their power, is by the most common arts. They proceed exactly as their ancestors of ambition have done before them. Trace them through all their artifices, frauds, and violences, you can find nothing at all that is new. They follow precedents and examples with the punctilious exactness of a pleader.[320] They never depart an iota from the authentic formulas of tyranny and usurpation. But in all the regulations relative to the public good, the spirit has been the very reverse of this. There they commit the whole to the mercy of untried speculations; they abandon the dearest interests of the public to those loose theories, to which none of them would chuse to trust the slightest of his private concerns. They make this difference, because in their desire of obtaining and securing power they are thoroughly in earnest; there they travel in the beaten road. The public interests, because about them they have no real solicitude, they abandon wholly to chance; I say to chance, because their schemes have nothing in experience to prove their tendency beneficial.

We must always see with a pity not unmixed with respect, the errors of those who are timid and doubtful of themselves with regard to points wherein the happiness of mankind is concerned. But in these gentlemen there is nothing of the tender parental solicitude which fears to cut up the infant for the sake of an experiment. In the vastness of their promises, and the confidence of their predictions, they far outdo all the boasting of

---

[319] *Prima fronte*: on the face of it, at first view.
[320] *Pleader*: a lawyer who draws up formal documents for presentation at a court hearing.

empirics. The arrogance of their pretensions, in a manner provokes, and challenges us to an enquiry into their foundation.

I am convinced that there are men of considerable parts among the popular leaders in the national assembly.[N] Some of them display eloquence in their speeches and their writings. This cannot be without powerful and cultivated talents. But eloquence may exist without a proportionable degree of wisdom. When I speak of ability, I am obliged to distinguish. What they have done towards the support of their system bespeaks no ordinary men. In the system itself, taken as the scheme of a republic constructed for procuring the prosperity and security of the citizen, and for promoting the strength and grandeur of the state, I confess myself unable to find out any thing which displays, in a single instance, the work of a comprehensive and disposing mind, or even the provisions of a vulgar prudence. Their purpose every where seems to have been to evade and slip aside from *difficulty*. This it has been the glory of the great masters in all the arts to confront, and to overcome; and when they had overcome the first difficulty, to turn it into an instrument for new conquests over new difficulties; thus to enable them to extend the empire of their science; and even to push forward beyond the reach of their original thoughts, the land marks of the human understanding itself. Difficulty is a severe instructor, set over us by the supreme ordinance of a parental guardian and legislator, who knows us better than we know ourselves, as he loves us better too. *Pater ipse colendi haud facilem esse viam voluit.*[321] He that wrestles with us strengthens our nerves, and sharpens our skill. Our antagonist is our helper. This amicable conflict with difficulty obliges us to an intimate acquaintance with our object, and compels us to consider it in all its relations. It will not suffer us to be superficial. It is the want of nerves of understanding for such a task; it is the degenerate fondness for tricking short-cuts, and little fallacious facilities, that has in so many parts of the world created governments with arbitrary powers. They have created the late arbitrary monarchy of France. They have created the arbitrary republic of Paris. With them defects in wisdom are to be supplied by the plenitude of force. They get nothing by it. Commencing their labours on a principle of sloth, they have the common fortune of slothful men. The difficulties which they rather had eluded than escaped, meet them again in their course; they multiply and thicken on them; they are involved,

---

[321] '[Our Founding] Father preferred the path of cultivation not to be easy' (Virgil, *Georgics*, 1.121–2).

through a labyrinth of confused detail, in an industry without limit, and without direction; and, in conclusion, the whole of their work becomes feeble, vitious, and insecure.

It is this inability to wrestle with difficulty which has obliged the arbitrary assembly of France to commence their schemes of reform with abolition and total destruction[xliv]. But is it in destroying and pulling down that skill is displayed? Your mob can do this as well at least as your assemblies. The shallowest understanding, the rudest hand, is more than equal to that task. Rage and phrenzy will pull down more in half an hour, than prudence, deliberation, and foresight can build up in an hundred years. The errors and defects of old establishments are visible and palpable. It calls for little ability to point them out; and where absolute power is given, it requires but a word wholly to abolish the vice and the establishment together. The same lazy but restless disposition, which loves sloth and hates quiet, directs these politicians, when they come to work, for supplying the place of what they have destroyed. To make every thing the reverse of what they have seen is quite as easy as to destroy. No difficulties occur in what has never been tried. Criticism is almost baffled in discovering the defects of what has not existed; and eager enthusiasm, and cheating hope, have all the wide field of imagination in which they may expatiate with little or no opposition.

At once to preserve and to reform is quite another thing. When the useful parts of an old establishment are kept, and what is superadded is to be fitted to what is retained, a vigorous mind, steady persevering attention, various powers of comparison and combination, and the resources of an understanding fruitful in expedients are to be exercised; they are to be

---

[xliv] A leading member of the assembly, M. Rabaud de St. Etienne, has expressed the principle of all their proceedings as clearly as possible. Nothing can be more simple:- '*Tous les établissemens en France couronnent le malheur du peuple: pour le rendre heureux il faut le renouveler; changer ses idées; changer ses loix; changer ses mœurs; . . . changer les hommes; changer les choses; changer les mots . . . tout détruire; oui, tout détruire; puisque tout est à recréer.*'[322] This gentlemen was chosen president in an assembly not sitting at the *Quinze vingt*, or the *Petites Maisons;*[323] and composed of persons giving themselves out to be rational beings; but neither his ideas, language, or conduct, differ in the smallest degree from the discourses, opinions, and actions of those within and without the assembly, who direct the operations of the machine now at work in France.

[322] 'All the establishments in France crown the unhappiness of the people: to make them happy they must be refashioned, have their ideas changed, their laws changed, their customs changed; . . . men changed; things changed; words changed; . . . everything destroyed; yes, destroy everything; since everything is to be made anew.'

[323] *Quinze Vingts*: the Paris hospital for the blind; *Petites Maisons*: a Parisian lunatic asylum.

exercised in a continued conflict with the combined force of opposite vices; with the obstinacy that rejects all improvement, and the levity that is fatigued and disgusted with every thing of which it is in possession. But you may object – 'A process of this kind is slow. It is not fit for an assembly, which glories in performing in a few months the work of ages. Such a mode of reforming, possibly might take up many years.' Without question it might; and it ought. It is one of the excellencies of a method in which time is amongst the assistants, that its operation is slow, and in some cases almost imperceptible. If circumspection and caution are a part of wisdom, when we work only upon inanimate matter, surely they become a part of duty too, when the subject of our demolition and construction is not brick and timber, but sentient beings, by the sudden alteration of whose state, condition, and habits, multitudes may be rendered miserable. But it seems as if it were the prevalent opinion in Paris, that an unfeeling heart, and an undoubting confidence, are the sole qualifications for a perfect legislator. Far different are my ideas of that high office. The true lawgiver ought to have an heart full of sensibility. He ought to love and respect his kind, and to fear himself. It may be allowed to his temperament to catch his ultimate object with an intuitive glance; but his movements towards it ought to be deliberate. Political arrangement, as it is a work for social ends, is to be only wrought by social means. There mind must conspire with mind. Time is required to produce that union of minds which alone can produce all the good we aim at. Our patience will atchieve more than our force. If I might venture to appeal to what is so much out of fashion in Paris, I mean, to experience, I should tell you, that in my course I have known, and, according to my measure, have co-operated with great men; and I have never yet seen any plan which has not been mended by the observations of those who were much inferior in understanding to the person who took the lead in the business. By a slow but well-sustained progress, the effect of each step is watched; the good or ill success of the first, gives light to us in the second; and so, from light to light, we are conducted with safety through the whole series. We see, that the parts of the system do not clash. The evils latent in the most promising contrivances are provided for as they arise. One advantage is as little as possible sacrificed to another. We compensate, we reconcile, we balance. We are enabled to unite into a consistent whole the various anomalies and contending principles that are found in the minds and affairs of men. From hence arises, not an excellence in simplicity, but one far superior, an excellence in composition. Where the great interests of mankind are concerned through a long succession of generations, that succession ought to be admitted into some share in the councils which are so deeply to affect them. If justice requires this, the work itself requires the aid of more minds than one age can furnish. It is from this view of things that the best legislators have been often satisfied with the establishment of some sure, solid, and ruling principle in government; a power like that which some of the philosophers have called a plastic nature;[324] and having fixed the principle, they have left it afterwards to its own operation.

To proceed in this manner, that is, to proceed with a presiding principle, and a prolific energy, is with me the criterion of profound wisdom. What your politicians think the marks of a bold, hardy genius, are only proofs of a deplorable want of ability. By their violent haste, and their defiance of the process of nature, they are delivered over blindly to every projector and adventurer, to every alchymist and empiric.[325] They despair of turning to account any thing that is common. Diet is nothing in their system of remedy. The worst of it is, that this their despair of curing common distempers by regular methods, arises not only from defect of comprehension, but, I fear, from some malignity of disposition. Your legislators seem to have taken their opinions of all professions, ranks, and offices, from the declamations and buffooneries of satirists; who would themselves be astonished if they were held to the letter of their own descriptions. By listening only to these, your leaders regard all things only on the side of their vices and faults, and view those vices and faults under every colour of exaggeration. It is undoubtedly true, though it may seem paradoxical; but in general, those who are habitually employed in finding and displaying faults, are unqualified for the work of reformation: because their minds are not only unfurnished with patterns of the fair and good, but by habit they come to take no delight in the contemplation of those things. By hating vices too much, they come to love men too little. It is therefore not wonderful, that they should be indisposed and unable to serve them. From hence arises the complexional disposition of some of your guides to pull every thing in pieces. At this malicious game they

---

[324] *Plastic nature*: This was a term coined by the Cambridge Platonist Ralph Cudworth (1617–89) in his *True Intellectual System of the Universe* (1678). To escape the alternative postulates of, on the one hand, a world under God's immediate and contingent will and superintendence and, on the other, a mechanical materialism: 'there is a plastic Nature in the Universe, as a subordinate instrument of divine providence' (*True Intellectual System*, 2nd edn (1743), Bk I, ch. 3, pp. 178ff.).

[325] *Alchymist*: student of alchemy, a magical predecessor of chemistry; *empiric*: a doctor without formal training who works from experience.

display the whole of their *quadrimanous* activity.[326] As to the rest, the paradoxes of eloquent writers, brought forth purely as a sport of fancy, to try their talents, to rouze attention, and excite surprize, are taken up by these gentlemen, not in the spirit of the original authors, as means of cultivating their taste and improving their style. These paradoxes become with them serious grounds of action, upon which they proceed in regulating the most important concerns of the state. Cicero ludicrously describes Cato as endeavouring to act in the commonwealth upon the school paradoxes which exercised the wits of the junior students in the stoic philosophy. If this was true of Cato, these gentlemen copy after him in the manner of some persons who lived about his time – *pede nudo Catonem*.[327] Mr. Hume told me, that he had from Rousseau himself the secret of his principles of composition. That acute, though eccentric, observer had perceived, that to strike and interest the public, the marvellous must be produced; that the marvellous of the heathen mythology had long since lost its effect; that giants, magicians, fairies, and heroes of romance which succeeded, had exhausted the portion of credulity which belonged to their age; that now nothing was left to a writer but that species of the marvellous, which might still be produced, and with as great an effect as ever, though in another way; that is, the marvellous in life, in manners, in characters, and in extraordinary situations, giving rise to new and unlooked-for strokes in politics and morals. I believe, that were Rousseau alive, and in one of his lucid intervals, he would be shocked at the practical phrenzy of his scholars, who in their paradoxes are servile imitators; and even in their incredulity discover an implicit faith.

Men who undertake considerable things, even in a regular way, ought to give us ground to presume ability. But the physician of the state, who, not satisfied with the cure of distempers, undertakes to regenerate constitutions, ought to shew uncommon powers. Some very unusual appearances of wisdom ought to display themselves on the face of the

---

[326] *Quadrimanous*: having four hands. The OED lists Burke's use here as the first. It refers to animals with prehensile feet, and by extension to monkeys, hence monkey-like in the sense of being destructively curious. Mitchell (*W&S*) suggests it may refer to a French *ancien régime* method of execution (applied to Louis XV's would-be assassin Damiens) in which the victim was dismembered by attaching their limbs to four horses pulling in different directions; but this form of execution had been abolished by the Revolution: it is unclear why it should characterise the revolutionaries.

[327] *Pede nudo Catonem*: 'with the bare feet of Cato'. A quotation used to hint at false displays of virtue. Mimicking the austere dress of Cato does not give one Cato's (legendary) ascetic virtue. Horace, *Epistles*, 1.19.12–14.

designs of those who appeal to no practice, and who copy after no model. Has any such been manifested? I shall take a view (it shall for the subject be a very short one) of what the assembly has done, with regard, first, to the constitution of the legislature; in the next place, to that of the executive power; then to that of the judicature; afterwards to the model of the army; and conclude with the system of finance, to see whether we can discover in any part of their schemes the portentous ability, which may justify these bold undertakers in the superiority which they assume over mankind.

It is in the model of the sovereign and presiding part of this new republic, that we should expect their grand display. Here they were to prove their title to their proud demands. For the plan itself at large, and for the reasons on which it is grounded, I refer to the journals of the assembly of the 29th of September 1789, and to the subsequent proceedings which have made any alterations in the plan.[328] So far as in a matter somewhat confused I can see light, the system remains substantially as it has been originally framed. My few remarks will be such as regard its spirit, its tendency, and its fitness for framing a popular commonwealth, which they profess theirs to be, suited to the ends for which any commonwealth, and particularly such a commonwealth, is made. At the same time, I mean to consider its consistency with itself, and its own principles.

Old establishments are tried by their effects. If the people are happy, united, wealthy, and powerful, we presume the rest. We conclude that to be good from whence good is derived. In old establishments various correctives have been found for their aberrations from theory. Indeed they are the results of various necessities and expediences. They are not often constructed after any theory; theories are rather drawn from them. In them we often see the end best obtained, where the means seem not perfectly reconcileable to what we may fancy was the original scheme. The means taught by experience may be better suited to political ends than those contrived in the original project. They again re-act upon the primitive constitution, and sometimes improve the design itself from which they seem to have departed. I think all this might be curiously exemplified in the British constitution. At worst, the errors and deviations

---

[328] The eventual legislative formulation of these proposals established the *Department* as the fundamental unit of sub-national government, and subsequently (26 Feb. 1790) divided France up into its 83 Departments (Decree establishing municipalities (14 Dec. 1789); Decree Establishing Electoral and Administrative Assemblies (22 Dec. 1789); Decree Dividing France into Departments (26 Feb. 1790), all in *DocS*, pp. 120, 127 and 137).

of every kind in reckoning are found and computed, and the ship proceeds in her course. This is the case of old establishments; but in a new and merely theoretic system, it is expected that every contrivance shall appear, on the face of it, to answer its end; especially where the projectors are no way embarrassed with an endeavour to accommodate the new building to an old one, either in the walls or on the foundations.

The French builders, clearing away as mere rubbish whatever they found, and, like their ornamental gardeners, forming every thing into an exact level,[329] propose to rest the whole local and general legislature on three bases of three different kinds; one geometrical, one arithmetical, and the third financial; the first of which they call the *basis of territory*; the second, the *basis of population*; and the third, the *basis of contribution*. For the accomplishment of the first of these purposes they divide the area of their country into eighty-three pieces, regularly square, of eighteen leagues by eighteen.[330] These large divisions are called *Departments*. These they portion, proceeding by square measurement, into seventeen hundred and twenty districts called *Communes*. These again they subdivide, still proceeding by square measurement, into smaller districts called *Cantons*, making in all 6,400.

At first view this geometrical basis of theirs presents not much to admire or to blame. It calls for no great legislative talents. Nothing more than an accurate land surveyor, with his chain, sight, and theodolite,[331] is requisite for such a plan as this. In the old divisions of the country various accidents at various times, and the ebb and flow of various properties and jurisdictions, settled their bounds. These bounds were not made upon any fixed system undoubtedly. They were subject to some inconveniencies; but they were inconveniencies for which use had found remedies, and habit had supplied accommodation and patience. In this new pavement of square within square, and this organisation and semiorganisation

---

329 The French style of gardening remained strictly formal and geometric, unlike the new British fashion for the picturesque imitation of the natural folds and undulations of the land.

330 This strict geometrical definition of the Departments was abandoned by the time the decree identifying them was promulgated on 26 Feb. 1790.

331 *Theodolite*: portable surveying instrument comprising a telescope mounted on a plain table, capable of accurately measuring angles subtended by features of the landscape. *Chain*: a means of measuring, and unit (*c*.20m) of length.

Burke is stressing the crude mechanical nature of the new Constitution, in contrast to the diverse, subtle cultural differences of the different parts of France.

made on the system of Empedocles[N] and Buffon,[332] and not upon any politic principle, it is impossible that innumerable local inconveniencies, to which men are not habituated, must not arise. But these I pass over, because it requires an accurate knowledge of the country, which I do not possess, to specify them.

When these state surveyors came to take a view of their work of measurement, they soon found, that in politics, the most fallacious of all things was geometrical demonstration. They had then recourse to another basis (or rather buttress) to support the building which tottered on that false foundation. It was evident, that the goodness of the soil, the number of the people, their wealth, and the largeness of their contribution, made such infinite variations between square and square as to render mensuration[333] a ridiculous standard of power in the commonwealth, and equality in geometry the most unequal of all measures in the distribution of men. However, they could not give it up. But dividing their political and civil representation into three parts, they allotted one of those parts to the square measurement, without a single fact or calculation to ascertain whether this territorial proportion of representation was fairly assigned, and ought upon any principle really to be a third. Having however given to geometry this portion (of a third for her dower[334]) out of compliment I suppose to that sublime science, they left the other two to be scuffled for between the other parts, population and contribution.

When they came to provide for population, they were not able to proceed quite so smoothly as they had done in the field of their geometry. Here their arithmetic came to bear upon their juridical metaphysics. Had they stuck to their metaphysic principles, the arithmetical process would be simple indeed. Men, with them, are strictly equal, and are entitled to equal rights in their own government. Each head, on this system, would have its vote, and every man would vote directly for the person who was

---

[332] *Buffon*: Georges Louis Leclerc, Comte de Buffon (1707–88), widely read French encyclopaedist, natural historian and author of the influential *Histoire Naturel* (1749), which includes his 'Discourse on the method of studying and treating natural history' advancing mathematics as a model of precision in science and the principle of utility. Amongst his views (for which his books were burnt in France) were that the solar system was formed by gravitational forces, the great antiquity of the earth, and the evolution of species in response to their environment. Burke cites him as exemplifying the atheistic materialist systematiser.

[333] *Mensuration*: measurement, or more specifically, quantitative geometry.

[334] *Dower*: a widow's portion of inheritance, in English law one-third of the estate (Blackstone, *Commentaries on the Laws of England*, II. vii. 116).

to represent him in the legislature. 'But soft – by regular degrees, not yet.'[335] This metaphysic principle, to which law, custom, usage, policy, reason, were to yield, is to yield itself to their pleasure. There must be many degrees, and some stages, before the representative can come in contact with his constituent. Indeed, as we shall soon see, these two persons are to have no sort of communion with each other. First, the voters in the *Canton*, who compose what they call *primary assemblies*, are to have a *qualification*. What! a qualification on the indefeasible rights of men? Yes; but it shall be a very small qualification. Our injustice shall be very little oppressive; only the local valuation of three days labour paid to the public. Why, this is not much, I readily admit, for any thing but the utter subversion of your equalising principle. As a qualification it might as well be let alone; for it answers no one purpose for which qualifications are established: and, on your ideas, it excludes from a vote, the man of all others whose natural equality stands the most in need of protection and defence; I mean the man who has nothing else but his natural equality to guard him. You order him to buy the right, which you before told him nature had given to him gratuitously at his birth, and of which no authority on earth could lawfully deprive him.[336] With regard to the person who cannot come up to your market, a tyrannous aristocracy, as against him, is established at the very outset, by you who pretend to be its sworn foe.

The gradation proceeds. These primary assemblies of the *Canton* elect deputies to the *Commune*; one for every two hundred qualified

---

335    'Behold! My Lord advances with majestic mein, [o'er the Green,]
        Smit with the mighty pleasure [,] to be seen:
        But soft – by regular approach – not yet –
        First thro' the length of yon hot Terras sweat;
             (Pope: *Epistle to the right Honourable Richard Earl of Burlington*,
                                                            ll. 127–30)

   Pope's epistle was a satire on neo-classical formal architecture and landscaping (the rectangular geometry of whose pathways commonly precluded direct passage from A to B, referring back to Burke's reference to the 'ornamental gardeners' (fn. 329). Burke is implicitly likening this to the revolutionaries' formalised constitution-making, and the indirection established between the constituent and the representative.

336 The Decree establishing the Assemblies and their electoral provisions introduced a distinction between active citizens, with the right to vote, and passive citizens, without such a right. Active citizens had to be (male) native or naturalised French*men* over 25, with a year's local residency, not personal servants and paying taxes valued at three days' labour (Decree establishing Electoral Assemblies, 22 Dec. 1789, Sect. 1,§3: *DocS*, p. 129). Burke points out the inconsistency of such qualifications with the universal principles claimed under the Declaration of the Rights of Man.

inhabitants. Here is the first medium put between the primary elector and the representative legislator; and here a new turnpike is fixed for taxing the rights of men with a second qualification: for none can be elected into the *Commune* who does not pay the amount of ten days labour. Nor have we yet done. There is still to be another gradation[xlv]. These *Communes*, chosen by the *Canton*, choose to the *Department*; and the deputies of the *Department* choose their deputies to the *National Assembly*.[N] Here is a third barrier of a senseless qualification. Every deputy to the national assembly must pay, in direct contribution, to the value of a *mark of silver*. Of all these qualifying barriers we must think alike; that they are impotent to secure independence; strong only to destroy the rights of men.

In all this process, which in its fundamental elements affects to consider only *population* upon a principle of natural right, there is a manifest attention to *property*; which, however just and reasonable on other schemes, is on theirs perfectly unsupportable.

When they come to their third basis, that of *Contribution*, we find that they have more completely lost sight of their rights of men. This last basis rests *entirely* on property. A principle totally different from the equality of men, and utterly irreconcileable to it, is thereby admitted; but no sooner is this principle admitted, than (as usual) it is subverted; and it is not subverted, (as we shall presently see,) to approximate the inequality of riches to the level of nature. The additional share in the third portion of representation, (a portion reserved exclusively for the higher contribution,) is made to regard the *district* only, and not the individuals in it who pay. It is easy to perceive, by the course of their reasonings, how much they were embarrassed by their contradictory ideas of the rights of men and the privileges of riches. The committee of constitution do as good as admit that they are wholly irreconcileable. 'The relation, with regard to the contributions, is without doubt *null* (say they) when the question is on the balance of the political rights as between individual and individual; without which *personal equality would be destroyed*, and

---

[xlv] [The assembly, in executing the plan of their committee, made some alterations. They have struck out one stage in these gradations; this removes a part of the objection: but the main objection, namely, that in their scheme the first constituent voter has no connection with the representative legislator, remains in all its force. There are other alterations, some possibly for the better, some certainly for the worse; but to the author the merit or demerit of these smaller alterations appear to be of no moment, where the scheme itself is fundamentally vitious and absurd.][337]

---

[337] Footnote absent from 1st edn.

*an aristocracy of the rich* would be established. But this inconvenience entirely disappears when the proportional relation of the contribution is only considered in the *great masses*, and is solely between province and province; it serves in that case only to form a just reciprocal proportion between the cities, without affecting the personal rights of the citizens.'[338]

Here the principle of *contribution*, as taken between man and man, is reprobated as *null*, and destructive to equality; and as pernicious too; because it leads to the establishment of an *aristocracy of the rich*. However, it must not be abandoned. And the way of getting rid of the difficulty is to establish the inequality as between department and department, leaving all the individuals in each department upon an exact par. Observe, that this parity between individuals had been before destroyed when the qualifications within the departments were settled; nor does it seem a matter of great importance whether the equality of men be injured by masses or individually. An individual is not of the same importance in a mass represented by a few, as in a mass represented by many. It would be too much to tell a man jealous of his equality, that the elector has the same franchise who votes for three members as he who votes for ten.

[Now[339] take it in the other point of view, and let us suppose their principle of representation according to contribution, that is according to riches, to be well imagined, and to be a necessary basis for their republic. In this their third basis they assume, that riches ought to be respected, and that justice and policy require that they should entitle men, in some mode or other, to a larger share in the administration of public affairs; it is now to be seen, how the assembly provides for the pre-eminence, or even for the security of the rich, by conferring, in virtue of their opulence, that larger measure of power to their district which is denied to them personally. I readily admit (indeed I should lay it down as a fundamental principle) that in a republican government, which has a democratic basis, the rich do require an additional security above what is necessary to them in monarchies. They are subject to envy, and through envy to oppression. On the present scheme, it is impossible to divine what advantage they derive from the aristocratic preference upon which the unequal representation of the masses is founded. The rich cannot feel it, either as a support to dignity, or as security to fortune: for the

[338] Burke's translation of the report of the committee published in *Le Moniteur*, 28-9 September 1789.
[339] The text from here down to ** on p. 183 was extensively revised and expanded by Burke in the third edition. For the text of the original three paragraphs, see Appendix.

aristocratic mass is generated from purely democratic principles; and the prevalence given to it in the general representation has no sort of reference to or connexion with the persons, upon account of whose property this superiority of the mass is established. If the contrivers of this scheme meant any sort of favour to the rich in consequence of their contribution, they ought to have conferred the privilege either on the individual rich, or on some class formed of rich persons (as historians represent Servius Tullius to have done in the early constitution of Rome);[340] because the contest between the rich and the poor is not a struggle between corporation and corporation, but a contest between men and men; a competition not between districts but between descriptions. It would answer its purpose better if the scheme were inverted; that the votes of the masses were rendered equal; and that the votes within each mass were proportioned to property.

Let us suppose one man in a district (it is an easy supposition) to contribute as much as an hundred of his neighbours. Against these he has but one vote. If there were but one representative for the mass, his poor neighbours would outvote him by an hundred to one for that single representative. Bad enough. But amends are to be made him. How? The district, in virtue of his wealth, is to choose, say, ten members instead of one: that is to say, by paying a very large contribution he has the happiness of being outvoted, an hundred to one, by the poor for ten representatives, instead of being outvoted exactly in the same proportion for a single member. In truth, instead of benefitting by this superior quantity of representation, the rich man is subjected to an additional hardship. The encrease of representation within his province sets up nine persons more, and as many more than nine as there may be democratic candidates, to cabal and intrigue, and to flatter the people at his expence and to his oppression. An interest is by this means held out to multitudes of the inferior sort, in obtaining a salary of eighteen livres a day (to them a vast object) besides the pleasure of a residence in Paris and their share in the government of the kingdom. The more the objects of ambition are multiplied and become democratic, just in that proportion the rich are endangered.

Thus it must fare between the poor and the rich in the province deemed aristocratic, which in its internal relation is the very reverse of

---

[340] *Servius Tullius (fl.* 578–*c.*535 BC): reforming King of Rome, credited with conducting the first census of Rome and admitting the Plebeians to civic and military rights. He established a political organisation of the city along residential divisions which cut across the previous ones based on lineage and status.

that character. In its external relation, that is, its relation to the other provinces, I cannot see how the unequal representation, which is given to masses on account of wealth, becomes the means of preserving the equipoise and the tranquillity of the commonwealth. For if it be one of the objects to secure the weak from being crushed by the strong (as in all society undoubtedly it is) how are the smaller and poorer of these masses to be saved from the tyranny of the more wealthy? Is it by adding to the wealthy further and more systematical means of oppressing them? When we come to a balance of representation between corporate bodies, provincial interests, emulations, and jealousies are full as likely to arise among them as among individuals; and their divisions are likely to produce a much hotter spirit of dissention, and something leading much more nearly to a war.

I see that these aristocratic masses are made upon what is called the principle of direct contribution. Nothing can be a more unequal standard than this. The indirect contribution, that which arises from duties on consumption, is in truth a better standard, and follows and discovers wealth more naturally than this of direct contribution. It is difficult indeed to fix a standard of local preference on account of the one, or of the other, or of both, because some provinces may pay the more of either or of both, on account of causes not intrinsic, but originating from those very districts over whom they have obtained a preference in consequence of their ostensible contribution. If the masses were independent sovereign bodies, who were to provide for a federative treasury by distinct contingents, and that the revenue had not (as it has) many impositions running through the whole, which affect men individually, and not corporately, and which, by their nature, confound all territorial limits, something might be said for the basis of contribution as founded on masses. But of all things, this representation, to be measured by contribution, is the most difficult to settle upon principles of equity in a country, which considers its districts as members of an whole. For a great city, such as Bourdeaux or Paris, appears to pay a vast body of duties, almost out of all assignable proportion to other places, and its mass is considered accordingly. But are these cities the true contributors in that proportion? No. The consumers of the commodities imported into Bourdeaux, who are scattered through all France, pay the import duties of Bourdeaux. The produce of the vintage in Guienne and Languedoc give to that city the means of its contribution growing out of an export commerce. The landholders who spend their estates in Paris, and are thereby the creators of that city, contribute for

Paris from the provinces out of which their revenue arise. Very nearly the same arguments will apply to the representative share given on account of *direct* contribution: because the direct contribution must be assessed on wealth real or presumed; and that local wealth will itself arise from causes not local, and which therefore in equity ought not to produce a local preference.

It is very remarkable, that in this fundamental regulation, which settles the representation of the mass upon the direct contribution, they have not yet settled how that direct contribution shall be laid, and how apportioned. Perhaps there is some latent policy towards the continuance of the present assembly in this strange procedure. However, until they do this, they can have no certain constitution. It must depend at last upon the system of taxation, and must vary with every variation in that system. As they have contrived matters, their taxation does not so much depend on their constitution, as their constitution on their taxation. This must introduce great confusion among the masses; as the variable qualification for votes within the district must, if ever real contested elections take place, cause infinite internal controversies.**]

To compare together the three bases, not on their political reason, but on the ideas on which the assembly works, and to try its consistency with itself, we cannot avoid observing, that the principle which the committee call the basis of *population*, does not begin to operate from the same point with the two other principles called the bases of *territory* and of *contribution*, which are both of an aristocratic nature. The consequence is, that where all three begin to operate together, there is the most absurd inequality produced by the operation of the former on the two latter principles. Every canton contains four square leagues, and is estimated to contain, on the average, 4,000 inhabitants, or 680 voters in the *primary assemblies*, which vary in numbers with the population of the canton, and send *one deputy* to the *commune* for every 200 voters. *Nine cantons* make a *commune*.

Now let us take a *canton* containing a *sea-port town of trade*, or *a great manufacturing town*. Let us suppose the population of this canton to be 12,700 inhabitants, or 2,193 voters, forming *three primary assemblies*, and sending *ten deputies* to the *commune*.

Oppose to this *one* canton *two* others of the remaining eight in the same commune. These we may suppose to have their fair population of 4,000 inhabitants, and 680 voters each, or 8,000 inhabitants and 1,360 voters, both together. These will form only *two primary assemblies*, and send only *six* deputies to the *commune*.

When the assembly of the *commune* comes to vote on the *basis of territory*, which principle is first admitted to operate in that assembly, the *single canton* which has *half* the territory of the *other two*, will have *ten* voices to *six* in the election of *three deputies* to the assembly of the department, chosen on the express ground of a representation of territory.

This inequality, striking as it is, will be yet highly aggravated, if we suppose, as we fairly may, the *several* other cantons of the *commune* to fall proportionably short of the average population, as much as the *principal canton* exceeds it. Now, as to *the basis of contribution*, which also is a principle admitted first to operate in the assembly of the *commune*. Let us again take *one* canton, such as is stated above. If the whole of the direct contributions paid by a great trading or manufacturing town be divided equally among the inhabitants, each individual will be found to pay much more than an individual living in the country according to the same average. The whole paid by the inhabitants of the former will be more than the whole paid by the inhabitants of the latter – we may fairly assume one third more. Then the 12,700 inhabitants, or 2,193 voters of the canton will pay as much as 19,050 inhabitants, or 3,289 voters of the *other cantons*, which are nearly the estimated proportion of inhabitants and voters of *five* other cantons. Now the 2,193 voters will, as I before said, send only *ten* deputies to the assembly; the 3,289 voters will send *sixteen*. Thus, for an *equal* share in the contribution of the whole *commune*, there will be a difference of *sixteen* voices to *ten* in voting for deputies to be chosen on the principle of representing the general contribution of the whole *commune*.

By the same mode of computation we shall find 15,875 inhabitants, or 2,741 voters of the *other* cantons, who pay *one-sixth* LESS to the contribution of the whole *commune*, will have *three* voices MORE than the 12,700 inhabitants, or 2,193 voters of the *one* canton.

Such is the fantastical and unjust inequality between mass and mass, in this curious repartition of the rights of representation arising out of *territory* and *contribution*. The qualifications which these confer are in truth negative qualifications, that give a right in an inverse proportion to the possession of them.

In this whole contrivance of the three bases, consider it in any light you please, I do not see a variety of objects, reconciled in one consistent whole, but several contradictory principles reluctantly and irreconcileably brought and held together by your philosophers, like wild beasts shut up in a cage, to claw and bite each other to their mutual destruction.

I am afraid I have gone too far into their way of considering the formation of a constitution. They have much, but bad, metaphysics; much, but bad, geometry; much, but false, proportionate arithmetic; but if it were all as exact as metaphysics, geometry, and arithmetic ought to be, and if their schemes were perfectly consistent in all their parts, it would make only a more fair and sightly vision. It is remarkable, that in a great arrangement of mankind, not one reference whatsoever is to be found to any thing moral or any thing politic; nothing that relates to the concerns, the actions, the passions, the interests of men. *Hominem non sapiunt.*[341]

You see I only consider this constitution as electoral, and leading by steps to the National Assembly.[N] I do not enter into the internal government of the Departments, and their genealogy through the Communes and Cantons. These local governments are, in the original plan, to be as nearly as possible composed in the same manner and on the same principles with the elective assemblies. They are each of them bodies perfectly compact and rounded in themselves.

You cannot but perceive in this scheme, that it has a direct and immediate tendency to sever France into a variety of republics, and to render them totally independent of each other, without any direct constitutional means of coherence, connection, or subordination, except what may be derived from their acquiescence in the determinations of the general congress of the ambassadors from each independent republic. Such in reality is the National Assembly, and such governments I admit do exist in the world, though in forms infinitely more suitable to the local and habitual circumstances of their people.[342] But such associations, rather than bodies politic, have generally been the effect of necessity, not choice; and I believe the present French power is the very first body of citizens, who, having obtained full authority to do with their country what they pleased, have chosen to dissever it in this barbarous manner.

It is impossible not to observe, that in the spirit of this geometrical distribution, and arithmetical arrangement, these pretended citizens treat France exactly like a country of conquest. Acting as conquerors, they

---

[341] Probably in contrast to an Epigram of Martial: *hominem pagina nostra sapit* ['our page is about humankind'] (*Epigrammata*, 10.4.10). Burke is claiming that the French constitution reveals no understanding of human nature.

[342] The Swiss Confederation was the main example of a federal republic in modern Europe. The American Federal Constitution, completed in September 1787, was barely two years old, and was still being ratified as *Reflections* was being composed.

have imitated the policy of the harshest of that harsh race. The policy of such barbarous victors, who contemn a subdued people, and insult their feelings, has ever been, as much as in them lay, to destroy all vestiges of the antient country, in religion, in polity, in laws, and in manners; to confound all territorial limits; to produce a general poverty; to put up their properties to auction; to crush their princes, nobles, and pontiffs; to lay low every thing which had lifted its head above the level, or which could serve to combine or rally, in their distresses, the disbanded people, under the standard of old opinion. They have made France free in the manner in which those sincere friends to the rights of mankind, the Romans, freed Greece, Macedon, and other nations. They destroyed the bonds of their union, under colour of providing for the independence of each of their cities.

When the members who compose these new bodies of cantons, com-munes, and departments, arrangements purposely produced through the medium of confusion, begin to act, they will find themselves, in a great measure, strangers to one another. The electors and elected through-out, especially in the rural *cantons*, will be frequently without any civil habitudes or connections, or any of that natural discipline which is the soul of a true republic. Magistrates and collectors of revenue are now no longer acquainted with their districts, bishops with their dioceses, or curates with their parishes. These new colonies of the rights of men bear a strong resemblance to that sort of military colonies which Tacitus has observed upon in the declining policy of Rome. In better and wiser days (whatever course they took with foreign nations) they were careful to make the elements of a methodical subordination and settlement to be coeval; and even to lay the foundations of civil discipline in the military[xlvi].

---

[xlvi] Non, ut olim, universæ legiones deducebantur cum tribunis, et centurionibus, et sui cujusque ordinis militibus, ut consensu et caritate rempublicam afficerent; sed ignoti inter se, diversis manipulis, sine rectore, sine affectibus mutuis, quasi ex alio genere mortalium, repente in unum collecti, numerus magis quam colonia. Tac. Annal. 1.14. sect. 27. All this will be still more applicable to the unconnected, rotatory, biennial national assemblies, in this absurd and senseless constitution.[343]

---

[343] 'Not, as once, were entire legions with their tribunes, centurions, and privates in their proper ranks all settled so as to make, by their unanimity and mutual concern, a civil community; but unknown to each other, from different platoons, without leaders, without mutual affection, as if from a different race of beings, unexpectedly drawn together in one, more a plurality than a community.' Tacitus (*Annales*, 1.14.27) is describing the failure of the late republic to continue the practice of founding veteran soldier colonies in their serving units so as to retain the sense of community created under arms.

But, when all the good arts had fallen into ruin, they proceeded, as your assembly does, upon the equality of men, and with as little judgment, and as little care for those things which make a republic tolerable or durable. But in this, as well as almost every instance, your new commonwealth is born, and bred, and fed, in those corruptions which mark degenerated and worn out republics. Your child comes into the world with the symptoms of death; the *facies Hippocratica*[344] forms the character of its physiognomy, and the prognostic of its fate.

The legislators who framed the antient republics knew that their business was too arduous to be accomplished with no better apparatus than the metaphysics of an undergraduate, and the mathematics and arithmetic of an exciseman.[345] They had to do with men, and they were obliged to study human nature. They had to do with citizens, and they were obliged to study the effects of those habits which are communicated by the circumstances of civil life. They were sensible that the operation of this second nature on the first produced a new combination; and thence arose many diversities amongst men, according to their birth, their education, their professions, the periods of their lives, their residence in towns or in the country, their several ways of acquiring and of fixing property, and according to the quality of the property itself, all which rendered them as it were so many different species of animals. From hence they thought themselves obliged to dispose their citizens into such classes, and to place them in such situations in the state as their peculiar habits might qualify them to fill, and to allot to them such appropriated privileges as might secure to them what their specific occasions required, and which might furnish to each description such force as might protect it in the conflict caused by the diversity of interests, that must exist, and must contend in all complex society: for the legislator would have been ashamed, that the coarse husbandman should well know how to assort and to use his sheep, horses, and oxen, and should have enough of common sense not to abstract and equalize them all into animals, without providing for each kind an appropriate food, care, and employment; whilst he, the œconomist, disposer, and shepherd of his own kindred, subliming

---

[344] Hippocrates (*c*.460–*c*.370 BC), ancient Greek medical practitioner and writer, a founder of scientific medicine presuming natural causes of illness. The *Facies Hippocratica* refers to his classic description of the appearance of the face immediately before death.

[345] Tom Paine had been an excise officer before emigrating to America. But there is no reason to believe Burke, at this stage, had Paine in his sights. Paine would compose his *Rights of Man* in response to Burke's work.

himself into an airy metaphysician, was resolved to know nothing of his flocks, but as men in general.[346] It is for this reason that Montesquieu observed very justly, that in their classification of the citizens, the great legislators of antiquity made the greatest display of their powers, and even soared above themselves.[347] It is here that your modern legislators have gone deep into the negative series, and sunk even below their own nothing. As the first sort of legislators attended to the different kinds of citizens, and combined them into one commonwealth, the others, the metaphysical and alchemistical legislators, have taken the direct contrary course. They have attempted to confound all sorts of citizens, as well as they could, into one homogeneous mass; and then they divided this their amalgama[348] into a number of incoherent republics. They reduce men to loose counters merely for the sake of simple telling,[349] and not to figures whose power is to arise from their place in the table. The elements of their own metaphysics might have taught them better lessons. The troll of their categorical table might have informed them that there was something else in the intellectual world besides *substance* and *quantity*. They might learn from the catechism of metaphysics that there were eight heads more[xlvii], in every complex deliberation, which they have never thought of, though these, of all the ten, are the subject on which the skill of man can operate any thing at all.[350]

So far from this able disposition of some of the old republican legislators, which follows with a solicitous accuracy, the moral conditions

---

[xlvii]   Qualitas, Relatio, Actio, Passio, Ubi, Quando, Situs, Habitus.

[346]  Despite the proximity of Montesquieu here the extended metaphor of the statesman as livestock farmer recalls several such in Plato's political works.

[347]  Montesquieu, *Spirit of the Laws* (Cambridge, 1989), vol. 2, p. 2: 'Great legislators have distinguished themselves by the way they have made this division, and upon it the duration and prosperity of democracies have always depended.'

[348]  *Amalgama* (*sc.* amalgam): a combination of mercury and another metal to form a soft mass; so by extension a mix of unlike elements.

[349]  *Telling*: counting.

[350]  In his work *The Categories*, Aristotle identified and analysed the ten fundamental categories of all propositions, that is to say the kinds of claims we can formulate about things. These were *Substance* (that which is) and the various classes of properties that could be predicated of a substance: *Quantity, Quality, Relation, Place, Time, Posture, Condition, Action* and *Affection (susceptibility)*. The table became a standard template for analysis in the medieval curriculum, and was still being taught in the undergraduate curriculum at Trinity College Dublin in Burke's day. Burke's intention is to associate the revolutionaries with scholastic and outmoded metaphysics, at which they are, in any case, incompetent.

and propensities of men, they have levelled and crushed together all the orders which they found, even under the coarse unartificial arrangement of the monarchy, in which mode of government the classing of the citizens is not of so much importance as in a republic. It is true, however, that every such classification, if properly ordered, is good in all forms of government; and composes a strong barrier against the excesses of despotism, as well as it is the necessary means of giving effect and permanence to a republic. For want of something of this kind, if the present project of a republic should fail, all securities to a moderated freedom fail along with it; all the indirect restraints which mitigate despotism are removed; insomuch that if monarchy should ever again obtain an entire ascendency in France, under this or under any other dynasty, it will probably be, if not voluntarily tempered at setting out, by the wise and virtuous counsels of the prince, the most completely arbitrary power that has ever appeared on earth. This is to play a most desperate game.[351]

The confusion, which attends on all such proceedings, they even declare to be one of their objects, and they hope to secure their constitution by a terror of a return of those evils which attended their making it. 'By this,' say they, 'its destruction will become difficult to authority, which cannot break it up without the entire disorganization of the whole state.' They presume, that if this authority should ever come to the same degree of power that they have acquired, it would make a more moderate and chastised use of it, and would piously tremble entirely to disorganise the state in the savage manner that they have done. They expect, from the virtues of returning despotism, the security which is to be enjoyed by the offspring of their popular vices.

[I wish, Sir, that you and my readers would give an attentive perusal to the work of M. de Calonne,[N] on this subject.[352] It is indeed not only an eloquent but an able and instructive performance. I confine myself to what he says relative to the constitution of the new state, and to the condition of the revenue. As to the disputes of this minister with his rivals, I do not wish to pronounce upon them. As little do I mean to hazard any opinion concerning his ways and means, financial or political, for taking his country out of its present disgraceful and deplorable situation of servitude, anarchy, bankruptcy, and beggary. I cannot speculate quite

---

[351] In 1st edn this and the preceding paragraph originally at **, p. 193 below.

[352] Charles Alexandre de Calonne, *De l'état de la France présent et à venir* (London, 1790). This paragraph was inserted in the 3rd edition, following Burke's reading of Calonne's important work, and two paragraphs were relocated; see previous fn.

so sanguinely as he does: but he is a Frenchman, and has a closer duty relative to those objects, and better means of judging of them, than I can have. I wish that the formal avowal which he refers to, made by one of the principal leaders in the assembly, concerning the tendency of their scheme to bring France not only from a monarchy to a republic, but from a republic to a mere confederacy, may be very particularly attended to.[353] It adds new force to my observations; and indeed M. de Calonne's work supplies my deficiencies by many new and striking arguments on most of the subjects of this Letter.[xlviii]]

It is this resolution, to break their country into separate republics, which has driven them into the greatest number of their difficulties and contradictions. If it were not for this, all the questions of exact equality, and these balances, never to be settled, of individual rights, population, and contribution, would be wholly useless. The representation, though derived from parts, would be a duty which equally regarded the whole. Each deputy to the assembly would be the representative of France, and of all its descriptions, of the many and of the few, of the rich and of the poor, of the great districts and of the small. All these districts would themselves be subordinate to some standing authority, existing independently of them; an authority in which their representation, and every thing that belongs to it, originated, and to which it was pointed.[354] This standing, unalterable, fundamental government would make, and it is the only thing which could make, that territory truly and properly an whole. With us, when we elect popular representatives, we send them to a council, in which each man individually is a subject, and submitted to a government complete in all its ordinary functions. With you the elective assembly is the sovereign, and the sole sovereign: all the members are therefore integral

[xlviii]  See L'Etat de la France, p. 363.

[353] Calonne followed most eighteenth-century political commentators in regarding the republican form as quite unworkable in a large state, such as France – an 'Empire' as he called it – and criticised the revolutionaries for a faddish pursuit of an unknown and untried model: the American United States.

[354] In a famous election speech at Bristol, Burke had maintained that MPs are not delegates – 'Your representative owes you, not his industry only, but his judgment; and he betrays, instead of serving you, if he sacrifices it to your opinion.' And he had insisted to them on the corporate character of Parliament: 'You chuse a Member indeed; but when you have chosen him, he is not Member of Bristol, but he is a Member of *Parliament*' (*Speech at the conclusion of the Poll*, 3 Nov. 1774; *W&S*, iii, p. 69). Here he emphasises an important underlying corollary of this, that, in England, it is the legislative body – the King in Parliament – that is the sovereign, not the people who elect to it.

parts of this sole sovereignty. But with us it is totally different. With us the representative, separated from the other parts, can have no action and no existence. The government is the point of reference of the several members and districts of our representation. This is the center of our unity. This government of reference is a trustee for the *whole*, and not for the parts. So is the other branch of our public council, I mean the house of lords. With us the king and the lords are several and joint securities for the equality of each district, each province, each city. When did you hear in Great Britain of any province suffering from the inequality of its representation; what district from having no representation at all?[355] Not only our monarchy and our peerage secure the equality on which our unity depends, but it is the spirit of the house of commons itself. The very inequality of representation, which is so foolishly complained of, is perhaps the very thing which prevents us from thinking or acting as members for districts. Cornwall elects as many members as all Scotland. But is Cornwall better taken care of than Scotland? Few trouble their heads about any of your bases, out of some giddy clubs. Most of those, who wish for any change, upon any plausible grounds, desire it on different ideas.

Your new constitution is the very reverse of ours in its principle; and I am astonished how any persons could dream of holding out any thing done in it as an example for Great Britain. With you there is little, or rather no, connection between the last representative and the first constituent. The member who goes to the national assembly[N] is not chosen by the people, nor accountable to them. There are three elections before he is chosen:[356] two sets of magistracy intervene between him and the primary assembly, so as to render him, as I have said, an ambassador of a state, and not the representative of the people within a state. By this the whole spirit of the election is changed; nor can any corrective your constitution-mongers have devised render him any thing else than what he is. The very attempt to do it would inevitably introduce a confusion, if possible, more horrid than the present. There is no way to make a connection between the original constituent and the representative, but by the circuitous means which may lead the candidate to apply in the

---

[355] Burke is here being disingenuous: a variety of reformers, including some of those active in the Revolution Society,[N] and the Society for Constitutional Information,[N] sought reform on precisely those grounds, and the Corresponding Societies would certainly do so, in addition, many of them, to seeking the extension of the franchise.

[356] As Burke conceded above (p. 179 n. xlv), this had been reduced to two in the eventual legislation.

first instance to the primary electors, in order that by their authoritative instructions (and something more perhaps) these primary electors may force the two succeeding bodies of electors to make a choice agreeable to their wishes. But this would plainly subvert the whole scheme. It would be to plunge them back into that tumult and confusion of popular election, which, by their interposed gradation elections, they mean to avoid, and at length to risque the whole fortune of the state with those who have the least knowledge of it, and the least interest in it. This is a perpetual dilemma, into which they are thrown by the vicious, weak, and contradictory principles they have chosen. Unless the people break up and level this gradation, it is plain that they do not at all substantially elect to the assembly; indeed they elect as little in appearance as reality.

What is it we all seek for in an election? To answer its real purposes, you must first possess the means of knowing the fitness of your man; and then you must retain some hold upon him by personal obligation or dependence. For what end are these primary electors complimented, or rather mocked, with a choice? They can never know any thing of the qualities of him that is to serve them, nor has he any obligation whatsoever to them. Of all the powers unfit to be delegated by those who have any real means of judging, that most peculiarly unfit is what relates to a *personal* choice. In case of abuse, that body of primary electors never can call the representative to an account for his conduct. He is too far removed from them in the chain of representation. If he acts improperly at the end of his two years lease, it does not concern him for two years more. By the new French constitution, the best and the wisest representatives go equally with the worst into this *Limbus Patrum*.[357] Their bottoms are supposed foul, and they must go into dock to be refitted. Every man who has served in an assembly is ineligible for two years after. Just as these magistrates begin to learn their trade, like chimney-sweepers,[358] they are disqualified for exercising it. Superficial, new, petulant acquisition, and interrupted, dronish, broken, ill recollection, is to be the destined character of all your future governors. Your constitution has too much of jealousy to have

---

357 *Limbus Patrum*: 'Limbo' is literally the edge or margin; *Limbus Patrum* refers, in medieval Catholic theology, to spaces at the margins of Hell where certain souls who died outside the Church await judgement. The *limbus infantium* was for unbaptised infants and the *limbus patrum* for the prophets and patriarchs who lived before Christ.

358 In the eighteenth and nineteenth centuries young children were employed as sweeps. When they grew too large to negotiate the chimneys they were made redundant.

much of sense in it. You consider the breach of trust in the representative so principally, that you do not at all regard the question of his fitness to execute it.

This purgatory interval is not unfavourable to a faithless representative, who may be as good a canvasser as he was a bad governor. In this time he may cabal himself into a superiority over the wisest and most virtuous. As, in the end, all the members of this elective constitution are equally fugitive, and exist only for the election, they may be no longer the same persons who had chosen him, to whom he is to be responsible when he solicits for a renewal of his trust. To call all the secondary electors of the *Commune* to account, is ridiculous, impracticable, and unjust; they may themselves have been deceived in their choice, as the third set of electors, those of the *Department*, may be in theirs. In your elections responsibility cannot exist.[359] * *

Finding no sort of principle of coherence with each other in the nature and constitution of the several new republics of France, I considered what cement the legislators had provided for them from any extraneous materials. Their confederations, their *spectacles*, their civic feasts, and their enthusiasm, I take no notice of;[360] They are nothing but mere tricks; but tracing their policy through their actions, I think I can distinguish the arrangements by which they propose to hold these republics together. The first, is the *confiscation*, with the compulsory paper currency annexed to it; the second, is the supreme power of the city of Paris; the third, is the general army of the state. Of this last I shall reserve what I have to say, until I come to consider the army as an head by itself.

As to the operation of the first (the confiscation and paper currency) merely as a cement, I cannot deny that these, the one depending on the other, may for some time compose some sort of cement, if their madness and folly in the management, and in the tempering of the parts together, does not produce a repulsion in the very outset. But allowing to the scheme some coherence and some duration, it appears to me, that if, after a while, the confiscation should not be found sufficient to support the paper coinage (as I am morally certain it will not) then, instead of cementing, it will add infinitely to the dissociation, distraction, and confusion of these

---

[359] Two paragraphs were cut from the 1st edition here and reinserted at pp. 187–89.

[360] From the first the revolutionary movement sought to generate public support and solidarity through celebrations, spectacles and festivities. See Mona Ozouf, *Festivals and the French Revolution* (1976; trs. Cambridge, Mass., 1988).

confederate republics, both with relation to each other, and to the several parts within themselves. But if the confiscation should so far succeed as to sink the paper currency, the cement is gone with the circulation. In the mean time its binding force will be very uncertain, and it will straiten or relax with every variation in the credit of the paper.

One thing only is certain in this scheme, which is an effect seemingly collateral, but direct, I have no doubt, in the minds of those who conduct this business, that is, its effect in producing an *Oligarchy* in every one of the republics. A paper circulation, not founded on any real money deposited or engaged for, amounting already to four-and-forty millions of English money, and this currency by force substituted in the place of the coin of the kingdom, becoming thereby the substance of its revenue, as well as the medium of all its commercial and civil intercourse, must put the whole of what power, authority, and influence is left, in any form whatsoever it may assume, into the hands of the managers and conductors of this circulation.

In England we feel the influence of the bank; though it is only the center of a voluntary dealing. He knows little indeed of the influence of money upon mankind, who does not see the force of the management of a monied concern, which is so much more extensive, and in its nature so much more depending on the managers than any of ours. [But this is not merely a money concern. There is another member in the system inseparably connected with this money management. It consists in the means of drawing out at discretion portions of the confiscated lands for sale; and carrying on a process of continual transmutation of paper into land, and land into paper. When we follow this process in its effects, we may conceive something of the intensity of the force with which this system must operate.][361] By this means the spirit of money-jobbing and speculation goes into the mass of land itself, and incorporates with it. By this kind of operation, that species of property becomes (as it were) volatilized; it assumes an unnatural and monstrous activity, and thereby throws into the hands of the several managers, principal and subordinate, Parisian and provincial, all the representative of money, and perhaps a full tenth part of all the land in France, which has now

---

[361] 1st edition here reads: 'But if we take into consideration the other part essentially connected with it (which consists in continually drawing out for sale portions of the confiscated land, this continual exchanging land for paper, and this mixing it into circulation) we may conceive something of the intensity of its operation.'

acquired the worst and most pernicious part of the evil of a paper circulation, the greatest possible uncertainty in its value. They have reversed the Latonian kindness to the landed property of Delos.[362] They have sent theirs to be blown about, like the light fragments of a wreck, *oras et littora circum.*[363]

The new dealers being all habitually adventurers, and without any fixed habits or local predilections, will purchase to job out again, as the market of paper, or of money, or of land shall present an advantage. For though an holy bishop thinks that agriculture will derive great advantages from the *'enlightened'* usurers who are to purchase the church confiscations, I, who am not a good, but an old farmer, with great humility beg leave to tell his late lordship, that usury is not a tutor of agriculture; and if the word 'enlightened' be understood according to the new dictionary, as it always is in your new schools, I cannot conceive how a man's not believing in God can teach him to cultivate the earth with the least of any additional skill or encouragement. 'Diis immortalibus sero,' said an old Roman,[364] when he held one handle of the plough, whilst Death held the other. Though you were to join in the commission all the directors of the two academies to the directors of the *Caisse d' Escompte,*[N365] one old experienced peasant is worth them all. I have got more information, upon a curious and interesting branch of husbandry, in one short conversation with a Carthusian monk,[366] than I have derived from all the Bank directors that I have ever conversed with. However, there is no cause for apprehension from the meddling of money-dealers with rural œconomy. These gentlemen are too wise in their generation. At first, perhaps, their tender and susceptible imaginations may be captivated with the innocent and unprofitable delights of a pastoral life; but in a little time they will find that agriculture is a trade much more laborious, and much less lucrative than that which they had left. After making its panegyric, they will turn

---

[362] *Latona* (Gr. Leto): A titan, mother of Apollo and Artemis by Zeus. When Leto was carrying Zeus' children, Hera, his jealous wife, commanded no land should give her refuge, so Zeus provided a floating island (Delos) for her to give birth on. The 'Latonian kindness' of Poseidon, god of the sea, was then to anchor Delos to the ocean floor.

[363] 'Around the shores and coasts' (Virgil, *Aeneid*, 3.75).

[364] Cicero, *De Senectute* (*On Old Age*), 7.25 (paraphrasing): 'I sow for the immortal Gods.'

[365] See above, fn. 256.

[366] *Carthusian*: a secluded and highly ascetic monastic order, founded in 1086, in which each monk occupied an individual cell with its own small garden plot.

their backs on it like their great precursor and prototype. – They may, like him, begin by singing '*Beatus ille*' – but what will be the end?

> *Hæc ubi locutus fænerator Alphius,*
> *Jam jam futurus rusticus*
> *Omnem relegit idibus pecuniam,*
> *Quærit calendis ponere.*[367]

They will cultivate the *Caisse d'Eglise*,[368] under the sacred auspices of this prelate, with much more profit than its vineyards or its corn-fields. They will employ their talents according to their habits and their interests. They will not follow the plough whilst they can direct treasuries, and govern provinces.

Your legislators, in every thing new, are the very first who have founded a commonwealth upon gaming,[369] and infused this spirit into it as its vital breath. The great object in these politics is to metamorphose France, from a great kingdom into one great play-table; to turn its inhabitants into a nation of gamesters; to make speculations as extensive as life; to mix it with all its concerns; and to divert the whole of the hopes and fears of the people from their useful channels, into the impulses, passions, and superstitions of those who live on chances. They loudly proclaim their opinion, that this their present system of a republic cannot possibly exist without this kind of gaming fund; and that the very thread of its life is spun out of the staple of these speculations. The old gaming in funds was mischievous enough undoubtedly; but it was so only to individuals. Even when it had

---

[367] Horace, *Epodes*, 2.67–70. The poem begins

> Happy the man who, far from business cares,
> Like the first race of mortals,
> Works with oxen his ancestral lands
> Free of all debt

and tells the story of the resolution, by the moneylender Alphius, to forsake his profession and return to that simple life. It ends with the quoted lines:

> When the moneylender Alphius had said this
> At the very beginning of his rustic future
> He called in all his monies on the *Ides*
> And on the *Kalends* sought to lend them out again.

(Thus forsaking his resolve to live the simple life of a farmer.)

[368] *Caisse d'Eglise*: the 'Church Bank' – a sardonic joke at the fact that the New Currency is based on the confiscated Church lands. Cf. the *Caisse d'Escompte*.[N]

[369] *Gaming*: i.e. on gambling.

its greatest extent, in the Mississippi and South Sea,[370] it affected but few, comparatively; where it extends further, as in lotteries, the spirit has but a single object. But [where the law, which in most circumstances forbids, and in none countenances gaming, is itself debauched, so as to reverse its nature and policy, and expressly to force the subject to this destructive table,][371] by bringing the [spirit and symbols][372] of gaming into the minutest matters, and engaging every body in it, and in every thing, a more dreadful epidemic distemper of that kind is spread than yet has appeared in the world. With you a man can neither earn nor buy his dinner, without a speculation. What he receives in the morning will not have the same value at night. What he is compelled to take as pay for an old debt, will not be received as the same [when he comes to pay a debt contracted by himself;][373] nor will it be the same when by prompt payment he would avoid contracting any debt at all. Industry must wither away. Œconomy must be driven from your country. Careful provision will have no existence. Who will labour without knowing the amount of his pay? Who will study to encrease what none can estimate? who will accumulate, when he does not know the value of what he saves? If you abstract it from its uses in gaming, to accumulate your paper wealth, would be not the providence of a man, but the distempered instinct of a jackdaw.

The truly melancholy part of the policy of systematically making a nation of gamesters is this; that tho' all are forced to play, few can understand the game; and fewer still are in a condition to avail themselves of the knowledge. The many must be the dupes of the few who conduct the machine of these speculations. What effect it must have on the country-people is visible. [The townsman can calculate from day to day: not so the inhabitant of the country.][374] When the peasant first brings his corn to market, the magistrate in the town obliges him to take the assignat at par; when he goes to the shop with this money, he finds it seven per cent. the worse for crossing the way. This market he will not readily resort to again.

---

[370] *Mississippi and South Sea*: Two notoriously disastrous early eighteenth-century financial bubbles in France and England respectively. Each generated fantastic speculative rises in the prices of their shares which were eventually seen to be worthless, resulting in huge losses for investors.

[371] Absent from 1st edn.      [372] 1st edn has 'currency'.

[373] Replaces 'when he is to contract a new one;' in 1st edn.

[374] This sentence transposed from three lines down, after 'not readily resort to again.' in 1st edn.

The townspeople will be inflamed! they will force the country-people to bring their corn. Resistance will begin, and the murders of Paris and St. Dennis may be renewed through all France.[375]

What signifies the empty compliment paid to the country by giving it perhaps more than its share in the theory of your representation? Where have you placed the real power over monied and landed circulation? Where have you placed the means of raising and falling the value of every man's freehold? [Those whose operations can take from, or add ten per cent. to, the possessions of every man in France, must be the masters of every man in France.][376] The whole of the power obtained by this revolution will settle in the towns among the burghers, and the monied directors who lead them. The landed gentlemen, the yeoman, and the peasant have, none of them, habits, or inclinations, or experience, which can lead them to any share in this the sole source of power and influence now left in France. The very nature of a country life, the very nature of landed property, in all the occupations, and all the pleasures they afford, render combination and arrangement (the sole way of procuring and exerting influence) in a manner impossible amongst country-people. Combine them by all the art you can, and all the industry, they are always dissolving into individuality. Any thing in the nature of incorporation is almost impracticable amongst them. Hope, fear, alarm, jealousy, the ephemerous tale that does its business and dies in a day, all these things, which are the reins and spurs by which leaders check or urge the minds of followers, are not easily employed, or hardly at all, amongst scattered people. They assemble, they arm, they act with the utmost difficulty, and at the greatest charge. Their efforts, if ever they can be commenced, cannot be sustained. They cannot proceed systematically. If the country gentlemen attempt an influence through the mere income of their property, what is it to that of those who have ten times their income to sell, and who can ruin their property by bringing their plunder to meet it at market. If the landed man wishes to mortgage, he falls the value of his land, and raises the value of assignats. He augments the power of his enemy by the very means he must take to contend with him. The country gentleman therefore, the officer by sea and land, the man of liberal views and habits, attached to no profession, will be as completely

---

[375] In the summer of 1789, following scares about famine, there were murders – including that of the Mayor of St Denis – of individuals supposedly seeking to hoard or benefit from food shortages. In late winter 1792 food shortages did indeed cause riots.

[376] This sentence appears at the end of the paragraph in 1st edn.

excluded from the government of his country as if he were legislatively proscribed. It is obvious, that in the towns, all the things which conspire against the country gentleman, combine in favour of the money manager and director. In towns combination is natural. The habits of burghers,[377] their occupations, their diversion, their business, their idleness, continually bring them into mutual contact. Their virtues and their vices are sociable; they are always in garrison; and they come embodied and half disciplined into the hands of those who mean to form them for civil, or for military action.[378]

All these considerations leave no doubt on my mind, that if this monster of a constitution can continue, France will be wholly governed by the agitators in corporations, by societies in the towns formed of directors of assignats, and trustees for the sale of church lands, attornies, agents, money-jobbers, speculators, and adventurers, composing an ignoble oligarchy founded on the destruction of the crown, the church, the nobility, and the people. Here end all the deceitful dreams and visions of the equality and rights of men. In the '*Serbonian bog*' of this base oligarchy they are all absorbed, sunk, and lost for ever.[379]

Though human eyes cannot trace them, one would be tempted to think some great offences in France must cry to heaven, which has thought fit to punish it with a subjection to a vile and inglorious domination, in which no comfort or compensation is to be found in any, even of those false splendours, which, playing about other tyrannies, prevent mankind from feeling themselves dishonoured even whilst they are oppressed. I must confess I am touched with a sorrow, mixed with some indignation, at the conduct of a few men, once of great rank, and still of great character, who, deluded with specious names, have engaged in a business too deep for the line of their understanding to fathom; who have lent their fair reputation, and the authority of their high-sounding names, to the designs of men with whom they could not be acquainted; and have thereby made their very virtues operate to the ruin of their country.

So far as to the first cementing principle.

---

377 *Burghers*: town dwellers. The propensity of commercial townspeople to collude had been famously stressed by Adam Smith, *Wealth of Nations*, I, x, c, 22.

378 Original (1st edn.) position of 'Those whose operations . . . masters of every man in France', subsequently moved to p. 198 above.

379 *Serbonian bog:* a reference to Lake Serbonis near the Nile Delta in Egypt. Often covered in sand, it mimicked dry land and supposedly swallowed up whole armies. It was first mentioned, as a lake marking the bounds of habitable Egypt, by Herodotus, and is referred to as a bog by Milton in *Paradise Lost*, 2.592.

The second material of cement for their new republic is the superiority of the city of Paris; and this I admit is strongly connected with the other cementing principle of paper circulation and confiscation. It is in this part of the project we must look for the cause of the destruction of all the old bounds of provinces and jurisdictions, ecclesiastical and secular, and the dissolution of all antient combinations of things, as well as the formation of so many small unconnected republics. The power of the city of Paris is evidently one great spring of all their politics. It is through the power of Paris, now become the center and focus of jobbing,[380] that the leaders of this faction direct, or rather command the whole legislative and the whole executive government. Every thing therefore must be done which can confirm the authority of that city over the other republics. Paris is compact; she has an enormous strength, wholly disproportioned to the force of any of the square republics; and this strength is collected and condensed within a narrow compass. Paris has a natural and easy connexion of its parts, which will not be affected by any scheme of a geometrical constitution, nor does it much signify whether its proportion of representation be more or less, since it has the whole draft of fishes in its drag-net. The other divisions of the kingdom being hackled and torn to pieces, and separated from all their habitual means, and even principles of union, cannot, for some time at least, confederate against her.[381] Nothing was to be left in all the subordinate members, but weakness, disconnection, and confusion. To confirm this part of the plan, the assembly has lately come to a resolution, that no two of their republics shall have the same commander in chief.

To a person who takes a view of the whole, the strength of Paris thus formed, will appear a system of general weakness. It is boasted, that the geometrical policy has been adopted, that all local ideas should be sunk, and that the people should no longer be Gascons, Picards, Bretons, Normans,[382] but Frenchmen, with one country, one heart, and one assembly. But instead of being all Frenchmen, the greater likelihood

---

[380] *Jobbing*: the buying and selling of financial securities.
[381] The following text removed from its original position here in the 1st edition: 'It was plain that the new incorporation of the city of Paris could not completely and conclusively domineer over France in any other way than by breaking, in every other part of it, those connections which might balance her power.'
[382] *Gascons*, etc.: inhabitants of the various French provinces – Gascony, Picardy, Brittany, Normandy. Burke believed that identification with the nation grew out of such provincial loyalties. The French were, in his view, wrong to destroy them in pursuit of a universalist 'French' identity.

is, that the inhabitants of that region will shortly have no country. No man ever was attached by a sense of pride, partiality, or real affection, to a description of square measurement. He never will glory in belonging to the Checquer, N° 71, or to any other badge-ticket. We begin our public affections in our families. No cold relation is a zealous citizen. We pass on to our neighbourhoods, and our habitual provincial connections. These are inns and resting-places. Such divisions of our country as have been formed by habit, and not by a sudden jerk of authority, were so many little images of the great country in which the heart found something which it could fill. The love to the whole is not extinguished by this subordinate partiality. Perhaps it is a sort of elemental training to those higher and more large regards, by which alone men come to be affected, as with their own concern, in the prosperity of a kingdom so extensive as that of France. In that general territory itself, as in the old name of provinces, the citizens are interested from old prejudices and unreasoned habits, and not on account of the geometric properties of its figure. The power and preeminence of Paris does certainly press down and hold these republics together, as long as it lasts. But, for the reasons I have already given you, I think it cannot last very long.

Passing from the civil creating, and the civil cementing principles of this constitution, to the national assembly,[N] which is to appear and act as sovereign, we see a body in its constitution with every possible power, and no possible external controul. We see a body without fundamental laws, without established maxims, without respected rules of proceeding, which nothing can keep firm to any system whatsoever. Their idea of their powers is always taken at the utmost stretch of legislative competency, and their examples for common cases, from the exceptions of the most urgent necessity. The future is to be in most respects like the present assembly; but, by the mode of the new elections and the tendency of the new circulations, it will be purged of the small degree of internal controul existing in a minority chosen originally from various interests, and preserving something of their spirit. If possible, the next assembly must be worse than the present. The present, by destroying and altering every thing, will leave to their successors apparently nothing popular to do. They will be roused by emulation and example to enterprises the boldest and the most absurd. To suppose such an assembly sitting in perfect quietude is ridiculous.

Your all-sufficient legislators, in their hurry to do every thing at once, have forgot one thing that seems essential, and which, I believe, never has been [before],[383] in the theory or the practice, omitted by any projector of a republic. They have forgot to constitute a *Senate*, or something of that nature and character. Never, before this time, was heard of a body politic composed of one legislative and active assembly, and its executive officers, without such a council; without something to which foreign states might connect themselves; something to which, in the ordinary detail of government, the people could look up; something which might give a bias and steadiness, and preserve something like consistency in the proceedings of state. Such a body kings generally have as a council. A monarchy may exist without it; but it seems to be in the very essence of a republican government. It holds a sort of middle place between the supreme power exercised by the people, or immediately delegated from them, and the mere executive. Of this there are no traces in your constitution; and in providing nothing of this kind, your Solons and Numas have,[384] as much as in any thing else, discovered a sovereign incapacity.

Let us now turn our eyes to what they have done towards the formation of an executive power. For this they have chosen a degraded king. This their first executive officer is to be a machine, without any sort of deliberative discretion in any one act of his function. At best he is but a channel to convey to the national assembly such matter as may import that body to know. If he had been made the exclusive channel, the power would not have been without its importance; though infinitely perilous to those who would choose to exercise it. But public intelligence and statement of facts may pass to the assembly, with equal authenticity, through any other conveyance. As to the means, therefore, of giving a direction to measures by the statement of an authorized reporter, this office of intelligence is as nothing.

---

[383] Not in 1st edn.

[384] *Solons and Numas*: famous lawgivers of antiquity.

*Solon* (*c.*630–560 BC): Athenian reformer and lawgiver. Aristotle identified his most famous and significant reforms as the abolition of slavery for debt, the right of citizens' access to law-courts, and the establishment of a popular tribunal of appeal.

*Numa*: Numa Pompilius (715–672 BC), Roman lawgiver and second king, successor to Romulus and reputed founder of Rome's calendar, her religio-legal state cult, property laws and the division of her population into occupational guilds.

Burke's invocation of these figures here is evidently quite unspecific – as wise lawmakers – since neither is associated with the establishment of a senate, or its foreign policy, for lack of which the French are here being criticised. Indeed, Numa was elected King by the senate of the time.

To consider the French scheme of an executive officer in its two natural divisions of civil and political – In the first it must be observed, that, according to the new constitution, the higher parts of judicature, in either of its lines, are not in the king. The king of France is not the fountain of justice. The judges, neither the original nor the appellate, are of his nomination. He neither proposes the candidates, nor has a negative on the choice. He is not even the public prosecutor. He serves only as a notary to authenticate the choice made of the judges in the several districts. By his officers he is to execute their sentence. When we look into the true nature of his authority, he appears to be nothing more than a chief of bumbailiffs, serjeants at mace, catchpoles,[385] jailers, and hangmen. It is impossible to place any thing called royalty in a more degrading point of view. A thousand times better it had been for the dignity of this unhappy prince, that he had nothing at all to do with the administration of justice, deprived as he is of all that is venerable, and all that is consolatory in that function, without power of originating any process; without a power of suspension, mitigation, or pardon. Every thing in justice that is vile and odious is thrown upon him. It was not for nothing that the assembly has been at such pains to remove the stigma from certain offices, when they were resolved to place the person who lately had been their king in a situation but one degree above the executioner, and in an office nearly of the same quality. It is not in nature, that situated as the king of the French now is, he can respect himself, or can be respected by others.

View this new executive officer on the side of his political capacity, as he acts under the orders of the national assembly. To execute laws is a royal office; to execute orders is not to be a king. However, a political executive magistracy, though merely such, is a great trust. It is a trust indeed that has much depending upon its faithful and diligent performance, both in the person presiding in it and in all his subordinates. Means of performing this duty ought to be given by regulation; and dispositions towards it ought to be infused by the circumstances attendant on the trust. It ought to be environed with dignity, authority, and consideration, and it ought to lead to glory. The office of execution is an office of exertion. It is not from impotence we are to expect the tasks of power. What sort of person is a king to command executory service, who has no means whatsoever

---

[385] *Bum-bailiff*: a collector of small debts; *catchpole*: a minor revenue officer; both are derogatory terms. *Serjeant at mace*: the bearer of a ceremonial mace – and thus a post carrying no power.

to reward it? Not in a permanent office; not in a grant of land; no, not in a pension of fifty pounds a year; not in the vainest and most trivial title. In France the king is no more the fountain of honour than he is the fountain of justice. All rewards, all distinctions are in other hands. Those who serve the king can be actuated by no natural motive but fear; by a fear of every thing except their master. His functions of internal coercion are as odious, as those which he exercises in the department of justice. If relief is to be given to any municipality, the assembly gives it. If troops are to be sent to reduce them to obedience to the assembly, the king is to execute the order; and upon every occasion he is to be spattered over with the blood of his people. He has no negative; yet his name and authority is used to enforce every harsh decree. Nay, he must concur in the butchery of those who shall attempt to free him from his imprisonment, or shew the slightest attachment to his person or to his antient authority.

Executive magistracy ought to be constituted in such a manner, that those who compose it should be disposed to love and to venerate those whom they are bound to obey. A purposed neglect, or, what is worse, a literal but perverse and malignant obedience, must be the ruin of the wisest counsels. In vain will the law attempt to anticipate or to follow such studied neglects and fraudulent attentions. To make men act zealously is not in the competence of law. Kings, even such as are truly kings, may and ought to bear the freedom of subjects that are obnoxious to them. They may too, without derogating from themselves, bear even the authority of such persons if it promotes their service. Louis the XIIIth[386] mortally hated the cardinal de Richlieu;[N] but his support of that minister against his rivals was the source of all the glory of his reign, and the solid foundation of his throne itself. Louis the XIVth,[N] when come to the throne, did not love the cardinal Mazarin;[387] but for his interests he preserved him in power. When old, he detested Louvois;[388] but for years, whilst he faithfully served his greatness, he endured his person. When George the IId

---

[386] *Louis XIII* (1601–43) succeeded in 1610, aged eight, under the regency of his mother Marie de Medici.

[387] *Mazarin*: Jules Mazarin (1602–61), Italian, naturalised French Cardinal and Chief Minister of France. Appointed Chief Minister by Louis XIII in 1642 following the death of Richelieu, his mentor, he was retained, on Louis' death a year later, by his wife, Anne of Austria, acting as regent for the future Louis XIV, then only in his fifth year. Far from Anne (or the younger Louis) being ill disposed to Mazarin there was a rumour she had secretly married him.

[388] *Louvois*: François Michel Letellier, Marquis de Louvois (1641–91). Minister of war to Louis XIV; one of the architects of the revocation of the Edict of Nantes (1685).

took Mr. Pitt, who certainly was not agreeable to him, into his councils, he did nothing which could humble a wise sovereign. But these ministers, who were chosen by affairs, not by affections, acted in the name of, and in trust for, kings; and not as their avowed, constitutional, and ostensible masters. I think it impossible that any king, when he has recovered his first terrors, can cordially infuse vivacity and vigour into measures which he knows to be dictated by those who he must be persuaded are in the highest degree ill affected to his person. Will any ministers, who serve such a king (or whatever he may be called) with but a decent appearance of respect, cordially obey the orders of those whom but the other day in his name they had committed to the Bastile? will they obey the orders of those whom, whilst they were exercising despotic justice upon them, they conceived they were treating with lenity; and for whom, in a prison, they thought they had provided an asylum? If you expect such obedience, amongst your other innovations and regenerations, you ought to make a revolution in nature, and provide a new constitution for the human mind. Otherwise, your supreme government cannot harmonize with its executory system. There are cases in which we cannot take up with names and abstractions. You may call half a dozen leading individuals, whom we have reason to fear and hate, the nation. It makes no other difference, than to make us fear and hate them the more. If it had been thought justifiable and expedient to make such a revolution by such means, and through such persons, as you have made yours, it would have been more wise to have completed the business of the fifth and sixth of October. The new executive officer would then owe his situation to those who are his creators as well as his masters; and he might be bound in interest, in the society of crime, and (if in crimes there could be virtues) in gratitude, to serve those who had promoted him to a place of great lucre and great sensual indulgence; and of something more: For more he must have received from those who certainly would not have limited an aggrandized creature, as they have done a submitting antagonist.

A king circumstanced as the present, if he is totally stupified by his misfortunes, so as to think it not the necessity, but the premium and privilege of life, to eat and sleep, without any regard to glory, never can be fit for the office. If he feels as men commonly feel, he must be sensible, that an office so circumstanced is one in which he can obtain no fame or reputation. He has no generous interest that can excite him to action. At best, his conduct will be passive and defensive. To inferior people such an office might be matter of honour. But to be raised to it, and to descend to it, are different things, and suggest different sentiments. Does he *really* name the ministers? They will have a sympathy with him. Are they forced upon him? The whole business between them and the nominal king will be mutual counteraction. In all other countries, the office of ministers of state is of the highest dignity. In France it is full of peril and incapable of glory. Rivals however they will have in their nothingness, whilst shallow ambition exists in the world, or the desire of a miserable salary is an incentive to short-sighted avarice. Those competitors of the ministers are enabled by your constitution to attack them in their vital parts, whilst they have not the means of repelling their charges in any other than the degrading character of culprits. The ministers of state in France are the only persons in that country who are incapable of a share in the national councils. What ministers! What councils! What a nation! – But they are responsible. It is a poor service that is to be had from responsibility. The elevation of mind, to be derived from fear, will never make a nation glorious. Responsibility prevents crimes. It makes all attempts against the laws dangerous. But for a principle of active and zealous service, none but idiots could think of it. Is the conduct of a war to be trusted to a man who may abhor its principle; who, in every step he may take to render it successful, confirms the power of those by whom he is oppressed? Will foreign states seriously treat with him who has no prerogative of peace or war; no, not so much as in a single vote by himself or his ministers, or by any one whom he can possibly influence. A state of contempt is not a state for a prince: better get rid of him at once.

I know it will be said, that these humours in the court and executive government will continue only through this generation; and that the king has been brought to declare the dauphin[389] shall be educated in a conformity to his situation. If he is made to conform to his situation, he will have no education at all. His training must be worse even than that of an arbitrary monarch. If he reads, – whether he reads or not, some good or evil genius will tell him his ancestors were kings. Thenceforward his object must be to assert himself, and to avenge his parents. This you will say is not his duty. That may be; but it is Nature; and whilst you pique Nature against you, you do unwisely to trust to Duty. In this futile scheme of polity, the state nurses in its bosom, for the present, a source of weakness, perplexity, counter-action, inefficiency, and decay; and it prepares the means of its final ruin. In short, I see nothing in the executive

---

[389] *Dauphin*: the heir to the French throne.

force (I cannot call it authority) that has even an appearance of vigour, or that has the smallest degree of just correspondence or symmetry, or amicable relation, with the supreme power, either as it now exists, or as it is planned for the future government.

You have settled, by an œconomy as perverted as the policy, two[xlix] establishments of government; one real, one fictitious. Both maintained at a vast expence; but the fictitious at, I think, the greatest. Such a machine as the latter is not worth the grease of its wheels. The expence is exorbitant; and neither the shew nor the use deserve the tenth part of the charge. Oh! but I don't do justice to the talents of the legislators. I don't allow, as I ought to do, for necessity. Their scheme of executive force was not their choice. This pageant must be kept. The people would not consent to part with it. Right; I understand you. You do, in spite of your grand theories, to which you would have heaven and earth to bend, you do know how to conform yourselves to the nature and circumstances of things. But when you were obliged to conform thus far to circumstances, you ought to have carried your submission farther, and to have made what you were obliged to take, a proper instrument, and useful to its end. That was in your power. For instance, among many others, it was in your power to leave to your king the right of peace and war. What! to leave to the executive magistrate the most dangerous of all prerogatives? I know none more dangerous; nor any one more necessary to be so trusted. I do not say that this prerogative ought to be trusted to your king, unless he enjoyed other auxiliary trusts along with it, which he does not now hold. But, if he did possess them, hazardous as they are undoubtedly, advantages would arise from such a constitution, more than compensating the risque. There is no other way of keeping the [several potentates of Europe][390] from intriguing distinctly and personally with the members of your assembly, from intermeddling in all your concerns, and fomenting, in the heart of your country, the most pernicious of all factions; factions in the interest and under the direction of foreign powers. From that worst of evils, thank God, we are still free. Your skill, if you had any, would be well employed to find out indirect correctives and controls upon this perilous trust. If you did not like those which in England we have chosen, your leaders might have exerted their abilities in contriving better. If it were necessary to exemplify the consequences of such an executive government as yours,

---

[xlix] [In reality three, to reckon with the provincial republican establishments.][391]

---

[390] 1st edn reads 'other potentates'.    [391] Footnote absent from 1st edn.

in the management of great affairs, I should refer you to the late reports of M. de Montmorin to the national assembly,[N] and all the other proceedings relative to the differences between Great Britain and Spain. It would be treating your understanding with disrespect to point them out to you.

I hear that the persons who are called ministers have signified an intention of resigning their places. I am rather astonished that they have not resigned long since. For the universe I would not have stood in the situation in which they have been for this last twelvemonth. They wished well, I take it for granted, to the Revolution. Let this fact be as it may, they could not, placed as they were upon an eminence, though an eminence of humiliation, but be the first to see collectively, and to feel each in his own department, the evils which have been produced by that revolution. In every step which they took, or forbore to take, they must have felt the degraded situation of their country, and their utter incapacity of serving it. They are in a species of subordinate servitude, in which no men before them were ever seen. Without confidence from their sovereign, on whom they were forced, or from the assembly who forced them upon him, all the noble functions of their office are executed by committees of the assembly, without any regard whatsoever to their personal, or their official authority. They are to execute, without power; they are to be responsible, without discretion; they are to deliberate, without choice. In their puzzled situation, under two sovereigns, over neither of whom they have any influence, they must act in such a manner as (in effect, whatever they may intend) sometimes to betray the one, sometimes the other, and always to betray themselves. Such has been their situation; such must be the situation of those who succeed them. I have much respect, and many good wishes, for Mr. Necker.[N] I am obliged to him for attentions. I thought when his enemies had driven him from Versailles, that his exile was a subject of most serious congratulation – *sed multæ urbes et publica vota vicerunt.*[392] He is now sitting on the ruins of the finances, and of the monarchy of France.[393]

---

[392] Juvenal, *Satires*, 10.284: 'but many cities and public prayers overcame him'. Said, iron-ically, of Pompey, who fought with Julius Caesar for control of the Roman Empire. Prior to Caesar's famous crossing of the Rubicon from Gaul, Pompey had fallen ill. The successful prayers for his recovery offered in many cities had only saved him for his eventual fate – defeat at the battle of Pharsalus and assassination in flight on the shore of Egypt. Necker, having been dismissed in 1781 and again in 1789, had been implored by the Assembly to return to office.

[393] No longer by the time *Reflections* was published. Necker had resigned on 9 September and retired to Coppet near Geneva.

A great deal more might be observed on the strange constitution of the executory part of the new government; but fatigue must give bounds to the discussion of subjects, which in themselves have hardly any limits.

As little genius and talent am I able to perceive in the plan of judicature formed by the national assembly.[N] According to their invariable course, the framers of your constitution have begun with the utter abolition of the parliaments.[N] These venerable bodies, like the rest of the old government, stood in need of reform, even though there should be no change made in the monarchy. They required several more alterations to adapt them to the system of a free constitution. But they had particulars in their constitution, and those not a few, which deserved approbation from the wise. They possessed one fundamental excellence; they were independent. The most doubtful circumstance attendant on their office, that of its being vendible, contributed however to this independency of character. They held for life. Indeed they may be said to have held by inheritance. Appointed by the monarch, they were considered as nearly out of his power. The most determined exertions of that authority against them only shewed their radical independence. They composed permanent bodies politic, constituted to resist arbitrary innovation; and from that corporate constitution, and from most of their forms, they were well calculated to afford both certainty and stability to the laws. They had been a safe asylum to secure these laws in all the revolutions of humour and opinion. They had saved that sacred deposit of the country during the reigns of arbitrary princes, and the struggles of arbitrary factions. They kept alive the memory and record of the constitution. They were the great security to private property; which might be said (when personal liberty had no existence) to be, in fact, as well guarded in France as in any other country. Whatever is supreme in a state, ought to have, as much as possible, its judicial authority so constituted as not only not to depend upon it, but in some sort to balance it. It ought to give a security to its justice against its power. It ought to make its judicature, as it were, something exterior to the state.

These parliaments had furnished, not the best certainly, but some considerable corrective to the excesses and vices of the monarchy. Such an independent judicature was ten times more necessary when a democracy became the absolute power of the country. In that constitution, elective, temporary, local judges, such as you have contrived, exercising their dependent functions in a narrow society, must be the worst of all tribunals. In them it will be vain to look for any appearance of justice towards strangers, towards the obnoxious rich, towards the minority of routed parties, towards all those who in the election have supported unsuccessful candidates. It will be impossible to keep the new tribunals clear of the worst spirit of faction. All contrivances by ballot, we know experimentally, to be vain and childish to prevent a discovery of inclinations. Where they may the best answer the purposes of concealment, they answer to produce suspicion, and this is a still more mischievous cause of partiality.

If the parliaments had been preserved, instead of being dissolved at so ruinous a charge to the nation, they might have served in this new commonwealth, perhaps not precisely the same (I do not mean an exact parallel) but near the same purposes as the court and senate of Areopagus[394] did in Athens; that is, as one of the balances and correctives to the evils of a light and unjust democracy. Every one knows, that this tribunal was the great stay of that state; every one knows with what care it was upheld, and with what a religious awe it was consecrated. The parliaments were not wholly free from faction, I admit; but this evil was exterior and accidental, and not so much the vice of their constitution itself, as it must be in your new contrivance of sexennial elective judicatories. Several English commend the abolition of the old tribunals, as supposing that they determined every thing by bribery and corruption. But they have stood the test of monarchic and republican scrutiny. The court was well disposed to prove corruption on those bodies when they were dissolved in 1771.[395] – Those who have again dissolved them would have done the same if they could – but both inquisitions having failed, I conclude, that gross pecuniary corruption must have been rather rare amongst them.

It would have been prudent, along with the parliaments, to preserve their antient power of registering, and of remonstrating at least, upon all the decrees of the national assembly,[N] as they did upon those which passed in the time of the monarchy. It would be a means of squaring the occasional decrees of a democracy to some principles of general jurisprudence. The vice of the antient democracies, and one cause of their ruin, was, that they

---

[394] *Areopagus*: hill in Athens where the Council comprising ex-officeholders met, and hence the name given to the Council.

[395] An attempt had been made to abolish the regional legal *parlements* in 1771 as a way of modernising the legal system, but a public outcry, possibly organised by the *parlements* themselves, complained of this as an invasion of liberties. Louis XVI had restored them. Having been suspended in Nov. 1789, they were abolished in Sept. 1790.

ruled, as you do, by occasional decrees, *psephismata*.[396] This practice soon broke in upon the tenour and consistency of the laws; it abated the respect of the people towards them; and totally destroyed them in the end.

Your vesting the power of remonstrance, which, in the time of the monarchy, existed in the parliament of Paris, in your principal executive officer, whom, in spite of common sense, you persevere in calling king, is the height of absurdity. You ought never to suffer remonstrance from him who is to execute. This is to understand neither council nor execution; neither authority nor obedience. The person whom you call king, ought not to have this power, or he ought to have more.

Your present arrangement is strictly judicial. Instead of imitating your monarchy, and seating your judges on a bench of independence, your object is to reduce them to the most blind obedience. As you have changed all things, you have invented new principles of order. You first appoint judges, who, I suppose, are to determine according to law, and then you let them know, that, at some time or other, you intend to give them some law by which they are to determine. Any studies which they have made (if any they have made) are to be useless to them. But to supply these studies, they are to be sworn to obey all the rules, orders, and instructions, which from time to time they are to receive from the national assembly.[N] These if they submit to, they leave no ground of law to the subject. They become complete, and most dangerous instruments in the hands of the governing power, which, in the midst of a cause, or on the prospect of it, may wholly change the rule of decision. If these orders of the National Assembly come to be contrary to the will of the people who locally choose those judges, such confusion must happen as is terrible to think of. For the judges owe their place to the local authority; and the commands they are sworn to obey come from those who have no share in their appointment. In the mean time they have the example of the court of *Chatelet*[397] to encourage and guide them in the exercise of their functions. That court is to try criminals sent to it by the National Assembly, or brought before it by other courses of delation. They sit under a guard, to save their own lives.

---

[396] *Psephismata*: decrees of the *ecclesia* or governing popular assembly in Athens. Contrasted with the higher laws or *nomoi*, which required a more elaborate legislative process. Democracies were regarded as dangerous to the rule of law because of the difficulty of resisting the popular will expressed in decrees (even those relating to the treatment of individuals), as opposed to general laws to which all were subject.

[397] *Chatelet*: a major Parisian Court of Justice in which royalists were tried for *lèse nation* (see fn. 147) from 1789.

They know not by what law they judge, nor under what authority they act, nor by what tenure they hold. It is thought that they are sometimes obliged to condemn at peril of their lives. This is not perhaps certain, nor can it be ascertained; but when they acquit, we know, they have seen the persons whom they discharge, with perfect impunity to the actors, hanged at the door of their court.

The assembly indeed promises that they will form a body of law, which shall be short, simple, clear, and so forth. That is, by their short laws, they will leave much to the discretion of the judge; whilst they have exploded the authority of all the learning which could make judicial discretion, (a thing perilous at best) deserving the appellation of a *sound* discretion.

It is curious to observe, that the administrative bodies are carefully exempted from the jurisdiction of these new tribunals. That is, those persons are exempted from the power of the laws, who ought to be the most entirely submitted to them. Those who execute public pecuniary trusts, ought of all men to be the most strictly held to their duty. One would have thought, that it must have been among your earliest cares, if you did not mean that those administrative bodies should be real sovereign independent states, to form an awful tribunal, like your late parliaments, or like our king's-bench, where all corporate officers might obtain protection in the legal exercise of their functions, and would find coercion if they trespassed against their legal duty. But the cause of the exemption is plain. These administrative bodies are the great instruments of the present leaders in their progress through democracy to oligarchy. They must therefore be put above the law. It will be said, that the legal tribunals which you have made are unfit to coerce them. They are undoubtedly. They are unfit for any rational purpose. It will be said too, that the administrative bodies will be accountable to the general assembly. This I fear is talking, without much consideration, of the nature of that assembly, or of these corporations. However, to be subject to the pleasure of that assembly is not to be subject to law, either for protection or for constraint.

[This establishment of judges as yet wants something to its completion. It is to be crowned by a new tribunal. This is to be a grand state judicature; and it is to judge of crimes committed against the nation, that is, against the power of the assembly. It seems as if they had something in their view of the nature of the high court of justice erected in England during the time of the great usurpation. As they have not yet finished this part of the scheme, it is impossible to form a direct judgment upon it. However, if great care is not taken to form it in a spirit very different from that which has guided them in their proceedings relative to state offences, this tribunal, subservient to their inquisition, *the committee of research*, will extinguish the last sparks of liberty in France, and settle the most dreadful and arbitrary tyranny ever known in any nation. If they wish to give to this tribunal any appearance of liberty and justice, they must not evoke from, or send to it, the causes relative to their own members, at their pleasure. They must also remove the seat of that tribunal out of the republic of Paris[l].]³⁹⁸

Has more wisdom been displayed in the constitution of your army than what is discoverable in your plan of judicature? The able arrangement of this part is the more difficult, and requires the greater skill and attention, not only as a great concern in itself, but as it is the third cementing principle in the new body of republics, which you call the French nation. Truly it is not easy to divine what that army may become at last. You have voted a very large one, and on good appointments, at least fully equal to your apparent means of payment. But what is the principle of its discipline? or whom is it to obey? You have got the wolf by the ears,³⁹⁹ and I wish you joy of the happy position in which you have chosen to place yourselves, and in which you are well circumstanced for a free deliberation, relatively to that army, or to any thing else.

The minister and secretary of state for the war department, is M. de la Tour du Pin.ᴺ This gentleman, like his colleagues in administration, is a most zealous assertor of the revolution, and a sanguine admirer of the new constitution, which originated in that event. His statement of facts, relative to the military of France, is important, not only from his official and personal authority, but because it displays very clearly the actual condition of the army in France, and because it throws light on the principles upon which the assembly proceeds in the administration of this critical object. It may enable us to form some judgment how far it may be expedient in this country to imitate the martial policy of France.

M. de la Tour du Pin, on the 4th of last June, comes to give an account of the state of his department, as it exists under the auspices of

---

[l] For further elucidations upon the subject of all these judicatures, and of the committee of research, see M. de Calonne's work.

³⁹⁸ This paragraph absent from 1st edn.

³⁹⁹ *Got the wolf by the ears*: a famous image used, according to Suetonius, by Tiberius to describe his difficulties in exercising power over the Roman Empire (Suetonius, *The Twelve Caesars*, 'Tiberius', c. 25).

the national assembly.ᴺ No man knows it so well; no man can express it better. Addressing himself to the National Assembly, he says, 'His Majesty has *this day* sent me to apprize you of the multiplied disorders of which *every day* he receives the most distressing intelligence. The army (le corps militaire) threatens to fall into the most turbulent anarchy. Entire regiments have dared to violate at once the respect due to the laws, to the King, to the order established by your decrees, and to the oaths which they have taken with the most awful solemnity. Compelled by my duty to give you information of these excesses, my heart bleeds when I consider who they are that have committed them. Those, against whom it is not in my power to withhold the most grievous complaints, are a part of that very soldiery which to this day have been so full of honour and loyalty, and with whom, for fifty years, I have lived the comrade and the friend.'

'What incomprehensible spirit of delirium and delusion has all at once led them astray? Whilst you are indefatigable in establishing uniformity in the empire, and moulding the whole into one coherent and consistent body; whilst the French are taught by you, at once the respect which the laws owe to the rights of man, and that which the citizens owe to the laws, the administration of the army presents nothing but disturbance and confusion. I see in more than one corps the bonds of discipline relaxed or broken; the most unheard of pretensions avowed directly and without any disguise; the ordinances without force; the chiefs without authority; the military chest and the colours carried off; the authority of the King himself [*risum teneatis*[400]] proudly defied; the officers despised, degraded, threatened, driven away, and some of them prisoners in the midst of their corps, dragging on a precarious life in the bosom of disgust and humiliation. To fill up the measure of all these horrors, the commandants of places have had their throats cut, under the eyes, and almost in the arms, of their own soldiers.'

'These evils are great; but they are not the worst consequences which may be produced by such military insurrections. Sooner or later they may menace the nation itself. *The nature of things requires*, that the army should never act but as *an instrument*. The moment that, erecting itself into a deliberative body, it shall act according to its own resolutions, the *government, be it what it may, will immediately degenerate into a military democracy*; a species of political monster, which has always ended by devouring those who have produced it.'

---

[400] 'Hold your laughter' (Burke's interpolation).

'After all this, who must not be alarmed at the irregular consultations, and turbulent committees, formed in some regiments by the common soldiers and non-commissioned officers, without the knowledge, or even in contempt of the authority of their superiors; although the presence and concurrence of those superiors could give no authority to such monstrous democratic assemblies [comices.[401]]'

It is not necessary to add much to this finished picture: finished as far as its canvas admits; but, as I apprehend, not taking in the whole of the nature and complexity of the disorders of this military democracy, which, the minister at war truly and wisely observes, wherever it exists, must be the true constitution of the state, by whatever formal appellation it may pass. For, though he informs the assembly, that the more considerable part of the army have not cast off their obedience, but are still attached to their duty, yet those travellers who have seen the corps whose conduct is the best, rather observe in them the absence of mutiny than the existence of discipline.

I cannot help pausing here for a moment, to reflect upon the expressions of surprise which this Minister has let fall, relative to the excesses he relates. To him the departure of the troops from their antient principles of loyalty and honour seems quite inconceivable. Surely those to whom he addresses himself know the causes of it but too well. They know the doctrines which they have preached, the decrees which they have passed, the practices which they have countenanced. The soldiers remember the 6th of October. They recollect the French guards. They have not forgot the taking of the King's castles in Paris, and at Marseilles. [That the governors in both places, were murdered with impunity,][402] is a fact that has not passed out of their minds. They do not abandon the principles laid down so ostentatiously and laboriously, of the equality of men. They cannot shut their eyes to the degradation of the whole noblesse of France; and the suppression of the very idea of a gentleman. The total abolition of titles and distinctions is not lost upon them. But Mr. du Pin is astonished at their disloyalty, when the doctors of the assembly have taught them at the same time the respect due to laws. It is easy to judge which of the two sorts of lessons men with arms in their hands are likely to learn. As to the authority of the King, we may collect from the minister himself

---

[401] *Comices/Comites*: group of comrades, especially soldiers, from the Latin. Burke retained this word from his translation of du Pin's original.
[402] 1st edn reads: 'That they murdered, with impunity, the governors in both places'.

(if any argument on that head were not quite superfluous) that it is not of more consideration with these troops, than it is with every body else. 'The King,' says he, 'has over and over again repeated his orders to put a stop to these excesses: but, in so terrible a crisis *your* [the assembly's][403] concurrence is become indispensably necessary to prevent the evils which menace the state. *You* unite to the force of the legislative power, *that of opinion* still more important.' To be sure the army can have no opinion of the power or authority of the king. Perhaps the soldier has by this time learned, that the assembly itself does not enjoy a much greater degree of liberty than that royal figure.

It is now to be seen what has been proposed in this exigency, one of the greatest that can happen in a state. The Minister requests the assembly to array itself in all its terrors, and to call forth all its majesty. He desires that the grave and severe principles announced by them may give vigour to the King's proclamation. After this we should have looked for courts civil and martial; breaking of some corps, decimating others, and all the terrible means which necessity has employed in such cases to arrest the progress of the most terrible of all evils; particularly, one might expect, that a serious inquiry would be made into the murder of commandants in the view of their soldiers. Not one word of all this, or of any thing like it. After they had been told that the soldiery trampled upon the decrees of the assembly promulgated by the King, the assembly pass new decrees; and they authorise the King to make new proclamations. After the Secretary at War had stated that the regiments had paid no regard to oaths *prêtés avec la plus imposante solemnité*[404] – they propose – what? More oaths. They renew decrees and proclamations as they experience their insufficiency, and they multiply oaths in proportion as they weaken, in the minds of men, the sanctions of religion. I hope that handy abridgments of the excellent sermons of Voltaire,[N] d'Alembert,[N] Diderot,[N] and Helvetius,[N] on the Immortality of the Soul, on a particular superintending Providence, and on a Future State of Rewards and Punishments, are sent down to the soldiers along with their civic oaths. Of this I have no doubt; as I understand, that a certain description of reading makes no inconsiderable part of their military exercises, and that they are full as well supplied with the ammunition of pamphlets as of cartridges.

To prevent the mischiefs arising from conspiracies, irregular consultations, seditious committees, and monstrous democratic assemblies

---

[403] Interpolation by Burke.  [404] 'Sworn with the most imposing solemnity'.

['comitia, comices']⁴⁰⁵ of the soldiers, and all the disorders arising from idleness, luxury, dissipation, and insubordination, I believe the most astonishing means have been used, that ever occurred to men, even in all the inventions of this prolific age. It is no less than this:– The King has promulgated in circular letters to all the regiments his direct authority and encouragement, that the several corps should join themselves with the clubs and confederations in the several municipalities, and mix with them in their feasts and civic entertainments! This jolly discipline, it seems, is to soften the ferocity of their minds; to reconcile them to their bottle companions of other descriptions; and to merge particular conspiracies in more general associations⁽ˡⁱ⁾. That this remedy would be pleasing to the soldiers, as they are described by Mr. de la Tour du Pin,ᴺ I can readily believe; and that, however mutinous otherwise, they will dutifully submit themselves to *these* royal proclamations. But I should question whether all this civic swearing, clubbing, and feasting, would dispose them more than at present they are disposed, to an obedience to their officers; or teach them better to submit to the austere rules of military discipline. It will make them admirable citizens after the French mode, but not quite so good soldiers after any mode. A doubt might well arise, whether the conversations at these good tables, would fit them a great deal the better for the character of *mere instruments*, which this veteran officer and statesman justly observes, the nature of things always requires an army to be.

Concerning the likelihood of this improvement in discipline, by the free conversation of the soldiers with the municipal festive societies, which is thus officially encouraged by royal authority and sanction, we may judge by the state of the municipalities themselves, furnished to us by

---

ˡⁱ Comme sa Majesté y a reconnu, non une systême d'associations particulières, mais une réunion de volontés de tous les François pour la liberté et la prosperité communes, ainsi pour le maintien de l'ordre publique; il a pensé qu'il convenoit que chacque regiment prit part a ces fêtes civiques pour multiplier les rapports, et reserrer les liens d'union entre les citoyens et les troupes. – Lest I should not be credited, I insert the words, authorising the troops to feast with the popular confederacies.⁴⁰⁶

⁴⁰⁵ Interpolation by Burke.

⁴⁰⁶ 'As his Majesty has acknowledged – this is not a system of private or local associations, but a coming together of the wills of all Frenchmen for common liberty and prosperity, and so for the maintenance of public order – he thought it suitable that each regiment take part in these civic celebrations so as to increase the connections, and strengthen the bonds of union between the citizens and the troops.' Burke quotes from Du Pin's address to the National Assembly, *Discours de M. de la Tour du Pin*, June 1790.

the war minister in this very speech. He conceives good hopes of the success of his endeavours towards restoring order *for the present* from the good disposition of certain regiments; but he finds something cloudy with regard to the future. As to preventing the return of confusion "for this, the administration (says he) cannot be answerable to you, as long as they see the municipalities arrogate to themselves an authority over the troops, which your institutions have reserved wholly to the monarch. You have fixed the limits of the military authority and the municipal authority. You have bounded the action, which you have permitted to the latter over the former, to the right of requisition; but never did the letter or the spirit of your decrees authorise the commons in these municipalities to break the officers, to try them, to give orders to the soldiers, to drive them from the posts committed to their guard, to stop them in their marches ordered by the King, or, in a word, to enslave the troops to the caprice of each of the cities or even market towns through which they are to pass."

Such is the character and disposition of the municipal society which is to reclaim the soldiery, to bring them back to the true principles of military subordination, and to render them machines in the hands of the supreme power of the country! Such are the distempers of the French troops! Such is their cure! As the army is, so is the navy. The municipalities supersede the orders of the assembly, and the seamen in their turn supersede the orders of the municipalities. From my heart I pity the condition of a respectable servant of the public, like this war minister, obliged in his old age to pledge the assembly in their civic cups, and to enter with a hoary head into all the fantastick vagaries of these juvenile politicians. Such schemes are not like propositions coming from a man of fifty years wear and tear amongst mankind. They seem rather such as ought to be expected from those grand compounders in politics, who shorten the road to their degrees in the state; and have a certain inward fanatical assurance and illumination upon all subjects; upon the credit of which one of their doctors has thought fit, with great applause, and greater success, to caution the assembly not to attend to old men, or to any persons who valued themselves upon their experience. I suppose all the ministers of state must qualify, and take this test; wholly abjuring the errors and heresies of experience and observation. Every man has his own relish. But I think, if I could not attain to the wisdom, I would at least preserve something of the stiff and peremptory dignity of age. These gentlemen deal in regeneration; but at any price I should hardly yield my rigid fibres to be regenerated by them; nor begin, in my grand climacteric, to squall in their new accents, or to stammer, in my second cradle, the elemental sounds of their barbarous metaphysics[lii]. *Si isti mihi largiantur ut repueriscam, et in eorum cunis vagiam, valde recusem!*[407]

The imbecility of any part of the puerile and pedantic system, which they call a constitution, cannot be laid open without discovering the utter insufficiency and mischief of every other part with which it comes in contact, or that bears any the remotest relation to it. You cannot propose a remedy for the incompetence of the crown, without displaying the debility of the assembly. You cannot deliberate on the confusion of the army of the state, without disclosing the worse disorders of the armed municipalities. The military lays open the civil, and the civil betrays the military anarchy. I wish every body carefully to peruse the eloquent speech (such it is) of Mons. de la Tour du Pin. He attributes the salvation of the municipalities to the good behaviour of some of the troops. These troops are to preserve the well-disposed part of those municipalities, which is confessed to be the weakest, from the pillage of the worst disposed, which is the strongest. But the municipalities affect a sovereignty and will command those troops which are necessary for their protection. Indeed they must command them or court them. The municipalities, by the necessity of their situation, and by the republican powers they have obtained, must, with relation to the military, be the masters, or the servants, or the confederates, or each successively; or they must make a jumble of all together, according to circumstances. What government is there to coerce the army but the municipality, or the municipality but the army? To preserve concord where authority is extinguished, at the hazard of all consequences, the assembly attempts to cure the distempers by the distempers themselves; and they hope to preserve themselves from a purely military democracy, by giving it a debauched interest in the municipal.

If the soldiers once come to mix for any time in the municipal clubs, cabals, and confederacies, an elective attraction will draw them to the lowest and most desperate part. With them will be their habits, affections, and sympathies. The military conspiracies, which are to be remedied

---

[lii] [This war-minister has since quitted the school and resigned his office.][408]

[407] Freely quoted from Cicero, *De Senectute* (*On Old Age*), 23.83: 'And if it was generously given to me that I might recover my youth, and wail in my cradle, I should vehemently refuse.'

[408] Footnote absent from 1st edn. Du Pin was replaced as minister for war on 16 November 1790.

by civic confederacies; the rebellious municipalities, which are to be rendered obedient by furnishing them with the means of seducing the very armies of the state that are to keep them in order; all these chimeras of a monstrous and portentous policy, must aggravate the confusions from which they have arisen. There must be blood. The want of common judgment manifested in the construction of all their descriptions of forces, and in all their kinds of civil and judicial authorities, will make it flow. Disorders may be quieted in one time and in one part. They will break out in others; because the evil is radical[409] and intrinsic. All these schemes of mixing mutinous soldiers with seditious citizens, must weaken still more and more the military connection of soldiers with their officers, as well as add military and mutinous audacity to turbulent artificers and peasants. To secure a real army, the officer should be first and last in the eye of the soldier; first and last in his attention, observance, and esteem. Officers it seems there are to be, whose chief qualification must be temper and patience. They are to manage their troops by electioneering arts. They must bear themselves as candidates not as commanders. But as by such means power may be occasionally in their hands, the authority by which they are to be nominated becomes of high importance.

What you may do finally, does not appear; nor is it of much moment, whilst the strange and contradictory relation between your army and all the parts of your republic, as well as the puzzled relation of those parts to each other and to the whole, remain as they are. You seem to have given the provisional nomination of the officers, in the first instance, to the king, with a reserve of approbation by the National Assembly.[N] Men who have an interest to pursue are extremely sagacious in discovering the true seat of power. They must soon perceive that those who can negative indefinitely, in reality appoint. The officers must therefore look to their intrigues in that assembly, as the sole certain road to promotion. Still, however, by your new constitution they must begin their solicitation at court. This double negotiation for military rank seems to me a contrivance as well adapted, as if it were studied for no other end, to promote faction in the assembly itself, relative to this vast military patronage; and then to poison the corps of officers with factions of a nature still more dangerous to the safety of government, upon any bottom on which it can be placed, and destructive in the end to the efficiency of the army itself. Those

---

[409] *Radical*: not yet in the political sense. Here meaning 'going to, or deriving from the root, systemic'.

officers, who lose the promotions intended for them by the crown, must become of a faction opposite to that of the assembly which has rejected their claims, and must nourish discontents in the heart of the army against the ruling powers. Those officers, on the other hand, who, by carrying their point through an interest in the assembly, feel themselves to be at best only second in the good-will of the crown, though first in that of the assembly, must slight an authority which would not advance, and could not retard their promotion. If to avoid these evils you will have no other rule for command or promotion than seniority, you will have an army of formality; at the same time it will become more independent, and more of a military republic. Not they but the king is the machine. A king is not to be deposed by halves. If he is not every thing in the command of an army, he is nothing. What is the effect of a power placed nominally at the head of the army, who to that army is no object of gratitude, or of fear? Such a cypher is not fit for the administration of an object of all things the most delicate, the supreme command of military men. They must be constrained (and their inclinations lead them to what their necessities require) by a real, vigorous, effective, decided, personal authority. The authority of the assembly itself suffers by passing through such a debilitating channel as they have chosen. The army will not long look to an assembly acting through the organ of false shew, and palpable imposition. They will not seriously yield obedience to a prisoner. They will either despise a pageant, or they will pity a captive king. This relation of your army to the crown will, if I am not greatly mistaken, become a serious dilemma in your politics.

It is besides to be considered, whether an assembly like yours, even supposing that it was in possession of another sort of organ through which its orders were to pass, is fit for promoting the obedience and discipline of an army. It is known, that armies have hitherto yielded a very precarious and uncertain obedience to any senate, or popular authority; and they will least of all yield it to an assembly which is to have only a continuance of two years. The officers must totally lose the characteristic disposition of military men, if they see with perfect submission and due admiration, the dominion of pleaders; especially when they find, that they have a new court to pay to an endless succession of those pleaders, whose military policy, and the genius of whose command (if they should have any) must be as uncertain as their duration is transient. In the weakness of one kind of authority, and in the fluctuation of all, the officers of an army will remain for some time mutinous and full of faction, until some popular general, who understands the art of conciliating the soldiery, and who possesses the true spirit of command, shall draw the eyes of all men upon himself. Armies will obey him on his personal account. There is no other way of securing military obedience in this state of things. But the moment in which that event shall happen, the person who really commands the army is your master; the master (that is little) of your king, the master of your assembly, the master of your whole republic.[410]

How came the assembly by their present power over the army? Chiefly, to be sure, by debauching the soldiers from their officers. They have begun by a most terrible operation. They have touched the central point, about which the particles that compose armies are at repose. They have destroyed the principle of obedience in the great essential critical link between the officer and the soldier, just where the chain of military subordination commences, and on which the whole of that system depends. The soldier is told, he is a citizen, and has the rights of man and citizen. The right of a man, he is told, is to be his own governor, and to be ruled only by those to whom he delegates that self-government. It is very natural he should think, that he ought most of all to have his choice where he is to yield the greatest degree of obedience. He will therefore, in all probability, systematically do, what he does at present occasionally; that is, he will exercise at least a negative in the choice of his officers. At present the officers are known at best to be only permissive, and on their good behaviour. In fact, there have been many instances in which they have been cashiered by their corps. Here is a second negative on the choice of the king; a negative as effectual at least as the other of the assembly. The soldiers know already that it has been a question, not ill received in the national assembly, whether they ought not to have the direct choice of their officers, or some proportion of them? When such matters are in deliberation, it is no extravagant supposition that they will incline to the opinion most favourable to their pretensions. They will not bear to be deemed the army of an imprisoned king, whilst another army in the same country, with whom too they are to feast and confederate, is to be considered as the free army of a free constitution. They will cast their eyes on the other and more permanent army; I mean the municipal. That corps, they well know, does actually elect its own officers. They may

---

[410] Possibly the most prescient of Burke's observations, born out by Napoleon Bonaparte's coup of 18th Brumaire (9 November) 1799.

not be able to discern the grounds of distinction on which they are not to elect a Marquis de la Fayette[411] (or what is his new name) of their own? If this election of a commander in chief be a part of the rights of men, why not of theirs? They see elective justices of peace, elective judges, elective curates, elective bishops, elective municipalities, and elective commanders of the Parisian army. – Why should they alone be excluded? Are the brave troops of France the only men in that nation who are not the fit judges of military merit, and of the qualifications necessary for a commander in chief? Are they paid by the state, and do they therefore lose the rights of men? They are a part of that nation themselves, and contribute to that pay. And is not the king, is not the national assembly, and are not all who elect the national assembly, likewise paid? Instead of seeing all these forfeit their rights by their receiving a salary, they perceive that in all these cases a salary is given for the exercise of those rights. All your resolutions, all your proceedings, all your debates, all the works of your doctors in religion and politics, have industriously been put into their hands; and you expect that they will apply to their own case just as much of your doctrines and examples as suits your pleasure.

Every thing depends upon the army in such a government as yours; for you have industriously destroyed all the opinions, and prejudices, and, as far as in you lay, all the instincts which support government. Therefore the moment any difference arises between your national assembly and any part of the nation, you must have recourse to force. Nothing else is left to you; or rather you have left nothing else to yourselves. You see by the report of your war minister, that the distribution of the army is in a great measure made with a view of internal coercion[liii].[412] You must rule by an army; and you have infused into that army by which

---

[liii] Courier François, 30 July, 1790. Assemblée Nationale. Numero 210.

[411] *Marquis de La Fayette*: Marie-Joseph Paul Yves Roch Gilbert du Motier, Marquis de La Fayette (1757–1834) descended from a long-established military family. LaFayette had fought for the Americans against the British in the American War of Independence. Abandoning his long family name and title he became known simply as LaFayette (hence Burke's jibe) and was elected to the house of the nobles in the Estates General,[N] joining those who withdrew to form the National Assembly,[N] of which he was elected vice president. He had been appointed Commander of the National Guard in July 1790. He would be imprisoned under the Jacobins and survive to become a figurehead of constitutionalism in the post-Napoleonic regimes.

[412] Resistance to the Revolution was expressed in several provincial towns and regions. The major town of Lyon was a particular worry to the new regime. Du Pin, the minister for

you rule, as well as into the whole body of the nation, principles which after a time must disable you in the use you resolve to make of it. The king is to call out troops to act against his people, when the world has been told, and the assertion is still ringing in our ears, that troops ought not to fire on citizens. The colonies assert to themselves an independent constitution and a free trade.[413] They must be constrained by troops. In what chapter of your code of the rights of men are they able to read, that it is a part of the rights of men to have their commerce monopolized and restrained for the benefit of others. As the colonists rise on you, the negroes rise on them. Troops again – Massacre, torture, hanging! These are your rights of men! These are the fruits of metaphysic declarations wantonly made, and shamefully retracted! It was but the other day that the farmers of land in one of your provinces refused to pay some sorts of rents to the lord of the soil. In consequence of this, you decree, that the country people shall pay all rents and dues, except those which as grievances you have abolished; and if they refuse, then you order the king to march troops against them. You lay down metaphysic propositions which infer universal consequences, and then you attempt to limit logic by despotism.[414] The leaders of the present system tell them of their rights, as men, to take fortresses, to murder guards, to seize on kings without the least appearance of authority even from the assembly, whilst, as the sovereign legislative body, that assembly was sitting in the name of the nation – and yet these leaders presume to order out the troops, which have acted in these very disorders, to coerce those who shall judge on the principles, and follow the examples, which have been guarantied by their own approbation.

war, had explained to the Assembly on 29 July the need for troops to be posted to the interior.

[413] Both colonists and slaves in France's Caribbean possessions had taken the Declaration of the Rights of Man in all seriousness, causing conflict both between Metropolitan France and the colonists (who set up their own assemblies), and between the enslaved Afro-Caribbeans (who sought emancipation) and the colonists. In late 1791, following a National Assembly[N] decree depriving all black inhabitants of citizenship, there was a full-scale uprising led by the ex-slave Toussaint l'Ouverture establishing the independence of Haiti. Slavery was abolished under the Convention in 1794, but re-imposed in 1802 by Napoleon, who attempted, unsuccessfully, to retake Haiti.

[414] The decree of 4 August declared: 'The National Assembly abolishes the feudal regime entirely, and decrees that both feudal and censual rights and dues deriving from . . . servitude . . . are abolished without indemnity . . . Those . . . which are not suppressed . . . , however, shall continue to be collected until reimbursement has been made.' (Art 1. August 4th Decree, *DocS*, p. 107)

The leaders teach the people to abhor and reject all feodality[415] as the barbarism of tyranny, and they tell them afterwards how much of that barbarous tyranny they are to bear with patience. As they are prodigal of light with regard to grievances, so the people find them sparing in the extreme with regard to redress. They know that not only certain quit-rents[416] and personal duties, which you have permitted them to redeem (but have furnished no money for the redemption) are as nothing to those burthens for which you have made no provision at all. They know, that almost the whole system of landed property in its origin is feudal; that it is the distribution of the possessions of the original proprietors, made by a barbarous conqueror to his barbarous instruments; and that the most grievous effects of conquest are the land rents of every kind, as without question they are.

The peasants, in all probability, are the descendants of these antient proprietors, Romans or Gauls. But if they fail, in any degree, in the titles which they make on the principles of antiquaries and lawyers, they retreat into the citadel of the rights of men. There they find that men are equal; and the earth, the kind and equal mother of all, ought not to be monopolized to foster the pride and luxury of any men, who by nature are no better than themselves, and who, if they do not labour for their bread, are worse. They find, that by the laws of nature the occupant and subduer of the soil is the true proprietor; that there is no prescription against nature; and that the agreements (where any there are) which have been made with their landlords, during the time of slavery, are only the effect of duresse and force; and that when the people re-entered into the rights of men, those agreements were made as void as every thing else which had been settled under the prevalence of the old feudal and aristocratic tyranny. They will tell you that they see no difference between an idler with a hat and a national cockade, and an idler in a cowl or in a rochet.[417] If you ground the title to rents on succession and prescription, they tell you, from the speech of Mr. *Camus*,[418] published by the national assembly[N]

---

[415] *Foedality*: relationships and institutions deriving from or characteristic of feudalism.

[416] *Quit-rent*: a fee paid by a feudal tenant to escape some obligation or liability attached to the tenure of the land – such as having to perform service for the freeholder, or allow hunting on it.

[417] *Cowl*: hood such as on a monk's habit; *rochet*: a loose over-garment, or surplice. Garments typical of ecclesiastical dress.

[418] *Camus, Armand-Gaston* (1740–1804): lawyer, member and archivist of the National Assembly. He drafted the Civil Constitution of the Clergy and argued that prescription – long-held possession – cannot vindicate property rights, the origins of which were

for their information, that things ill begun cannot avail themselves of prescription; that the title of these lords was vicious in its origin; and that force is at least as bad as fraud. As to the title by succession, they will tell you, that the succession of those who have cultivated the soil is the true pedigree of property, and not rotten parchments and silly substitutions; that the lords have enjoyed their usurpation too long; and that if they allow to these lay monks any charitable pension, they ought to be thankful to the bounty of the true proprietor, who is so generous towards a false claimant to his goods.

When the peasants give you back that coin of sophistic reason, on which you have set your image and superscription, you cry it down as base money, and tell them you will pay for the future with French guards, and dragoons, and hussars. You hold up, to chastise them, the second-hand authority of a king, who is only the instrument of destroying, without any power of protecting either the people or his own person. Through him it seems you will make yourselves obeyed. They answer, You have taught us that there are no gentlemen; and which of your principles teach us to bow to kings whom we have not elected? We know, without your teaching, that lands were given for the support of feudal dignities, feudal titles, and feudal offices. When you took down the cause as a grievance, why should the more grievous effect remain? As there are now no hereditary honours, and no distinguished families, why are we taxed to maintain what you tell us ought not to exist? You have sent down our old aristocratic landlords in no other character, and with no other title, but that of exactors under your authority. Have you endeavoured to make these your rent-gatherers respectable to us? No. You have sent them to us with their arms reversed, their shields broken,[419] their impresses defaced; and so displumed, degraded, and metamorphosed, such unfeathered two-legged things, that we no longer know them.[420] They are strangers to us. They do not even go by the names of our ancient lords. Physically they may be the same men; though we are not quite sure of that, on your new philosophic doctrines of personal identity. In all other respects they are totally changed. We do not see why we have not as good a right to refuse them their rents, as you have to abrogate all their honours, titles, and

morally compromised; in this way legitimating the appropriation of Church lands – a doctrine that Burke predicts will be used by peasants against current secular landowners.

[419] *Shields broken*: the treatment accorded to a defeated enemy.

[420] Plato (*Statesman*, 267) had defined humans as featherless bipeds. Burke is insinuating that the dispossessed landlords are no longer recognisable as human beings.

distinctions. This we have never commissioned you to do; and it is one instance, among many indeed, of your assumption of undelegated power. We see the burghers of Paris, through their clubs, their mobs, and their national guards, directing you at their pleasure, and giving that as law to you, which, under your authority, is transmitted as law to us. Through you, these burghers dispose of the lives and fortunes of us all. Why should not you attend as much to the desires of the laborious husbandman with regard to our rent, by which we are affected in the most serious manner, as you do to the demands of these insolent burghers, relative to distinctions and titles of honour, by which neither they nor we are affected at all? But we find you pay more regard to their fancies than to our necessities. Is it among the rights of man to pay tribute to his equals? Before this measure of yours, we might have thought we were not perfectly equal. We might have entertained some old, habitual, unmeaning prepossession in favour of those landlords; but we cannot conceive with what other view than that of destroying all respect to them, you could have made the law that degrades them. You have forbidden us to treat them with any of the old formalities of respect, and now you send troops to sabre and to bayonet us into a submission to fear and force, which you did not suffer us to yield to the mild authority of opinion.

The ground of some of these arguments is horrid and ridiculous to all rational ears; but to the politicians of metaphysics who have opened schools for sophistry, and made establishments for anarchy, it is solid and conclusive. It is obvious, that on a mere consideration of the right, the leaders in the assembly would not in the least have scrupled to abrogate the rents along with the titles and family ensigns. It would be only to follow up the principle of their reasonings, and to complete the analogy of their conduct. But they had newly possessed themselves of a great body of landed property by confiscation. They had this commodity at market; and the market would have been wholly destroyed, if they were to permit the husbandmen to riot in the speculations with which they so freely intoxicated themselves. The only security which property enjoys in any one of its descriptions, is from the interests of their rapacity with regard to some other. They have left nothing but their own arbitrary pleasure to determine what property is to be protected and what subverted.[421]

Neither have they left any principle by which any of their municipalities can be bound to obedience; or even conscientiously obliged not to separate

---

[421] No paragraph break in 1st edn.

from the whole, to become independent, or to connect itself with some other state. The people of Lyons, it seems, have refused lately to pay taxes. Why should they not? What lawful authority is there left to exact them? The king imposed some of them. The old states, methodised by orders, settled the more antient. They may say to the assembly, Who are you, that are not our kings, nor the states we have elected, nor sit on the principles on which we have elected you? And who are we, that when we see the gabelles,[422] which you have ordered to be paid, wholly shaken off, when we see the act of disobedience afterwards ratified by yourselves, who are we, that we are not to judge what taxes we ought or ought not to pay, and who are not to avail ourselves of the same powers, the validity of which you have approved in others? To this the answer is, We will send troops. The last reason of kings, is always the first with your assembly. This military aid may serve for a time, whilst the impression of the increase of pay remains, and the vanity of being umpires in all disputes is flattered. But this weapon will snap short, unfaithful to the hand that employs it. The assembly keep a school where, systematically, and with unremitting perseverance, they teach principles, and form regulations destructive to all spirit of subordination, civil and military – and then they expect that they shall hold in obedience an anarchic people by an anarchic army.

The municipal army, which, according to their new policy, is to balance this national army, if considered in itself only, is of a constitution much more simple, and in every respect less exceptionable. It is a mere democratic body, unconnected with the crown or the kingdom; armed, and trained, and officered at the pleasure of the districts to which the corps severally belong; and the personal service of the individuals, who compose, or the fine in lieu of personal service, are directed by the same authority[liv]. Nothing is more uniform. If, however, considered in any relation to the crown, to the national assembly,[N] to the public tribunals, or to the other army, or considered in a view to any coherence or connection between its parts, it seems a monster, and can hardly fail to terminate its perplexed movements in some great national calamity. It is a worse preservative of a general constitution, than the systasis of Crete, or

---

[liv] I see by Mr. Necker's account, that the national guards of Paris have received, over and above the money levied within their own city, about 145,000*l.* sterling out of the public treasure. Whether this be an actual payment for the nine months of their existence, or an estimate of their yearly charge, I do not clearly perceive. It is of no great importance, as certainly they may take whatever they please.

[422] *Gabelle*: a notoriously unpopular tax levied on salt.

the confederation of Poland,[423] or any other ill-devised corrective which has yet been imagined, in the necessities produced by an ill-constructed system of government.

Having concluded my few remarks on the constitution of the supreme power, the executive, the judicature, the military, and on the reciprocal relation of all these establishments, I shall say something of the ability shewed by your legislators with regard to the revenue.

In their proceedings relative to this object, if possible, still fewer traces appear of political judgment or financial resource. When the states met, it seemed to be the great object to improve the system of revenue, to enlarge its connection, to cleanse it of oppression and vexation, and to establish it on the most solid footing. Great were the expectations entertained on that head throughout Europe. It was by this grand arrangement that France was to stand or fall; and this became, in my opinion, very properly, the test by which the skill and patriotism of those who ruled in that assembly would be tried. The revenue of the state is the state. In effect all depends upon it, whether for support or for reformation. The dignity of every occupation wholly depends upon the quantity and the kind of virtue that may be exerted in it. As all great qualities of the mind which operate in public, and are not merely suffering and passive, require force for their display, I had almost said for their unequivocal existence, the revenue, which is the spring of all power, becomes in its administration the sphere of every active virtue. Public virtue, being of a nature magnificent and splendid, instituted for great things, and conversant about great concerns, requires abundant scope and room, and cannot spread and grow under confinement, and in circumstances straitened, narrow, and sordid. Through the revenue alone the body politic can act in its true genius and character, and therefore it will display just as much of its collective virtue, and as much of that virtue which may characterise those who move it, and are, as it were, its life and guiding principle, as it is possessed of a just revenue. For from hence, not only magnanimity, and liberality, and beneficence, and fortitude, and providence, and the

---

[423] All examples of unworkably decentralised constitutions. *Systasis of Crete*: an alliance of hitherto warring Cretan states in the Roman period. *Confederation of Poland*: a reference to the Polish Constitution consolidated by an act ('Nihil Novi') of the *Sejm* (parliament) in 1505 according to which any new legislation required unanimity amongst the assembly of the nobility. As a result the state was sometimes referred to as a confederation. This made concerted action notoriously difficult and enabled neighbouring powers to partition the country in the eighteenth century.

tutelary protection of all good arts, derive their food, and the growth of their organs, but continence, and self-denial, and labour, and vigilance, and frugality, and whatever else there is in which the mind shews itself above the appetite, are no where more in their proper element than in the provision and distribution of the public wealth. It is therefore not without reason that the science of speculative and practical finance, which must take to its aid so many auxiliary branches of knowledge, stands high in the estimation not only of the ordinary sort, but of the wisest and best men; and as this science has grown with the progress of its object, the prosperity and improvement of nations has generally encreased with the encrease of their revenues; and they will both continue to grow and flourish, as long as the balance between what is left to strengthen the efforts of individuals, and what is collected for the common efforts of the state, bear to each other a due reciprocal proportion, and are kept in a close correspondence and communication. And perhaps it may be owing to the greatness of revenues, and to the urgency of state necessities, that old abuses in the constitution of finances are discovered, and their true nature and rational theory comes to be more perfectly understood; insomuch, that a smaller revenue might have been more distressing in one period than a far greater is found to be in another; the proportionate wealth even remaining the same. In this state of things, the French assembly found something in their revenues to preserve, to secure, and wisely to administer, as well as to abrogate and alter. Though their proud assumption might justify the severest tests, yet in trying their abilities on their financial proceedings, I would only consider what is the plain obvious duty of a common finance minister, and try them upon that, and not upon models of ideal perfection.

The objects of a financier are, then, to secure an ample revenue; to impose it with judgment and equality; to employ it œconomically; and when necessity obliges him to make use of credit, to secure its foundations in that instance, and for ever, by the clearness and candour of his proceedings, the exactness of his calculations, and the solidity of his funds. On these heads we may take a short and distinct view of the merits and abilities of those in the national assembly, who have taken to themselves the management of this arduous concern. Far from any encrease of revenue in their hands, I find, by a report of M. Vernier.[424] from the

---

[424] *Vernier*: Théodore Vernier, Comte de Montorient (1731–1818), one of the consummate political survivors of the Revolution. He escaped the Terror and survived the Thermidor, serving in May 1795 as president of the National Assembly, and was later president of the Council of Elders (the Upper House) under the Directory.

committee of finances, of the second of August last, that the amount of the national revenue, as compared with its produce before the revolution, was diminished by the sum of two hundred millions, or *eight millions sterling* of the annual income, considerably more than one-third of the whole!

If this be the result of great ability, never surely was ability displayed in a more distinguished manner, or with so powerful an effect. No common folly, no vulgar incapacity, no ordinary official negligence, even no official crime, no corruption, no peculation, hardly any direct hostility which we have seen in the modern world, could in so short a time have made so complete an overthrow of the finances, and with them, of the strength of a great kingdom. – *Cedò quî vestram rempublicam tantam amisistis tam cito?*[425]

The sophisters and declaimers, as soon as the assembly met, began with decrying the ancient constitution of the revenue in many of its most essential branches, such as the public monopoly of salt. They charged it, as truly as unwisely, with being ill-contrived, oppressive, and partial. This representation they were not satisfied to make use of in speeches preliminary to some plan of reform; they declared it in a solemn resolution or public sentence, as it were judicially, passed upon it; and this they dispersed throughout the nation. At the time they passed the decree, with the same gravity they ordered this same absurd, oppressive, and partial tax to be paid, until they could find a revenue to replace it. The consequence was inevitable. The provinces which had been always exempted from this salt monopoly, some of whom were charged with other contributions, perhaps equivalent, were totally disinclined to bear any part of the burthen, which by an equal distribution was to redeem the others. As to the assembly, occupied as it was with the declaration and violation of the rights of men, and with their arrangements for general confusion, it had neither leisure nor capacity to contrive, nor authority to enforce any plan of any kind relative to the replacing the tax or equalizing it, or compensating the provinces, or for conducting their minds to any scheme of accommodation with the other districts which were to be relieved.

The people of the salt provinces, impatient under taxes damned by the authority which had directed their payment, very soon found their

---

[425] Cicero, *De Senectute*, 6.20: 'Tell us, how did you let such a state as yours collapse so quickly?' The reply in Cicero is: 'New orators appeared, silly little adolescents [*stulti adulescentuli*].'

patience exhausted. They thought themselves as skilful in demolishing as the assembly could be. They relieved themselves by throwing off the whole burthen. Animated by this example, each district, or part of a district, judging of its own grievance by its own feeling, and of its remedy by its own opinion, did as it pleased with other taxes.

We are next to see how they have conducted themselves in contriving equal impositions, proportioned to the means of the citizens, and the least likely to lean heavy on the active capital employed in the generation of that private wealth, from whence the public fortune must be derived. By suffering the several districts, and several of the individuals in each district, to judge of what part of the old revenue they might withhold, instead of better principles of equality, a new inequality was introduced of the most oppressive kind. Payments were regulated by dispositions. The parts of the kingdom which were the most submissive, the most orderly, or the most affectionate to the commonwealth, bore the whole burthen of the state. Nothing turns out to be so oppressive and unjust as a feeble government. To fill up all the deficiencies in the old impositions, and the new deficiencies of every kind which were to be expected, what remained to a state without authority? The national assembly called for a voluntary benevolence; for a fourth part of the income of all the citizens, to be estimated on the honour of those who were to pay. They obtained something more than could be rationally calculated, but what was, far indeed, from answerable to their real necessities, and much less to their fond expectations. Rational people could have hoped for little from this their tax in the disguise of a benevolence; a tax, weak, ineffective, and unequal; a tax by which luxury, avarice, and selfishness were screened, and the load thrown upon productive capital, upon integrity, generosity, and public spirit – a tax of regulation upon virtue. At length the mask is thrown off, and they are now trying means (with little success) of exacting their benevolence by force.

This benevolence, the ricketty offspring of weakness, was to be supported by another resource, the twin brother of the same prolific imbecility. The patriotic donations were to make good the failure of the patriotic contribution. John Doe was to become security for Richard Roe.[426] By this scheme they took things of much price from the giver, comparatively of small value to the receiver; they ruined several trades; they pillaged

---

[426] *John Doe . . . Richard Roe*: dummy names used in fictional legal cases illustrative of the law.

the crown of its ornaments, the churches of their plate, and the people of their personal decorations. The invention of these juvenile pretenders to liberty, was in reality nothing more than a servile imitation of one of the poorest resources of doting despotism. They took an old huge full-bottomed perriwig out of the wardrobe of the antiquated frippery of Louis XIV,<sup>N</sup> to cover the premature baldness of the national assembly. They produced this old-fashioned formal folly, though it had been so abundantly exposed in the Memoirs of the Duke de St. Simon, if to reasonable men it had wanted any arguments to display its mischief and insufficiency. A device of the same kind was tried in my memory by Louis XV. but it answered at no time.[427] However, the necessities of ruinous wars were some excuse for desperate projects. The deliberations of calamity are rarely wise. But here was a season for disposition and providence. It was in a time of profound peace, then enjoyed for five years, and promising a much longer continuance, that they had recourse to this desperate trifling. They were sure to lose more reputation by sporting, in their serious situation, with these toys and playthings of finance, which have filled half their journals, than could possibly be compensated by the poor temporary supply which they afforded. It seemed as if those who adopted such projects were wholly ignorant of their circumstances, or wholly unequal to their necessities. Whatever virtue may be in these devices, it is obvious that neither the patriotic gifts, nor the patriotic contribution, can ever be resorted to again. The resources of public folly are soon exhausted. The whole indeed of their scheme of revenue is to make, by any artifice, an appearance of a full reservoir for the hour, whilst at the same time they cut off the springs and living fountains of perennial supply. The account not long since furnished by Mr. Necker was meant, without question, to be favourable. He gives a flattering view of the means of getting through the year; but he expresses, as it is natural he should, some apprehension for that which was to succeed. On this last prognostic, instead of entering into the grounds of this apprehension, in order by a proper foresight, to prevent the prognosticated evil, Mr. Necker receives a sort of friendly reprimand from the president of the assembly.

As to their other schemes of taxation, it is impossible to say any thing of them with certainty; because they have not yet had their operation; but nobody is so sanguine as to imagine they will fill up any perceptible

---

[427] References to emergency direct taxes and forced loans imposed by Louis XIV and XV.

part of the wide gaping breach which their incapacity has made in their revenues. At present the state of their treasury sinks every day more and more in cash, and swells more and more in fictitious representation. When so little within or without is now found but paper, the representative not of opulence but of want, the creature not of credit but of power, they imagine that our flourishing state in England is owing to that bank-paper, and not the bank-paper to the flourishing condition of our commerce, to the solidity of our credit, and to the total exclusion of all idea of power from any part of the transaction. They forget that, in England, not one shilling of paper-money of any description is received but of choice; that the whole has had its origin in cash actually deposited; and that it is convertible, at pleasure, in an instant, and without the smallest loss, into cash again. Our paper is of value in commerce, because in law it is of none. It is powerful on Change, because in Westminster-hall it is impotent.[428] In payment of a debt of twenty shillings, a creditor may refuse all the paper of the bank of England. Nor is there amongst us a single public security, of any quality or nature whatsoever, that is enforced by authority. In fact it might be easily shewn, that our paper wealth, instead of lessening the real coin, has a tendency to encrease it; instead of being a substitute for money, it only facilitates its entry, its exit, and its circulation; that it is the symbol of prosperity, and not the badge of distress. Never was a scarcity of cash, and an exuberance of paper, a subject of complaint in this nation.

Well! but a lessening of prodigal expences, and the œconomy which has been introduced by the virtuous and sapient assembly, makes amends for the losses sustained in the receipt of revenue. In this at least they have fulfilled the duty of a financier. Have those, who say so, looked at the expences of the national assembly itself? of the municipalities,[429] of the city of Paris? of the increased pay of the two armies? of the new police? of the new judicatures? Have they even carefully compared the present pension-list with the former? These politicians have been cruel, not œconomical. Comparing the expences of the former prodigal government and its relation to the then revenues with the expences of this new system as

---

[428] *Change*: Change Alley in the City of London, site of the original Stock Exchange; *Westminster-hall*: the law courts. Burke is pointing out that English paper money is powerful in the market because its value is freely accepted, convertible, and not imposed by law.

[429] 1st edn has '?' in place of the comma.

opposed to the state of its new treasury, I believe the present will be found beyond all comparison more chargeable[lv].

It remains only to consider the proofs of financial ability, furnished by the present French managers when they are to raise supplies on credit. Here I am a little at a stand; for credit, properly speaking, they have none. The credit of the antient government was not indeed the best: but they could always, on some terms, command money, not only at home, but from most of the countries of Europe where a surplus capital was accumulated; and the credit of that government was improving daily. The establishment of a system of liberty would of course be supposed to give it new strength; and so it would actually have done, if a system of liberty had been established. What offers has their government of pretended liberty had from Holland, from Hamburgh, from Switzerland, from Genoa, from England, for a dealing in their paper? Why should these nations of commerce and œconomy enter into any pecuniary dealings with a people who attempt to reverse the very nature of things; amongst whom they see the debtor prescribing, at the point of the bayonet, the medium of his solvency to the creditor; discharging one of his engagements with another; turning his very penury into his resource; and paying his interest with his rags?

Their fanatical confidence in the omnipotence of church plunder, has induced these philosophers to overlook all care of the public estate, just as the dream of the philosopher's stone induces dupes, under the more plausible delusion of the hermetic art, to neglect all rational means of improving their fortunes. With these philosophic financiers, this universal medicine made of church mummy[430] is to cure all the evils of the state.

---

[lv] [The reader will observe, that I have but lightly touched (my plan demanded nothing more) on the condition of the French finances, as connected with the demands upon them. If I had intended to do otherwise, the materials in my hands for such a task are not altogether perfect. On this subject I refer the reader to M. de Calonne's work; and the tremendous display that he has made of the havock and devastation in the public estate, and in all the affairs of France, caused by the presumptious good intentions of ignorance and incapacity. Such effects, those causes will always produce. Looking over that account with a pretty strict eye, and, with perhaps too much rigour, deducting every thing which may be placed to the account of a financier out of place, who might be supposed by his enemies desirous of making the most of his cause, I believe it will be found, that a more salutary lesson of caution against the daring spirit of innovators than what has been supplied at the expence of France, never was at any time furnished to mankind.][431]

430 *Church mummy*: a medicine prepared from ground-up mummies, punning on the money created from the break-up of the Church estates.
431 Footnote absent from 1st edn.

These gentlemen perhaps do not believe a great deal in the miracles of piety; but it cannot be questioned, that they have an undoubting faith in the prodigies of sacrilege. Is there a debt which presses them – Issue *assignats*.[N] – Are compensations to be made, or a maintenance decreed to those whom they have robbed of their freehold in their office, or expelled from their profession – *Assignats*. Is a fleet to be fitted out – *Assignats*. If sixteen millions sterling of these *assignats*, forced on the people, leave the wants of the state as urgent as ever – issue, says one, thirty millions sterling of *assignats* – says another, issue fourscore millions more of *assignats*. The only difference among their financial factions is on the greater or the lesser quantity of *assignats* to be imposed on the publick sufferance. They are all professors of *assignats*. Even those, whose natural good sense and knowledge of commerce, not obliterated by philosophy, furnish decisive arguments against this delusion, conclude their arguments, by proposing the emission of *assignats*. I suppose they must talk of *assignats*, as no other language would be understood. All experience of their inefficacy does not in the least discourage them. Are the old *assignats* depreciated at market? What is the remedy? Issue new *assignats*. – *Mais si maladia, opiniatria, non vult se garire, quid illi facere? assignare – postea assignare; ensuita assignare*.[432] The word is a trifle altered. The Latin of your present doctors may be better than that of your old comedy; their wisdom, and the variety of their resources, are the same. They have not more notes in their song than the cuckow; though, far from the softness of that harbinger of summer and plenty, their voice is as harsh and as ominous as that of the raven.[433]

---

[432] 'But if the malady is stubborn, and will not be cured, what is to be done with it? – assignats; then assignats; and following that more assignats.'

Burke here adapts a quotation from the last scene in Molière's comedy about a hypochondriac, *Le Malade imaginaire*. The parallel with his view of the French revolutionaries – trying to restore a constitution which in Burke's view was in good health – is clear. Here an unimpressive candidate doctor is undergoing his examination in dog Latin. The treatment he suggests for every illness about which he is questioned is:

> Clysterium donare, [adminster an enema]
> Postea seignare, [Then let blood]
> Ensuita purgare. [and then purge]

'The word a trifle altered' to which Burke refers is thus the invented word *assignare*, 'to make *assignats*', in place of *saignare*, 'to let blood'.

[433] The *cuckoo* notoriously possesses only two notes. The *raven*'s harsh croak made it a proverbially bad songster, as well as a 'bird of ill omen'.

Who but the most desperate adventurers in philosophy and finance could at all have thought of destroying the settled revenue of the state, the sole security for the public credit, in the hope of rebuilding it with the materials of confiscated property? If, however, an excessive zeal for the state should have led a pious and venerable prelate (by anticipation a father of the church)[lvi], to pillage his own order, and, for the good of the church and people, to take upon himself the place of grand financier of confiscation, and comptroller general of sacrilege, he and his coadjutors were, in my opinion, bound to shew, by their subsequent conduct, that they knew something of the office they assumed. When they had resolved to appropriate to the *Fisc*, a certain portion of the landed property of their conquered country, it was their business to render their bank a real fund of credit; as far as such a bank was capable of becoming so.

To establish a current circulating credit upon any *Land-bank*, under any circumstances whatsoever, has hitherto proved difficult at the very least. The attempt has commonly ended in bankruptcy.[434] But when the assembly were led, through a contempt of moral, to a defiance of œconomical principles, it might at least have been expected, that nothing would be omitted on their part to lessen this difficulty, to prevent any aggravation of this bankruptcy. It might be expected that to render your *Land-bank* tolerable, every means would be adopted that could display openness and candour in the statement of the security; every thing which could aid the recovery of the demand. To take things in their most favourable point of view, your condition was that of a man of a large landed estate, which he wished to dispose of for the discharge of a debt, and the supply of certain services. Not being able instantly to sell, you wished to mortgage. What would a man of fair intentions, and a commonly clear understanding, do in such circumstances? Ought he not first to ascertain the gross value of the estate; the charges of its management and disposition; the encumbrances perpetual and temporary of all kinds that

---

[lvi] La Bruyere of Bossuet.[435]

[434] A Land-Bank had been floated in 1696 by Tories, hoping to counter the new Bank of England, which they saw as a Whig device for aligning interests with the new regime, but it was undersubscribed.

[435] *La Bruyere*: Jean de La Bruyère (1645–96), French moral essayist, the author of the epithet 'pious and venerable' applied to the seventeenth-century bishop Jacques-Bénigne Bossuet (1627–1704). The phrase is here applied, in satiric contrast, to Talleyrand, Bishop of Autun, who had proposed the Civil Constitution of the Clergy and presided over the appropriation of Church lands.

affect it; then, striking a net surplus, to calculate the just value of the security? When that surplus (the only security to the creditor) had been clearly ascertained, and properly vested in the hands of trustees; then he would indicate the parcels to be sold, and the time, and conditions of sale; after this, he would admit the public creditor, if he chose it, to subscribe his stock into this new fund; or he might receive proposals for an *assignat* from those who would advance money to purchase this species of security.

This would be to proceed like men of business, methodically and rationally; and on the only principles of public and private credit that have an existence. The dealer would then know exactly what he purchased; and the only doubt which could hang upon his mind would be, the dread of the resumption of the spoil, which one day might be made (perhaps with an addition of punishment) from the sacrilegious gripe of those execrable wretches who could become purchasers at the auction of their innocent fellow-citizens.

An open and exact statement of the clear value of the property, and of the time, the circumstances, and the place of sale, were all necessary, to efface as much as possible the stigma that has hitherto been branded on every kind of Land-bank. It became necessary on another principle, that is, on account of a pledge of faith previously given on that subject, that their future fidelity in a slippery concern might be established by their adherence to their first engagement. When they had finally determined on a state resource from church booty, they came, on the 14th of April 1790, to a solemn resolution on the subject; and pledged themselves to their country, 'that in the statement of the public charges for each year there should be brought to account a sum sufficient for defraying the expences of the R.C.A. religion, the support of the ministers at the altars, the relief of the poor, the pensions to the ecclesiastics, secular as well as regular, of the one and of the other sex, *in order that the estates and goods which are at the disposal of the nation may be disengaged of all charges, and employed by the representatives, or the legislative body, to the great and most pressing exigencies of the state.*' They further engaged, on the same day, that the sum necessary for the year 1791 should be forthwith determined.

In this resolution they admit it their duty to show distinctly the expence of the above objects, which, by other resolutions, they had before engaged should be first in the order of provision. They admit that they ought to shew the estate clear and disengaged of all charges, and that they should shew it immediately. Have they done this immediately, or at any time? Have they ever furnished a rent-roll of the immoveable estates, or given in an inventory of the moveable effects which they confiscate to their assignats? In what manner they can fulfil their engagements of holding out to public service 'an estate disengaged of all charges,' without authenticating the value of the estate, or the *quantum* of the charges, I leave it to their English admirers to explain. Instantly upon this assurance, and previously to any one step towards making it good, they issue, on the credit of so handsome a declaration, sixteen millions sterling of their paper. This was manly. Who, after this masterly stroke, can doubt of their abilities in finance? – But then, before any other emission of these financial *indulgences*, they took care at least to make good their original promise! – If such estimate, either of the value of the estate or the amount of the incumbrances, has been made, it has escaped me. I never heard of it.[436]

[At length they have spoken out, and they have made a full discovery of their abominable fraud, in holding out the church lands as a security for any debts or any service whatsoever. They rob only to enable them to cheat; but in a very short time they defeat the ends both of the robbery and the fraud, by making out accounts for other purposes, which blow up their whole apparatus of force and of deception. I am obliged to M. de Calonne[N] for his reference to the document which proves this extraordinary fact: it had, by some means, escaped me. Indeed it was not necessary to make out my assertion as to the breach of faith on the declaration of the 14th of April 1790. By a report of their Committee it now appears, that the charge of keeping up the reduced ecclesiastical establishments, and other expences attendant on religion, and maintaining the religious of both sexes, retained or pensioned, and the other concomitant expences of the same nature, which they have brought upon themselves by this convulsion in property, exceeds the income of the estates acquired by it in the enormous sum of two millions sterling annually; besides a debt of seven millions and upwards. These are the calculating powers of imposture! This is the finance of philosophy! This is the result of all the delusions held out to engage a miserable people in rebellion, murder, and sacrilege, and to make them prompt and zealous instruments in the ruin of their country! Never did a state, in any case, enrich itself by the confiscations of the

---

[436] The following sentence appeared in the first edition but was later removed: 'They have however done one thing, which in the gross is clear, obscure, as usual, in the detail.'

citizens.[437] This new experiment has succeeded like all the rest. Every honest mind, every true lover of liberty and humanity must rejoice to find that injustice is not always good policy, nor rapine the high road to riches. I subjoin with pleasure, in a note, the able and spirited observations of M. de Calonne on this subject[lvii].

[lvii] [Ce n'est point à l'assemblée entière que je m'adresse ici; je ne parle qu'à ceux qui l'égarent, en lui cachant sous des gazes séduisantes le but où ils l'entraînent. C'est à eux que je dis: votre objet, vous n'en disconviendrez pas, c'est d'ôter tout espoir au clergé, & de consommer sa ruine; c'est là, en ne vous soupçonnant d'aucune combinaison de cupidité, d'aucun regard sur le jeu des effets publics, c'est là ce qu'on doit croire que vous avez en vue dans la terrible opération que vous proposez; c'est ce qui doit en être le fruit. Mais le peuple que vous y intéressez, quel avantage peut-il y trouver? En vous servant sans cesse de lui, que faites vous pour lui? Rien, absolument rien; &, au contraire, vous faites ce qui ne conduit qu'a l'accabler de nouvelles charges. Vous avez rejeté, à son prejudice, une offre de 400 millions, dont l'acceptation pouvoit devenir un moyen de soulagement en sa faveur; & à cette ressource, aussi profitable que legitime, vous avez substitué une injustice ruineuse, qui, de votre propre aveu, charge le trésor public, & par conséquent le peuple, d'un surcroit de depense annuelle de 50 millions au moins, & d'un remboursement de 150 millions.

'Malheureux peuple, voilà ce que vous vaut en dernier résultat l'expropriation de l'Eglise, & la dureté des décrets taxateurs du traitement des ministres d'une religion bienfaisante; & desormais ils seront à votre charge: leurs charités soulageoient les pauvres; vous allez être imposés pour subvenir à leur entretien!' – *De l'Etat de la* France, p. 81, See also p. 92, and the following pages.][438]

---

[437] The expropriation of the monasteries under Henry VIII and of Loyalist property by Americans after the War of Independence, of both of which Burke was aware, must surely bear comparison.

[438] [Footnote absent from 1st edn.] 'It is not at all to the whole assembly that I address myself here; I speak only to those who lead it astray whilst concealing from it, beneath beguiling veils, the end to which they are drawing it. It is to them that I say: your object – you cannot deny it – is to strip the clergy of all hope, and to consummate their ruin; it is that – without suspecting you of any greedy scheme, or of casting eyes on the lottery of government securities – which one must believe you had in view throughout this terrible project that you are proposing; that is what must be the fruit of it. But the people that you involve in this, what advantage will they find in it? In constantly making use of them, what do you do for them? Nothing, absolutely nothing; and on the contrary, what you do can only lead to crushing them with new expenses. You have rejected, to their disadvantage, an offer of 400 million, the acceptance of which could have provided a means of relief in their favour; and in place of this resource, as beneficial as it was legitimate, you have substituted a ruinous injustice, which, on your own admission, burdens the public treasury, and in consequence the people, with an additional annual expense of at least 50 million, and a repayment of 150 million.

'Unhappy people, here is what you have earned as the end result of the expropriation of the Church, and the severity of the taxation measures in treatment of the ministers of a benign religion, and henceforth they will be a charge on you: their charity used to support the poor; [now] you will be taxed to provide for their maintenance.'

In order to persuade the world of the bottomless resource of ecclesiastical confiscation, the assembly have proceeded to other confiscations of estates in offices, which could not be done with any common colour without being compensated out of this grand confiscation of landed property.][439] They have thrown upon this fund, which was to shew a surplus, disengaged of all charges, a new charge; namely, the compensation to the whole body of the disbanded judicature; and of all suppressed offices and estates; a charge which I cannot ascertain, but which unquestionably amounts to many French millions. Another of the new charges, is an annuity of four hundred and eighty thousand pounds sterling, to be paid (if they choose to keep faith) by daily payments, for the interest of the first assignats. Have they ever given themselves the trouble to state fairly the expence of the management of the church lands in the hands of the municipalities, to whose care, skill, and diligence, and that of their legion of unknown under agents, they have chosen to commit the charge of the forfeited estates, and the consequence of which had been so ably pointed out by the bishop of Nancy?[440]

But it is unnecessary to dwell on these obvious heads of incumbrance. Have they made out any clear state of the grand incumbrance of all, I mean the whole of the general and municipal establishments of all sorts, and compared it with the regular income by revenue? Every deficiency in these becomes a charge on the confiscated estate, before the creditor can plant his cabbages on an acre of church property. There is no other prop than this confiscation to keep the whole state from tumbling to the ground. In this situation they have purposely covered all that they ought industriously to have cleared, with a thick fog; and then, blindfold themselves, like bulls that shut their eyes when they push, they drive, by the point of the bayonets, their slaves, blindfolded indeed no worse than their lords, to take their fictions for currencies, and to swallow down paper pills by thirty-four millions sterling at a dose. Then they proudly lay in their claim to a future credit, on failure of all their past engagements, and at a time when (if in such a matter any thing can be clear) it is clear that the surplus estates will never answer even the first of their mortgages, I mean that of the four hundred million (or sixteen millions sterling) of *assignats*. In all this procedure I can discern neither the solid sense of

---

[439] The previous paragraph, and this paragraph to this point were added after the 1st edn.

[440] *Bishop of Nancy [and Sens]*: Ann-Louis-Henri de la Fare (1732–1804), Member of the National Assembly,[N] who opposed the appropriation of Church lands. He was later a Cardinal.

plain-dealing, nor the subtle dexterity of ingenious fraud. The objection within the assembly to pulling up the flood-gates for this inundation of fraud, are unanswered; but they are thoroughly refuted by an hundred thousand financiers in the street. These are the numbers by which the metaphysic arithmeticians compute. These are the grand calculations on which a philosophical public credit is founded in France. They cannot raise supplies; but they can raise mobs. Let them rejoice in the applauses of the club at Dundee,[441] for their wisdom and patriotism in having thus applied the plunder of the citizens to the service of the state. I hear of no address upon this subject from the directors of the Bank of England; though their approbation would be of a *little* more weight in the scale of credit than that of the club at Dundee. But, to do justice to the club, I believe the gentlemen who compose it to be wiser than they appear; that they will be less liberal of their money than of their addresses; and that they would not give a dog's-ear of their most rumpled and ragged Scotch paper for twenty of your fairest assignats.

Early in this year the assembly issued paper to the amount of sixteen millions sterling: What must have been the state into which the assembly has brought your affairs, that the relief afforded by so vast a supply has been hardly perceptible? This paper also felt an almost immediate depreciation of five per cent. which in little time came to about seven. The effect of these assignats on the receipt of the revenue is remarkable. Mr. Necker[N] found that the collectors of the revenue, who received in coin, paid the treasury in *assignats*. The collectors made seven per cent. by thus receiving in money, and accounting in depreciated paper. It was not very difficult to foresee, that this must be inevitable. It was, however, not the less embarrassing. Mr. Necker was obliged (I believe, for a considerable part, in the market of London) to buy gold and silver for the mint, which amounted to about twelve thousand pounds above the value of the commodity gained. That minister was of opinion, that whatever their secret nutritive virtue might be, the state could not live upon *assignats* alone; that some real silver was necessary, particularly for the satisfaction of those, who having iron in their hands, were not likely to distinguish themselves for patience, when they should perceive that whilst an encrease of pay was held out to them in real money, it was again to be fraudulently drawn back by depreciated paper. The minister,

---

[441] The Dundee 'Friends of Liberty' had been amongst those sending congratulatory letters to the National Assembly.

in this very natural distress, applied to the assembly, that they should order the collectors to pay in specie what in specie they had received. It could not escape him, that if the treasury paid 3 per cent. for the use of a currency, which should be returned seven per cent. worse than the minister issued it, such a dealing could not very greatly tend to enrich the public. The assembly took no notice of his recommendation. They were in this dilemma – If they continued to receive the assignats, each must become an alien to their treasury: If the treasury should refuse those paper *amulets*,[442] or should discountenance them in any degree, they must destroy the credit of their sole resource. They seem then to have made their option; and to have given some sort of credit to their paper by taking it themselves; at the same time in their speeches they made a sort of swaggering declaration, something, I rather think, above legislative competence; that is, that there is no difference in value between metallic money and their assignats. This was a good stout proof article of faith, pronounced under an anathema, by the venerable fathers of this philosophic synod. *Credat* who will – certainly not *Judaeus Apella*.[443]

A noble indignation rises in the minds of your popular leaders, on hearing the magic lanthorn in their shew of finance compared to the fraudulent exhibitions of Mr. Law.[444] They cannot bear to hear the sands of his Mississippi compared with the rock of the church, on which they build their system. Pray let them suppress this glorious spirit, until they shew to the world what piece of solid ground there is for their assignats, which they have not pre-occupied by other charges. They do injustice to that great, mother fraud, to compare it with their degenerate imitation. It is not true, that Law built solely on a speculation concerning the Mississippi. He added the East India trade; he added the African trade; he added the farms of all the farmed revenue of France. All these together unquestionably could not support the structure which the public enthusiasm, not he, chose to build upon these bases. But these were,

---

[442] *Amulet*: a charm worn about the person to prevent evils.

[443] *Credat Iudaeus Apella, non ego*: 'let Apella the Jew believe it, I don't' (Horace, *Satires*, 1.5.100). Apella the Jew was a fictional and proverbially credulous character.

[444] *Mr. Law*: John Law (1671–1729), Scots banker and financier. Exiled from Britain following a duel, he successfully promoted his projects in France where, as Controller-General of Finances, he established a paper currency issued originally by his own bank, which later became the French national bank. National debt was secured against the value of stock in his trading company, the Mississippi Company, whilst speculation drove up the price of shares, but it, and with it the value of the paper currency and the national finances, collapsed in 1720 once it was realised there was no real value behind the company.

however, in comparison, generous delusions. They supposed, and they aimed at, an increase of the commerce of France. They opened to it the whole range of the two hemispheres. They did not think of feeding France from its own substance. A grand imagination found in this flight of commerce something to captivate. It was wherewithal to dazzle the eye of an eagle. It was not made to entice the smell of a mole, nuzzling and burying himself in his mother earth, as yours is. Men were not then quite shrunk from their natural dimensions by a degrading and sordid philosophy, and fitted for low and vulgar deceptions. Above all remember, that in imposing on the imagination, the then managers of the system made a compliment to the freedom of men. In their fraud there was no mixture of force. This was reserved to our time, to quench the little glimmerings of reason which might break in upon the solid darkness of this enlightened age.

On recollection, I have said nothing of a scheme of finance which may be urged in favour of the abilities of these gentlemen, and which has been introduced with great pomp, though not yet finally adopted in the national assembly.[N] It comes with something solid in aid of the credit of the paper circulation; and much has been said of its utility and its elegance. I mean the project for coining into money the bells of the suppressed churches. This is their alchymy. There are some follies which baffle argument; which go beyond ridicule; and which excite no feeling in us but disgust; and therefore I say no more upon it.

It is as little worth remarking any farther upon all their drawing and re-drawing, on their circulation for putting off the evil day, on the play between the treasury and the *Caisse d' Escompte*,[N] and on all these old exploded contrivances of mercantile fraud, now exalted into policy of state. The revenue will not be trifled with. The prattling about the rights of men will not be accepted in payment for a biscuit or a pound of gunpowder. Here then the metaphysicians descend from their airy spec-ulations, and faithfully follow examples. What examples? the examples of bankrupts. But, defeated, baffled, disgraced, when their breath, their strength, their inventions, their fancies desert them, their confidence still maintains its ground. In the manifest failure of their abilities they take credit for their benevolence. When the revenue disappears in their hands, they have the presumption, in some of their late proceedings, to value *themselves* on the relief given to the people. They did not relieve the peo-ple. If they entertained such intentions, why did they order the obnoxious taxes to be paid? The people relieved themselves in spite of the assembly.

But waiving all discussion on the parties, who may claim the merit of this fallacious relief, has there been, in effect, any relief to the people, in any form? Mr. Bailly,[N] one of the grand agents of paper circulation, lets you into the nature of this relief. His speech to the National Assembly[N] contained an high and laboured panegyric on the inhabitants of Paris for the constancy and unbroken resolution with which they have borne their distress and misery. A fine picture of public felicity! What! great courage and unconquerable firmness of mind to endure benefits, and sustain redress! One would think from the speech of this learned Lord Mayor, that the Parisians, for this twelvemonth past, had been suffering the straits of some dreadful blockade; that Henry the Fourth[N] had been stopping up the avenues to their supply, and Sully[N] thundering with his ordnance at the gates of Paris; when in reality they are besieged by no other enemies than their own madness and folly, their own credulity and perverseness. But Mr. Bailly will sooner thaw the eternal ice of his atlantic regions, than restore the central heat to Paris, whilst it remains 'smitten with the cold, dry, petrifick mace' of a false and unfeeling philosophy. Some time after this speech, that is, on the thirteenth of last August, the same magistrate, giving an account of his government at the bar of the same assembly, expresses himself as follows: 'In the month of July 1789,' (the period of everlasting commemoration) 'the finances of the city of Paris were *yet* in good order; the expenditure was counterbalanced by the receipt, and she had at that time a million (forty thousand pounds sterling) in bank. The expences which she has been constrained to incur, *subsequent to the revolution*, amount to 2,500,000 livres. From these expences, and the great falling off in the product of the *free gifts*, not only a momentary but a *total* want of money has taken place.' This is the Paris upon whose nourishment, in the course of the last year, such immense sums, drawn from the vitals of all France, has been expended. As long as Paris stands in the place of antient Rome, so long she will be maintained by the subject provinces. It is an evil inevitably attendant on the dominion of sovereign democratic republics. As it happened in Rome, it may survive that republican domination which gave rise to it. In that case despotism itself must submit to the vices of popularity. Rome, under her emperors, united the evils of both systems; and this unnatural combination was one great cause of her ruin.

To tell the people that they are relieved by the dilapidation of their public estate, is a cruel and insolent imposition. Statesmen, before they valued themselves on the relief given to the people, by the destruction of their revenue, ought first to have carefully attended to the solution of this problem:– Whether it be more advantageous to the people to pay considerably, and to gain in proportion; or to gain little or nothing, and to be disburthened of all contribution? My mind is made up to decide in favour of the first proposition. Experience is with me, and, I believe, the best opinions also. To keep a balance between the power of acquisition on the part of the subject, and the demands he is to answer on the part of the state, is a fundamental part of the skill of a true politician. The means of acquisition are prior in time and in arrangement. Good order is the foundation of all good things. To be enabled to acquire, the people, without being servile, must be tractable and obedient. The magistrate must have his reverence, the laws their authority. The body of the people must not find the principles of natural subordination by art rooted out of their minds. They must respect that property of which they cannot partake. They must labour to obtain what by labour can be obtained; and when they find, as they commonly do, the success disproportioned to the endeavour, they must be taught their consolation in the final proportions of eternal justice. Of this consolation, whoever deprives them, deadens their industry, and strikes at the root of all acquisition as of all conservation. He that does this is the cruel oppressor, the merciless enemy of the poor and wretched; at the same time that by his wicked speculations he exposes the fruits of successful industry, and the accumulations of fortune, to the plunder of the negligent, the disappointed, and the unprosperous.

Too many of the financiers by profession are apt to see nothing in revenue, but banks, and circulations, and annuities on lives, and tontines,[445] and perpetual rents, and all the small wares of the shop. In a settled order of the state, these things are not to be slighted, nor is the skill in them to be held of trivial estimation. They are good, but then only good, when they assume the effects of that settled order, and are built upon it. But when men think that these beggarly contrivances may supply a resource for the evils which result from breaking up the foundations of public order, and from causing or suffering the principles of property to be subverted, they will, in the ruin of their country, leave a melancholy and lasting monument of the effect of preposterous politics, and presumptuous, short-sighted, narrow-minded wisdom.

---

[445] *Tontine:* An early form of life insurance, named after Lorenzo de Tonti, a seventeenth-century Neapolitan banker.

The effects of the incapacity shewn by the popular leaders in all the great members of the commonwealth are to be covered with the 'all-atoning name' of liberty.[446] In some people I see great liberty indeed; in many, if not in the most, an oppressive degrading servitude. But what is liberty without wisdom, and without virtue? It is the greatest of all possible evils; for it is folly, vice, and madness, without tuition or restraint. Those who know what virtuous liberty is, cannot bear to see it disgraced by incapable heads, on account of their having high-sounding words in their mouths. Grand, swelling sentiments of liberty, I am sure I do not despise. They warm the heart; they enlarge and liberalise our minds; they animate our courage in a time of conflict. Old as I am, I read the fine raptures of Lucan[N] and Corneille[447] with pleasure. Neither do I wholly condemn the little arts and devices of popularity. They facilitate the carrying of many points of moment; they keep the people together; they refresh the mind in its exertions; and they diffuse occasional gaiety over the severe brow of moral freedom. Every politician ought to sacrifice to the graces; and to join compliance with reason. But in such an undertaking as that in France, all these subsidary sentiments and artifices are of little avail. To make a government requires no great prudence. Settle the seat of power; teach obedience: and the work is done. To give freedom is still more easy. It is not necessary to guide; it only requires to let go the rein. But to form a *free government*; that is, to temper together these opposite elements of liberty and restraint in one consistent work, requires much thought, deep reflection, a sagacious, powerful, and combining mind. This I do not find in those who take the lead in the national assembly.[N] Perhaps they are not so miserably deficient as they appear. I rather believe it. It would put them below the common level of human understanding. But when the leaders choose to make themselves bidders at an auction of popularity, their talents, in the construction of the state, will be of no service. They will become flatterers instead of legislators; the instruments, not the guides of the people. If any of them should happen to propose a scheme of liberty, soberly limited, and defined with proper qualifications, he will be immediately outbid by

---

[446] *All-atoning*: all forgiving, but effectively meaningless. At the start of Dryden's *Absalom and Achitophel*, the latter:

> seiz'd with Fear, yet still affecting Fame,
> Assum'd a Patriot's All-atoning Name.

[447] *Corneille*: Pierre Corneille (1606–84), French dramatist, famous for his tragedies in revived high classical style.

his competitors, who will produce something more splendidly popular. Suspicions will be raised of his fidelity to his cause. Moderation will be stigmatized as the virtue of cowards; and compromise as the prudence of traitors; until, in hopes of preserving the credit which may enable him to temper and moderate on some occasions, the popular leader is obliged to become active in propagating doctrines, and establishing powers, that will afterwards defeat any sober purpose at which he ultimately might have aimed.

But am I so unreasonable as to see nothing at all that deserves commendation in the indefatigable labours of this assembly? I do not deny that among an infinite number of acts of violence and folly, some good may have been done. They who destroy every thing certainly will remove some grievance. They who make every thing new, have a chance that they may establish something beneficial. To give them credit for what they have done in virtue of the authority they have usurped, or which can excuse them in the crimes by which that authority has been acquired, it must appear, that the same things could not have been accomplished without producing such a revolution. Most assuredly they might; because almost every one of the regulations made by them, which is not very equivocal, was either in the cession of the king, voluntarily made at the meeting of the states, or in the concurrent instructions to the orders. Some usages have been abolished on just grounds; but they were such that if they had stood as they were to all eternity, they would little detract from the happiness and prosperity of any state. The improvements of the national assembly are superficial, their errors fundamental.

Whatever they are, I wish my countrymen rather to recommend to our neighbours the example of the British constitution, than to take models from them for the improvement of our own. In the former they have got an invaluable treasure. They are not, I think, without some causes of apprehension and complaint; but these they do not owe to their constitution, but to their own conduct. I think our happy situation owing to our constitution; but owing to the whole of it, and not to any part singly; owing in a great measure to what we have left standing in our several reviews and reformations, as well as to what we have altered or superadded. Our people will find employment enough for a truly patriotic, free, and independent spirit, in guarding what they possess, from violation. I would not exclude alteration neither; but even when I changed, it should be to preserve. I should be led to my remedy by a great grievance. In what I did, I should follow the example of our ancestors. I would make the reparation as nearly as possible in the style of the building. A politic caution, a guarded circumspection, a moral rather than a complexional timidity were among the ruling principles of our forefathers in their most decided conduct.[448] Not being illuminated with the light of which the gentlemen of France tell us they have got so abundant a share, they acted under a strong impression of the ignorance and fallibility of mankind. He that had made them thus fallible, rewarded them for having in their conduct attended to their nature. Let us imitate their caution, if we wish to deserve their fortune, or to retain their bequests. Let us add, if we please, but let us preserve what they have left; and, standing on the firm ground of the British constitution, let us be satisfied to admire rather than attempt to follow in their desperate flights the aëronauts of France.[449]

I have told you candidly my sentiments. I think they are not likely to alter yours. I do not know that they ought. You are young; you cannot guide, but must follow the fortune of your country. But hereafter they may be of some use to you, in some future form which your commonwealth may take. In the present it can hardly remain; but before its final settlement it may be obliged to pass, as one of our poets says, 'through great varieties of untried being,'[450] and in all its transmigrations to be purified by fire and blood.

I have little to recommend my opinions, but long observation and much impartiality. They come from one who has been no tool of power, no flatterer of greatness; and who in his last acts does not wish to belye the tenour of his life. They come from one, almost the whole of whose public exertion has been a struggle for the liberty of others; from one in whose breast no anger durable or vehement has ever been kindled, but by what he considered as tyranny; and who snatches from his share in the endeavours which are used by good men to discredit opulent oppression, the hours he has employed on your affairs; and who in so doing persuades himself he has not departed from his usual office: they come from one who desires honours, distinctions, and emoluments, but little; and who expects them not at all; who has no contempt for fame, and no fear of obloquy; who shuns contention, though he will hazard an opinion: from one who wishes to preserve consistency; but who would preserve consistency by varying

---

[448] *Moral . . . complexional*: a timidity based on strength of evidence rather than disposition.

[449] *Aëronauts*: Ascents in hot air balloons were famous recent innovations. Burke likens the French constitutional experiments to such hazardous adventures, possibly playing on the 'hot air' as well as the risk involved.

[450] Addison, *Cato*, v, I, 11.

his means to secure the unity of his end; and, when the equipoise of the vessel in which he sails, may be endangered by overloading it upon one side, is desirous of carrying the small weight of his reasons to that which may preserve its equipoise.

FINIS

# The first
# Letter on a
# Regicide Peace

# TWO LETTERS

ADDRESSED TO

## A MEMBER

OF

## THE PRESENT PARLIAMENT,

ON THE PROPOSALS FOR

# PEACE

WITH THE

## REGICIDE DIRECTORY

OF

## FRANCE.

———————

BY THE RIGHT HON. EDMUND BURKE.

———————

London:

PRINTED FOR F. AND C. RIVINGTON,

ST. PAUL'S CHURCH-YARD.

1796.

# LETTER I.

## On the Overtures of Peace.

MY DEAR SIR,

OUR last conversation, though not in the tone of absolute despondency, was far from chearful. We could not easily account for some unpleasant appearances. They were represented to us as indicating the state of the popular mind; and they were not at all what we should have expected from our old ideas even of the faults and vices of the English character. The disastrous events,[1] which have followed one upon another in a long unbroken funereal train, moving in a procession, that seemed to have no end, these were not the principal causes of our dejection. We feared more from what threatened to fail within, than what menaced to oppress us from abroad. To a people who have once been proud and great, and great because they were proud, a change in the national spirit is the most terrible of all revolutions.

I shall not live to behold the unravelling of the intricate plot, which saddens and perplexes the awful drama of Providence, now acting on the moral theatre of the world. Whether for thought or for action, I am at the end of my career. You are in the middle of yours. In what part of it's orbit

---

[1] *Disastrous events*: the triumphs of the French Revolutionary Army in Belgium, the Nether-lands and the Rhineland, followed by the withdrawal of members from the anti-French counter-revolutionary coalition to make separate peace treaties with the French. Only Britain and Austria were still at war with France.

the nation, with which we are carried along, moves at this instant, it is not easy to conjecture. It may, perhaps, be far advanced in its aphelion.[2] – But when to return?

Not to lose ourselves in the infinite void of the conjectural world, our business is with what is likely to be affected for the better or the worse by the wisdom or weakness of our plans. In all speculations upon men and human affairs, it is of no small moment to distinguish things of accident from permanent causes, and from effects that cannot be altered. It is not every irregularity in our movement that is a total deviation from our course. I am not quite of the mind of those speculators, who seem assured, that necessarily, and by the constitution of things, all States have the same periods of infancy, manhood, and decrepitude, that are found in the individuals who compose them. Parallels of this sort rather furnish similitudes to illustrate or to adorn, than supply analogies from whence to reason. The objects which are attempted to be forced into an analogy are not found in the same classes of existence. Individuals are physical beings, subject to laws universal and invariable. The immediate cause acting in these laws may be obscure: The general results are subjects of certain calculation. But commonwealths are not physical but moral essences. They are artificial combinations; and, in their proximate efficient cause, the arbitrary productions of the human mind. We are not yet acquainted with the laws which necessarily influence the stability of that kind of work made by that kind of agent. There is not in the physical order (with which they do not appear to hold any assignable connexion) a distinct cause by which any of those fabrics must necessarily grow, flourish, or decay; nor, in my opinion, does the moral world produce any thing more determinate on that subject, than what may serve as an amusement (liberal indeed, and ingenious, but still only an amusement) for speculative men. I doubt whether the history of mankind is yet complete enough, if ever it can be so, to furnish grounds for a sure theory on the internal causes which necessarily affect the fortune of a State. I am far from denying the operation of such causes: But they are infinitely uncertain, and much more obscure, and much more difficult to trace, than the foreign causes that tend to raise, to depress, and sometimes to overwhelm a community.

It is often impossible, in these political enquiries, to find any proportion between the apparent force of any moral causes we may assign and their

---

[2] *Aphelion*: point farthest from the sun (or centre) in any eccentrically orbiting body such as a comet.

known operation. We are therefore obliged to deliver up that operation to mere chance, or, more piously (perhaps more rationally) to the occasional interposition and the irresistible hand of the Great Disposer. We have seen States of considerable duration, which for ages have remained nearly as they have begun, and could hardly be said to ebb or flow. Some appear to have spent their vigour at their commencement. Some have blazed out in their glory a little before their extinction. The meridian of some has been the most splendid. Others, and they the greatest number, have fluctuated, and experienced at different periods of their existence a great variety of fortune. At the very moment when some of them seemed plunged in unfathomable abysses of disgrace and disaster, they have suddenly emerged. They have begun a new course and opened a new reckoning; and even in the depths of their calamity, and on the very ruins of their country, have laid the foundations of a towering and durable greatness. All this has happened without any apparent previous change in the general circumstances which had brought on their distress. The death of a man at a critical juncture, his disgust, his retreat, his disgrace, have brought innumerable calamities on a whole nation. A common soldier, a child, a girl at the door of an inn, have changed the face of fortune, and almost of Nature.[3]

Such, and often influenced by such causes, has commonly been the fate of Monarchies of long duration. They have their ebbs and their flows. This has been eminently the fate of the Monarchy of France. There have been times in which no Power has ever been brought so low. Few have ever flourished in greater glory. By turns elevated and depressed, that Power had been, on the whole, rather on the encrease; and it continued not only powerful but formidable to the hour of the total ruin of the Monarchy. This fall of the Monarchy was far from being preceded by any exterior symptoms of decline. The interior were not visible to every eye;

---

[3] *The death of a man . . .* : Payne suggests the episodes and figures that Burke may have had in mind here that 'changed the face of fortune': the death of Pericles during the Peloponnesian war; the disgust of Coriolanus at having to seek popular election; the retreat of Pitt the Elder from public life; the treason against his King Francis I, and disgrace of Charles de Bourbon (1490–1572), constable of France; the common soldier: Arnold von Winkelreid, a Swiss militiaman who, according to legend, broke the ranks of Leopold III's Austrian army at the battle of Sempach (1386), leading to the Duke's death and the Austrian's expulsion from Switzerland; the child: the infant Hannibal who begged to be allowed to campaign with his father and swore eternal enmity to Rome; and the girl at the door of the inn: Joan of Arc (1412–31), supposedly originally an inn-servant (*Select Works of Edmund Burke*, ed. E. J. Payne, repr. with intro. by F. Canavan, 4 vols (Indianapolis, 1999), vol. 3, notes to p. 64).

and a thousand accidents might have prevented the operation of what the most clear-sighted were not able to discern, nor the most provident to divine. A very little time before its dreadful catastrophe, there was a kind of exterior splendour in the situation of the Crown, which usually adds to Government strength and authority at home. The Crown seemed then to have obtained some of the most splendid objects of state ambition. None of the Continental Powers of Europe were the enemies of France. They were all, either tacitly disposed to her, or publickly connected with her; and in those who kept the most aloof, there was little appearance of jealousy; of animosity there was no appearance at all. The British Nation, her great preponderating rival, she had humbled; to all appearance she had weakened; certainly had endangered, by cutting off a very large, and by far the most growing part of her empire.[4] In that it's acmé of human prosperity and greatness, in the high and palmy state of the Monarchy of France, it fell to the ground without a struggle. It fell without any of those vices in the Monarch, which have sometimes been the causes of the fall of kingdoms, but which existed, without any visible effect on the state, in the highest degree in many other Princes; and, far from destroying their power, had only left some slight stains on their character. The financial difficulties were only pretexts and instruments of those who accomplished the ruin of that Monarchy. They were not the causes of it.

Deprived of the old Government, deprived in a manner of all Government, France fallen as a Monarchy, to common speculators might have appeared more likely to be an object of pity or insult, according to the disposition of the circumjacent powers, than to be the scourge and terror of them all: But out of the tomb of the murdered Monarchy in France, has arisen a vast, tremendous, unformed spectre,[5] in a far more terrific guise than any which ever yet have overpowered the imagination, and subdued the fortitude of man. Going straight forward to it's end,

---

[4] *Cutting off . . . empire*: a reference to the role of the French in supporting the Americans in the War of Independence.

[5] *A vast, tremendous, unformed spectre*: a quotation from Virgil's *Aeneid*. Achaemenides, the marooned companion of Ulysses, has just told Aeneas about the blinding of the giant Cyclops Polyphemus when they catch sight of him:

> pastorem Polyphemum et litora nota petentem,
> monstrum horrendum, informe, ingens, cui lumen ademptum.
> ['The shepherd Polyphemus, seeking his familiar shore,
> A dreadful spectre, vast, deformed, from whom the light was gone.']
> (*Aeneid*, 3.657–8)

unappalled by peril, unchecked by remorse, despising all common maxims and all common means, that hideous phantom overpowered those who could not believe it was possible she could at all exist, except on the principles, which habit rather than nature had persuaded them were necessary to their own particular welfare and to their own ordinary modes of action. But the constitution of any political being, as well as that of any physical being, ought to be known, before one can venture to say what is fit for it's conservation, or what is the proper means of it's power. The poison of other States is the food of the new Republick. That bankruptcy, the very apprehension of which is one of the causes assigned for the fall of the Monarchy, was the capital on which she opened her traffick with the world.

The Republick of Regicide with an annihilated revenue, with defaced manufactures, with a ruined commerce, with an uncultivated and half depopulated country, with a discontented, distressed, enslaved, and famished people, passing with a rapid, eccentrick, incalculable course from the wildest anarchy to the sternest despotism, has actually conquered the finest parts of Europe, has distressed, disunited, deranged, and broke to pieces all the rest; and so subdued the minds of the rulers in every nation, that hardly any resource presents itself to them, except that of entitling themselves to a contemptuous mercy by a display of their imbecility and meanness. Even in their greatest military efforts and the greatest display of their fortitude, they seem not to hope, they do not even appear to wish, the extinction of what subsists to their certain ruin. Their ambition is only to be admitted to a more favoured class in the order of servitude under that domineering power.

This seems the temper of the day. At first the French force was too much despised. Now it is too much dreaded. As inconsiderate courage has given way to irrational fear, so it may be hoped, that through the medium of deliberate sober apprehension, we may arrive at steady fortitude. Who knows whether indignation may not succeed to terror, and the revival of high sentiment, spurning away the delusion of a safety purchased at the expence of glory, may not yet drive us to that generous despair, which has often subdued distempers in the State for which no remedy could be found in the wisest counsels.

Other great States, having been without any regular certain course of elevation, or decline, we may hope that the British fortune may fluctuate also; because the public mind, which greatly influences that fortune, may have it's changes. We are therefore never authorized to abandon our country to it's fate, or to act or advise as if it had no resource. There is no reason to apprehend, because ordinary means threaten to fail, that no others can spring up. Whilst our heart is whole, it will find means, or make them. The heart of the citizen is a perennial spring of energy to the State. Because the pulse seems to intermit, we must not presume that it will cease instantly to beat. The publick must never be regarded as incurable. I remember in the beginning of what has lately been called the seven years war, that an eloquent writer and ingenious speculator, Dr. Brown, upon some reverses which happened in the beginning of that war, published an elaborate philosophical discourse[6] to prove that the distinguishing features of the people of England had been totally changed, and that a frivolous effeminacy was become the national character. Nothing could be more popular than that work. It was thought a great consolation to us the light people of this country (who were and are light, but who were not and are not effeminate) that we had found the causes of our misfortunes in our vices. Pythagoras could not be more pleased with his leading discovery.[7] But whilst in that splenetick mood we amused ourselves in a sour critical speculation, of which we were ourselves the objects, and in which every man lost his particular sense of the publick disgrace in the epidemic nature of the distemper; whilst, as in the Alps *Goitre* kept *Goitre* in countenance;[8] whilst we were thus abandoning ourselves to a direct confession of our inferiority to France, and whilst many, very many, were ready to act upon a sense of that inferiority, a few months effected a total change in our variable minds. We emerged from the gulph of that speculative despondency; and were buoyed up to the highest point

---

[6] *Dr Brown . . . elaborate philosophical discourse*: John Brown (1715–66), *An Estimate of the manners and principles of the times*, 2 vols. (London, 1757–8). Burke had reviewed the book in the periodical he edited, *The Annual Register*, in 1758, pp. 445–53.

[7] *Pythagoras* (c.570–c.475 BC): famous Greek mathematician and geometer. His 'leading discovery' was the proof of the theorem that bears his name, that 'the square on the hypotenuse of a right-angled triangle equals the sum of the squares on the other two sides'. However, there is no record of his especial pleasure at this discovery. This may be a misplaced allusion to another Greek, Archimedes (287–212 BC), who had supposedly run naked through the streets of Syracuse crying 'Eureka!' ('I've found it!') on formulating – whilst in his bath – the principle of displacement.

[8] *Goitre*: a swelling of the thyroid gland brought on by iodine deficiency, and hence common in the Alps, the waters of which are deficient in that element. Juvenal had famously used this as a metaphor for any immorality which had become so commonplace as to fail to excite comment. *Quis tumidum guttur miratur in Alpibus?* ['Whoever wonders at goitre in the Alps?'] (*Satires*, 13.1.162). Burke is implying that the French revolutionary pathology had become so normal that many in England wanted to imitate it.

of practical vigour. Never did the masculine spirit of England display itself with more energy, nor ever did it's genius soar with a prouder pre-eminence over France, than at the time when frivolity and effeminacy had been at least tacitly acknowledged as their national character, by the good people of this kingdom.

For one (if they be properly treated) I despair neither of the publick fortune nor of the publick mind. There is much to be done undoubtedly, and much to be retrieved. We must walk in new ways, or we can never encounter our enemy in his devious march. We are not at an end of our struggle, nor near it. Let us not deceive ourselves: we are at the beginning of great troubles. I readily acknowledge that the state of publick affairs is infinitely more unpromising than at the period I have just now alluded to, and the position of all the Powers of Europe, in relation to us, and in relation to each other, is more intricate and critical beyond all comparison. Difficult indeed is our situation. In all situations of difficulty men will be influenced in the part they take, not only by the reason of the case, but by the peculiar turn of their own character. The same ways to safety do not present themselves to all men, nor to the same men in different tempers. There is a courageous wisdom: there is also a false reptile prudence, the result not of caution but of fear. Under misfortunes it often happens that the nerves of the understanding are so relaxed, the pressing peril of the hour so completely confounds all the faculties, that no future danger can be properly provided for, can be justly estimated, can be so much as fully seen. The eye of the mind is dazzled and vanquished.[9] An abject distrust of ourselves, an extravagant admiration of the enemy, present us with no hope but in a compromise with his pride, by a submission to his will. This short plan of policy is the only counsel which will obtain a hearing. We plunge into a dark gulph with all the rash precipitation of fear. The nature of courage is, without a question, to be conversant with danger; but in the palpable night of their terrors, men under consternation suppose, not that it is the danger, which, by a sure instinct, calls out the courage to resist it, but that it is the courage which produces the danger. They therefore seek for a refuge from their fears in the fears themselves, and consider a temporizing meanness as the only source of safety.

---

[9] *Dazzled and vanquished*: a reference to the power of morale. Tacitus, *Germania* §43: *nam primi in omnibus proeliis oculi vincuntur* ['For in all conflicts the eyes are the first to be overcome'].

The rules and definitions of prudence can rarely be exact; never universal. I do not deny that in small truckling states a timely compromise with power has often been the means, and the only means, of drawling out their puny existence: But a great state is too much envied, too much dreaded, to find safety in humiliation. To be secure, it must be respected. Power, and eminence, and consideration, are things not to be begged. They must be commanded: and they who supplicate for mercy from others can never hope for justice thro' themselves. What justice they are to obtain, as the alms of an enemy, depends upon his character; and that they ought well to know before they implicitly confide.

Much controversy there has been in Parliament, and not a little amongst us out of doors,[10] about the instrumental means of this nation towards the maintenance of her dignity, and the assertion of her rights. On the most elaborate and correct detail of facts, the result seems to be, that at no time has the wealth and power of Great Britain been so considerable as it is at this very perilous moment. We have a vast interest to preserve, and we possess great means of preserving it: But it is to be remembered that the artificer may be incumbered by his tools, and that resources may be among impediments. If wealth is the obedient and laborious slave of virtue and of publick honour, then wealth is in it's place, and has it's use: But if this order is changed, and honor is to be sacrificed to the conservation of riches, riches which have neither eyes nor hands, nor any thing truly vital in them, cannot long survive the being of their vivifying powers, their legitimate masters, and their potent protectors. If we command our wealth, we shall be rich and free: If our wealth commands us, we are poor indeed.[11] We are bought by the enemy with the treasure from our own coffers. Too great a sense of the value of a subordinate interest may be the very source of it's danger, as well as the certain ruin of interests of a superiour order. Often has a man lost his all because he would not submit to hazard all in defending it. A display of our wealth before robbers is not the way to restrain their boldness, or to lessen their rapacity. This display is made, I know, to persuade the people of England that thereby we shall awe the enemy, and improve the terms of our capitulation: it is made, not that we should fight with more animation, but that we should supplicate

---

[10]  *Out of doors*: i.e. those not in Parliament.

[11]  *Wealth commands us*...: a much-repeated sentiment in early modern, moralising literature. Pliny, *Letters*, 9.30: *Ea invasit homines habendi cupido ut possederi magis quam possidere videamur.* ['The desire for ownership so takes men over that they seem more possessed than possessors.']

with better hopes. We are mistaken. We have an enemy to deal with who never regarded our contest as a measuring and weighing of purses. He is the Gaul that puts his *sword* into the scale.[12] He is more tempted with our wealth as booty, than terrified with it as power. But let us be rich or poor, let us be either in what proportion we may, nature is false or this is true, that where the essential publick force, (of which money is but a part,) is in any degree upon a par in a conflict between nations, that state which is resolved to hazard it's existence rather than to abandon it's objects, must have an infinite advantage over that which is resolved to yield rather than to carry it's resistance beyond a certain point. Humanly speaking, that people which bounds it's efforts only with it's being, must give the law to that nation which will not push it's opposition beyond its convenience.

If we look to nothing but our domestick condition, the state of the nation is full even to plethory;[13] but if we imagine that this country can long maintain it's blood and it's food, as disjoined from the community of mankind, such an opinion does not deserve refutation as absurd, but pity as insane.

I do not know that such an improvident and stupid selfishness, deserves the discussion, which, perhaps, I may bestow upon it hereafter. We cannot arrange with our enemy in the present conjuncture, without abandoning the interest of mankind. If we look only to our own petty peculium in the war,[14] we have had some advantages; advantages ambiguous in their nature, and dearly bought. We have not in the slightest degree, impaired the strength of the common enemy, in any one of those points in which his particular force consists; at the same time that new enemies to ourselves, new allies to the Regicide Republick, have been made out of the wrecks and fragments of the general confederacy. So far as to the selfish part. As composing a part of the community of Europe, and interested in it's fate, it is not easy to conceive a state of things more doubtful and perplexing. When Louis the XIVth[N] had made himself master of one of the largest and most important provinces of Spain; when he had in a manner over-run

---

[12] *Sword into the scale*: After the Gauls' capture of Rome in 390 BC, the Romans agreed to ransom the city for a certain weight of gold. When the Romans protested that the Gauls had used heavier weights than agreed, the Gaulish chief, Brennus, insolently added his sword to the scales to further *increase* the amount of gold required (Livy, *History of Rome*, 5.48). Burke implies that however many concessions are made, the revolutionaries will always increase their demands.

[13] *Plethory*: *sc.* plethora, an over-fullness.    [14] *Petty peculium*: a small sum of money.

Lombardy, and was thundering at the gates of Turin; when he had mastered almost all Germany on this side the Rhine; when he was on the point of ruining the august fabrick of the Empire; when with the Elector of Bavaria in his alliance, hardly any thing interposed between him and Vienna; when the Turk hung with a mighty force over the Empire on the other side; I do not know, that in the beginning of 1704 (that is in the third year of the renovated war with Louis the XIV) the state of Europe was so truly alarming.[15] To England it certainly was not. Holland (and Holland is a matter to England of value inestimable) was then powerful, was then independent, and though greatly endangered, was then full of energy and spirit. But the great resource of Europe was in England: Not in a sort of England detached from the rest of the world, and amusing herself with the puppet shew of a naval power, (it can be no better, whilst all the sources of that power, and of every sort of power, are precarious) but in that sort of England, who considered herself as embodied with Europe; but in that sort of England, who, sympathetick with the adversity or the happiness of mankind, felt that nothing in human affairs was foreign to her. We may consider it as a sure axiom that, as on the one hand no confederacy of the least effect or duration can exist against France, of which England is not only a part, but the head, so neither can England pretend to cope with France but as connected with the body of Christendom.

Our account of the war, *as a war of communion*, to the very point in which we began to throw out lures, oglings,[16] and glances for peace, was a war of disaster and of little else. The independant advantages obtained by us at the beginning of the war, and which were made at the expence of that common cause, if they deceive us about our largest and our surest interest, are to be reckoned amongst our heaviest losses.[17]

The allies, and Great Britain amongst the rest, (perhaps amongst the foremost) have been miserably deluded by this great fundamental error;

[15] *Truly alarming*: Burke describes what for most European politicians was the nightmare scenario – the unification of the thrones of Spain and France (and their associated possessions), and the further suppression or incorporation of the Holy Roman Empire, leading to the breakdown of the European 'balance of power' and the achievement of 'universal empire'. Desire to avoid this had already led to the War of the Spanish Succession (1701-14) but had in fact fuelled many European conflicts since Francis I's war with the Emperor Charles V.

[16] *Oglings*: desirous looks.

[17] *Advantages obtained . . . at the expence of that common cause*: Britain had captured a number of French island colonies in the Americas at the start of the war – Tobago, St Pierre (Newfoundland), Martinique etc. – much against Burke's urgings that the war should be prosecuted in mainland France.

that it was in our power to make peace with this monster of a State, whenever we chose to forget the crimes that made it great, and the designs that made it formidable. People imagined that their ceasing to resist was the sure way to be secure. This 'pale cast of thought sicklied over all their enterprizes and turned all their politicks awry.'[18] They could not, or rather they would not read, in the most unequivocal declarations of the enemy, and in his uniform conduct, that more safety was to be found in the most arduous war, than in the friendship of that kind of being. It's hostile amity can be obtained on no terms that do not imply an inability hereafter to resist it's designs. This great prolific error (I mean that peace was always in our power) has been the cause that rendered the allies indifferent about the *direction* of the war; and persuaded them that they might always risque a choice, and even a change in it's objects. They seldom improved any advantage; hoping that the enemy, affected by it, would make a proffer of peace. Hence it was, that all their early victories have been followed almost immediately with the usual effects of a defeat; whilst all the advantages obtained by the Regicides, have been followed by the consequences that were natural. The discomfitures, which the Republick of Assassins has suffered, have uniformly called forth new exertions, which not only repaired old losses, but prepared new conquests. The losses of the allies, on the contrary, (no provision having been made on the speculation of such an event) have been followed by desertion, by dismay, by disunion, by a dereliction of their policy, by a flight from their principles, by an admiration of the enemy, by mutual accusations, by a distrust in every member of the alliance of it's fellow, of it's cause, it's power, and it's courage.

Great difficulties in consequence of our erroneous policy, as I have said, press upon every side of us. Far from desiring to conceal or even to palliate the evil in the representation, I wish to lay it down as my foundation, that never greater existed. In a moment when sudden panick is apprehended, it may be wise, for a while to conceal some great publick disaster, or to reveal it by degrees, until the minds of the people have

---

[18] *Pale cast of thought* . . . : a misremembered quotation from Hamlet's famous soliloquy at Act III, i.85:

> 'And thus the native hue of resolution
> Is sicklied o'er with the pale cast of thought,
> And enterprises of great pith and moment
> With this regard their currents turn awry,
> And lose the name of action . . . '

time to be re-collected, that their understanding may have leisure to rally, and that more steady counsels may prevent their doing something desperate under the first impressions of rage or terror. But with regard to a *general* state of things, growing out of events and causes already known in the gross, there is no piety in the fraud that covers it's true nature; because nothing but erroneous resolutions can be the result of false representations. Those measures which in common distress might be available, in greater, are no better than playing with the evil. That the effort may bear a proportion to the exigence, it is fit it should be known; known in it's quality, in it's extent, and in all the circumstances which attend it. Great reverses of fortune, there have been, and great embarrassments in council: a principled Regicide enemy possessed of the most important part of Europe and struggling for the rest: within ourselves a total relaxation of all authority, whilst a cry is raised against it, as if it were the most ferocious of all despotism: a worse phænomenon; – our government disowned by the most efficient member of it's tribunals; ill supported by any of their constituent parts; and the highest tribunal of all (from causes not for our present purpose to examine) deprived of all that dignity and all that efficiency which might enforce, or regulate, or if the case required it, might supply the want of every other court.[19] Public prosecutions are become little better than schools for treason; of no use but to improve the dexterity of criminals in the mystery of evasion; or to shew with what compleat impunity men may conspire against the Commonwealth; with what safety assassins may attempt it's awful head.[20] Every thing is secure, except what the laws have made sacred; every thing is tameness and languor that is not fury and faction. Whilst the distempers of a relaxed fibre prognosticate and prepare all the morbid force of convulsion in the body of the State the steadiness of

[19] *Highest tribunal of all*: probably a reference to the House of Lords sitting as a court of impeachment, which had acquitted Warren Hastings in April 1795 – a prosecution to which Burke had unsuccessfully devoted huge energy over the previous seven years.

[20] *With what compleat impunity men may conspire against the commonwealth*: a reference to the successful defences by Thomas Hardy, John Horne Tooke and John Thelwall, at their trials for high treason in 1794. Their acquittal forced the Crown to abandon the prosecution of some thirty further political activists. The 'impunity' was not quite complete: similar trials in Scotland the previous year had, with the benefit of carefully picked juries, resulted in the conviction and transportation of Thomas Muir, the Revd Thomas Fyshe Palmer, Maurice Margarot, Thomas Skirving and Joseph Gerrald and for similar political activity. The presiding Judge, Lord Braxfield, had *defined* campaigning for parliamentary reform as seditious.

the physician is overpowered by the very aspect of the disease.[i] The doctor of the Constitution, pretending to under-rate what he is not able to contend with, shrinks from his own operation. He doubts and questions the salutary but critical terrors of the cautery[21] and the knife. He takes a poor credit even from his defeat; and covers impotence under the mask of lenity. He praises the moderation of the laws, as, in his hands, he sees them baffled and despised. Is all this, because in our day the statutes of the kingdom are not engrossed in as firm a character, and imprinted in as black and legible a type as ever? No! the law is a clear, but it is a dead letter. Dead and putrid, it is insufficient to save the State, but potent to infect, and to kill. Living law, full of reason, and of equity and justice, (as it is, or it should not exist) ought to be severe and awful too; or the words of menace, whether written on the parchment roll of England, or cut into the brazen tablet of Rome, will excite nothing but contempt. How comes it, that in all the State prosecutions of magnitude, from the Revolution to within these two or three years, the Crown has scarcely ever retired disgraced and defeated from it's Courts? Whence this alarming change? By a connexion easily felt, and not impossible to be traced to it's cause, all the parts of the State have their correspondence and consent. They who bow to the enemy abroad will not be of power to subdue the conspirator at home. It is impossible not to observe, that in proportion as we approximate to the poisonous jaws of anarchy, the fascination grows irresistible. In proportion as we are attracted towards the focus of illegality, irreligion, and desperate enterprize, all the venomous and blighting insects of the State are awakened into life. The promise of the year is blasted, and shrivelled, and burned up before them. Our most salutary and most beautiful institutions yield nothing but dust and smut: the harvest of our law is no more than stubble. It is in the nature of these eruptive diseases in the State to sink in by fits and re-appear. But the fuel of the malady remains; and in my opinion is not in the smallest degree mitigated in it's malignity, though it waits the favourable moment of a freer communication with the source of Regicide to exert and to encrease it's force.

---

[i] "Mussabat tacito medicina timore."[22]

---

[21] *Cautery*: cauterisation, the sealing of amputated limbs with red hot irons.
[22] 'Medicine muttered in silent fear': Lucretius, *De Rerum Natura*, 6.1179, describing the effects of the plague in Athens.

Is it that the people are changed, that the Commonwealth cannot be protected by its laws? I hardly think it. On the contrary, I conceive, that these things happen because men are not changed, but remain always what they always were; they remain what the bulk of us must ever be, when abandoned to our vulgar propensities, without guide, leader or controul: That is, made to be full of a blind elevation in prosperity; to despise untried dangers; to be overpowered with unexpected reverses; to find no clue in a labyrinth of difficulties; to get out of a present inconvenience with any risque of future ruin; to follow and to bow to fortune; to admire successful though wicked enterprize, and to imitate what we admire; to contemn the government which announces danger from sacrilege and regicide, whilst they are only in their infancy and their struggle, but which finds nothing that can alarm in their adult state and in the power and triumph of those destructive principles. In a mass we cannot be left to ourselves. We must have leaders. If none will undertake to lead us right, we shall find guides who will contrive to conduct us to shame and ruin.

We are in a war of a *peculiar* nature. It is not with an ordinary community, which is hostile or friendly as passion or as interest may veer about; not with a State which makes war through wantonness, and abandons it through lassitude. We are at war with a system, which, by it's essence, is inimical to all other Governments, and which makes peace or war, as peace and war may best contribute to their subversion. It is with an *armed doctrine*, that we are at war. It has, by it's essence, a faction of opinion, and of interest, and of enthusiasm, in every country. To us it is a Colossus which bestrides our channel.[23] It has one foot on a foreign shore, the other upon the British soil. Thus advantaged, if it can at all exist, it must finally prevail. Nothing can so compleatly ruin any of the old Governments, ours in particular, as the acknowledgment, directly or by implication, of any kind of superiority in this new power. This acknowledgment we make, if in a bad or doubtful situation of our affairs, we solicit peace; or if we yield to the modes of new humiliation, in which alone she is content to give us an hearing. By that means the terms cannot be of our choosing; no, not in any part.

---

[23] *Colossus which bestrides our channel*: The Colossus of Rhodes, one of the wonders of the ancient world, was a statue of the titan Helios at the entrance to the harbour of the ancient Greek city of Rhodes. In Burke's day it was thought to have stood with one foot on either side of the harbour entrance (hence 'bestrides our channel'), a posture which modern scholars now consider improbable.

It is laid in the unalterable constitution of things: – none can aspire to act greatly, but those who are of force greatly to suffer. They who make their arrangements in the first run of misadventure, and in a temper of mind the common fruit of disappointment and dismay, put a seal on their calamities. To their power they take a security against any favours which they might hope from the usual inconstancy of fortune. I am therefore, my dear friend, invariably of your opinion (though full of respect for those who think differently) that neither the time chosen for it, nor the manner of soliciting a negotiation, were properly considered; even though I had allowed (I hardly shall allow) that with the horde of Regicides we could by any selection of time, or use of means, obtain any thing at all deserving the name of peace.

In one point we are lucky. The Regicide has received our advances with scorn. We have an enemy, to whose virtues we can owe nothing; but on this occasion we are infinitely obliged to one of his vices. We owe more to his insolence than to our own precaution. The haughtiness by which the proud repel us, has this of good in it; that in making us keep our distance, they must keep their distance too. In the present case, the pride of the Regicide may be our safety. He has given time for our reason to operate; and for British dignity to recover from it's surprise. From first to last he has rejected all our advances. Far as we have gone he has still left a way open to our retreat.

There is always an augury to be taken of what a peace is likely to be, from the preliminary steps that are made to bring it about. We may gather something from the time in which the first overtures are made; from the quarter whence they come; from the manner in which they are received. These discover the temper of the parties. If your enemy offers peace in the moment of success, it indicates that he is satisfied with something. It shews that there are limits to his ambition or his resentment. If he offers nothing under misfortune, it is probable, that it is more painful to him to abandon the prospect of advantage than to endure calamity. If he rejects solicitation, and will not give even a nod to the suppliants for peace, until a change in the fortune of the war threatens him with ruin, then I think it evident, that he wishes nothing more than to disarm his adversary to gain time. Afterwards a question arises, which of the parties is likely to obtain the greater advantages, by continuing disarmed and by the use of time.

With these few plain indications in our minds, it will not be improper to re-consider the conduct of the enemy together with our own, from the day that a question of peace has been in agitation. In considering this part of the question, I do not proceed on my own hypothesis. I suppose, for a moment, that this body of Regicide, calling itself a Republick, is a politick person, with whom something deserving the name of peace may be made.[24] On that supposition, let us examine our own proceeding. Let us compute the profit it has brought, and the advantage that it is likely to bring hereafter. A peace too eagerly sought, is not always the sooner obtained. The discovery of vehement wishes generally frustrates their attainment; and your adversary has gained a great advantage over you when he finds you impatient to conclude a treaty. There is in reserve, not only something of dignity, but a great deal of prudence too. A sort of courage belongs to negotiation as well as to operations of the field. A negotiator must often seem willing to hazard the whole issue of his treaty, if he wishes to secure any one material point.

The Regicides were the first to declare war.[25] We are the first to sue for peace. In proportion to the humility and perseverance we have shewn in our addresses, has been the obstinacy of their arrogance in rejecting our suit. The patience of their pride seems to have been worn out with the importunity of our courtship. Disgusted as they are with a conduct so different from all the sentiments by which they are themselves filled, they think to put an end to our vexatious solicitation by redoubling their insults.

It happens frequently, that pride may reject a public advance, while interest listens to a secret suggestion of advantage. The opportunity has been afforded. At a very early period in the diplomacy of humiliation, a gentleman was sent on an errand[ii], of which, from the motive of it, whatever the event might be, we can never be ashamed. Humanity cannot be degraded by humiliation. It is it's very character to submit to such things. There is a consanguinity between benevolence and humility. They are virtues of the same stock. Dignity is of as good a race; but it belongs to the family of Fortitude. In the spirit of that benevolence, we

---

[ii] Mr. Bird sent to state the real situation of the Duc de Choiseul.[26]

[24] *Not . . . on my own hypothesis . . . suppose [the Republic] a politick person*: Burke did not consider the Republic a properly constituted legal entity ('politick person'), but even supposing it were . . .

[25] On 1 February 1793.

[26] *Mr Bird*: Christopher Bird, British Commissioner with the royalist army in the Vendée, on a mission to Paris in December 1795 to secure the release of the Duc de Choiseul, had been curtly refused (*Corr.* viii, p. 376).

sent a gentleman to beseech the Directory of Regicide, not to be quite so prodigal as their Republick had been of judicial murder. We solicited them to spare the lives of some unhappy persons of the first distinction, whose safety at other times could not have been an object of solicitation.[27] They had quitted France on the faith of the declaration of the rights of citizens. They never had been in the service of the Regicides, nor at their hands had received any stipend. The very system and constitution of government that now prevails, was settled subsequent to their emigration. They were under the protection of Great Britain, and in his Majesty's pay and service. Not an hostile invasion, but the disasters of the sea had thrown them upon a shore, more barbarous and inhospitable than the inclement ocean under the most pitiless of it's storms. Here was an opportunity to express a feeling for the miseries of war; and to open some sort of conversation, which (after our publick overtures had glutted their pride), at a cautious and jealous distance, might lead to something like an accommodation. What was the event? A strange uncouth thing, a theatrical figure of the opera, his head shaded with three-coloured plumes, his body fantastically habited,[28] strutted from the back scenes, and after a short speech, in the mock-heroic falsetto of stupid tragedy, delivered the gentleman who came to make the representation into the custody of a guard, with directions not to lose sight of him for a moment; and then ordered him to be sent from Paris in two hours.

Here it is impossible, that a sentiment of tenderness should not strike athwart the sternness of politicks, and make us recal to painful memory, the difference between this insolent and bloody theatre, and the temperate, natural majesty of a civilized court, where the afflicted family of Asgill did not in vain solicit the mercy of the highest in rank, and the most compassionate of the compassionate sex.[29]

In this intercourse, at least, there was nothing to promise a great deal of success in our future advances. Whilst the fortune of the field was wholly with the Regicides, nothing was thought of but to follow where

---

[27] *Object of solicitation*: The Duc de Choiseul and other émigrés escaping to England had been shipwrecked on the French coast, and the English government was asking they be given asylum.

[28] *Fantastically habited*: Burke ridicules the gaudy black and red costume prescribed for French Ministers under the 1795 constitution.

[29] *Asgill*: In a famous postscript to the American War of Independence, Grenadier Charles Asgill, a British prisoner of war, sentenced to death in reprisal for the execution of an American officer, had been released, following the successful intervention on his behalf of the French foreign minister, at the request of Asgill's mother.

it led; and it led to every thing. Not so much as a talk of treaty. Laws were laid down with arrogance. The most moderate politician in their clan[iii] was chosen as the organ, not so much for prescribing limits to their claims, as to mark what, for the present, they are content to leave to others. They made, not laws, not conventions, not late possession, but physical nature, and political convenience, the sole foundation of their claims.[30] The Rhine, the Mediterranean, and the ocean were the bounds which, for the time, they assigned to the Empire of Regicide. What was the Chamber of Union of Louis the Fourteenth, which astonished and provoked all Europe, compared to this declaration? In truth, with these limits, and their principle, they would not have left even the shadow of liberty or safety to any nation. This plan of empire was not taken up in the first intoxication of unexpected success. You must recollect, that it was projected, just as the report has stated it, from the very first revolt of the faction against their Monarchy; and it has been uniformly pursued, as a standing maxim of national policy, from that time to this. It is, generally, in the season of prosperity that men discover their real temper, principles, and designs. But this principle suggested in their first struggles, fully avowed in their prosperity, has, in the most adverse state of their affairs, been tenaciously adhered to. The report, combined with their conduct, forms an infallible criterion of the views of this Republick.

In their fortune there has been some fluctuation. We are to see how their minds have been affected with a change. Some impression it made on them undoubtedly. It produced some oblique notice of the submissions that were made by suppliant nations. The utmost they did, was to make some of those cold, formal, general professions of a love of peace which no Power has ever refused to make; because they mean little, and cost nothing. The first paper I have seen (the publication at Hamburgh) making a shew of that pacific disposition, discovered a rooted animosity against this nation, and an incurable rancour, even more than any one of their hostile acts. In this Hamburgh declaration, they choose to suppose, that the war, on the

---

[iii] Boissy d'Anglas.

[30] Boissy d'Anglas (1756–1828), then a member of the Committee of Public Safety, had reported to the Convention on 30 January 1795 that a solid and endurable peace required France's military expansion to her 'natural' geographical boundaries – the Alps, the Pyrenees, the Rhine, the Atlantic and Mediterranean coast.

part of England, *is a war of Government, begun and carried on against the sense and interests of the people*; thus sowing in their very overtures towards peace the seeds of tumult and sedition: for they never have abandoned, and never will they abandon, in peace, in war, in treaty, in any situation, or for one instant, their old steady maxim of separating the people from their Government.[31] Let me add – and it is with unfeigned anxiety for the character and credit of Ministers that I do add – if our Government perseveres, in its as uniform course, of acting under instruments with such preambles, it pleads guilty to the charges made by our enemies against it, both on it's own part, and on the part of Parliament itself. The enemy must succeed in his plan for loosening and disconnecting all the internal holdings of the kingdom.

It was not enough, that the Speech from the Throne in the opening of the session in 1795, threw out oglings and glances of tenderness. Lest this coquetting should seem too cold and ambiguous, without waiting for it's effect, the violent passion for a relation to the Regicides, produced a direct Message from the Crown, and it's consequences from the two Houses of Parliament.[32] On the part of the Regicides these declarations could not be entirely passed by without notice: but in that notice they discovered still more clearly the bottom of their character. The offer made to them by the message to Parliament was hinted at in their answer; but in an obscure and oblique manner as before. They accompanied their notice of the indications manifested on our side, with every kind of insolent and taunting reflection. The Regicide Directory, on the day which, in their gipsey jargon, they call the 5th of Pluviose,[33] in return for our advances, charge us with eluding our declarations under 'evasive formalities and frivolous pretexts.' What these pretexts and evasions were, they do not

---

[31] *Separating the people from their Government*: In their propaganda war the revolutionaries not infrequently expressed their deep friendship toward the English people, blaming the war on its misguided government. Letters between the Corresponding Societies in England and Scotland reinforced this view.

[32] Both the King's speech at the start of the parliamentary session, and a letter from the King to the House of Commons, had expressed a willingness to negotiate a peace should the conditions prove right, an initiative which had reinforced Burke's concerns about a 'Regicide Peace'.

[33] *Pluviose*: In 1793, as part of their de-Christianisation programme, the revolutionaries established a new calendar, dating years not from the birth of Christ but from the establishment of the Republic – 1792 became year 1 – and renaming the months of the year after their natural properties. Pluviôse, (the 'month of rain') ran from 20 Jan. to 18 Feb.

say, and I have never heard. But they do not rest there. They proceed to charge us, and, as it should seem, our allies in the mass, with direct *perfidy*; they are so conciliatory in their language as to hint that this perfidious character is not new in our proceedings. However, notwithstanding this our habitual perfidy, they will offer peace 'on conditions *as* moderate' – as what? as reason and as equity require? No! as moderate 'as are suitable to their *national dignity*.' National dignity in all treaties I do admit is an important consideration. They have given us an useful hint on that subject: but dignity, hitherto, has belonged to the mode of proceeding, not to the matter of a treaty. Never before has it been mentioned as the standard for rating the conditions of peace; no, never by the most violent of conquerors. Indemnification is capable of some estimate; dignity has no standard. It is impossible to guess what acquisitions pride and ambition may think fit for their *dignity*. But lest any doubt should remain on what they think for their dignity, the Regicides in the next paragraph tell us 'that they will have no peace with their enemies, until they have reduced them to a state, which will put them under an *impossibility* of pursuing their wretched projects;' that is, in plain French or English, until they have accomplished our utter and irretrievable ruin. This is their *pacific* language. It flows from their unalterable principle in whatever language they speak, or whatever steps they take, whether of real war, or of pretended pacification. They have never, to do them justice, been at much trouble in concealing their intentions. We were as obstinately resolved to think them not in earnest: but I confess jests of this sort, whatever their urbanity may be, are not much to my taste.

To this conciliatory and amicable publick communication, our sole answer, in effect, is this – 'Citizen Regicides! whenever *you* find yourselves in the humour, you may have a peace with *us*. That is a point you may always command. We are constantly in attendance, and nothing you can do shall hinder us from the renewal of our supplications. You may turn us out at the door; but we will jump in at the window.'

To those, who do not love to contemplate the fall of human greatness, I do not know a more mortifying spectacle, than to see the assembled majesty of the crowned heads of Europe waiting as patient suitors in the anti-chamber of Regicide. They wait, it seems, until the sanguinary tyrant *Carnot*,[N] shall have snorted away the fumes of the indigested blood of his Sovereign. Then, when sunk on the down of usurped pomp, he shall have sufficiently indulged his meditations with what Monarch he shall next glut his ravening maw,[34] he may condescend to signify that it is his pleasure to be awake; and that he is at leisure to receive the proposals of his high and mighty clients for the terms on which he may respite the execution of the sentence he has passed upon them. At the opening of those doors, what a sight it must be to behold the plenipotentiaries[35] of royal impotence, in the precedency which they will intrigue to obtain, and which will be granted to them according to the seniority of their degradation, sneaking into the Regicide presence, and with the reliques of the smile, which they had dressed up for the levee of their masters, still flickering on their curled lips, presenting the faded remains of their courtly graces, to meet the scornful, ferocious, sardonic grin of a bloody ruffian, who, whilst he is receiving their homage, is measuring them with his eye, and fitting to their size the slider of his Guillotine! These ambassadors may easily return as good courtiers as they went; but can they ever return from that degrading residence, loyal and faithful subjects; or with any true affection to their master, or true attachment to the constitution, religion, or laws of their country? There is great danger that they who enter smiling into this Trophonian Cave,[36] will come out of it sad and serious conspirators; and such will continue as long as they live. They will become true conductors of contagion to every country, which has had the misfortune to send them to the source of that electricity. At best they will become totally indifferent to good and evil, to one institution or another. This species of indifference is but too generally distinguishable in those who have been much employed in foreign Courts; but in the present case the evil must be aggravated without measure; for they go from their country, not with the pride of the old character, but in a state of the lowest degradation; and what must happen in their place of residence can have no effect in raising them to the level of true dignity, or of chaste self estimation, either as men, or as representatives of crowned heads.

---

[34] *Ravening maw*: the mouth and gullet of any voracious wild beast.

[35] *Plenipotentiary*: one invested (often by delegation) with full and unconstrained discretionary power.

[36] *Trophonian Cave*: Trophonius was a mythical Greek character, son of either Apollo or Erginis, King of Orchomenus. Burke refers to Pausanius' account of the cult of Trophonius in which individuals could consult an oracle by fasting, then descending into the deep cave associated with Trophonius at Lebadae, where they would drink the waters of forgetfulness (Lethe) and memory (Mnemosyne) and emerge terrified and disoriented, to have their ravings interpreted by the priests. So to enter the Trophonian cave is to undergo a terrifying and personality-altering experience.

Our early proceeding, which has produced these returns of affront, appeared to me totally new, without being adapted to the new circumstances of affairs. I have called to my mind the speeches and messages in former times. I find nothing like these. You will look in the journals to find whether my memory fails me. Before this time, never was a ground of peace laid, (as it were, in a parliamentary record,) until it had been as good as concluded. This was a wise homage paid to the discretion of the Crown. It was known how much a negotiation must suffer by having any thing in the train towards it prematurely disclosed. But when those parliamentary declarations were made, not so much as a step had been taken towards a negotiation in any mode whatever. The measure was an unpleasant and unseasonable discovery.

I conceive that another circumstance in that transaction has been as little authorised by any example; and that it is as little prudent in itself; I mean the formal recognition of the French Republick. Without entering, for the present, into a question on the good faith manifested in that measure, or on it's general policy, I doubt, upon mere temporary considerations of prudence, whether it was perfectly adviseable. It is not within the rules of dexterous conduct to make an acknowledgment of a contested title in your enemy, before you are morally certain that your recognition will secure his friendship. Otherwise it is a measure worse than thrown away. It adds infinitely to the strength, and consequently to the demands of the adverse party. He has gained a fundamental point without an equivalent. It has happened as might have been foreseen. No notice whatever was taken of this recognition. In fact, the Directory never gave themselves any concern about it; and they received our acknowledgment with perfect scorn. With them, it is not for the States of Europe to judge of their title: But in their eye the title of every other power depends wholly on their pleasure.

Preliminary declarations of this sort, thrown out at random, and sown, as it were, broad-cast, were never to be found in the mode of our proceeding with France and Spain, whilst the great Monarchies of France and Spain existed. I do not say, that a diplomatick measure ought to be, like a parliamentary or a judicial proceeding, according to strict precedent. I hope I am far from that pedantry: But this I know, that a great state ought to have some regard to it's antient maxims; especially where they indicate it's dignity; where they concur with the rules of prudence; and above all, where the circumstances of the time require that a spirit of innovation should be resisted, which leads to the humiliation of sovereign powers.

It would be ridiculous to assert, that those powers have suffered nothing in their estimation. I admit, that the greater interests of state will for a moment supersede all other considerations: but if there was a rule that a sovereign never should let down his dignity without a sure payment to his interest, the dignity of Kings would be held high enough. At present, however, fashion governs in more serious things than furniture and dress. It looks as if sovereigns abroad were emulous in bidding against their estimation. It seems as if the pre-eminence of Regicide was acknowledged; and that Kings tacitly ranked themselves below their sacrilegious murderers, as natural magistrates and judges over them. It appears as if dignity were the prerogative of crime; and a temporising humiliation the proper part for venerable authority. If the vilest of mankind are resolved to be the most wicked, they lose all the baseness of their origin, and take their place above Kings. This example in foreign Princes, I trust, will not spread. It is the concern of mankind, that the destruction of order should not be a claim to rank: that crimes should not be the only title to pre-eminence and honour.

At this second stage of humiliation, (I mean the insulting declaration in consequence of the message to both Houses of Parliament) it might not have been amiss to pause; and not to squander away the fund of our submissions, until we know what final purposes of public interest they might answer. The policy of subjecting ourselves to further insults is not to me quite apparent. It was resolved however, to hazard a third trial. Citizen Barthelemi[37] had been established on the part of the new Republick, at Basle; where, with his proconsulate of Switzerland and the adjacent parts of Germany, he was appointed as a sort of factor to deal in the degradation of the crowned heads of Europe. At Basle it was thought proper, in order to keep others, I suppose, in countenance, that Great Britain should appear at this market, and bid with the rest, for the mercy of the People-King.

On the 6th of March 1796 Mr. Wickham,[38] in consequence of authority, was desired to sound France on her disposition towards a general pacification; to know whether she would consent to send Ministers to a Congress at such a place as might be hereafter agreed upon; to know

---

[37] *Citizen Barthelemi*: Francois Marie, Marquis de Barthélemy (1747–1830) was French minister representative in Switzerland, where he had negotiated the Peace of Basle (1795) with Prussia, Spain and Hesse, previously members of the anti-revolutionary coalition.

[38] *Mr. Wickham*: William Wickham (1761–1840), an English diplomat, had studied in Switzerland and was appointed ambassador there in 1795.

whether they would communicate the general grounds of a pacification such as France (the diplomatick name of the Regicide power) would be willing to propose, as a foundation for a negociation for peace with his Majesty *and his allies*: but he had no authority to enter into any negociation or discussion with citizen Barthelemi upon these subjects.

On the part of Great Britain this measure was a voluntary act, wholly uncalled for on the part of Regicide. Suits of this sort are at least strong indications of a desire for accommodation. Any other body of men but the Directory would be somewhat soothed with such advances. They could not however begin their answer, which was given without much delay, and communicated on the 28th of the same month, without a preamble of insult and reproach. 'They doubt the sincerity of the pacific intentions of this Court.' She did not begin, say they, yet to 'know her real interests,' 'she did not seek peace with *good faith*.' This, or something to this effect, has been the constant preliminary observation, (now grown into a sort of office-form) on all our overtures to this power: a perpetual charge on the British Government of fraud, evasion, and habitual perfidy.

It might be asked, from whence did these opinions of our insincerity and ill faith arise? It was because the British Ministry (leaving to the Directory however to propose a better mode) proposed a *Congress* for the purpose of a general pacification, and this they said "would render negociation endless." From hence they immediately inferred a fraudulent intention in the offer. Unquestionably their mode of giving the law would bring matters to a more speedy conclusion. As to any other method more agreeable to them than a Congress, an alternative expressly proposed to them, they did not condescend to signify their pleasure.

This refusal of treating conjointly with the powers allied against this Republick, furnishes matter for a great deal of serious reflexion. They have hitherto constantly declined any other than a treaty with a single power. By thus dissociating every State from every other, like deer separated from the herd, each power is treated with, on the merit of his being a deserter from the common cause. In that light the Regicide power finding each of them insulated and unprotected, with great facility gives the law to them all. By this system for the present, an incurable distrust is sown amongst confederates; and in future all alliance is rendered impracticable. It is thus they have treated with Prussia, with Spain, with Sardinia, with

Bavaria, with the Ecclesiastical State,[39] with Saxony; and here we see them refuse to treat with Great Britain in any other mode. They must be worse than blind who do not see with what undeviating regularity of system, in this case and in all cases, they pursue their scheme for the utter destruction of every independent power; especially the smaller, who cannot find any refuge whatever but in some common cause.

Renewing their taunts and reflections, they tell Mr. Wickham, 'that *their* policy has no guides but openness and good faith, and that their conduct shall be conformable to these principles.' They say concerning their Government, that 'yielding to the ardent desire by which it is animated to procure peace for the French Republick, and for all nations, it will not *fear to declare itself openly.* Charged by the Constitution with the execution of the *laws*, it cannot *make* or *listen* to any proposal that would be contrary to them. The constitutional act does not permit it to consent to any alienation of that which, according to the existing laws, constitutes the territory of the Republick.'[40]

'With respect to the countries *occupied by the French armies and which have not been united to France*, they, as well as other interests political and commercial, may become the subject of a negociation, which will present to the Directory the means of proving how much it desires to attain speedily to a happy pacification. That the Directory is ready to receive in this respect any overtures that shall be just, reasonable, and compatible *with the dignity of the Republick.*' On the head of what is *not* to be the subject of negotiation, the Directory is clear and open. As to what may be a matter of treaty, all this open dealing is gone. She retires into her shell. There she expects overtures from *you* – and you are to guess what she shall judge just, reasonable, and above all, *compatible with her dignity.*

In the records of pride there does not exist so insulting a declaration. It is insolent in words, in manner, but in substance it is not only insulting but alarming. It is a specimen of what may be expected from the masters we are preparing for our humbled country. Their openness and candour consist in a direct avowal of their despotism and ambition. We know that their declared resolution had been to surrender no object belonging to

---

[39] *Ecclesiastical State*: The area of central Italy ruled directly by the Vatican in its capacity as a secular power.

[40] The quoted passages are from a letter written by Barthelemy conveying the Directory's response to the British peace overtures (*Commons Journals*, lii, 243–4).

France previous to the war. They had resolved, that the Republick was entire, and must remain so.[41] As to what she has conquered from the allies and united to the same indivisible body, it is of the same nature. That is, the allies are to give up whatever conquests they have made or may make upon France, but all which she has violently ravished from her neighbours and thought fit to appropriate, are not to become so much as objects of negociation.

In this unity and indivisibility of possession are sunk ten immense and wealthy provinces, full of strong, flourishing and opulent cities, (the Austrian Netherlands),[42] the part of Europe the most necessary to preserve any communication between this kingdom and its natural allies, next to Holland the most interesting to this country, and without which Holland must virtually belong to France. Savoy and Nice,[43] the keys of Italy, and the citadel in her hands to bridle Switzerland, are in that consolidation. The important territory of Leige is torn out of the heart of the Empire.[44] All these are integrant parts of the Republick, not to be subject to any discussion, or to be purchased by any equivalent. Why? because there is a law which prevents it. What law? The law of nations? The acknowledged public law of Europe? Treaties and conventions of parties? No! not a pretence of the kind. It is a declaration not made in consequence of any prescription on her side, not on any cession or dereliction, actual or tacit, of other powers. It is a declaration *pendente lite*[45] in the middle of a war, one principal object of which was originally the defence, and has since been the recovery of these very countries.

This strange law is not made for a trivial object, not for a single port, or for a single fortress; but for a great kingdom; for the religion, the morals, the laws, the liberties, the lives and fortunes of millions of human creatures, who without their consent, or that of their lawful government, are, by an arbitrary act of this regicide and homicide Government, which they call a law, incorporated into their tyranny.

---

[41] *Entire*: the phrase 'one and indivisible' had gained currency with Abbé Sieyes'[N] pamphlets of 1789. The first article of title II of the constitution of 1791 had declared 'The Kingdom is one and indivisible'; Article One of the Constitutions of 1793 and of Year 3 (1795) both stated: 'The French Republic is one and indivisible' (*DocS*, pp. 233, 458, 574).

[42] *The Austrian Netherlands* – roughly modern Belgium – had been annexed by France in Oct. 1795.

[43] *Savoy and Nice*: both annexed in Nov. 1792. 'Interesting' here meaning 'concerning our political or economic interests'.

[44] *Liège*: annexed in Oct. 1795.   [45] *Pendente lite*: whilst the case is undecided.

In other words, their will is the law, not only at home, but as to the concerns of every nation. Who has made that law but the Regicide Republick itself, whose laws, like those of the Medes and Persians,[46] they cannot alter or abrogate, or even so much as take into consideration? Without the least ceremony or compliment, they have sent out of the world whole sets of laws and lawgivers. They have swept away the very constitutions under which the Legislatures acted, and the Laws were made. Even the fundamental sacred rights of man they have not scrupled to profane. They have set this holy code at naught with ignominy and scorn.[47] Thus they treat all their domestick laws and constitutions, and even what they had considered as a Law of Nature; but whatever they have put their seal on for the purposes of their ambition, and the ruin of their neighbours, this alone is invulnerable, impassible, immortal. Assuming to be masters of every thing human and divine, here, and here alone, it seems they are limited, 'cooped and cabined in;'[48] and this omnipotent legislature finds itself wholly without the power of exercising it's favourite attribute, the love of peace. In other words, they are powerful to usurp, impotent to restore; and equally by their power and their impotence they aggrandize themselves, and weaken and impoverish you and all other nations.

Nothing can be more proper or more manly than the state publication called a *note* on this proceeding, dated Downing-street, the 10th of April, 1796. Only that it is better expressed, it perfectly agrees with the opinion I have taken the liberty of submitting to your consideration.[iv] I place it below at full length as my justification in thinking that this astonishing

---

iv 'This Court has seen, with regret, how far the tone and spirit of that answer, the nature and extent of the demands which it contains, and the manner of announcing them, are remote from any dispositions for peace.

'The inadmissible pretension is there avowed of appropriating to France all that the laws existing there may have comprised under the denomination of French territory. To a demand such as this, is added an express declaration that no proposal contrary to it will be made, or even listened to. And even this, under the pretence of an internal regulation, the provisions of which are wholly foreign to all other nations.

46 *Medes and Persians*: Following a reference in the Old Testament Book of Esther (1:19), the laws of the Medes and the Persians were proverbially unalterable.

47 *Set this holy code at naught* . . . : the original *Declaration of the rights of men and of citizens* had been reformulated and recast in each of the subsequent constitutions. For a survey of the numerous *declarations* see Christine Fauré, *Les Declarations des Droits de l'Homme de 1789* (Paris, 1992).

48 *Macbeth*, 3.iv.24–5: 'But now I am cabin'd, cribb'd, confined, bound in To saucy doubts and fears.'

paper from the Directory is not only a direct negative, to all treaty, but is a rejection of every principle upon which treaties could be made. To admit it for a moment were to erect this power, usurped at home, into a Legislature to govern mankind. It is an authority that on a thousand occasions they have asserted in claim, and whenever they are able, exerted in practice. The dereliction of this whole scheme of policy became, therefore, an indispensable previous condition to all renewal of treaty. The remark of the British Cabinet on this arrogant and tyrannical claim is natural and unavoidable. Our Ministry state, '*That while these dispositions shall be persisted in, nothing is left for the King but to prosecute a war that is just and necessary.*'

It was of course, that we should wait until the enemy shewed some sort of disposition on his part to fulfil this condition. It was hoped indeed that our suppliant strains might be suffered to steal into the august ear in a more propitious season. That season, however, invoked by so many vows, conjurations and prayers, did not come. Every declaration of hostility renovated, and every act pursued with double animosity – the over-running of Lombardy – the subjugation of Piedmont – the possession of its impregnable fortresses – the seizing on all the neutral states of Italy – our expulsion from Leghorn[49] – instances for ever renewed, for our expulsion from Genoa – Spain rendered subject to them and hostile to us – Portugal bent under the yoke – half the Empire over-run and ravaged, were the only signs which this mild Republick thought proper to manifest of her pacific sentiments. Every demonstration of an implacable rancour and an untameable pride were the only encouragements we received to the renewal of our supplications.

'While these dispositions shall be persisted in, nothing is left for the King, but to prosecute a war equally just and necessary.

'Whenever his enemies shall manifest more pacific sentiments, his Majesty will, at all times, be eager to concur in them, by lending himself, in concert with his allies, to all such measures as shall be calculated to re-establish general tranquillity on conditions just, honourable and permanent, either by the establishment of a general Congress, which has been so happily the means of restoring peace to Europe, or by a preliminary discussion of the principles which may be proposed, on either side, as a foundation of a general pacification; or, lastly, by an impartial examination of any other way which may be pointed out to him for arriving at the same salutary end.'

Downing-Street, April 10, 1796.

[49] *Expulsion from Leghorn*: Leghorn – modern Livorno – had been, under the Medici, a 'Free' (i.e. not taxed or subject to restrictions) trading city, with an international commercial community. Occupation by the French Revolutionary Armies in June 1796 caused the British residents to leave.

Here therefore they and we were fixed. Nothing was left to the British Ministry but "to prosecute a war just and necessary" – a war equally just as at the time of our engaging in it – a war become ten times more necessary by every thing which happened afterwards. This resolution was soon, however, forgot. It felt the heat of the season and melted away. New hopes were entertained from supplication. No expectations, indeed, were then formed from renewing a direct application to the French Regicides through the Agent General for the humiliation of Sovereigns. At length a step was taken in degradation which even went lower than all the rest. Deficient in merits of our own, a Mediator was to be sought – and we looked for that Mediator at Berlin! The King of Prussia's merits in abandoning the general cause might have obtained for him some sort of influence in favour of those whom he had deserted – but I have never heard that his Prussian Majesty had lately discovered so marked an affection for the Court of St. James's, or for the Court of Vienna, as to excite much hope of his interposing a very powerful mediation to deliver them from the distresses into which he had brought them.[50]

If humiliation is the element in which we live, if it is become not only our occasional policy but our habit, no great objection can be made to the modes in which it may be diversified; though, I confess, I cannot be charmed with the idea of our exposing our lazar sores[51] at the door of every proud servitor of the French Republick, where the court-dogs will not deign to lick them. We had, if I am not mistaken, a minister at that court, who might try it's temper, and recede and advance as he found backwardness or encouragement. But to send a gentleman there on no other errand than this, and with no assurance whatever that he should not find, what he did find, a repulse, seems to me to go far beyond all the demands of a humiliation merely politick. I hope, it did not arise from a predilection for that mode of conduct.

The cup of bitterness was not, however, drained to the dregs. Basle and Berlin were not sufficient. After so many and so diversified repulses, we were resolved to make another experiment, and to try another Mediator.

[50] *His Prussian Majesty*: Frederick William II, originally a member of the anti-revolutionary coalition, had sought (and got) acquiescence in the partition of Poland, and a large subsidy, as the price for remaining in the alliance. Following withdrawal of the subsidy, Frederick had begun unilateral peace negotiations with the French in Oct. 1794, signing a peace treaty at Basle in April 1795. Burke refers here to British overtures, led by George Hammond in Berlin in summer 1796, to involve Prussia in a general European settlement.
[51] *Lazar*: a destitute, diseased person. Beggars would exhibit sores to excite pity and elicit cash from passers-by.

Among the unhappy gentlemen in whose persons Royalty is insulted and degraded at the seat of plebeian pride, and upstart insolence, there is a minister from Denmark at Paris.[52] Without any previous encouragement to that, any more than the other steps, we sent through this turnpike[53] to demand a passport for a person who on our part was to solicit peace in the metropolis, at the footstool of Regicide itself. It was not to be expected that any one of those degraded beings could have influence enough to settle any part of the terms in favour of the candidates for further degradation; besides, such intervention would be a direct breach in their system, which did not permit one sovereign power to utter a word in the concerns of his equal. – Another repulse. – We were desired to apply directly in our persons. – We submitted and made the application.

It might be thought that here, at length, we had touched the bottom of humiliation; our lead[54] was brought up covered with mud. But 'in the lowest deep, a lower deep'[55] was to open for us still more profound abysses of disgrace and shame. However, in we leaped. We came forward in our own name. The passport, such a passport and safe conduct as would be granted to thieves who might come in to betray their accomplices, and no better, was granted to British supplication. To leave no doubt of it's spirit, as soon as the rumour of this act of condescension could get abroad, it was formally announced with an explanation from authority, containing an invective against the Ministry of Great Britain, their habitual frauds, their proverbial, *punick*[N] perfidy. No such State Paper, as a preliminary to a negociation for peace has ever yet appeared. Very few declarations of war have ever shewn so much and so unqualified animosity. I place it below[v] as a diplomatick curiosity, and in order to be better understood, in the few remarks I have to make upon a piece which indeed defies all description – 'None but itself can be it's parallel.'

---

[v] Official Note, extracted from the Journal of the Defenders of the Country.
    Executive Directory.
    'Different Journals have advanced that an English Plenipotentiary had reached Paris, and had presented himself to the Executive Directory, but that his propositions not having appeared satisfactory, he had received orders instantly to quit France.
    'All these assertions are equally false.

[52] *Minister from Denmark:* Johan Könemann, Danish Chargé d'Affaires in Paris.
[53] *Turnpike*: a kind of revolving gate or turnstile, commonly set at the entrance to toll roads, hence any barrier that had to be negotiated.
[54] *Lead*: referring to the practice of seafarers in unknown waters dropping a lead weight smeared with fat on a line from the bow of the ship to test the depth and nature of the sea bed.
[55] *Paradise Lost*, 4.76.

I pass by all the insolence and contumely of the performance, as it comes from them. The present question is not now how we are to be affected with it in regard to our dignity. That is gone. I shall say no more about it. Light lie the earth on the ashes of English pride. I shall only observe upon it *politically*, and as furnishing a direction for our own conduct in this low business.

The very idea of a negociation for peace, whatever the inward sentiments of the parties may be, implies some confidence in their faith, some degree of belief in the professions which are made concerning it. A temporary and occasional credit, at least, is granted. Otherwise men stumble on the very threshold. I therefore wish to ask what hope we can have of

'The notices given, in the English Papers, of a Minister having been sent to Paris, there to treat of peace, bring to recollection the overtures of Mr. Wickham to the Ambassador of the Republick at Basle, and the rumours circulated relative to the mission of Mr. Hammond to the Court of Prussia. The *insignificance*, or rather the *subtle duplicity*, the *PUNICK stile of* Mr. Wickham's note, is not forgotten. According to the partizans of the English Ministry, it was to Paris that Mr. Hammond was to come to speak for peace: when his destination became publick, and it was known that he went to Prussia, the same writer repeated that it was to accelerate a peace, and notwithstanding the object, now well known, of this negociation, was to engage Prussia to break her treaties with the Republick, and to return into the coalition – The Court of Berlin, faithful to its engagements, repulsed these *perfidious* propositions. But in converting this intrigue into a mission for peace, the English Ministry joined to the hope of giving a new enemy to France, *that of justifying the continuance of the war in the eyes of the English nation, and of throwing all the odium of it on the French Government*. Such was also the aim of Mr. Wickham's note. *Such is still that of the notices given at this time in the English papers.*

'This aim will appear evident, if we reflect how difficult it is, that the ambitious Government of England should sincerely wish for a peace that would *snatch from it it's maritime preponderancy, would re-establish the freedom of the seas, would give a new impulse to the Spanish, Dutch, and French marines*, and would carry to the highest degree of prosperity the industry and commerce of those nations in which it has always found *rivals*, and which it has considered as *enemies* of it's commerce, when they were tired of being it's *dupes*.

'But there will no longer be any credit given to the pacific intentions of the English Ministry, when it is known, that it's gold and it's intrigues, it's open practices, and it's insinuations, besiege more than ever the Cabinet of Vienna, and are one of the principal obstacles to the negotiation which that Cabinet would of itself be induced to enter on for peace.

'They will no longer *be credited*, finally, when the moment of the rumour of these overtures being circulated is considered. *The English nation supports impatiently the continuance of the war, a reply must be made to it's complaints, it's reproaches*: the Parliament is about to re-open it's sittings, the mouths of the orators who will declaim against the war must be shut, the demand of new taxes must be justified; and to obtain these results, it is necessary to be enabled to advance, that the French Government refuses every reasonable proposition of peace.'[56]

[56] *Le Moniteur Universel*, 1 Oct. 1796. *Le Moniteur* was a record of political proceedings from the start of the Revolution, later (in 1799) becoming the official Government newspaper.

their good faith, who, as the very basis of the negociation, assume the ill faith and treachery of those they have to deal with? The terms, as against us, must be such as imply a full security against a treacherous conduct – that is, what this Directory stated in it's first declaration, to place us 'in an utter impossibility of executing our wretched projects.' This is the omen, and the sole omen, under which we have consented to open our treaty.

The second observation I have to make upon it, (much connected undoubtedly with the first,) is, that they have informed you of the result they propose from the kind of peace they mean to grant you; that is to say, the union they propose among nations with the view, of rivalling our trade and destroying our naval power: and this they suppose (and with good reason too) must be the inevitable effect of their peace. It forms one of their principal grounds for suspecting our Ministers could not be in good earnest in their proposition. They make no scruple beforehand to tell you the whole of what they intend; and this is what we call, in the modern style, the acceptance of a proposition for peace! In old language it would be called a most haughty, offensive, and insolent rejection of all treaty.

Thirdly, they tell you what they conceive to be the perfidious policy which dictates your delusive offer; that is, the design of cheating not only them, but the people of England, against whose interest and inclination this war is supposed to be carried on.

If we proceed in this business, under this preliminary declaration, it seems to me, that we admit, (now for the third time) by something a great deal stronger than words, the truth of the charges of every kind which they make upon the British Ministry, and the grounds of those foul imputations. The language used by us, which in other circumstances would not be exceptionable, in this case tends very strongly to confirm and realize the suspicion of our enemy. I mean the declaration, that if we do not obtain such terms of peace as suits our opinion of what our interests require, *then*, and in *that* case, we shall continue the war with vigour. This offer so reasoned plainly implies, that without it, our leaders themselves entertain great doubts of the opinion and good affections of the British people; otherwise there does not appear any cause, why we should proceed under the scandalous construction of our enemy, upon the former offer made by Mr. Wickham, and on the new offer made directly at Paris. It is not, therefore, from a sense of dignity, but from the danger of radicating[57] that false sentiment in the breasts of the enemy, that I think, under the auspices of this declaration, we cannot, with the least hope of a good event, or, indeed, with any regard to the common safety, proceed in the train of this negociation. I wish Ministry would seriously consider the importance of their seeming to confirm the enemy in an opinion, that his frequent appeals to the people against their Government has not been without it's effect. If it puts an end to this war, it will render another impracticable.

Whoever goes to the directorial presence under this passport, with this offensive comment, and foul explanation, goes, in the avowed sense of the Court to which he is sent; as the instrument of a Government dissociated from the interests and wishes of the Nation, for the purpose of cheating both the people of France and the people of England. He goes out the declared emissary of a faithless Ministry. He has perfidy for his credentials. He has national weakness for his full powers. I yet doubt whether any one can be found to invest himself with that character. If there should, it would be pleasant to read his instructions on the answer which he is to give to the Directory, in case they should repeat to him the substance of the Manifesto which he carries with him in his portfolio.

So much for the *first* Manifesto of the Regicide Court which went along with the passport. Lest this declaration should seem the effect of haste, or a mere sudden effusion of pride and insolence, on full deliberation about a week after comes out a second. This manifesto, is dated the fifth of October, one day before the speech from the Throne, on the vigil of the festive day of cordial unanimity so happily celebrated by all parties in the British Parliament. In this piece the Regicides, our worthy friends, (I call them by advance and by courtesy what by law I shall be obliged to call them hereafter) our worthy friends, I say, renew and enforce the former declaration concerning our faith and sincerity, which they pinned to our passport.[58] On three other points which run through all their declarations, they are more explicit than ever.

First, they more directly undertake to be the real representatives of the people of this kingdom: and on a supposition in which they agree with our parliamentary reformers, that the House of Commons is not that

---

[57] *Radicating*: implanting, setting root.

[58] *Our passport*: The French press had reported the British request for a passport for an ambassador to discuss peace, and that the Directory indicated they would reply only if he were granted full powers to conclude peace.

Representative, the function being vacant, they, as our true constitutional organ, inform his Majesty and the world of the sense of the nation. They tell us that 'the English people see with regret his Majesty's Government squandering away the funds which had been granted to him.' This astonishing assumption of the publick voice of England, is but a slight foretaste of the usurpation which, on a peace, we may be assured they will make of all the powers in all the parts of our vassal constitution. 'If they do these things in the green tree, what shall be done in the dry?'

Next they tell us, as a condition to our treaty, that 'this Government must abjure the unjust hatred it bears to them, and at last open it's ears to the voice of humanity.' – Truly this is, even from them, an extraordinary demand. Hitherto it seems we have put wax into our ears to shut them up against the tender, soothing strains, in the *affettuoso*[59] of humanity, warbled from the throats of Reubel, Carnot,[N] Tallien,[N,60] and the whole chorus of Confiscators, domiciliary Visitors, Committee-men of Research, Jurors and Presidents of Revolutionary Tribunals, Regicides, Assassins, Massacrers, and Septembrizers.[61] It is not difficult to discern what sort of humanity our Government is to learn from these syren singers.[62] Our Government also, I admit with some reason, as a step towards the proposed fraternity, is required to abjure the unjust hatred which it bears to this body of honour and virtue. I thank God I am neither a Minister nor a leader of Opposition. I protest I cannot do what they desire, if I were under the guillotine, or as they ingeniously and pleasantly express it, "looking out of the little national window." Even at that opening I could receive none of their light. I am fortified against all such affections by the declaration of the Government, which I must yet consider as lawful, made on the 29th of October 1793[vi], and still

---

[vi] 'In their place has succeeded a system destructive of all publick order, maintained by proscriptions, exiles, and confiscations without number: by arbitrary imprisonment; by

[59] *Affettuoso*: Italian musical term indicating the piece to be played with affection, tenderly. Here ironic, with overtones of hypocrisy: affec*tat*ion.

[60] *Reubel, Carnot, Tallien*: leaders of the Thermidorian reaction which overthrew Robespierre and the Jacobins. The first two were subsequently members of the governing French Directory of five.

[61] *Septembrizer*: later 'septembrist', one who took part in the September 1792 'massacres', imprisoning the royal family.

[62] *Syren* (Siren): Greek myths describe the Sirens as bird-women who lured sailors to their deaths by singing songs of irresistible beauty. In Homer's *Odyssey* (xii) Odysseus escapes the lure of their isle by binding himself to the mast and plugging his sailors' ears with beeswax, so they could not hear the siren's beguiling songs, nor his commands to change course should he yield to them.

ringing in my ears. This declaration was transmitted not only to all our commanders by sea and land, but to our Ministers in every Court of Europe. It is the most eloquent and highly finished in the style, the most judicious in the choice of topicks, the most orderly in the arrangement, and the most rich in the colouring, without employing the smallest degree of exaggeration, of any state paper that has ever yet appeared.[63] An ancient writer, Plutarch,[64] I think it is, quotes some verses on the eloquence of

massacres which cannot be remembered without horror; and at length by the execrable murder of a just and beneficent Sovereign, and of the illustrious Princess, who, with an unshaken firmness, has shared all the misfortunes of her Royal Consort, his protracted sufferings, his cruel captivity and his ignominious death.' – 'They (the allies) have had to encounter acts of aggression without pretext, open violations of all treaties, unprovoked declarations of war; in a word, whatever corruption, intrigue or violence could effect for the purpose so openly avowed, of subverting all the institutions of society, and of extending over all the nations of Europe that confusion, which has produced the misery of France.' – 'This state of things cannot exist in France without involving all the surrounding powers in one common danger, without giving them the right, without imposing it upon them as a duty, to stop the progress of an evil, which exists only by the successive violation of all law and all property, and which attacks the fundamental principles by which mankind is united in the bonds of civil society.' – 'The King would impose none other than equitable and moderate conditions, not such as the expence, the risques and the sacrifices of the war might justify; but such as his Majesty thinks himself under the indispensable necessity of requiring, with a view to these considerations, and still more to that of his own security and of the future tranquillity of Europe. His Majesty desires nothing more sincerely than thus to terminate a war, which he in vain endeavoured to avoid, and all the calamities of which, as now experienced by France, are to be attributed only to the ambition, the perfidy and the violence of those, whose crimes have involved their own country in misery, and disgraced all civilized nations.' – 'The King promises on his part the suspension of hostilities, friendship, and (as far as the course of events will allow, of which the will of man cannot dispose) security and protection to all those who, by declaring for a monarchical form of Government, shall shake off the yoke of sanguinary anarchy; of that anarchy which has broken all the most sacred bonds of society, dissolved all the relations of civil life, violated every right, confounded every duty; which uses the name of liberty to exercise the most cruel tyranny, to annihilate all property, to seize on all possessions; which founds it's power on the pretended consent of the people, and itself carries fire and sword through extensive provinces for having demanded their laws, their religion and their lawful Sovereign.'

Declaration sent by his Majesty's command to the Commanders of his Majesty's fleets and armies employed against France, and to his Majesty's Ministers employed at foreign Courts.

*Whitehall, Oct.* 29, 1793.

---

[63] Burke, at that time close to the Government, had sought unsuccessfully to be involved in the writing of the paper (*Corr.* vii, pp. 465, 468).

[64] *Plutarch*: Lucius Mestrius Plutarch (AD 46–120), Roman historian and essayist, of Greek origin. Most famous for his biographical essays: 'Lives' pairing famous Greeks with famous Romans, including an essay on Pericles, the Athenian leader and orator during the Peloponnesian war.

Pericles, who is called 'the only orator that left stings in the minds of his hearers.'[65] Like his, the eloquence of the declaration, not contradicting, but enforcing sentiments of the truest humanity, has left stings that have penetrated more than skin-deep into my mind; and never can they be extracted by all the surgery of murder; never can the throbbings they have created, be assuaged by all the emollient cataplasms of robbery and confiscation. I *cannot* love the Republick.

The third point which they have more clearly expressed than ever, is of equal importance with the rest; and with them furnishes a complete view of the Regicide system. For they demand as a condition, without which our ambassador of obedience cannot be received with any hope of success, that he shall be 'provided with full powers to negociate a peace between the French Republick and Great Britain, and to conclude it *definitively* between the TWO powers.' With their spear they draw a circle about us. They will hear nothing of a joint treaty. We must make a peace separately from our allies. We must, as the very first and preliminary step, be guilty of that perfidy towards our friends and associates, with which they reproach us in our transactions with them our enemies. We are called upon scandalously to betray the fundamental securities to ourselves and to all nations. In my opinion, (it is perhaps but a poor one) if we are meanly bold enough to send an ambassador such as this official note of the enemy requires, we cannot even dispatch our emissary without danger of being charged with a breach of our alliance. Government now understand the full meaning of the passport.

Strange revolutions have happened in the ways of thinking and in the feelings of men. But it requires a very extraordinary coalition of parties indeed, and a kind of unheard-of unanimity in publick Councils, which can impose this new-discovered system of negociation, as sound national policy, on the understanding of a spectator of this wonderful scene, who judges on the principles of any thing he ever before saw, read, or heard of, and above all, on the understanding of a person who has had in his eye the transactions of the last seven years.

I know it is supposed, that if good terms of capitulation are not granted, after we have thus so repeatedly hung out the white flag, the national spirit will revive with tenfold ardour. This is an experiment cautiously to be

---

[65] The quotation is not from Plutarch, but from Cicero's *De Oratore*, 3.34: *dixerunt tantamque in eodem vim fuisse, ut in eorum mentibus, qui audissent, quasi aculeos quosdam relinqueret.* ['They said that he made such a powerful impression that it was as if he left a sting [or thorn] in the minds of those who had heard him.']

made. *Reculer pour mieux sauter*,[66] according to the French by-word, cannot be trusted to as a general rule of conduct. To diet a man into weakness and languor, afterwards to give him the greater strength, has more of the empirick than the rational physician. It is true that some persons have been kicked into courage; and this is no bad hint to give to those who are too forward and liberal in bestowing insults and outrages on their passive companions. But such a course does not at first view appear a well-chosen discipline to form men to a nice sense of honour, or a quick resentment of injuries. A long habit of humiliation does not seem a very good preparative to manly and vigorous sentiment. It may not leave, perhaps, enough of energy in the mind fairly to discern what are good terms or what are not. Men low and dispirited may regard those terms as not at all amiss, which in another state of mind they would think intolerable: if they grew peevish in this state of mind, they may be roused, not against the enemy whom they have been taught to fear, but against the Ministry[vii],[67] who are more within their reach, and who have refused conditions that are not unreasonable, from power that they have been taught to consider as irresistible.

If all that for some months I have heard have the least foundation, I hope it has not, the Ministers are, perhaps, not quite so much to be blamed, as their condition is to be lamented. I have been given to understand, that these proceedings are not in their origin properly theirs. It is said that there is a secret in the House of Commons. It is said that Ministers act not according to the votes, but according to the dispositions, of the majority. I hear that the minority has long since spoken the general sense of the nation; and that to prevent those who compose it from having the open and avowed lead in that house, or perhaps in both Houses, it was necessary to pre-occupy their ground, and to take their propositions out of their mouths, even with the hazard of being afterwards reproached with a compliance which it was foreseen would be fruitless.

If the general disposition of the people be, as I hear it is, for an immediate peace with Regicide, without so much as considering our publick and solemn engagements to the party in France whose cause we had espoused, or the engagements expressed in our general alliances, not only without

---

[vii] Ut lethargicus hic, cum fit pugil, et medicum urget. – HOR.

[66] 'Draw back, the better to leap forward.'

[67] 'So it is with a man in a lethargy, when he becomes a boxer, and turns on his doctor.' (Horace, *Satires*, 2.3.30)

an enquiry into the terms, but with a certain knowledge that none but the worst terms will be offered, it is all over with us. It is strange, but it may be true, that as the danger from Jacobinism[N] is increased in my eyes and in yours, the fear of it is lessened in the eyes of many people who formerly regarded it with horror. It seems, they act under the impression of terrors of another sort, which have frightened them out of their first apprehensions. But let their fears or their hopes, or their desires, be what they will, they should recollect, that they who would make peace without a previous knowledge of the terms, make a surrender. They are conquered. They do not treat; they receive the law. Is this the disposition of the people of England? Then the people of England are contented to seek in the kindness of a foreign systematick enemy combined with a dangerous faction at home, a security which they cannot find in their own patriotism and their own courage. They are willing to trust to the sympathy of Regicides, the guarantee of the British Monarchy. They are content to rest their religion on the piety of atheists by establishment. They are satisfied to seek in the clemency of practised murderers the security of their lives. They are pleased to confide their property to the safeguard of those who are robbers by inclination, interest, habit, and system. If this be our deliberate mind, truly we deserve to lose, what it is impossible we should long retain, the name of a nation.

In matters of State, a constitutional competence to act, is in many cases the smallest part of the question. Without disputing (God forbid I should dispute) the sole competence of the King and the Parliament, each in it's province, to decide on war and peace, I venture to say, no war *can* be long carried on against the will of the people. This war, in particular, cannot be carried on unless they are enthusiastically in favour of it. Acquiescence will not do. There must be zeal. Universal zeal in such a cause, and at such a time as this is, cannot be looked for; neither is it necessary. A zeal in the larger part carries the force of the whole. Without this, no Government, certainly not our Government, is capable of a great war. None of the ancient regular Governments have wherewithal to fight abroad with a foreign foe, and at home to overcome repining, reluctance, and chicane. It must be some portentous thing, like Regicide France, that can exhibit such a prodigy. Yet even she, the mother of monsters, more prolifick than the country of old called *Ferax monstrorum*,[68] shews symptoms of being

---

[68] *Ferax monstrorum*: possibly *miraculorum ferax* ['a richness of wonders'] (Pliny, *Letters*, 8.20.2 (to Gallus)). There are in fact a number of countries referred to as productive

almost effete already; and she will be so, unless the fallow of a peace comes to recruit her fertility. But whatever may be represented concerning the meanness of the popular spirit, I, for one, do not think so desperately of the British nation. Our minds, as I said, are light, but they are not depraved. We are dreadfully open to delusion and to dejection; but we are capable of being animated and undeceived.

It cannot be concealed. We are a divided people. But in divisions, where a part is to be taken, we are to make a muster of our strength. I have often endeavoured to compute and to class those who, in any political view, are to be called the people. Without doing something of this sort we must proceed absurdly. We should not be much wiser, if we pretended to very great accuracy in our estimate: But I think, in the calculation I have made, the error cannot be very material. In England and Scotland, I compute that those of adult age, not declining in life, of tolerable leisure for such discussions, and of some means of information, more or less, and who are above menial dependence, (or what virtually is such) may amount to about four hundred thousand.[69] There is such a thing as a natural representative of the people. This body is that representative; and on this body, more than on the legal constituent, the artificial representative depends. This is the British publick; and it is a publick very numerous. The rest, when feeble, are the objects of protection; when strong, the means of force. They who affect to consider that part of us in any other light, insult while they cajole us; they do not want us for counsellors in deliberation, but to list us as soldiers for battle.

Of these four hundred thousand political citizens, I look upon one fifth, or about eighty thousand, to be pure Jacobins;[N] utterly incapable of amendment; objects of eternal vigilance; and when they break out, of legal constraint. On these, no reason, no argument, no example, no venerable authority, can have the slightest influence. They desire a change; and they will have it if they can. If they cannot have it by English cabal,[70] they will make no sort of scruple of having it by the cabal of France,

---

of wonders. The full quote reads: *quae si tulisset Achaia Aegyptos Asia aliave quaelibet miraculorum ferax commendatrixque terra* ['[curiosities] which if they had had come from Greece, or Egypt, or Asia, or any other country which commends itself as a fertile source of wonders'].

[69] *The class... to be called the people*: For Burke and many of his contemporaries, 'The People' did not mean the inhabitants, it meant all those of a reasonable degree of economic independence and who were informed about public affairs. The figure of 400,000 is an estimate that also appears elsewhere in Burke's writings.

[70] *Cabal*: a small secretive political clique.

into which already they are virtually incorporated. It is only their assured and confident expectation of the advantages of French fraternity and the approaching blessings of Regicide intercourse, that skins over their mischievous dispositions with a momentary quiet.

This minority is great and formidable. I do not know whether if I aimed at the total overthrow of a kingdom, I should wish to be encumbered with a larger body of partizans. They are more easily disciplined and directed than if the number were greater. These, by their spirit of intrigue, and by their restless agitating activity, are of a force far superior to their numbers; and if times grew the least critical, have the means of debauching or intimidating many of those who are now sound, as well as of adding to their force large bodies of the more passive part of the nation. This minority is numerous enough to make a mighty cry for peace, or for war, or for any object they are led vehemently to desire. By passing from place to place with a velocity incredible, and diversifying their character and description, they are capable of mimicking the general voice. We must not always judge of the generality of the opinion by the noise of the acclamation.

The majority, the other four fifths, is perfectly sound; and of the best possible disposition to religion, to government, to the true and undivided interest of their country. Such men are naturally disposed to peace. They who are in possession of all they wish are languid and improvident. With this fault, (and I admit it's existence in all it's extent) they would not endure to hear of a peace that led to the ruin of every thing for which peace is dear to them. However, the desire of peace is essentially the weak side of that kind of men. All men that are ruined, are ruined on the side of their natural propensities. There they are unguarded. Above all, good men do not suspect that their destruction is attempted through their virtues. This their enemies are perfectly aware of: And accordingly, they, the most turbulent of mankind, who never made a scruple to shake the tranquillity of their country to it's center, raise a continual cry for peace with France. Peace with Regicide, and war with the rest of the world, is their motto. From the beginning, and even whilst the French gave the blows, and we hardly opposed the *vis inertiæ*[71] to their efforts, from that day to this hour, like importunate Guinea-fowls crying one note day and night, they have called for peace.

[71] *Vis inertiae*: inertial force.

In this they are, as I confess in all things they are, perfectly consistent. They who wish to unite themselves to your enemies, naturally desire, that you should disarm yourself by a peace with these enemies. But it passes my conception, how they, who wish well to their country on its antient system of laws and manners, come not to be doubly alarmed, when they find nothing but a clamor for peace, in the mouths of the men on earth the least disposed to it in their natural or in their habitual character.

I have a good opinion of the general abilities of the Jacobins: not that I suppose them better born than others; but strong passions awaken the faculties. They suffer not a particle of the man to be lost. The spirit of enterprise gives to this description the full use of all their native energies. If I have reason to conceive that my enemy, who, as such, must have an interest in my destruction, is also a person of discernment and sagacity, then I must be quite sure, that in a contest, the object he violently pursues, is the very thing by which my ruin is likely to be the most perfectly accomplished. Why do the Jacobins cry for peace? Because they know, that this point gained, the rest will follow of course. On our part, why are all the rules of prudence, as sure as the laws of material nature, to be at this time reversed? How comes it, that now for the first time, men think it right to be governed by the counsels of their enemies? Ought they not rather to tremble, when they are persuaded to travel on the same road; and to tend to the same place of rest?

The minority I speak of, is not susceptible of an impression from the topics of argument, to be used to the larger part of the community. I therefore do not address to them any part of what I have to say. The more forcibly I drive my arguments against their system, so as to make an impression where I wish to make it, the more strongly I rivet them in their sentiments. As for us, who compose the far larger, and what I call the far better part of the people; let me say, that we have not been quite fairly dealt with when called to this deliberation. The Jacobin minority have been abundantly supplied with stores and provisions of all kinds towards their warfare. No sort of argumentative materials, suited to their purposes, have been withheld. False they are, unsound, sophistical; but they are regular in their direction. They all bear one way; and they all go to the support of the substantial merits of their cause. The others have not had the question so much as fairly stated to them.

There has not been in this century, any foreign peace or war, in it's origin, the fruit of popular desire; except the war that was made with Spain in 1739.[72] Sir Robert Walpole[N] was forced into the war by the people, who were inflamed to this measure by the most leading politicians, by the first orators, and the greatest poets of the time. For that war, Pope sung his dying notes.[73] For that war, Johnson, in more energetic strains, employed the voice of his early genius.[74] For that war, Glover distinguished himself in the way in which his muse was the most natural and happy.[75] The crowd readily followed the politicians in the cry for a war, which threatened little bloodshed, and which promised victories that were attended with something more solid than glory. A war with Spain was a war of plunder. In the present conflict with Regicide, Mr. Pitt[N] has not hitherto had, nor will perhaps for a few days have, many prizes to hold out in the lottery of war, to tempt the lower part of our character. He can only maintain it by an appeal to the higher; and to those, in whom that higher part is the most predominant, he must look the most for his support. Whilst he holds out no inducements to the wise, nor bribes to the avaricious, he may be forced by a vulgar cry into a peace ten times more ruinous than the most disastrous war. The weaker he is in the fund of motives which apply to our avarice, to our laziness, and to our lassitude, if he means to carry the war to any end at all, the stronger he ought to be in his addresses to our magnanimity and to our reason.

In stating that Walpole was driven by a popular clamour into a measure not to be justified, I do not mean wholly to excuse his conduct. My time of observation did not exactly coincide with that event; but I read much of the controversies then carried on. Several years after the contests of parties had ceased, the people were amused, and in a degree warmed with them. The events of that æra seemed then of magnitude, which the revolutions of our time have reduced to parochial importance; and the debates, which then shook the nation, now appear of no higher moment

---

[72] *War... of popular desire*: Walpole had been unwillingly pressed into declaring war on Spain in 1739, partly as a result of its threat to Britain's lucrative transatlantic slave-trade.

[73] *Pope*: Alexander Pope (1688–1744), poet and satirist, latterly explicitly critical of Walpole; 'his dying notes' possibly refers to dialogue II of the *Epilogue to the Satires*.

[74] *Johnson*: Samuel Johnson (1709–84), writer, wit and literary and social commentator, compiler of the famous *Dictionary*. Burke refers to Johnson's opposition, in his first major published essay 'London' (1738), to the peace overtures pursued by Walpole, and, more generally to his likening of the decline of liberty in British politics to that of Rome under the early emperors.

[75] *Glover*: Richard Glover (1712–85), English poet and (1761) MP for Weymouth. Famous for his jeremiad *London, or the Progress of Commerce* (1739), and *Admiral Hosier's Ghost* (1740), written against Walpole's peace policy.

than a discussion in a vestry. When I was very young, a general fashion told me I was to admire some of the writings against that Minister;[76] a little more maturity taught me as much to despise them. I observed one fault in his general proceeding. He never manfully put forward the entire strength of his cause. He temporized; he managed; and adopting very nearly the sentiments of his adversaries, he opposed their inferences. This, for a political commander, is the choice of a weak post. His adversaries had the better of the argument, as he handled it, not as the reason and justice of his cause enabled him to manage it. I say this, after having seen, and with some care examined, the original documents concerning certain important transactions of those times. They perfectly satisfied me of the extreme injustice of that war, and of the falsehood of the colours, which to his own ruin, and guided by a mistaken policy, he suffered to be daubed over that measure. Some years after, it was my fortune to converse with many of the principal actors against that Minister, and with those who principally excited that clamour. None of them, no not one, did in the least defend the measure, or attempt to justify their conduct. They condemned it as freely as they would have done in commenting upon any proceeding in history, in which they were totally unconcerned. Thus it will be. They who stir up the people to improper desires, whether of peace or war, will be condemned by themselves. They who weakly yield to them will be condemned by history.

In my opinion, the present Ministry are as far from doing full justice to their cause in this war, as Walpole was from doing justice to the peace which at that time he was willing to preserve. They throw the light on one side only of their case; though it is impossible they should not observe, that the other side which is kept in the shade, has it's importance too. They must know, that France is formidable, not only as she is France, but as she is Jacobin[N] France. They knew from the beginning that the Jacobin party was not confined to that country. They knew, they felt, the strong disposition of the same faction in both countries to communicate and to co-operate. For some time past, these two points have been kept, and even industriously kept, out of sight. France is considered as merely a foreign Power; and the seditious English only as a domestic faction. The merits of the war with the former have been argued solely

---

[76] *Writings against that minister*: a reference to the famous campaign against Walpole waged by *The Craftsman* (1726–52), edited by the pseudonymous Caleb d'Anvers (Nicholas Amhurst) and funded by Bolingbroke[N] and William Pultney, later Earl of Bath (1684–1764). Contributors included Henry Fielding and Alexander Pope.

on political grounds. To prevent the mischievous doctrines of the latter, from corrupting our minds, matter and argument have been supplied abundantly, and even to surfeit, on the excellency of our own government. But nothing has been done to make us feel in what manner the safety of that Government is connected with the principle and with the issue of this war. For any thing, which in the late discussion has appeared, the war is entirely collateral to the state of Jacobinism; as truly a foreign war to us and to all our home concerns, as the war with Spain in 1739, about *Garda-Costas*, the Madrid Convention,[77] and the fable of Captain *Jenkins's* ears.[78]

Whenever the adverse party has raised a cry for peace with the Regicide, the answer has been little more than this, 'that the Administration wished for such a peace, full as much as the Opposition; but that the time was not convenient for making it.' Whatever else has been said was much in the same spirit. Reasons of this kind never touched the substantial merits of the war. They were in the nature of dilatory pleas, exceptions of form, previous questions. Accordingly all the arguments against a compliance with what was represented as the popular desire, (urged on with all possible vehemence and earnestness by the Jacobins) have appeared flat and languid, feeble and evasive. They appeared to aim only at gaining time. They never entered into the peculiar and distinctive character of the war. They spoke neither to the understanding nor to the heart. Cold as ice themselves, they never could kindle in our breasts a spark of that zeal, which is necessary to a conflict with an adverse zeal; much less were they made to infuse into our minds, that stubborn persevering spirit, which alone is capable of bearing up against those vicissitudes of fortune, which will probably occur, and those burthens which must be inevitably borne in a long war. I speak it emphatically, and with a desire that it should be marked, in a *long* war; because, without such a war, no experience has yet told us, that a dangerous power has ever been reduced to measure or to reason. I do not throw back my view to the Peloponnesian war of

---

[77] *Guarda Costas* (Coast-guards): light, fast vessels used to intercept and check on the cargoes of British ships, whose right to trade in the Spanish Caribbean was being disputed. The Madrid Convention (1713) gave to the British the right to ship African slaves to Spanish America.

[78] *Jenkins's ears*: notorious international incident in 1731 in which Robert Jenkins, the captain of an English merchant ship, stopped and searched in the Caribbean by a Spanish excise cutter ('Garda-Costas'), had had his ear cut off. The incident was used against Walpole's peace-policy by supporters of war with Spain in 1739. Some doubted the truth of his story – hence Burke's reference to a 'fable'.

twenty-seven years;[79] nor to two of the Punic wars,[N] the first of twenty-four, the second of eighteen; nor to the more recent war concluded by the treaty of Westphalia,[80] which continued, I think, for thirty. I go to what is but just fallen behind living memory, and immediately touches our own country. Let the portion of our history from the year 1689 to 1713 be brought before us. We shall find, that in all that period of twenty-four years, there were hardly five that could be called a season of peace; and the interval between the two wars was in reality, nothing more than a very active preparation for renovated hostility. During that period, every one of the propositions of peace came from the enemy: The first, when they were accepted, at the peace of Ryswick;[N] The second, when they were rejected at the congress at Gertruydenburgh;[81] The last, when the war ended by the treaty of Utrecht. Even then, a very great part of the nation, and that which contained by far the most intelligent statesmen, was against the conclusion of the war. I do not enter into the merits of that question as between the parties. I only state the existence of that opinion as a fact, from whence you may draw such an inference as you think properly arises from it.

It is for us at present to recollect what we have been; and to consider what, if we please, we may be still. At the period of those wars, our principal strength was found in the resolution of the people; and that in the resolution of a part only of the then whole, which bore no proportion to our existing magnitude. England and Scotland were not united at the beginning of that mighty struggle.[82] When, in the course of the contest, they were conjoined, it was in a raw, an ill-cemented, an unproductive union. For the whole duration of the war, and long after, the names, and other outward and visible signs of approximation, rather augmented than diminished our insular feuds. They were rather the causes of new

---

[79] *Peloponnesian war*: One of the most famous wars of antiquity, between Athens and Sparta (431–404 BC), recorded by Thucydides in his *History*.

[80] *Treaty [Peace] of Westphalia*: collective name given to the treaties of Osnabrück and Münster (1648), ending respectively the Thirty Years' War within the Holy Roman Empire, and the eighty-year Dutch War of Independence. Traditionally regarded as initiating the modern European system of state sovereignty, although many commentators now accord this to the Treaty of Utrecht[N] (1714).

[81] *Gertruydenburgh*: Unsuccessful peace talks to end the War of the Spanish Succession were held in Geertruidenberg (Brabant) in 1710.

[82] *Not united*: Although England and Scotland had shared the same monarch since the accession of James I of England/ VI of Scotland in 1603, the political union and the consolidation of a national parliament did not take place until the Act of Union in 1707.

discontents and new troubles, than promoters of cordiality and affection. The now single and potent Great Britain was then not only two countries, but, from the party heats in both, and the divisions formed in each of them, each of the old kingdoms within itself in effect was made up of two hostile nations. Ireland, now so large a source of the common opulence and power, which wisely managed might be made much more beneficial and much more effective, was then the heaviest of the burthens. An army not much less than forty thousand men, was drawn from the general effort, to keep that kingdom in a poor, unfruitful, and resourceless subjection.

Such was the state of the empire. The state of our finances was worse, if possible. Every branch of the revenue became less productive after the Revolution. Silver, not as now a sort of counter, but the body of the current coin, was reduced so low as not to have above three parts in four of the value in the shilling. It required a dead expence of three millions sterling to renew the coinage.[83] Publick credit, that great but ambiguous principle, which has so often been predicted as the cause of our certain ruin, but which for a century has been the constant companion, and often the means, of our prosperity and greatness, had it's origin, and was cradled, I may say, in bankruptcy and beggary. At this day we have seen parties contending to be admitted, at a moderate premium, to advance eighteen millions to the Exchequer. For infinitely smaller loans, the Chancellor of the Exchequer of that day, Montagu,[84] the father of publick credit, counter-securing the State by the appearance of the city, with the Lord-Mayor of London at his side, was obliged, like an agent at an election, to go cap in hand from shop to shop, to borrow an hundred pound and even smaller sums. When made up in driblets as they could, their best securities were at an interest of 12 per cent. Even the paper of the Bank (now at par with cash, and even sometimes preferred to it) was often at a discount of twenty per cent. By this the state of the rest may be judged.

---

[83] *Renew the coinage*: What is known as 'The Great Re-coinage' took place in the late 1690s, when the much debased and clipped silver coinage was recalled and re-minted to a standard weight and purity, and non-coinage silver marked at an equal standard to discourage the melting down of coin.

[84] *Montagu*: Charles Montague, 1st Earl Halifax (1661–1715), Chancellor of the Exchequer under William and Mary and First Lord of the Treasury under George I. 'Father of public credit' because it was under his term as Chancellor that the Bank of England was established by subscription of investors who lent the Government £1.2m, thereby initiating the National Debt.

As to our commerce, the imports and exports of the nation, now six and forty million, did not then amount to ten. The inland trade, which is commonly passed by in this sort of estimates, but which, in part growing out of the foreign, and connected with it, is more advantageous, and more substantially nutritive to the State, is not only grown in a proportion of near five to one as the foreign, but has been augmented, at least, in a tenfold proportion. When I came to England,[85] I remember but one river navigation, the rate of carriage on which was limited by an Act of Parliament. It was made in the reign of William the Third;[N] I mean that of the Aire and Calder.[86] The rate was settled at thirteen pence. So high a price demonstrated the feebleness of these beginnings of our inland intercourse. In my time, one of the longest and sharpest contests I remember in your House, and which rather resembled a violent contention amongst national parties than a local dispute, was, as well as I can recollect, to hold the price up to threepence. Even this, which a very scanty justice to the proprietors required, was done with infinite difficulty. As to private credit, there were not, as I best remember, twelve Bankers shops at that time out of London. In this their number, when I first saw the country, I cannot be quite exact; but certainly those machines of domestick credit were then very few indeed. They are now in almost every market town: and this circumstance (whether the thing be carried to an excess or not) demonstrates the astonishing encrease of private confidence, of general circulation, and of internal commerce; an encrease out of all proportion to the growth of the foreign trade. Our naval strength in the time of King William's[N] war was nearly matched by that of France; and though conjoined with Holland, then a maritime Power hardly inferior to our own, even with that force we were not always victorious. Though finally superior, the allied fleets experienced many unpleasant reverses on their own element. In two years three thousand vessels were taken from the English trade. On the continent we lost almost every battle we fought.

In 1697, (it is not quite an hundred years ago,) in that state of things, amidst the general debasement of the coin, the fall of the ordinary revenue,

---

[85] *When I came to England*: In early 1750, following graduation from Trinity College Dublin, Burke came to London to study Law.

[86] *Aire and Calder*: In 1699 an Act of Parliament provided for the construction of weirs on the rivers Aire and Calder raising their levels, and for 'cuts', entered by locks to bypass the weirs, rendering the rivers navigable, thereby connecting Leeds with the Ouse, York, and ultimately the Trent and the north-central midlands. It initiated a century and more of canalisation of major rivers which transformed inland transport in north-central England.

the failure of all the extraordinary supplies, the ruin of commerce and the almost total extinction of an infant credit, the Chancellor of the Exchequer himself whom we have just seen begging from door to door – came forward to move a resolution, full of vigour, in which far from being discouraged by the generally adverse fortune, and the long continuance of the war, the Commons agreed to address the Crown in the following manly, spirited, and truly animating style.[87]

> 'This is the EIGHTH year in which your Majesty's most dutiful and loyal subjects the Commons in Parliament assembled, have assisted your Majesty with large supplies for carrying on a just and necessary war, in defence of our religion, and preservation of our laws, and vindication of the rights and liberties of the people of England.'

Afterwards they proceed in this manner:-

> 'To shew to your Majesty and all Christendom, that the Commons of England will not be *amused* or diverted from their firm resolutions of obtaining by WAR, a safe and honourable peace, we do in the name of those we represent, renew our assurances to support your Majesty and your Government against all your enemies at home and abroad; and that we will effectually assist you in carrying on the war against France.'

The amusement and diversion they speak of, was the suggestion of a treaty *proposed by the enemy*, and announced from the Throne. Thus the people of England felt in the *eighth*, not in the *fourth* year of the war. No sighing or panting after negociation; no motions from the Opposition to force the Ministry into a peace; no messages from Ministers to palsy and deaden the resolution of Parliament or the spirit of the nation. They did not so much as advise the King to listen to the propositions of the enemy, nor to seek for peace but through the mediation of a vigorous war. This address was moved in an hot, a divided, a factious, and in a great part, disaffected House of Commons, and it was carried *nemine contradicente*.[88]

While that first war (which was ill smothered by the treaty of Ryswick[N]) slept in the thin ashes of a seeming peace, a new conflagration was in it's immediate causes. A fresh and a far greater war was in preparation. A year had hardly elapsed when arrangements were made for renewing the

---

[87] 22 October 1697, *Commons Journals*, xi, 568.
[88] *Nemine contradicente*: with no-one contradicting.

contest with tenfold fury. The steps which were taken, at that time, to compose, to reconcile, to unite, and to discipline all Europe against the growth of France, certainly furnish to a statesman the finest and most interesting part in the history of that great period. It formed the master-piece of King William's policy, dexterity, and perseverance. Full of the idea of preserving, not only a local civil liberty, united with order, to our country, but to embody it in the political liberty, the order, and the independence of nations united under a natural head, the King called upon his Parliament to put itself into a posture '*To preserve to England the weight and influence it at present had on the councils and affairs* ABROAD. It will be requisite Europe should see you will not be wanting to yourselves.'[89]

Baffled as that Monarch was, and almost heart-broken at the disap-pointment he met with in the mode he first proposed for that great end, he held on his course. He was faithful to his object; and in councils, as in arms, over and over again repulsed, over and over again he returned to the charge. All the mortifications he had suffered from the last Parliament, and the greater he had to apprehend from that newly chosen, were not capable of relaxing the vigour of his mind. He was in Holland when he combined the vast plan of his foreign negociations. When he came to open his design to his Ministers in England, even the sober firmness of Somers,[N] the undaunted resolution of Shrewsbury, and the adventur-ous spirit of Montagu and Orford,[90] were staggered. They were not yet mounted to the elevation of the King. The Cabinet met on the subject at Tunbridge Wells the 28th of August, 1698; and there, Lord Somers holding the pen, after expressing doubts on the state of the continent, which they ultimately refer to the King, as best informed, they give him a most discouraging portrait of the spirit of this nation. 'So far as relates to England,' say these Ministers,

> 'it would be want of duty not to give your Majesty this clear account, that *there* is a *deadness and want of spirit in the nation universally*, so as not to be at all disposed to *entering into a new war*. That they seem to

---

[89] King William's Speech from the Throne, 9 Dec. 1698 (*Commons Journals* xii, 348).

[90] *Shrewsbury*: Charles, Duke of Shrewsbury (1660–1718), Secretary of State 1690–1 and 1694–6; *Orford*: Edward Russell, Earl of Orford, First Lord of the Admiralty 1694–9. Two of the 'immortal seven' notables who wrote to William of Orange inviting him to supplant the Catholic James II. *Montagu*: Baron Ralph Montagu (1638–1709), 'adventur-ous' presumably because of his volatile but successful political career. Having supported Monmouth's claim to the throne, and the Exclusion Bill, he nevertheless found favour with James II, only then successfully to welcome William and Mary, by whom he was created Earl.

be *tired out with taxes* to a degree beyond what was discerned, till it appeared upon occasion of the *late elections*. This is the truth of the fact upon which your Majesty will determine what resolution ought to be taken.'

His Majesty did determine; and did take and pursue his resolution. In all the tottering imbecility of a new Government, and with Parliament totally unmanageable, he persevered. He persevered to expel the fears of his people, by his fortitude – To steady their fickleness, by his constancy – To expand their narrow prudence, by his enlarged wisdom – To sink their factious temper in his public spirit. – In spite of his people he resolved to make them great and glorious; to make England, inclined to shrink into her narrow self, the Arbitress of Europe, the tutelary Angel of the human race. In spite of the Ministers, who staggered under the weight that his mind imposed upon theirs, unsupported as they felt themselves by the popular spirit, he infused into them his own soul; he renewed in them their ancient heart; he rallied them in the same cause.

It required some time to accomplish this work. The people were first gained, and through them their distracted representatives. Under the influence of King William[N] Holland had rejected the allurements of every seduction, and had resisted the terrors of every menace. With Hannibal at her gates, she had nobly and magnanimously refused all separate treaty, or any thing which might for a moment appear to divide her affection or her interest, or even to distinguish her in identity from England. Having settled the great point of the consolidation (which he hoped would be eternal) of the countries made for a common interest, and common sentiment, the King, in his message to both Houses, calls their attention to the affairs of the *States General*[N]. The House of Lords was perfectly sound, and entirely impressed with the wisdom and dignity of the King's proceedings. In answer to the message, which you will observe was narrowed to a single point, (the danger of the States General) after the usual professions of zeal for his service, the Lords opened themselves at large. They go far beyond the demands of the message. They express themselves as follows:

'We take this occasion *further* to assure your Majesty, that we are sensible of the *great and imminent danger to which the States General are exposed. And we perfectly agree with them in believing that their safety and ours are so inseparably united, that whatsoever is ruin to the one must be fatal to the other.*

'We humbly desire your Majesty will be pleased, *not only* to make good all the articles of any *former* treaties to the States General, but that you will enter into a strict league, offensive and defensive, with them, *for their common preservation: and that you will invite into it all Princes and States who are concerned in the present visible danger, arising from the union of France and Spain.*

'And we further desire your Majesty, that you will be pleased to enter into such alliances with the *Emperor*, as your Majesty shall think fit, pursuant to the ends of the treaty of 1689; towards all which we assure your Majesty of our hearty and sincere assistance; not doubting, but whenever your Majesty shall be obliged to be engaged for the defence of your allies, *and securing the liberty and quiet of Europe*, Almighty God will protect your sacred person in so righteous a cause. And that the unanimity, wealth, and courage of your subjects will carry your Majesty with honour and success *through all the difficulties of a* JUST WAR.'[91]

The House of Commons was more reserved; the late popular disposition was still in a great degree prevalent in the representative, after it had been made to change in the constituent body. The principle of the Grand Alliance was not directly recognized in the resolution of the Commons, nor the war announced, though they were well aware the alliance was formed for the war. However, compelled by the returning sense of the people, they went so far as to fix the three great immoveable pillars of the safety and greatness of England, as they were then, as they are now, and as they must ever be to the end of time. They asserted in general terms the necessity of supporting Holland; of keeping united with our allies; and maintaining the liberty of Europe; though they restricted their vote to the succours stipulated by actual treaty.[92] But now they were fairly embarked; they were obliged to go with the course of the vessel; and the whole nation, split before into an hundred adverse factions, with a King at it's head evidently declining to his tomb, the whole nation, Lords, Commons, and People, proceeded as one body, informed by one soul. Under the British union, the union of Europe was consolidated; and it long held together with a degree of cohesion, firmness, and fidelity not known before or since in any political combination of that extent.

[91] *Lords Journals*, xvi, 677 (10 May 1710).  [92] *Commons Journals*, xiii, 523.

Just as the last hand was given to this immense and complicated machine, the master workman died.[93] But the work was formed on true mechanical principles; and it was as truly wrought. It went by the impulse it had received from the first mover. The man was dead: But the grand alliance survived, in which King William lived and reigned. That heartless and dispirited people, whom Lord Somers[N] had represented, about two years before, as dead in energy and operation, continued that war to which it was supposed they were unequal in mind, and in means, for near thirteen years.[94]

For what have I entered into all this detail? To what purpose have I recalled your view to the end of the last century? It has been done to shew that the British Nation was then a great people – to point out how and by what means they came to be exalted above the vulgar level, and to take that lead which they assumed among mankind. To qualify us for that pre-eminence, we had then an high mind, and a constancy unconquerable; we were then inspired with no flashy passions; but such as were durable as well as warm; such as corresponded to the great interests we had at stake. This force of character was inspired, as all such spirit must ever be, from above. Government gave the impulse. As well may we fancy, that, of itself the sea will swell, and that without winds the billows will insult the adverse shore, as that the gross mass of the people will be moved, and elevated, and continue by a steady and permanent direction to bear upon one point, without the influence of superior authority, or superior mind.

This impulse ought, in my opinion, to have been given in this war; and it ought to have been continued to it at every instant. It is made, if ever war was made, to touch all the great springs of action in the human breast. It ought not to have been a war of apology. The Minister had, in this conflict, wherewithal to glory in success; to be consoled in adversity; to hold high his principle in all fortunes. If it were not given him to support the falling edifice, he ought to bury himself under the ruins of the civilized world. All the art of Greece, and all the pride and power of eastern Monarchs, never heaped upon their ashes so grand a monument.

[93] *Master workman died*: William III died on 8 March 1702.
[94] *Thirteen years*: The War of the Spanish Succession (1701–14) was fought between the Grand Alliance of Archduke Charles of Spain, The Holy Roman Emperor and Great Britain, and the Two Crowns, the Spanish King Philip V, France and Bavaria, to prevent the possible union of the Spanish and French Crowns. It was concluded by the Treaty of Utrecht[N].

There were days when his great mind was up to the crisis of the world he is called to act in[viii]. His manly eloquence was equal to the elevated wisdom of such sentiments. But the little have triumphed over the great; an unnatural, (as it should seem) not an unusual victory. I am sure you cannot forget with how much uneasiness we heard in conversation, the language of more than one gentleman at the opening of this contest, 'that he was willing to try the war for a year or two, and if it did not succeed, then to vote for peace.' As if war was a matter of experiment! As if you could take it up or lay it down as an idle frolick! As if the dire goddess that presides over it, with her murderous spear in her hand, and her gorgon at her breast, was a coquette to be flirted with![95] We ought with reverence to approach that tremendous divinity, that loves courage, but commands counsel. War never leaves, where it found a nation. It is never to be entered into without a mature deliberation; not a deliberation lengthened out into a perplexing indecision, but a deliberation leading to a sure and fixed judgment. When so taken up it is not to be abandoned without reason as valid, as fully, and as extensively considered. Peace may be made as unadvisedly as war. Nothing is so rash as fear; and the counsels of pusillanimity[96] very rarely put off, whilst they are always sure to aggravate, the evils from which they would fly.

In that great war carried on against Louis the XIVth, for near eighteen years, Government spared no pains to satisfy the nation, that though they were to be animated by a desire of glory, glory was not their ultimate object: but that every thing dear to them, in religion, in law, in liberty, every thing which as freemen, as Englishmen, and as citizens of the great commonwealth of Christendom, they had at heart, was then at stake. This was to know the true art of gaining the affections and confidence of an high-minded people; this was to understand human nature. A danger to avert a danger – a present inconvenience and suffering to prevent a foreseen future, and a worse calamity – these are the motives that belong to an animal, who, in his constitution, is at once adventurous and provident; circumspect and daring; whom his Creator has made, as the Poet says, "of large discourse, looking before and after."[97] But never can

---

[viii]  See the Declaration.

[95]  *Dire goddess*: Athena, Greek goddess of wisdom and of war, invariably depicted armed, with a gorgon's head on her shield and sometimes with a spear. The gorgon was a mythical creature with hair of snakes and a face that turned to stone those who looked on it.

[96]  *Pusillanimity*: cowardliness.    [97]  *Hamlet*, 4.iv.36–7 (freely quoted).

a vehement and sustained spirit of fortitude be kindled in a people by a war of calculation. It has nothing that can keep the mind erect under the gusts of adversity. Even where men are willing, as sometimes they are, to barter their blood for lucre, to hazard their safety for the gratification of their avarice, the passion which animates them to that sort of conflict, like all the short-sighted passions, must see it's objects distinct and near at hand. The passions of the lower order are hungry and impatient. Speculative plunder; contingent spoil; future, long adjourned, uncertain booty; pillage which must enrich a late posterity, and which possibly may not reach to posterity at all; these, for any length of time, will never support a mercenary war. The people are in the right. The calculation of profit in all such wars is false. On balancing the account of such wars, ten thousand hogsheads of sugar are purchased at ten thousand times their price.[98] The blood of man should never be shed but to redeem the blood of man. It is well shed for our family, for our friends, for our God, for our country, for our kind. The rest is vanity; the rest is crime.

In the war of the Grand Alliance, most of these considerations voluntarily and naturally had their part. Some were pressed into the service. The political interest easily went in the track of the natural sentiment. In the reverse course the carriage does not follow freely. I am sure the natural feeling, as I have just said, is a far more predominant ingredient in this war, than in that of any other that ever was waged by this kingdom.

If the war made to prevent the union of two crowns upon one head was a just war, this, which is made to prevent the tearing all crowns from all heads which ought to wear them, and with the crowns to smite off the sacred heads themselves, this is a just war.

If a war to prevent Louis the XIVth[N] from imposing his religion was just,[99] a war to prevent the murderers of Louis the XVIth from imposing their irreligion upon us is just; a war to prevent the operation of a system, which makes life without dignity, and death without hope, is a just war.

If to preserve political independence and civil freedom to nations, was a just ground of war; a war to preserve national independence, property, liberty, life, and honour, from certain universal havock, is a war just,

---

[98] *Hogshead*: a large barrel and hence a unit of volume (of approx. 239 litres).

[99] *War to prevent... imposing his religion*: Louis XIV's famous revocation of the Edict of Nantes involved the murder, forced conversion or expulsion of French Protestants, a policy extended to lands incorporated in France. Burke suggests this was part of the reason for, and hence justification of, the War of the Spanish Succession.

necessary, manly, pious; and we are bound to persevere in it by every principle, divine and human, as long as the system which menaces them all, and all equally, has an existence in the world.

You, who have looked at this matter with as fair and impartial an eye as can be united with a feeling heart, you will not think it an hardy assertion, when I affirm, that it were far better to be conquered by any other nation, than to have this faction for a neighbour. Before I felt myself authorised to say this, I considered the state of all the countries in Europe for these last three hundred years, which have been obliged to submit to a foreign law. In most of those I found the condition of the annexed countries even better, certainly not worse, than the lot of those which were the patrimony of the conquerour. They wanted some blessings-but they were free from many very great evils. They were rich and tranquil. Such was Artois, Flanders, Lorrain, Alsatia,[100] under the old Government of France. Such was Silesia under the King of Prussia.[101] They who are to live in the vicinity of this new fabrick, are to prepare to live in perpetual conspiracies and seditions; and to end at last in being conquered, if not to her dominion, to her resemblance. But when we talk of conquest by other nations, it is only to put a case. This is the only power in Europe by which it is *possible* we should be conquered. To live under the continual dread of such immeasurable evils is itself a grievous calamity. To live without the dread of them is to turn the danger into the disaster. The influence of such a France is equal to a war; it's example, more wasting than an hostile irruption. The hostility with any other power is separable and accidental; this power, by the very condition of it's existence, by it's very essential constitution, is in a state of hostility with us, and with all civilized people.[ix]

A Government of the nature of that set up at our very door has never been hitherto seen, or even imagined, in Europe. What our relation to it will be cannot be judged by other relations. It is a serious thing to have a connexion with a people, who live only under positive, arbitrary, and changeable institutions; and those not perfected nor supplied, nor

---

[ix] See declaration, Whitehall, October 29, 1793.

[100] *Artois, Flanders, Lorraine, Alsatia* [Alsace]: all provinces acquired by the French *ancien régime* in the seventeenth or (in the case of Lorraine) eighteenth centuries.

[101] *Silesia*: a quasi-independent Duchy situated in the southwest of modern Poland, conquered by Prussia in 1740-1, and annexed in 1742.

explained, by any common acknowledged rule of moral science. I remember that in one of my last conversations with the late Lord Camden,[102] we were struck much in the same manner with the abolition in France of the law, as a science of methodized and artificial equity. France, since her Revolution, is under the sway of a sect, whose leaders have deliberately, at one stroke, demolished the whole body of that jurisprudence which France had pretty nearly in common with other civilized countries.[103] In that jurisprudence were contained the elements and principles of the law of nations, the great ligament of mankind.[104] With the law they have of course destroyed all seminaries in which jurisprudence was taught, as well as all the corporations established for it's conservation. I have not heard of any country, whether in Europe or Asia, or even in Africa on this side of Mount Atlas, which is wholly without some such colleges and such corporations, except France. No man, in a publick or private concern, can divine by what rule or principle her judgments are to be directed; nor is there to be found a professor in any University, or a practitioner in any Court, who will hazard an opinion of what is or is not law in France, in any case whatever. They have not only annulled all their old treaties; but they have renounced the law of nations from whence treaties have their force. With a fixed design they have outlawed themselves, and to their power outlawed all other nations.

Instead of the religion and the law by which they were in a great politick communion with the Christian world, they have constructed their Republick on three bases, all fundamentally opposite to those on which the communities of Europe are built. It's foundation is laid in Regicide; in Jacobinism;[N] and in Atheism; and it has joined to those principles, a body of systematick manners which secures their operation.

If I am asked, how I would be understood in the use of these terms, Regicide, Jacobinism, Atheism, and a system of correspondent manners, and their establishment, I will tell you.

---

[102] *Lord Camden*: Charles Pratt, 1st Earl Camden (1714–94), Whig politician and Lord Chancellor 1766–70.

[103] *Demolished ... jurisprudence*: Starting with the Assembly's abolition of nobility and reorganisation of judiciary in the summer of 1790, through to September 1793 when law schools were closed and the profession of attorney was abolished, the Revolution progressively abolished the entire inherited legal system.

[104] *Law of nations* refers originally to that part of Roman law which sought to synthesise legal customs, common to different peoples, and hence to an embryonic 'international law' recognised by different legal jurisdictions as applying to their interactions.

I call a commonwealth *Regicide*, which lays it down as a fixed law of nature, and a fundamental right of man, that all government, not being a democracy, is an usurpation[x]. That all Kings, as such, are usurpers; and for being Kings, may and ought to be put to death, with their wives, families, and adherents. The commonwealth which acts uniformly upon those principles; and which after abolishing every festival of religion, chooses the most flagrant act of a murderous Regicide treason for a feast of eternal commemoration, and which forces all her people to observe it – – – This I call *Regicide by establishment*.

Jacobinism[N] is the revolt of the enterprising talents of a country against it's property. When private men form themselves into associations for the purpose of destroying the pre-existing laws and institutions of their country; when they secure to themselves an army by dividing amongst the people of no property, the estates of the ancient and lawful proprietors; when a state recognizes those acts; when it does not make confiscations for crimes, but makes crimes for confiscations; when it has it's principal strength, and all it's resources in such a violation of property; when it stands chiefly upon such a violation; massacring by judgments, or otherwise, those who make any struggle for their old legal government, and their legal, hereditary, or acquired possessions – I call this *Jacobinism by Establishment*.

I call it *Atheism by Establishment*, when any State, as such, shall not acknowledge the existence of God as a moral Governor of the World; when it shall offer to Him no religious or moral worship; – when it shall abolish the Christian religion by a regular decree; – when it shall persecute with a cold, unrelenting, steady cruelty, by every mode of confiscation, imprisonment, exile, and death, all it's ministers; – when it shall generally shut up, or pull down, churches; when the few buildings which remain of this kind shall be opened only for the purpose of making a profane apotheosis of monsters, whose vices and crimes have no parallel

---

[x] Nothing could be more solemn than their promulgation of this principle as a preamble to the destructive code of their famous articles for the decomposition of society into whatever country they should enter. 'La Convention Nationale, après avoir entendu le rapport de ses Comittés de Finances, de la guerre, & diplomatiques réunis, fidèle *au principe de souveraineté de peuples qui ne lui permet pas de reconnoitre aucune institution qui y porte atteinte*,' &c. &c.[105] Decret sur le Rapport de Cambon, Dec. 18, 1792, and see the subsequent proclamation.

[105] 'The National Convention, after having heard the report of its Committees of finance, war, and diplomatic links, faithful to the principle of the sovereignty of the people which does not permit it to recognise any other institution which undermines it, etc. etc.'

amongst men,[106] and whom all other men consider as objects of general detestation, and the severest animadversion of law.[107] When, in the place of that religion of social benevolence, and of individual self-denial, in mockery of all religion, they institute impious, blasphemous, indecent theatric rites, in honour of their vitiated, perverted reason, and erect altars to the personification of their own corrupted and bloody Republick; – when schools and seminaries are founded at publick expence to poison mankind, from generation to generation, with the horrible maxims of this impiety;[108] – when wearied out with incessant martyrdom, and the cries of a people hungering and thirsting for religion, they permit it, only as a tolerated evil – I call this *Atheism by Establishment*.

When to these establishments of Regicide, of Jacobinism, and of Atheism, you add the *correspondent system of manners*, no doubt can be left on the mind of a thinking man, concerning their determined hostility to the human race. Manners are of more importance than laws. Upon them, in a great measure the laws depend. The law touches us but here and there, and now and then. Manners are what vex or sooth, corrupt or purify, exalt or debase, barbarize or refine us, by a constant, steady, uniform, insensible operation, like that of the air we breathe in. They give their whole form and colour to our lives. According to their quality, they aid morals, they supply them, or they totally destroy them. Of this the new French Legislators were aware; therefore, with the same method, and under the same authority, they settled a system of manners, the most licentious, prostitute, and abandoned that ever has been known, and at

---

[106] *Opened only for the purpose*... : a reference to the neo-classical church, Ste Geneviève, which was renamed the Panthéon, in imitation of the pagan temple in Ancient Rome, and to which were removed the bodies of Revolutionary heroes such as Marat, and Enlightenment figures such as those of Voltaire and Rousseau, retrospectively claimed as such by the revolutionaries. Burke is being heavily ironic: apotheosis' literal meaning being 'the ascription of divine status'.

[107] *Animadversion*: a critical observation or judgement, esp. in a legal context, a judgment.

[108] *Impious... rites... maxims of impiety*: From autumn 1793 a series of measures later known as 'De-Christianisation' had been introduced. The principal innovations involved the marking of the years from the founding of the Republic instead of the birth of Christ (1792 = Year 1) (5 Oct. 1793); the substitution of the Republican Calendar for the Christian one, with ten-day weeks and months named after their natural properties (24 Nov. 1793); the establishment of a 'civil religion': state worship of 'The Supreme Being' with appropriate annual festivals based on important revolutionary events (7 May 1794); and the Decree on the Exercise of Worship which, whilst guaranteeing freedom of worship, prescribed close supervision and licensing of ministers of religion and religious meetings, and a complete ban on religious symbols being worn or displayed outside the home, churches or religious meeting-houses (29 September 1795).

the same time the most coarse, rude, savage, and ferocious. Nothing in the Revolution, no, not to a phrase or a gesture, not to the fashion of a hat or a shoe, was left to accident. All has been the result of design; all has been matter of institution. No mechanical means could be devised in favour of this incredible system of wickedness and vice, that has not been employed. The noblest passions, the love of glory, the love of country, have been debauched into means of it's preservation and it's propagation. All sorts of shews and exhibitions calculated to inflame and vitiate the imagination, and pervert the moral sense, have been contrived. They have sometimes brought forth five or six hundred drunken women, calling at the bar of the Assembly for the blood of their own children, as being royalists or constitutionalists. Sometimes they have got a body of wretches, calling themselves fathers, to demand the murder of their sons; boasting that Rome had but one Brutus, but that they could shew five hundred.[109] There were instances, in which they inverted, and retaliated the impiety, and produced sons, who called for the execution of their parents. The foundation of their Republick is laid in moral paradoxes. Their patriotism is always prodigy. All those instances to be found in history, whether real or fabulous, of a doubtful publick spirit, at which morality is perplexed, reason is staggered, and from which affrighted nature recoils, are their chosen, and almost sole examples for the instruction of their youth.

The whole drift of their institution is contrary to that of the wise Legislators of all countries, who aimed at improving instincts into morals, and at grafting the virtues on the stock of the natural affections. They, on the contrary, have omitted no pains to eradicate every benevolent and noble propensity in the mind of men. In their culture it is a rule always to graft virtues on vices. They think everything unworthy of the name of publick virtue, unless it indicates violence on the private. All their

---

[109] *But one Brutus*: The promulgation of a classical Roman republican aesthetic and morality (presaged and exemplified in the austere neo-classical style and subjects of the artist Jacques-Louis David) was a deliberate ideological project, evidently taken up by many enthusiastic supporters. The example of Lucius Junius Brutus, who slew the last King of Rome and founded the Roman republic, and who supposedly executed his own sons for failing in their military duty, became an emblem of the republican ethic of putting the polity before family, and subject of a famous painting by David. The busts of classical regicides were placed in the Convention Hall, where also, mothers supposedly gathered, pleading for their sons to be sent to fight in the revolutionary wars. Burke considered the provision of divorce to be a deliberate attempt to elevate political above family loyalties. See the following passages.

new institutions, (and with them every thing is new) strike at the root of our social nature. Other Legislators, knowing that marriage is the origin of all relations, and consequently the first element of all duties, have endeavoured, by every art, to make it sacred. The Christian Religion, by confining it to the pairs, and by rendering that relation indissoluble, has, by these two things, done more towards the peace, happiness, settlement, and civilization of the world, than by any other part in this whole scheme of Divine Wisdom. The direct contrary course has been taken in the Synagogue of Antichrist, I mean in that forge and manufactory of all evil, the sect which predominated in the Constituent Assembly of 1789. Those monsters employed the same, or greater industry, to desecrate and degrade that State, which other Legislators have used to render it holy and honourable. By a strange, uncalled for declaration, they pronounced, that marriage was no better than a common, civil contract. It was one of their ordinary tricks, to put their sentiments into the mouths of certain personated characters, which they theatrically exhibited at the bar of what ought to be a serious Assembly. One of these was brought out in the figure of a prostitute, whom they called by the affected name of 'a mother without being a wife.' This creature they made to call for a repeal of the incapacities, which in civilized States are put upon bastards. The prostitutes of the Assembly gave to this their puppet the sanction of their greater impudence. In consequence of the principles laid down, and the manners authorised, bastards were not long after put on the footing of the issue of lawful unions. Proceeding in the spirit of the first authors of their constitution, succeeding assemblies went the full length of the principle, and gave a licence to divorce at the mere pleasure of either party, and at a month's notice.[110] With them the matrimonial connexion is brought into so degraded a state of concubinage, that, I believe, none of the wretches in London, who keep warehouses of infamy, would give out one of their victims to private custody on so short and insolent a tenure. There was indeed a kind of profligate equity in thus giving to women the same licentious power. The reason they assigned was as infamous as the act; declaring that women had been too long under the tyranny of parents and of husbands. It is not necessary to observe upon the

---

[110] *Licence to divorce*: The Decree of 20 September 1792 provided for divorce, claiming it to be 'a consequence of individual liberty', and defined marriage as 'only a civil contract'. Divorce proceedings could be initiated by mutual consent, or unilaterally on grounds of incompatibility of character, insanity, criminality, cruelty, dissolute morals, desertion, absence or emigration. Divorce was all but impossible in England at the time.

horrible consequences of taking one half of the species wholly out of the guardianship and protection of the other.

The practice of divorce, though in some countries permitted, has been discouraged in all. In the East, polygamy and divorce are in discredit; and the manners correct the laws. In Rome, whilst Rome was in it's integrity, the few causes allowed for divorce amounted in effect to a prohibition.[111] They were only three. The arbitrary was totally excluded; and accordingly some hundreds of years passed, without a single example of that kind. When manners were corrupted, the laws were relaxed; as the latter always follow the former, when they are not able to regulate them, or to vanquish them. Of this circumstance the Legislators of vice and crime were pleased to take notice, as an inducement to adopt their regulation; holding out an hope, that the permission would as rarely be made use of. They knew the contrary to be true; and they had taken good care, that the laws should be well seconded by the manners. Their law of divorce, like all their laws, had not for it's object the relief of domestick uneasiness, but the total corruption of all morals, the total disconnection of social life.

It is a matter of curiosity to observe the operation of this encouragement to disorder. I have before me the Paris paper, correspondent to the usual register of births, marriages, and deaths. Divorce, happily, is no regular head of registry among civilized nations. With the Jacobins it is remarkable, that divorce is not only a regular head, but it has the post of honour. It occupies the first place in the list. In the three first months of the year 1793, the number of divorces in that city amounted to 562. The marriages were 1785; so that the proportion of divorces to marriages was not much less than one to three; a thing unexampled, I believe, among mankind. I caused an enquiry to be made at Doctor's Commons,[112] concerning the number of divorces; and found, that all the divorces, (which, except by

---

[111] Burke misrepresents the position. Although divorce became more common under the 'corrupt manners' of the later Empire, late Republican Roman law clearly provided for divorce, by the 'repudiation' of either party, and even at the initiative of the father of the couple (P. Buckland and P. Stein, *A Textbook of Roman Law* (Cambridge, 1963), pp. 117ff.).

[112] *Doctor's Commons*: The law college devoted to civil (i.e. Roman) law in London. All the other Inns of Court taught English common law. Divorce (and the treatment of Wills) were originally an ecclesiastical matter dealt with in Church courts whose practice derived from canon (i.e. Church, and ultimately Roman) law. Roman influence continued in these areas of law after the abolition of the lay jurisdiction of Church courts. Domestic international law relating to trade and the seaways also derived from Roman law (the law of nations) giving rise to the otherwise bizarre English High Court division of *Probate, Divorce, and Admiralty*.

special Act of Parliament, are separations, and not proper divorces) did not amount in all those Courts, and in an hundred years, to much more than one fifth of those that passed, in the single city of Paris, in three months. I followed up the enquiry relative to that city through several of the subsequent months until I was tired, and found the proportions still the same. Since then I have heard that they have declared for a revisal of these laws: but I know of nothing done. It appears as if the contract that renovates the world was under no law at all. From this we may take our estimate of the havock that has been made through all the relations of life. With the Jacobins of France, vague intercourse is without reproach; marriage is reduced to the vilest concubinage; children are encouraged to cut the throats of their parents; mothers are taught that tenderness is no part of their character; and to demonstrate their attachment to their party, that they ought to make no scruple to rake with their bloody hands in the bowels of those who came from their own.

To all this let us join the practice of *cannibalism*, with which, in the proper terms, and with the greatest truth, their several factions accuse each other. By cannibalism, I mean their devouring, as a nutriment of their ferocity, some part of the bodies of those they have murdered; their drinking the blood of their victims, and forcing the victims themselves to drink the blood of their kindred slaughtered before their faces. By cannibalism, I mean also to signify all their nameless, unmanly, and abominable insults on the bodies of those they slaughter.[113]

As to those whom they suffer to die a natural death, they do not permit them to enjoy the last consolations of mankind, or those rights of sepulture,[114] which indicate hope, and which meer nature has taught to mankind in all countries, to soothe the afflictions, and to cover the infirmity of mortal condition. They disgrace men in the entry into life; they vitiate and enslave them through the whole course of it; and they

---

[113] *Cannibalism:* Burke persistently asserted the existence of cannibalism in the Revolution, on the basis of some few sensationalist press reports. However there may have been a forensic motive. Lord Bacon – a favourite author of Burke's – cites cannibalism as one of the grounds for just offensive wars. In his *An Advertisement touching an Holy War* (in *Works of Francis Bacon*, ed. J. Spedding, R. L. Ellis and D. D. Heath, 15 vols. (1900–), vol. 13, p. 121) he writes that the Incas' human sacrifice and cannibalism 'did make it lawful for the Spaniards to invade their territory, forfeited by the law of nature, and either reduce them or displant them'. Burke possessed a copy of *The Works of Francis Bacon* (ed. Mallet), 3 vols. (London, 1753), which contains this essay. Payne draws attention to textual parallels between this essay and Burke's prose (*Select Works*, vol. 3, note to p. 122).

[114] *Sepulture*: burial.

deprive them of all comfort at the conclusion of their dishonoured and depraved existence. Endeavouring to persuade the people that they are no better than beasts, the whole body of their institution tends to make them beasts of prey, furious and savage. For this purpose the active part of them is disciplined into a ferocity which has no parallel. To this ferocity there is joined not one of the rude, unfashioned virtues, which accompany the vices, where the whole are left to grow up together in the rankness of uncultivated nature. But nothing is left to nature in their systems.

The same discipline which hardens their hearts relaxes their morals. Whilst courts of justice were thrust out by revolutionary tribunals, and silent churches were only the funeral monuments of departed religion, there were no fewer than nineteen or twenty theatres, great and small, most of them kept open at the publick expence, and all of them crowded every night. Among the gaunt, haggard forms of famine and nakedness, amidst the yells of murder, the tears of affliction, and the cries of despair, the song, the dance, the mimick scene, the buffoon laughter, went on as regularly as in the gay hour of festive peace. I have it from good authority, that under the scaffold of judicial murder, and the gaping planks that poured down blood on the spectators, the space was hired out for a shew of dancing dogs. I think, without concert, we have made the very same remark on reading some of their pieces, which being written for other purposes, let us into a view of their social life. It struck us that the habits of Paris had no resemblance to the finished virtues, or to the polished vice, and elegant, though not blameless luxury, of the capital of a great empire. Their society was more like that of a den of outlaws upon a doubtful frontier; of a lewd tavern for the revels and debauches of banditti, assassins, bravos, smugglers, and their more desperate paramours, mixed with bombastick players, the refuse and rejected offal of strolling theatres, puffing out ill-sorted verses about virtue, mixed with the licentious and blasphemous songs, proper to the brutal and hardened course of life belonging to that sort of wretches. This system of manners in itself is at war with all orderly and moral society, and is in it's neighbourhood unsafe. If great bodies of that kind were any where established in a bordering territory, we should have a right to demand of their Governments the suppression of such a nuisance. What are we to do if the Government and the whole community is of the same description? Yet that Government has thought proper to invite ours to lay by its unjust hatred, and to listen to the voice of humanity as taught by their example.

The operation of dangerous and delusive first principles obliges us to have recourse to the true ones. In the intercourse between nations, we are apt to rely too much on the instrumental part. We lay too much weight upon the formality of treaties and compacts. We do not act much more wisely when we trust to the interests of men as guarantees of their engagements. The interests frequently tear to pieces the engagements; and the passions trample upon both. Entirely to trust to either, is to disregard our own safety, or not to know mankind. Men are not tied to one another by papers and seals. They are led to associate by resemblances, by conformities, by sympathies. It is with nations as with individuals. Nothing is so strong a tie of amity between nation and nation as correspondence in laws, customs, manners, and habits of life. They have more than the force of treaties in themselves. They are obligations written in the heart. They approximate men to men, without their knowledge, and sometimes against their intentions. The secret, unseen, but irrefragable bond of habitual intercourse, holds them together, even when their perverse and litigious nature sets them to equivocate, scuffle, and fight about the terms of their written obligations.

As to war, if it be the means of wrong and violence, it is the sole means of justice amongst nations. Nothing can banish it from the world. They who say otherwise, intending to impose upon us, do not impose upon themselves. But it is one of the greatest objects of human wisdom to mitigate those evils which we are unable to remove. The conformity and analogy of which I speak, incapable, like every thing else, of preserving perfect trust and tranquillity among men, has a strong tendency to facilitate accommodation, and to produce a generous oblivion of the rancour of their quarrels. With this similitude, peace is more of peace, and war is less of war. I will go further. There have been periods of time in which communities, apparently in peace with each other, have been more perfectly separated than, in later times, many nations in Europe have been in the course of long and bloody wars. The cause must be sought in the similitude throughout Europe of religion, laws, and manners. At bottom, these are all the same. The writers on public law have often called this *aggregate* of nations a Commonwealth. They had reason. It is virtually one great state having the same basis of general law; with some diversity of provincial customs and local establishments. The nations of Europe have had the very same christian religion, agreeing in the fundamental parts, varying a little in the ceremonies and in the subordinate doctrines. The whole of the polity and œconomy of every country in Europe has been derived from the same sources. It was drawn from the old Germanic or Gothic custumary;[115] from the feudal institutions which must be considered as an emanation from that custumary; and the whole has been improved and digested into system and discipline by the Roman law. From hence arose the several orders, with or without a Monarch (which are called States) in every European country; the strong traces of which, where Monarchy predominated, were never wholly extinguished or merged in despotism. In the few places where Monarchy was cast off, the spirit of European Monarchy was still left. Those countries still continued countries of States; that is, of classes, orders, and distinctions, such as had before subsisted, or nearly so. Indeed the force and form of the institution called States, continued in greater perfection in those republican communities than under Monarchies. From all those sources arose a system of manners and of education which was nearly similar in all this quarter of the globe; and which softened, blended, and harmonized the colours of the whole.[116] There was little difference in the form of the Universities for the education of their youth, whether with regard to faculties, to sciences, or to the more liberal and elegant kinds of erudition. From this resemblance in the modes of intercourse, and in the whole form and fashion of life, no citizen of Europe could be altogether an exile in any part of it. There was nothing more than a pleasing variety to recreate and instruct the mind; to enrich the imagination; and to meliorate the heart. When a man travelled or resided for health, pleasure, business or necessity, from his own country, he never felt himself quite abroad.

The whole body of this new scheme of manners in support of the new scheme of politicks, I consider as a strong and decisive proof of determined ambition and systematick hostility. I defy the most refining

[115] *Custumary*: a set of customs or customary laws, hence *Gothic custumary*: the set of customs and laws supposedly characteristic of Gothic, i.e. pre-Renaissance Germanic, European feudal society. These include the idea of a society of different social orders ('[e]states') with representative bodies limiting the power of the Monarch.

[116] Burke here schematically incorporates many of the insights of certain of the Scottish Enlightenment thinkers about the general processes involved in European political and social development: the idea that modern liberty and the institutions that preserved it were a Gothic, and not a classical inheritance, the idea that a gradation of ranks constituted states, the idea that chivalry and Christianity created a greater delicacy and refinement of manners, to which Burke adds the pervasive influence of Roman Law (true of Scotland, but less so of England see above, fn. 112). These influences were so uniform throughout Europe, writes Burke, that they render it almost a single 'commonwealth'. All these refining influences, he claims, are being rejected by the Jacobins.

ingenuity to invent any other cause for the total departure of the Jacobin[N] Republick from every one of the ideas and usages, religious, legal, moral, or social, of this civilized world, and for her tearing herself from its communion with such studied violence, but from a formed resolution of keeping no terms with that world. It has not been, as has been falsely and insidiously represented, that these miscreants had only broke with their old Government. They made a schism with the whole universe; and that schism extended to almost every thing great and small. For one, I wish, since it is gone thus far, that the breach had been so compleat, as to make all intercourse impracticable; but partly by accident, partly by design, partly from the resistance of the matter, enough is left to preserve intercourse, whilst amity is destroyed or corrupted in it's principle.

This violent breach of the community of Europe, we must conclude to have been made, (even if they had not expressly declared it over and over again) either to force mankind into an adoption of their system, or to live in perpetual enmity with a community the most potent we have ever known. Can any person imagine, that in offering to mankind this desperate alternative, there is no indication of a hostile mind, because men in possession of the ruling authority are supposed to have a right to act without coercion in their own territories? As to the right of men to act any where according to their pleasure, without any moral tie, no such right exists. Men are never in a state of *total* independence of each other. It is not the condition of our nature: nor is it conceivable how any man can pursue a considerable course of action without it's having some effect upon others; or, of course, without producing some degree of responsibility for his conduct. The *situations* in which men relatively stand produce the rules and principles of that responsibility, and afford directions to prudence in exacting it.

Distance of place does not extinguish the duties or the rights of men; but it often renders their exercise impracticable. The same circumstance of distance renders the noxious effects of an evil system in any community less pernicious. But there are situations where this difficulty does not occur; and in which, therefore, these duties are obligatory, and these rights are to be asserted. It has ever been the method of publick jurists to draw a great part of the analogies on which they form the law of nations, from the principles of law which prevail in civil community. Civil laws are not all of them merely positive. Those which are rather conclusions of legal reason, than matters of statutable provision, belong to universal equity, and are

universally applicable. Almost the whole prætorian law is such.[117] There
is a *Law of Neighbourhood* which does not leave a man perfect master on
his own ground. When a neighbour sees a *new erection*, in the nature of a
nuisance, set up at his door, he has a right to represent it to the judge; who,
on his part, has a right to order the work to be staid; or if established,
to be removed. On this head, the parent law is express and clear; and
has made many wise provisions, which, without destroying, regulate and
restrain the right of *ownership*, by the right of *vicinage*.[118] No *innovation*
is permitted that may redound, even secondarily, to the prejudice of a
neighbour. The whole doctrine of that important head of prætorian law,
'*De novi operis nunciatione*,'[119] is founded on the principle, that no *new* use
should be made of a man's private liberty of operating upon his private
property, from whence a detriment may be justly apprehended by his
neighbour. This law of denunciation is prospective. It is to anticipate what
is called *damnum infectum*, or *damnum nondum factum*,[120] that is a damage
justly apprehended but not actually done. Even before it is clearly known,
whether the innovation be damageable or not, the judge is competent
to issue a prohibition to innovate, until the point can be determined.

[117] *Prætorian law*: In Republican Rome the praetor enforced the law. The Roman citizens
were governed by the *ius civile* – local custom and the twelve tablets of the law, which was
imposed by the *praetor urbanus*. But the second praetor, the *praetor peregrinus* (the praetor
for foreigners, whom Burke evidently has in mind here), was responsible for adjudications
amongst non-citizens, who did not have access to the *ius civile*. His prescriptions had to
be drawn from practices thought to be shared by the various foreigners resident in Rome,
and involved a degree of creative discretion. Such shared practices constituted the law of
nations – laws common to many nations. The commonality of practices were thought –
influenced by Stoic thinking – to be due to reason, the common factor amongst different
cultures. This gives rise to the idea that the 'law of nations' bears a relationship to the
law of 'nature' similarly derived from reason.

[118] *Vicinage*: neighbourhood.

[119] *De novi operis nunciatione* ('Concerning the declaration of new works'): Heading 39.1.0.
of Justinian's *Digest* of Roman law. This was a *stipulatio* – a precautionary legal remedy –
available to private citizens, who could petition the praetor to stop a neighbour from
starting works on a property that might damage their own, or exact a surety from them
to indemnify any damage resulting from such works.

[120] The *missio in possessionem damni infecti* ('The dismissal of injurious uncompleted works')
was a legal action described in Justinian's *Digest* (39.2.0. *De damno infecto et de suggrundis
et proiectionibus* ['concerning injurious construction, encroachments and projections'])
to appeal to a magistrate to intervene to prevent some injury apprehended from the
behaviour of another party such as a neighbour whose property was shown to be so
dilapidated as to constitute a danger to the complainant. It could even result in the
petitioner gaining possession of the offending property. On both legal instruments see
Buckland and Stein, *A Textbook of Roman Law*, pp. 724–8.

This prompt interference is grounded on principles favourable to both parties. It is preventive of mischief difficult to be repaired, and of ill blood difficult to be softened. The rule of law, therefore, which comes before the evil, is amongst the very best parts of equity, and justifies the promptness of the remedy; because, as it is well observed, *Res damni infecti celeritatem desiderat & periculosa est dilatio.*[121] This right of denunciation does not hold, when things continue, however inconveniently to the neighbourhood, according to the *antient* mode. For there is a sort of presumption against novelty, drawn out of a deep consideration of human nature and human affairs; and the maxim of jurisprudence is well laid down, *Vetustas pro lege semper habetur.*[122]

Such is the law of civil vicinity. Now where there is no constituted judge, as between independent states there is not, the vicinage itself is the natural judge. It is, preventively, the assertor of its own rights; or remedially, their avenger. Neighbours are presumed to take cognizance of each other's acts. '*Vicini, vicinorum facta presumuntur scire.*'[123] This principle, which, like the rest, is as true of nations, as of individual men, has bestowed on the grand vicinage of Europe, a duty to know, and a right to prevent, any capital innovation which may amount to the erection of a dangerous nuisance.[xi] Of the importance of that innovation, and the mischief of that nuisance, they are, to be sure, bound to judge not litigiously: but it is in their competence to judge. They have uniformly acted on this right. What in civil society is a ground of action, in politick society is a ground of war. But the exercise of that competent jurisdiction is a matter of moral prudence. As suits in civil society, so war in the political, must ever be a matter of great deliberation. It is not this or that particular proceeding, picked out here and there, as a subject of quarrel, that will do. There must be an aggregate of mischief. There must be marks of deliberation; there must be traces of design; there must be indications

---

[xi] 'This state of things cannot exist in France without involving all the surrounding powers in one common danger, without giving them the right, without imposing it on them as a duty, to stop the progress of an evil which attacks the fundamental principles by which mankind is united in civil society.' Declaration, 29th Oct. 1793.

[121] 'Matters importing danger must be quickly dealt with and delay is dangerous.'
[122] 'Antiquity is always held to have the force of law.'
[123] 'Neighbours are presumed to know what is done in the neighbourhood.' Coke, *The Fourth Part of the Institutes of the Laws of England* (London, 1797 [1628–44]), Cap. 31, p. 172, note h.

of malice; there must be tokens of ambition.[124] There must be force in the body where they exist; there must be energy in the mind. When all these circumstances combine, or the important parts of them, the duty of the vicinity calls for the exercise of it's competence; and the rules of prudence do not restrain, but demand it.

In describing the nuisance erected by so pestilential a manufactory,[125] by the construction of so infamous a brothel, by digging a night cellar for such thieves, murderers, and house-breakers, as never infested the world, I am so far from aggravating, that I have fallen infinitely short of the evil. No man who has attended to the particulars of what has been done in France, and combined them with the principles there asserted, can possibly doubt it. When I compare with this great cause of nations, the trifling points of honour, the still more contemptible points of interest, the light ceremonies, the undefinable punctilios,[126] the disputes about precedency, the lowering or the hoisting of a sail, the dealing in a hundred or two of wild cat-skins on the other side of the Globe, which have often kindled up the flames of war between nations,[127] I stand astonished at those persons, who do not feel a resentment, not more natural than politick, at the atrocious insults that this monstrous compound offers to the dignity of every nation, and who are not alarmed with what it threatens to their safety.

I have therefore been decidedly of opinion, with our declaration at Whitehall, in the beginning of this war, that the vicinage of Europe had not only a right, but an indispensable duty, and an exigent interest, to denunciate this new work before it had produced the danger we have so sorely felt, and which we shall long feel. The example of what is done by France is too important not to have a vast and extensive influence; and that example backed with it's power, must bear with great force on those

---

[124] Burke's reasoning here recalls Locke's claim about the conditions for the invocation of universal abstract principles in a similar absence of positive law – that is, in the dispute between the people and the ruler: 'The examples of particular Injustice, or Oppression of here and there an unfortunate Man, moves them not. But if they universally have a perswasion, grounded upon manifest evidence, that designs are carrying on against their Liberties, and the general course and tendency of things cannot but give them strong suspicions of the evil intention . . . ' (John Locke, *Two Treatises of Government*(London, 1690), Second Treatise, §230).

[125] *Pestilential*: a source of disease or infection.

[126] *Punctilio*: a pedantic or over-precise point or distinction.

[127] *Lowering or hoisting of sail*: The willingness to lower sail (to be inspected by those claiming monopolies on trade), and disputes about trapping rights had both proved sources of international conflict in the eighteenth century.

who are near it; especially on those who shall recognize the pretended Republick on the principle upon which it now stands. It is not an old structure which you have found as it is, and are not to dispute of the original end and design with which it had been so fashioned. It is a recent wrong, and can plead no prescription. It violates the rights upon which not only the community of France, but those on which all communities are founded. The principles on which they proceed are *general* principles, and are as true in England as in any other country. They who (though with the purest intentions) recognize the authority of these Regicides and robbers upon principle, justify their acts, and establish them as precedents. It is a question not between France and England. It is a question between property and force. The property claims; and it's claim has been allowed. The property of the nation is the nation. They who massacre, plunder, and expel the body of the proprietary, are murderers and robbers. The State, in it's essence, must be moral and just: and it may be so, though a tyrant or usurper should be accidentally at the head of it. This is a thing to be lamented: but this notwithstanding, the body of the commonwealth may remain in all it's integrity and be perfectly sound in it's composition. The present case is different. It is not a revolution in government. It is not the victory of party over party. It is a destruction and decomposition of the whole society; which never can be made of right by any faction, however powerful, nor without terrible consequences to all about it, both in the act and in the example. This pretended Republick is founded in crimes, and exists by wrong and robbery; and wrong and robbery, far from a title to any thing, is war with mankind. To be at peace with robbery is to be an accomplice with it.

Mere locality does not constitute a body politick. Had Cade and his gang got possession of London,[128] they would not have been the Lord-Mayor, Aldermen, and Common Council. The body politick of France existed in the majesty of it's throne; in the dignity of it's nobility; in the honour of it's gentry; in the sanctity of it's clergy; in the reverence of it's magistracy; in the weight and consideration due to it's landed

---

[128] *Cade and his gang*: Jack Cade, an ex-soldier, led the 'Kentish Rebellion' in 1450 protesting against the hardships caused by the Hundred Years War and the taxation policies of Henry VI. With about 5,000 men he entered London, murdered some of Henry's officials and associates and declared himself mayor. Although he was persuaded to disband on promise of a pardon by John Kemp, Chancellor and Archbishop of York, the King issued a reward for his arrest or death and he was subsequently killed in Lewes, Sussex.

property in the several bailliages;[129] in the respect due to it's moveable substance represented by the corporations of the kingdom. All these particular *moleculæ* united, form the great mass of what is truly the body politick in all countries. They are so many deposits and receptacles of justice; because they can only exist by justice. Nation is a moral essence, not a geographical arrangement, or a denomination of the nomenclator. France, though out of her territorial possession, exists; because the sole possible claimant, I mean the proprietary, and the Government to which the proprietary adheres, exists and claims. God forbid, that if you were expelled from your house by ruffians and assassins, that I should call the material walls, doors and windows of ——, the ancient and honourable family of ——. Am I to transfer to the intruders, who not content to turn you out naked to the world, would rob you of your very name, all the esteem and respect I owe to you? The Regicides in France are not France. France is out of her bounds, but the kingdom is the same.[130]

To illustrate my opinions on this subject, let us suppose a case, which, after what has happened, we cannot think absolutely impossible, though the augury is to be abominated, and the event deprecated with our most ardent prayers. Let us suppose then, that our gracious Sovereign was sacrilegiously murdered; his exemplary Queen, at the head of the matronage of this land, murdered in the same manner: That those Princesses whose beauty and modest elegance are the ornaments of the country, and who are the leaders and patterns of the ingenuous youth of their sex, were put to a cruel and ignominious death, with hundreds of others, mothers and daughters, ladies of the first distinction; ——— that the Prince of Wales and the Duke of York, princes the hope and pride of the nation, with all their brethren, were forced to fly from the knives of assassins ——— that the whole body of our excellent Clergy were either massacred or robbed of all, and transported – the Christian Religion, in all its denominations, forbidden and persecuted; the law totally, fundamentally, and in all it's parts destroyed – the judges put to death by revolutionary tribunals – the Peers and Commons robbed to the last acre of their estates; massacred if they staid, or obliged to seek life in flight, in exile, and in beggary – that the whole landed property should share the very same fate – that

---

[129] *Bailliage*: The area of responsibility of a particular bailiff or legal competence or jurisdiction of a court.

[130] *Out of her bounds . . .*: the French nation (i.e. the émigrés who hold to the original constitution of France) is outside of her geographical boundaries, but it remains the same.

every military and naval officer of honour and rank, almost to a man, should be placed in the same description of confiscation and exile – that the principal merchants and bankers should be drawn out, as from an hen-coop, for slaughter – that the citizens of our greatest and most flourishing cities, when the hand and the machinery of the hangman were not found sufficient, should have been collected in the publick squares, and massacred by thousands with cannon; – if three hundred thousand others should have been doomed to a situation worse than death in noisome and pestilential prisons; – in such a case, is it in the faction of robbers I am to look for my country? Would this be the England that you and I, and even strangers, admired, honoured, loved, and cherished? Would not the exiles of England alone be my Government and my fellow citizens? Would not their places of refuge be my temporary country? Would not all my duties and all my affections be there and there only? Should I consider myself as a traitor to my country, and deserving of death, if I knocked at the door and heart of every Potentate in Christendom to succour my friends, and to avenge them on their enemies? Could I, in any way, shew myself more a Patriot? What should I think of those Potentates who insulted their suffering brethren; who treated them as vagrants, or at least as mendicants; and could find no allies, no friends, but in Regicide murderers and robbers? What ought I to think and feel, if being geographers instead of Kings, they recognized the desolated cities, the wasted fields, and the rivers polluted with blood, of this geometrical measurement, as the honourable member of Europe, called England? In that condition what should we think of Sweden, Denmark, or Holland, or whatever Power afforded us a churlish and treacherous hospitality, if they should invite us to join the standard of our King, our Laws, and our Religion, if they should give us a direct promise of protection, ––– if after all this, taking advantage of our deplorable situation, which left us no choice, they were to treat us as the lowest and vilest of all mercenaries? If they were to send us far from the aid of our King, and our suffering Country, to squander us away in the most pestilential climates for a venal enlargement of their own territories, for the purpose of trucking them, when obtained, with those very robbers and murderers they had called upon us to oppose with our blood? What would be our sentiments, if in that miserable service we were not to be considered either as English, or as Swedes, Dutch, Danes, but as outcasts of the human race? Whilst we were fighting those battles of their interest, and as their soldiers, how should we feel if we were to be excluded from all their cartels? How must we feel, if the pride and flower of the English Nobility and Gentry, who might escape the pestilential clime, and the devouring sword, should, if taken prisoners, be delivered over as rebel subjects, to be condemned as rebels, as traitors, as the vilest of all criminals, by tribunals formed of Maroon negroe slaves,[131] covered over with the blood of their masters, who were made free and organized into judges, for their robberies and murders? What should we feel under this inhuman, insulting, and barbarous protection of Muscovites, Swedes or Hollanders? Should we not obtest Heaven,[132] and whatever justice there is yet on Earth? Oppression makes wise men mad;[133] but the distemper is still the madness of the wise, which is better than the sobriety of fools. Their cry is the voice of sacred misery, exalted, not into wild raving, but into the sanctified phrensy of prophecy and inspiration ——— in that bitterness of soul, in that indignation of suffering virtue, in that exaltation of despair, would not persecuted English Loyalty cry out, with an awful warning voice, and denounce the destruction that waits on Monarchs, who consider fidelity to them as the most degrading of all vices; who suffer it to be punished as the most abominable of all crimes; and who have no respect but for rebels, traitors, Regicides, and furious negro slaves, whose crimes have broke their chains? Would not this warm language of high indignation have more of sound reason in it, more of real affection, more of true attachment, than all the lullabies of flatterers, who would hush Monarchs to sleep in the arms of death? Let them be well convinced, that if ever this example should prevail in it's whole extent, it will have it's full operation. Whilst Kings stand firm on their base, though under that base there is a sure-wrought mine, there will not be wanting to their levees a single person of those who are attached to their fortune, and not to their persons or cause: But hereafter none will support a tottering throne. Some will fly for fear of being crushed under the ruin; some will join in making it. They will seek in the destruction of Royalty, fame, and power, and wealth, and the homage of Kings, with *Reubel*, with *Carnot*,[N] with *Revelliere*, and with the *Merlins* and the *Talliens*,[N] rather than suffer exile and beggary with the *Condés*,[N] or the *Broglios*, the *Castries*, the *D'Avrais*, the *Serrents*, the *Cazalés*, and the long line of loyal, suffering Patriot Nobility, or to be butchered with the oracles and the victims of the laws, the *D'Ormesons*,

---

[131] *Maroon negro slaves*: armed communities of escaped slaves in the Caribbean islands.
[132] *Obtest*: to call upon, or bear witness (to an injustice).
[133] Ecclesiastes 7:7.

the *d'Espremenils*, and the *Malesherbes*.[134] This example we shall give, if instead of adhering to our fellows in a cause which is an honour to us all, we abandon the lawful Government and lawful corporate body of France, to hunt for a shameful and ruinous fraternity, with this odious usurpation that disgraces civilized society and the human race.

And is then example nothing? It is every thing. Example is the school of mankind, and they will learn at no other. This war is a war against that example. It is not a war for Louis the Eighteenth, or even for the property, virtue, fidelity of France. It is a war for George the Third, for Francis the Second, and for all the dignity, property, honour, virtue, and religion of England, of Germany, and of all nations.[135]

I know that all I have said of the systematick unsociability of this new-invented species of republick, and the impossibility of preserving peace, is answered by asserting that the scheme of manners, morals, and even of maxims and principles of state, is of no weight in a question of peace or war between communities. This doctrine is supported by example. The case of Algiers is cited, with an hint, as if it were the stronger case.[136] I

---

[134] *Reubel*, *Carnot* and *Revellière* were members of the Directory (see below, fn. 143); *Merlin* and *Tallien* were prominent in the Thermidor and members of the Council of 500, the legislative chamber under the Directory.

The Prince de *Condé*, commander of the royalist army, Duc *de Broglie*, Marshal of France, and the Marquis de *Castries*, also Marshal of France and his son, all served in the émigré armies. They, along with the Duc *d'Avrais*, who had been a member of the National Assembly, the Duc de *Serent* and Jacques-Antoine-Marie de *Cazalès* were all members of prominent families who went into exile following the execution of the King.

The Marquis *d'Ormesson* (Louis-François de Paul le Fèvre) died a natural death in 1789, but his son Anne-Louis d'Ormesson, along with Jean-Jacques d'*Esprémesnil*, counsellor of the Parlement de Paris, and Chrétien-Guillaume de *Malesherbes*, the retired secretary of the King and defendant at his trial, along with several members of his family, had all been guillotined in the Terror in April 1794.

[135] *Louis the Eighteenth*: the then pretender to the French throne, brother of the executed French King Louis XVI (whose son had died in 1795); *George the Third* (1738–1820): then King of Great Britain. *Francis the Second* (1768–1835): then Holy Roman Emperor, a title he would lose following defeat by Napoleon at Austerlitz in 1805. Burke is urging the view that the war is not limited to the reinstatement of the French monarchy but involves the defence of all of the monarchies of Europe.

[136] *The case of Algiers*: Burke addresses here the question whether entering into diplomatic relations with a state presupposes recognition of the legitimacy of its government. Fox (*The Parliamentary History of England from the Norman Conquest ... to 1803*, ed. William Cobbett, 36 vols. (London, 1806–20), vol. 30, cols. 80–1) had pointed out that the fact that there was a British Consul in Algiers did not imply support for its government (which provided a notorious base and haven for piracy in the Mediterranean). On this basis Fox had urged the propriety of diplomatic negotiation with the revolutionaries. Burke sees it as a dangerous concession: 'Because we have done one humiliating act, we ought, with infinite caution, to admit more.'

should take no notice of this sort of inducement, if I had found it only where first it was. I do not want respect for those from whom I first heard it – but having no controversy at present with them, I only think it not amiss to rest on it a little, as I find it adopted with much more of the same kind, by several of those on whom such reasoning had formerly made no apparent impression. If it had no force to prevent us from submitting to this necessary war, it furnishes no better ground for our making an unnecessary and ruinous peace.

This analogical argument drawn from the case of Algiers would lead us a good way. The fact is, we ourselves with a little cover, others more directly, pay a *tribute* to the Republick of Algiers. Is it meant to reconcile us to the payment of a *tribute* to the French Republick?[137] That this, with other things more ruinous, will be demanded hereafter, I little doubt; but for the present, this will not be avowed ––– though our minds are to be gradually prepared for it. In truth, the arguments from this case are worth little, even to those who approve the buying an Algerine forbearance of piracy. There are many things which men do not approve, that they must do to avoid a greater evil. To argue from thence, that they are to act in the same manner in all cases, is turning necessity into a law. Upon what is matter of prudence, the argument concludes the contrary way. Because we have done one humiliating act, we ought, with infinite caution, to admit more acts of the same nature, lest humiliation should become our habitual state. Matters of prudence are under the dominion of circumstances, and not of logical analogies. It is absurd to take it otherwise.

I, for one, do more than doubt the policy of this kind of convention with Algiers. On those who think as I do, the argument *ad hominem* can make no sort of impression. I know something of the Constitution and composition of this very extraordinary Republick. It has a Constitution, I admit, similar to the present tumultuous military tyranny of France, by which an handful of obscure ruffians domineer over a fertile country, and a brave people. For the composition, too, I admit, the Algerine community resembles that of France; being formed out of the very scum, scandal, disgrace, and pest of the Turkish Asia. The grand Seignor, to disburthen the country, suffers the Dey to recruit, in his dominions, the corps of Janisaries, or Asaphs, which form the Directory and Council of Elders of

---

[137] *Tribute*: Britain paid a sum, 'tribute', to the ruler – the Dey – of Algeria to purchase immunity for its ships from piracy. Burke argues that if we take the Algerian analogy all the way we would finish up buying off the French to prevent them exporting revolution.

the African Republick one and indivisible.[138] But notwithstanding this resemblance, which I allow, I never shall so far injure the Janisarian Republick of Algiers, as to put it in comparison for every sort of crime, turpitude, and oppression with the Jacobin Republick of Paris. There is no question with me to which of the two I should choose to be a neighbour or a subject. But situated as I am, I am in no danger of becoming to Algiers either the one or the other. It is not so in my relation to the atheistical fanaticks of France. I *am* their neighbour; I *may* become their subject. Have the Gentlemen who borrowed this happy parallel, no idea of the different conduct to be held with regard to the very same evil at an immense distance, and when it is at your door? when it's power is enormous, as when it is comparatively as feeble as it's distance is remote? when there is a barrier of language and usages, which prevents corruption through certain old correspondences and habitudes, from the contagion of the horrible novelties that are introduced into every thing else? I can contemplate, without dread, a royal or a national tyger on the borders of Pegu.[139] I can look at him, with an easy curiosity, as prisoner within bars in the menagerie of the Tower.[140] But if, by Habeas Corpus,[141] or otherwise, he was to come into the Lobby of the House of Commons whilst your door was open, any of you would be more stout than wise, who would not gladly make your escape out of the back windows. I certainly should dread more from a wild cat in my bed-chamber, than from all the lions that roar in the deserts behind Algiers. But in this parallel it is the cat that is at a distance, and the lions and tygers that are in our anti-chambers and our lobbies. Algiers is not near; Algiers is not powerful; Algiers is not our neighbour; Algiers is not infectious. Algiers, whatever it may be, is an old creation; and we have good data to calculate all the mischief to be apprehended from it. When I find Algiers transferred to Calais, I will tell you what I think of that point. In the mean time, the case quoted from the Algerine reports, will not apply as authority. We shall put it out of

---

[138] Algeria was nominally a part of the Turkish Empire but the Dey was elected by the professional soldiery, the Janissaries. *Asaphs*: possibly from the Hebrew verb 'to gather', hence those gathered, i.e. a council, or those doing the gathering (i.e. collecting revenue), but either way an elite body.

[139] *Pegu*: now Bago, a town and district in south central Burma (Myanmar).

[140] *Menagerie of the Tower*: The Tower of London housed the royal menagerie, or collection of wild animals (often presented by sovereigns to each other as gifts). This was opened to the public in the eighteenth century – and moved to the Zoological Gardens in Regent's Park in the 1830s.

[141] *Habeas Corpus*: the requirement that anyone arrested be brought before a magistrate.

court; and so far as that goes, let the counsel for the Jacobin[N] peace take nothing by their motion.

When we voted, as you and I did, with many more whom you and I respect and love, to resist this enemy, we were providing for dangers that were direct, home, pressing, and not remote, contingent, uncertain, and formed upon loose analogies. We judged of the danger with which we were menaced by Jacobin France, from the whole tenor of her conduct; not from one or two doubtful or detached acts or expressions. I not only concurred in the idea of combining with Europe in this war; but to the best of my power even stimulated Ministers to that conjunction of interests and of efforts. I joined them with all my soul, on the principles contained in that manly and masterly state-paper, which I have two or three times referred to,[xii] and may still more frequently hereafter. The diplomatick collection never was more enriched than with this piece. The historick facts justify every stroke of the master. 'Thus painters write their names at Co.'[142]

Various persons may concur in the same measure on various grounds. They may be various, without being contrary to, or exclusive of each other. I thought the insolent, unprovoked aggression of the Regicide upon our Ally of Holland, a good ground of war. I think his manifest attempt to overturn the balance of Europe, a good ground of war. As a good ground of war, I consider his declaration of war on his Majesty and his kingdom. But though I have taken all these to my aid, I consider them as nothing more than as a sort of evidence to indicate the treasonable mind within. Long before their acts of aggression, and their declaration of war, the faction in France had assumed a form, had adopted a body of principles and maxims, and had regularly and systematically acted on them, by which she virtually had put herself in a posture, which was in itself a declaration of war against mankind.

---

[xii] Declaration, Whitehall, Oct. 29, 1793.

[142] Mathew Prior, 'Protogenes and Appelles', in *Poems on Several Occasions*, 2 vols. (Dublin, 1768), p. 81. The poem is based on the account (in Pliny, *Hist. Nat.* 35.91ff.) of the rivalry between the painters Protogenes and Apelles of Kos. In the poem's version Apelles announces himself to a maidservant of Protogenes by drawing a perfect circle freehand, saying:

> And will you please, sweet heart, said he,
> To shew your master this from me
> By it he shall presently know
> How painters write their names in Co.

It is said by the Directory[143] in their several manifestoes, that we of the people are tumultuous for peace; and that Ministers pretend negociation to amuse us. This they have learned from the language of many amongst ourselves, whose conversations have been one main cause of whatever extent the opinion for peace with Regicide may be. But I who think the Ministers unfortunately to be but too serious in their proceedings, find myself obliged to say a little more on this subject of the popular opinion.

Before our opinions are quoted against ourselves, it is proper that, from our serious deliberation, they may be worth quoting. It is without reason we praise the wisdom of our Constitution, in putting under the discretion of the Crown, the awful trust of war and peace, if the Ministers of the Crown virtually return it again into our hands. The trust was placed there as a sacred deposit, to secure us against popular rashness in plunging into wars, and against the effects of popular dismay, disgust, or lassitude in getting out of them as imprudently as we might first engage in them. To have no other measure in judging of those great objects than our momentary opinions and desires, is to throw us back upon that very democracy which, in this part, our Constitution was formed to avoid.[144]

It is no excuse at all for a minister, who at our desire, takes a measure contrary to our safety, that it is our own act. He who does not stay the hand of suicide, is guilty of murder. On our part I say, that to be instructed, is not to be degraded or enslaved. Information is an advantage to us; and we have a right to demand it. He that is bound to act in the dark cannot be said to act freely. When it appears evident to our governors that our desires and our interests are at variance, they ought not to gratify the former at the expence of the latter. Statesmen are placed on an eminence, that they may have a larger horizon than we can possibly command. They have a whole before them, which we can contemplate only in the parts, and even without the necessary relations. Ministers are not only our natural rulers but our natural guides. Reason clearly and manfully delivered, has in itself a mighty force: but reason in the mouth of legal authority, is, I may fairly say, irresistible.

I admit that reason of state will not, in many circumstances, permit the disclosure of the true ground of a public proceeding. In that case silence

---

[143] *Directory*: Name of the constitution that succeeded the National Convention in 1795, so called because the executive comprised five Directors, chosen by the elected chambers.

[144] *The democracy our constitution was formed to avoid*: 'Unconstitutional' democracy was a continual majoritarian referendum, and offended against the rule of law. See Burke's earlier discussion, pp. 210–11.

is manly and it is wise. It is fair to call for trust when the principle of reason itself suspends it's public use. I take the distinction to be this: The ground of a particular measure, making a part of a plan, it is rarely proper to divulge; All the broader grounds of policy on which the general plan is to be adopted, ought as rarely to be concealed. They who have not the whole cause before them, call them politicians, call them people, call them what you will, are no judges. The difficulties of the case, as well as it's fair side, ought to be presented. This ought to be done: and it is all that can be done. When we have our true situation distinctly presented to us, if then we resolve with a blind and headlong violence, to resist the admonitions of our friends, and to cast ourselves into the hands of our potent and irreconcileable foes, then, and not till then, the ministers stand acquitted before God and man, for whatever may come.

Lamenting as I do, that the matter has not had so full and free a discussion as it requires, I mean to omit none of the points which seem to me necessary for consideration, previous to an arrangement which is for ever to decide the form and the fate of Europe. In the course, therefore, of what I shall have the honour to address to you, I propose the following questions to your serious thoughts. 1. Whether the present system, which stands for a Government in France, be such as in peace and war affects the neighbouring States in a manner different from the internal Government that formerly prevailed in that country? 2. Whether that system, supposing it's views hostile to other nations, possesses any means of being hurtful to them peculiar to itself? 3. Whether there has been lately such a change in France, as to alter the nature of it's system, or it's effect upon other Powers? 4. Whether any publick declarations or engagements exist, on the part of the allied Powers, which stand in the way of a treaty of peace, which supposes the right and confirms the power of the Regicide faction in France? 5. What the state of the other Powers of Europe will be with respect to each other, and their colonies, on the conclusion of a Regicide Peace? 6. Whether we are driven to the absolute necessity of making that kind of peace?

These heads of enquiry will enable us to make the application of the several matters of fact and topicks of argument, that occur in this vast discussion, to certain fixed principles. I do not mean to confine myself to the order in which they stand. I shall discuss them in such a manner as shall appear to me the best adapted for shewing their mutual bearings and relations. Here then I close the public matter of my Letter; but before I have done, let me say one word in apology for myself.

In wishing this nominal peace not to be precipitated, I am sure no man living is less disposed to blame the present Ministry than I am. Some of my oldest friends, (and I wish I could say it of more of them) make a part in that Ministry. There are some indeed, 'whom my dim eyes in vain explore.' In my mind, a greater calamity could not have fallen on the publick than the exclusion of one of them. But I drive away that, with other melancholy thoughts. A great deal ought to be said upon that subject or nothing. As to the distinguished persons to whom my friends who remain, are joined, if benefits, nobly and generously conferred, ought to procure good wishes, they are intitled to my best vows; and they have them all. They have administered to me the only consolation I am capable of receiving, which is to know that no individual will suffer by my thirty years service to the publick. If things should give us the comparative happiness of a struggle, I shall be found, I was going to say fighting, (that would be foolish) but dying by the side of Mr. Pitt.[N] I must add, that if any thing defensive in our domestick system can possibly save us from the disasters of a Regicide peace, he is the man to save us. If the finances in such a case can be repaired, he is the man to repair them. If I should lament any of his acts, it is only when they appear to me to have no resemblance to acts of his. But let him not have a confidence in himself, which no human abilities can warrant. His abilities are fully equal (and that is to say much for any man) to those which are opposed to him. But if we look to him as our security against the consequences of a Regicide Peace, let us be assured, that a Regicide Peace and a Constitutional Ministry are terms that will not agree. With a Regicide Peace the King cannot long have a Minister to serve him, nor the Minister a King to serve. If the Great Disposer, in reward of the royal and the private virtues of our Sovereign, should call him from the calamitous spectacles, which will attend a state of amity with Regicide, his successor will surely see them, unless the same Providence greatly anticipates the course of nature. Thinking thus, (and not, as I conceive, on light grounds) I dare not flatter the reigning Sovereign, nor any Minister he has or can have, nor his Successor Apparent, nor any of those who may be called to serve him, with what appears to me a false state of their situation. We cannot have them and that Peace together.

I do not forget that there had been a considerable difference between several of our friends, (with my insignificant self) and the great man at the head of Ministry, in an early stage of these discussions. But I am sure there was a period in which we agreed better in the danger of a Jacobin[N] existence in France. At one time, he and all Europe seemed to feel it. But why am not I converted with so many great Powers, and so many great Ministers? It is because I am old and slow. – I am in this year, 1796, only where all the powers of Europe were in 1793. I cannot move with this procession of the Equinoxes,[145] which is preparing for us the return of some very old, I am afraid no golden æra, or the commencement of some new æra that must be denominated from some new metal. In this crisis I must hold my tongue, or I must speak with freedom. Falsehood and delusion are allowed in no case whatever: But, as in the exercise of all the virtues, there is an œconomy of truth.[146] It is a sort of temperance, by which a man speaks truth with measure that he may speak it the longer. But as the same rules do not hold in all cases – what would be right for you, who may presume on a series of years before you, would have no sense for me, who cannot, without absurdity, calculate on six months of life.[147] What I say, I *must* say at once. Whatever I write is in it's nature testamentary. It may have the weakness, but it has the sincerity of a dying declaration. For the few days I have to linger here, I am removed completely from the busy scene of the world; but I hold myself to be still responsible for every thing that I have done whilst I continued on the place of action. If the rawest Tyro[148] in politicks has been influenced by the authority of my grey hairs, and led by any thing in my speeches, or my writings, to enter into this war, he has a right to call upon me to know why I have changed my opinions, or why, when those I voted with, have adopted better notions, I persevere in exploded errour?

When I seem not to acquiesce in the acts of those I respect in every degree short of superstition, I am obliged to give my reasons fully. I cannot set my authority against their authority. But to exert reason is

---

[145] *Procession of the Equinoxes*: The equinoxes are conventionally those dates in the Earth's annual orbit round the sun when day and night are of equal lengths. Because the Earth's rotational axis is not constantly related to the plane of its path round the sun – it wobbles – the equinoctial points are not stable but return to their original points in a cycle of approximately 26,000 years. This 'procession' (properly 'precession') was known to the ancient Greeks such as Aristarchos of Samos (third century BC) and is sometimes linked to Plato's 'great year'. So Burke here refers to great periods of time and invokes Platonic ideas of social and historical recurrence.

[146] *Oeconomy of truth*: Aristotle famously asserted that virtue was the midpoint of any quality between its excess and deficiency (*Nicomachean Ethics*, 2.2 [1104a]). Burke claims, in a now-famous phrase, the same moderation applies to truth-telling.

[147] *Six months of life*: Burke was only slightly pessimistic. These words were probably written towards the end of composition, which was completed in early October 1796. He was to die within a year, early on 9 July 1797.

[148] *Tyro*: a beginner or novice in any field of expertise.

not to revolt against authority. Reason and authority do not move in the same parallel. That reason is an *amicus curiæ* who speaks *de plano*, not *pro tribunali*.[149] It is a friend who makes an useful suggestion to the Court, without questioning it's jurisdiction. Whilst he acknowledges it's competence, he promotes it's efficiency. I shall pursue the plan I have chalked out in my Letters that follow this.[150].

---

[149] *Amicus curiae*: a friend of the court, or meeting. *De plano:* from the level ground, i.e. without claiming higher authority. *Pro tribunali*: as if from the chair.

[150] *Letters that follow this*: This and the second were published as *Two letters... on the proposals for Peace with the Regicide Directory of France...* in 1796. It seems likely that he projected at least another one, and his literary executors eventually published two further letters. Subsequent editions often refer to the *Four Letters on a Regicide Peace*, which is not a title Burke would have recognised. See the Introduction for a history of these texts.

# Variant readings

## Variant reading from *Reflections*

*The following text was removed by Burke for the third edition (16 November 1790) and replaced with the text between pp. 180 and 183 in the present edition (see fn 339).*

Now take in the other point of view, and suppose their principle of representation according to contribution, that is, according to *riches*, to be well founded, and to be a necessary basis for the republic, how have they provided for the rich by giving to the district, that is to say, to the poor in the district of *Canton* and *Commune*, who are the majority, the power of making an additional number of members on account of the superior contribution of the wealthy? Suppose one man (it is an easy supposition) to contribute ten times more than ten of his neighbours. For this contribution he has one vote out of ten. The poor outvote him by nine voices in virtue of his superior contribution, for (say) *ten* members, instead of out-voting him for only one member. Why are the rich complimented with an aristocratic preference, which they can never feel either as a gratification to pride, or as a security to fortune? The rich indeed require an additional security from the dangers to which they are exposed when a popular power is prevalent; but it is impossible to divine, on this system of unequal masses, how they are protected; because the aristocratic mass is generated from democratic principles; and the prevalence in the general representation has no sort of connection with those on account of whose property this superiority is given. If the contrivers of this scheme meant any sort of favour to the rich in consequence of their contribution, they ought to have conferred the privilege either on the individual rich, or on some class formed of rich persons; because the contest between the rich and the poor is not a struggle between corporation and corporation, but a contest between men and men; a competition not between districts, but between descriptions. It would answer its purpose better if the scheme was inverted; that the votes of the masses were rendered equal; and that the votes within each mass were proportioned to property. In any other light, I see nothing but danger from the inequality of the masses.

If indeed the masses were to provide for the general treasury by distinct contingents, and that the revenue had not (as it has) many impositions running through the whole, which affect men individually, and not corporately, and which, by their nature, confound all territorial limits, something might be said for the basis of contribution as founded on masses. But of all things, this representation, to be measured by contribution, is the most difficult to settle upon principles of equity, in a country which considers its districts as members of an whole. For a great city, such as Bordeaux or Paris, appears to pay a vast body of duties, almost out of all assignable proportion to other places, and its mass is considered accordingly. But are these cities the true contributors in that proportion? No. The consumers of the commodities imported into Bordeaux, who are scattered through all France, pay the import duties of Bordeaux. The produce of the vintage in Guienne and Languedoc give to that city the means of its contribution growing out of an export commerce. The landholders who spend their estates in Paris, and are thereby the creators of that city, contribute for Paris from the provinces out of which their revenues arise.

If in equity this basis of contribution, as locally ascertained by masses, be inequitable, it is impolitic too. If it be one of the objects to preserve the weak from being crushed by the strong (as in all society undoubtedly it is) how are the smaller and poorer of these masses to be saved from the tyranny of the more wealthy? Is it by adding to their means of oppressing them? When we come to a balance of representation between corporate bodies, provincial interests, emulations, and jealousies are full as likely to arise among them as among individuals; and their divisions are likely to produce much hotter dissention, and something leading much more nearly to a war.

## Variant reading from *A Regicide Peace*

*The following passage appears on pp. 63–6 in the pirated edition of the first* Letter on a Regicide Peace, *published without Burke's permission by his printer, John Owen, from Burke's preliminary draft (which had been in proof as early as April) as* Thoughts on the Prospect of a Regicide Peace, *in a series of letters (October 1796). The passage, which followed the paragraph ending 'and of all nations' at p. 326, line 11 of this edition and was eventually removed, probably on advice, by Burke from his final text, emphasises the great importance Burke places on the management of political beliefs, and even advances a pragmatic justification of the suppression of free expression.*

But, say some, you force opinion. You can never extirpate opinion without extirpating a whole nation. Nay, by pursuing it, you only increase its partizans. Opinions are things out of human jurisdiction. I have formerly heard this from the mouths of great men with, more surprize than satisfaction. They alledge as a proof of their doctrine, the wars of Charles the Fifth, and some of his successors, against the Reformation.

It is so common, though so unreasonable, it is hardly worth remarking, that no persons pursue more fiercely with criminal process, and with every kind of coercion, the publication of opinions contrary to their own, than those do, who claim in this respect the most unbounded latitude to themselves. If it were not for this inconsistency, then war against opinions might be justified as all others, more or less, according to the reason of the case: for the case judged on by moral prudence, and not by any universal abstract principle of right, is to guide government in this delicate point.

As to the mere matter of extirpation of all kinds of opinions, whether right or wrong, without the extirpation of a people, it is a thing so very common, that would be clouded and obscured rather than illustrated by examples. Every revolution in the predominant opinion made by the force of domestic legal government, by the force of any usurpation, by the force of any conquest, is a proof to the contrary; – and there is no nation which has not experienced those changes. Instances enough may be furnished of people who have enthusiastically, and with force, propagated those opinions, which some time before they resisted with their blood. Rarely have ever great changes in opinion taken place without the application of force, more or less. Like every thing else in human life and human affairs, it is not universally true, that a persecution of opinions lessens or increases the number of their votaries. In finding where it may or may not have gathered these effects, the sagacity of Government shines or is disgraced, as well as in the time, the manner, the choice of the opinions on which it ought to use or forbear the sword of domestic or of foreign justice. But it is a false maxim, that opinions ought to be indifferent to us, either as men or as a State. Opinion is the rudder of human action; and as the opinion is wise or foolish, vicious or moral, the cause of action is noxious or salutary. It has even been the great primary object of speculative and doctrinal philosophy to regulate opinion. It is the great object of political philosophy to promote that which is sound; and to extirpate what is mischievous, and which directly tends to render men bad citizens in the community, and mischievous neighbours out of it. Opinions are of infinite consequence. They make the manners – in fact, they make the laws: they make the Lagislator. They are, therefore, of all things, those to which provident Government ought to look most to in their beginnings. After a time they may look to them in vain. When, therefore, I am told that this is a war of opinions, I am told that it is the most important of all wars.

# Index

# CAMBRIDGE TEXTS IN THE HISTORY OF POLITICAL THOUGHT

*Titles published in the series thus far*

Aquinas *Political Writings* (edited by R. W. Dyson)
   978 0 521 37595 5 paperback
Aristotle *The Politics* and *The Constitution of Athens* (edited by
   Stephen Everson)
   978 0 521 48400 8 paperback
Arnold *Culture and Anarchy and Other Writings* (edited by Stefan Collini)
   978 0 521 37796 6 paperback
Astell *Political Writings* (edited by Patricia Springborg)
   978 0 521 42845 3 paperback
Augustine *The City of God against the Pagans* (edited by R. W. Dyson)
   978 0 521 46843 5 paperback
Augustine *Political Writings* (edited by E. M. Atkins and R. J. Dodaro)
   978 0 521 44697 6 paperback
Austin *The Province of Jurisprudence Determined* (edited by
   Wilfrid E. Rumble)
   978 0 521 44756 0 paperback
Bacon *The History of the Reign of King Henry VII* (edited by
   Brian Vickers)
   978 0 521 58663 4 paperback
Bagehot *The English Constitution* (edited by Paul Smith)
   978 0 521 46942 5 paperback
Bakunin *Statism and Anarchy* (edited by Marshall Shatz)
   978 0 521 36973 2 paperback
Baxter *Holy Commonwealth* (edited by William Lamont)
   978 0 521 40580 5 paperback
Bayle *Political Writings* (edited by Sally L. Jenkinson)
   978 0 521 47677 5 paperback
Beccaria *On Crimes and Punishments and Other Writings* (edited by
   Richard Bellamy)
   978 0 521 47982 0 paperback
Bentham *Fragment on Government* (introduction by Ross Harrison)
   978 0 521 35929 0 paperback
Bernstein *The Preconditions of Socialism* (edited by Henry Tudor)
   978 0 521 39808 4 paperback
Bodin *On Sovereignty* (edited by Julian H. Franklin)
   978 0 521 34992 5 paperback
Bolingbroke *Political Writings* (edited by David Armitage)
   978 0 521 58697 9 paperback

Bossuet *Politics Drawn from the Very Words of Holy Scripture* (edited by Patrick
 Riley)
  978 0 521 36807 0 paperback
*The British Idealists* (edited by David Boucher)
  978 0 521 45951 8 paperback
Burke *Pre-Revolutionary Writings* (edited by Ian Harris)
  978 0 521 36800 1 paperback
Cavendish *Political Writings* (edited by Susan James)
  978 0 521 63350 5 paperback
Christine De Pizan *The Book of the Body Politic* (edited by Kate Langdon
 Forhan)
  978 0 521 42259 8 paperback
Cicero *On Duties* (edited by M. T. Griffin and E. M. Atkins)
  978 0 521 34835 5 paperback
Cicero *On the Commonwealth* and *On the Laws* (edited by James E. G. Zetzel)
  978 0 521 45959 4 paperback
Comte *Early Political Writings* (edited by H. S. Jones)
  978 0 521 46923 4 paperback
*Conciliarism and Papalism* (edited by J. H. Burns and Thomas M. Izbicki)
  978 0 521 47674 4 paperback
Condorcet *Political Writings* (edited by Steven Lukes and Nadia Urbinati)
  978 1 107 02101 3 hardback
  978 1 107 60539 8 paperback
Constant *Political Writings* (edited by Biancamaria Fontana)
  978 0 521 31632 3 paperback
Dante *Monarchy* (edited by Prue Shaw)
  978 0 521 56781 7 paperback
Diderot *Political Writings* (edited by John Hope Mason and Robert Wokler)
  978 0 521 36911 4 paperback
*The Dutch Revolt* (edited by Martin van Gelderen)
  978 0 521 39809 1 paperback
*Early Greek Political Thought from Homer to the Sophists* (edited by Michael
 Gagarin and Paul Woodruff)
  978 0 521 43768 4 paperback
*The Early Political Writings of the German Romantics* (edited by Frederick C.
 Beiser)
  978 0 521 44951 9 paperback
Emerson *Political Writings* (edited by Kenneth S. Sacks)
  978 0 521 71002 2 paperback
*The English Levellers* (edited by Andrew Sharp)
  978 0 521 62511 1 paperback
Erasmus *The Education of a Christian Prince* (edited by Lisa Jardine)
  978 0 521 58811 9 paperback

Hooker *Of the Laws of Ecclesiastical Polity* (edited by A. S. McGrade)
    978 0 521 37908 3 paperback
Hume *Political Essays* (edited by Knud Haakonssen)
    978 0 521 46639 4 paperback
King James VI and I *Political Writings* (edited by Johann P. Sommerville)
    978 0 521 44729 4 paperback
Jefferson *Political Writings* (edited by Joyce Appleby and Terence Ball)
    978 0 521 64841 7 paperback
John of Salisbury *Policraticus* (edited by Cary Nederman)
    978 0 521 36701 1 paperback
Kant *Political Writings* (edited by H. S. Reiss and H. B. Nisbet)
    978 0 521 39837 4 paperback
Knox *On Rebellion* (edited by Roger A. Mason)
    978 0 521 39988 3 paperback
Kropotkin *The Conquest of Bread and Other Writings* (edited by Marshall Shatz)
    978 0 521 45990 7 paperback
Lawson *Politica sacra et civilis* (edited by Conal Condren)
    978 0 521 54341 5 paperback
Leibniz *Political Writings* (edited by Patrick Riley)
    978 0 521 35899 6 paperback
*The Levellers* (edited by Andrew Sharp)
    978 0 521 62511 4 paperback
Lincoln *Political Writings and Speeches* (edited by Terence Ball)
    978 0 521 89728 0 hardback
    978 0 521 72226 1 paperback
Locke *Political Essays* (edited by Mark Goldie)
    978 0 521 47861 8 paperback
Locke *Two Treatises of Government* (edited by Peter Laslett)
    978 0 521 35730 2 paperback
Loyseau *A Treatise of Orders and Plain Dignities* (edited by Howell A. Lloyd)
    978 0 521 45624 1 paperback
*Luther and Calvin on Secular Authority* (edited by Harro Höpfl)
    978 0 521 34986 4 paperback
Machiavelli *The Prince* (edited by Quentin Skinner and Russell Price)
    978 0 521 34993 2 paperback
de Maistre *Considerations on France* (edited by Isaiah Berlin and Richard Lebrun)
    978 0 521 46628 8 paperback
Maitland *State, Trust and Corporation* (edited by David Runciman and Magnus Ryan)
    978 0 521 526302 paperback
Malthus *An Essay on the Principle of Population* (edited by Donald Winch)
    978 0 521 42972 6 paperback

Marsilius of Padua *Defensor minor* and *De translatione Imperii* (edited by Cary Nederman)
978 0 521 40846 6 paperback
Marsilius of Padua *The Defender of the Peace* (edited and translated by Annabel Brett)
978 0 521 78911 0 paperback
Marx *Early Political Writings* (edited by Joseph O'Malley)
978 0 521 34994 9 paperback
Marx *Later Political Writings* (edited by Terrell Carver)
978 0 521 36739 4 paperback
James Mill *Political Writings* (edited by Terence Ball)
978 0 521 38748 4 paperback
J. S. Mill *On Liberty*, with *The Subjection of Women* and *Chapters on Socialism* (edited by Stefan Collini)
978 0 521 37917 5 paperback
Milton *Political Writings* (edited by Martin Dzelzainis)
978 0 521 34866 9 paperback
Montesquieu *The Spirit of the Laws* (edited by Anne M. Cohler, Basia Carolyn Miller and Harold Samuel Stone)
978 0 521 36974 9 paperback
More *Utopia* (edited by George M. Logan and Robert M. Adams)
978 0 521 52540 4 paperback
Morris *News from Nowhere* (edited by Krishan Kumar)
978 0 521 42233 8 paperback
Nicholas of Cusa *The Catholic Concordance* (edited by Paul E. Sigmund)
978 0 521 56773 2 paperback
Nietzsche *On the Genealogy of Morality* (edited by Keith Ansell-Pearson)
978 0 521 69163 5 paperback
Paine *Political Writings* (edited by Bruce Kuklick)
978 0 521 66799 9 paperback
Plato *Gorgias, Menexenus* and *Protagoras* (edited by Malcolm Schofield and Tom Griffith)
978 0 521 54600 3 paperback
Plato *The Republic* (edited by G. R. F. Ferrari and Tom Griffith)
978 0 521 48443 5 paperback
Plato *Statesman* (edited by Julia Annas and Robin Waterfield)
978 0 521 44778 2 paperback
Price *Political Writings* (edited by D. O. Thomas)
978 0 521 40969 8 paperback
Priestley *Political Writings* (edited by Peter Miller)
978 0 521 42561 2 paperback
Proudhon *What is Property?* (edited by Donald R. Kelley and Bonnie G. Smith)
978 0 521 40556 0 paperback

Pufendorf *On the Duty of Man and Citizen according to Natural Law* (edited by
James Tully)
978 0 521 35980 1 paperback
*The Radical Reformation* (edited by Michael G. Baylor)
978 0 521 37948 9 paperback
Rousseau *The Discourses and Other Early Political Writings* (edited by
Victor Gourevitch)
978 0 521 42445 5 paperback
Rousseau *The Social Contract and Other Later Political Writings* (edited by Victor
Gourevitch)
978 0 521 42446 2 paperback
Seneca *Moral and Political Essays* (edited by John Cooper and John Procope)
978 0 521 34818 8 paperback
Sidney *Court Maxims* (edited by Hans W. Blom, Eco Haitsma Mulier and
Ronald Janse)
978 0 521 46736 0 paperback
Sorel *Reflections on Violence* (edited by Jeremy Jennings)
978 0 521 55910 2 paperback
Spencer *Political Writings* (edited by John Offer)
978 0 521 43740 0 paperback
Stirner *The Ego and Its Own* (edited by David Leopold)
978 0 521 45647 0 paperback
Thoreau *Political Writings* (edited by Nancy Rosenblum)
978 0 521 47675 1 paperback
Thucydides *The War of the Peloponnesians and the Athenians* (edited by Jeremy
Mynott)
978 0 521 8 4774 2 hardback
978 0 521 61258 6 paperback
Tocqueville *The Ancien Régime and the French Revolution* (edited by
Jon Elster)
978 0 521 88980 3 hardback
978 0 521 71891 2 paperback
Tönnies *Community and Civil Society* (edited by Jose Harris and
Margaret Hollis)
978 0 521 56782 4 paperback
*Utopias of the British Enlightenment* (edited by Gregory Claeys)
978 0 521 45590 9 paperback
Vico *The First New Science* (edited by Leon Pompa)
978 0 521 38726 2 paperback
Vitoria *Political Writings* (edited by Anthony Pagden and Jeremy Lawrance)
978 0 521 36714 1 paperback
Voltaire *Political Writings* (edited by David Williams)
978 0 521 43727 1 paperback

Weber *Political Writings* (edited by Peter Lassman and Ronald Speirs)
   978 0 521 39719 3 paperback
William of Ockham *A Letter to the Friars Minor and Other Writings* (edited by
   A. S. McGrade and John Kilcullen)
   978 0 521 35804 0 paperback
William of Ockham *A Short Discourse on Tyrannical Government* (edited by
   A. S. McGrade and John Kilcullen)
   978 0 521 35803 3 paperback
Wollstonecraft *A Vindication of the Rights of Men* and *A Vindication of the Rights
   of Woman* (edited by Sylvana Tomaselli)
   978 0 521 43633 5 paperback

CPSIA information can be obtained
at www.ICGtesting.com
Printed in the USA
LVHW050314231121
704214LV00011B/486

9  780